MALTA:
BLITZED BUT NOT BEATEN

Philip Vella

Printed and Published
by
Progress Press Co. Ltd.,
Valletta, Malta G.C.
for
The National War Museum Association.

ISBN 0-907930-33-6

1st edition 1985
2nd edition 1987
3rd edition 1989
4th edition 1991

Cover lay-out:
Richard J. Caruana

© *Philip Vella 1985*

All rights reserved. No part of this book may be reproduced, stored in a retrieval system, or transmitted in any form or by any means, electronic, electrostatic, magnetic tape, mechanical, photo-copying, recording or otherwise, without permission in writing from the publishers.

To all those
who died or suffered
during the Battle for Malta
this book is
dedicated

CONTENTS

	Page
Preface	x
Acknowledgements	xi
List of Illustrations	xiii
List of Maps	xviii

Chapter One — 1

Declaration of war by Italy — Inadequacy of local defences — First air attacks and casualties — Civil Defence — First convoy to Malta — Hurricane reinforcements — *Luftwaffe's* arrival in Sicily

Chapter Two — 24

Attack on HMS *Illustrious* — Recovery of unexploded radio-controlled bomb

Chapter Three — 32

Capture of Italian floatplane — First British Airborne operation — Conscription — The *Luftwaffe* withdraws — Lloyd succeeds Maynard as Air Officer Commanding — Malta Night Fighter Unit — General Dobbie appointed Governor — Rationing — Sinking of MV *Moor* — Heinkel floatplanes at Malta

Chapter Four — 41

E-boat attack: radar detection, engagement by coastal batteries, mopping up by Hurricanes, capture of assaultmen

Chapter Five — 48

Supplies to Malta by convoys, submarines and unescorted vessels — Offensive Operations — Loss of HMS *Upholder*

Chapter Six — 55

Resumption of attacks by *Luftwaffe* — Threat of invasion — Widespread destruction — Regent Cinema tragedy — Arrival of first Spitfires

Chapter Seven   65

   Scuttling of *Talabot* — Evacuation of parts of Floriana — Life in shelters — The red flag — The role of Boy Scouts, Girl Guides, Women's Auxiliary Reserve and VADs — Victory Kitchens — Aircraft protective pens

Chapter Eight   83

   Radar — Ancillary and Service Corps — Royal Tank Regiment — Malta Police Force

Chapter Nine   87

   Internment of enemy aliens and a number of Maltese — Deportation to Uganda — Repatriation to Malta

Chapter Ten   91

   Digging of more shelters — Tragedies in shelters — Massive attacks on Ta' Qali

Chapter Eleven   101

   Start of Spring Blitz — Anti-aircraft defence — King George VI assumes Colonelcy-in-Chief of The Royal Malta Artillery

Chapter Twelve   111

   Blitz intensified — Royal Opera House destroyed — Mosta Dome bomb episode — Submarines withdraw from Malta — Award of George Cross to Malta

Chapter Thirteen   123

   Bomb disposal — Hospitals and Dressing Stations — Bombing of hospitals

Chapter Fourteen   132

   Lord Gort relieves General Dobbie — Aerial defence reaches a nadir — USS *Wasp* ferries Spitfires — The Glorious 10th of May

Chapter Fifteen   142

   Borg Pisani lands in Malta: his capture, trial and execution

Chapter Sixteen   145

   Efforts to supply Malta — Gozitan contribution — Attacks on seacraft plying between Malta and Gozo — Travel restrictions — Entertainment — Malta's top fighter ace

Chapter Seventeen   155

   Air-Sea rescue operations — Projected invasion of Malta — Park succeeds Lloyd as Air Officer Commanding — First aerial hijack

Chapter Eighteen — 163

The *Santa Marija* convoy — Malta Convoy Fund — Malta and the Desert Campaign — Failure of the October Blitz — Shortage of essential commodities — Lifting of the siege

Chapter Nineteen — 177

Offensive operations — Royal Air Force claims 1,000th victim — Invasion of Pantelleria and smaller islands — Preparations for invasion of Sicily — Construction of airstrips at Gozo

Chapter Twenty — 184

King George VI visits Malta: welcome by population, tour of the Island, presentation of Field Marshal's baton to Lord Gort

Chapter Twenty-One — 187

Allied Commanders arrive for invasion of Sicily — General Eisenhower's message to Malta — Last civilian victim through aerial bombardment — Mussolini's downfall

Chapter Twenty-Two — 192

Italy's surrender — Churchill and Roosevelt visit Malta — Allied Chiefs of Staff meet at Malta — Churchill and Roosevelt revisit Malta prior to Yalta Conference — Reconstruction — End of hostilities in Europe and Far East

Sources and Notes — 207

Appendices:

A.	British Army Units serving in Malta during the Second World War	213
B.	Presentation Spitfires *Malta* W3210 and *Ghawdex* W3212	216
C.	Convoys to Malta: 1940-1942	221
D.	Honours and Awards	224
E.	Successes by Malta-based submarines	227
F.	Transfer of Government Departments	228
G.	Civilian ration entitlements — 1942	229
H.	Daily Army rations — Spring/Autumn 1942	230
I.	Order of Deportation	231
J.	Month-by-month summary of enemy aircraft destroyed or damaged over Malta	232
K.	Anti-aircraft successes and ammunition expenditure	233
L.	HM ships, merchant vessels and other craft sunk at or near Malta	234
M.	Historical buildings — Destroyed or damaged	235
N.	Other buildings — Destroyed or damaged	238
O.	Aircraft flown to Malta from aircraft carriers: 1940-42	239
P.	Top-scoring 'Malta' fighter pilots	240
Q.	Men and equipment to be landed during Operation C 3	241
R.	Operation 'Pedestal' — Escorting Forces	242
S.	Operation 'Husky' — Order of Battle, RAF Malta	244
T.	Military Formation Signs in Malta	245
U.	Italian naval units surrendered in Malta	247
V.	Summary of air raid alerts over Malta	249
W.	Governors and Service Commanders: 1939-1945	250

X.	RAF, SAAF, RAAF, RCAF and USAAF Squadrons and Detachments based at Malta between June 1940 and December 1943	252
Y.	Royal Navy Ships, Fleet Air Arm Squadrons and Motor Launches granted the 'Malta Convoys' Battle Honour	255
Z.	Code names of Operations destined to, or originating from, Malta	257

The War Memorial	261
The Commonwealth Air Forces Memorial	262
Roll of Honour:	
Civilians	265
Royal Navy	292
Royal Malta Artillery	296
King's Own Malta Regiment	298
Malta Pioneer Group	298
Malta Auxiliary Corps	298
Royal Regiment of Artillery — 12th Field Regt	299
Royal Regiment of Artillery — 4th Coast Regt	299
Royal Regiment of Artillery — 4th HAA Regt	299
Royal Regiment of Artillery — 7th HAA Regt	300
Royal Regiment of Artillery — 10th (later 68th) HAA Regt	300
Royal Regiment of Artillery — 32nd LAA Regt	301
Royal Regiment of Artillery — 65th LAA Regt	301
Royal Regiment of Artillery — 74th LAA Regt	302
Royal Regiment of Artillery — 26th Defence Regt	302
Royal Regiment of Artillery — 4th S/L Regt RA/RMA	302
Royal Regiment of Artillery — Miscellaneous	303
Army Dental Corps	303
Army — Miscellaneous	303
4th Bn The Buffs (Royal East Kent Regiment)	304
8th Bn The King's Own Royal Regiment (Lancaster)	304
2nd Bn The Devonshire Regiment	304
11th Bn The Lancashire Fusiliers	305
1st Bn The Cheshire Regiment	305
1st Bn The Hampshire Regiment	305
1st Bn The Dorsetshire Regiment	306
2nd Bn The Queen's Own Royal West Kent Regiment	306
8th Bn The Manchester Regiment	307
1st Bn The Durham Light Infantry	307
2nd Bn The Royal Irish Fusiliers	307
Royal Engineers	308
Royal Corps of Signals	308
Royal Army Service Corps	308
Royal Army Medical Corps	309
Royal Army Ordnance Corps	309
Royal Electrical and Mechanical Engineers	309
Corps of Military Police	309

Royal Army Pay Corps	309
Royal Air Force	310
Navy, Army and Air Force Institutes	318
Merchant Navy	319
Bibliography	323
Index	325

Preface

On 29th July, 1974, a group of Maltese enthusiasts met to form The National War Museum Association, a purely voluntary organisation. What brought them together was the realisation that, despite the lapse of thirty years since the end of the Second World War, no tangible steps had been taken to record Malta's ordeal.

The aim of the Association is twofold: to establish and maintain a National War Museum; to set up a reference library comprising an archive and a photographic collection. The success achieved has been due to the dedicated efforts of the Members of the Association, who have found co-operation from the various Ministers responsible for Culture, the Department of Museums, the Armed Forces of Malta, overseas museums and local and overseas donors. Numerous photographs have been received whilst several books, documents and hitherto unpublished material have also been made available. Moreover, many persons, who took part in the Battle for Malta, were interviewed.

This has led to the publication of this book, which relates the story of Malta during the Second World War as seen through the eyes of Maltese civilians and servicemen, and of British Commonwealth sailors, soldiers and airmen.

The opportunity has been taken to include the Roll of Honour of Maltese civilians and servicemen. The memory of servicemen from Britain and the Commonwealth, who lost their life in the defence of Malta, is also recorded.

To those who were in Malta during the war years, this book will revive memories; to those who were not, it will show how the Maltese were blitzed but not beaten.

4th February, 1985   Philip Vella

Acknowledgements

In the compilation of material and the subsequent writing of this book, I have received encouragement and assistance from my colleagues on the Committee of The National War Museum Association, as well as from other sources. It is impossible to name each one individually but I feel that some deserve special mention.

My gratitude goes to Mr Frederick R. Galea, who took a deep interest in this work and collaborated closely with me at all stages. I am likewise indebted to Mr Louis F. Tortell for the processing of photographs and to Sqn Ldr Peter E.G. Durnford DFM TD for compiling the Index.

The updating of the Roll of Honour, published by the Commonwealth War Graves Commission, was undertaken by Mr John A. Agius. With unlimited patience and perseverance, he delved through reports, newspapers and other documents to make the lists as complete as possible.

I am also grateful to the Trustees of the Imperial War Museum, the Board of Directors of Allied Newspapers Limited and to Cav. Nicola Malizia for permission to use photographs from their respective collections.

The book has been enhanced by photographs and extracts from interviews given by various individuals, to whom I am indebted.

LIST OF ILLUSTRATIONS

	Page
The Maltese Islands	XX
Piazza Venezia, Rome, on 10th June, 1940	1
Submarine shelters at Marsamxett Harbour	2
Fougasse at Salina Bay	3
Parabolic Acoustic Mirror	4
Officers of The King's Own Malta Regiment	5
Barbed-wire defences at Mistra, St Paul's Bay	6
Camouflaged beach-post at St Paul's Bay	7
HMS *Terror* in Lazaretto Creek	7
Italian bombs on Hal Far on 11th June, 1940	8
First air raid victims — 11th June, 1940	9
Bombed-out families leaving Floriana	10
Aerial view of north-east Malta showing military targets	11
First Italian bomber destroyed on 22nd June, 1940	12
Grave of Flt Lt Peter Keeble at Kalkara	12
Italian S.79 trailing smoke over Valletta	13
Tarxien First Aid and Decontamination Centre	14
Home Guard, Zebbug Group	15
Brigadier C.T. Beckett MC inspecting Home Guard	15
Selection of armbands	16
Special Constabulary	17
Malta Presentation Spitfires	18
Commemorative plaque to Anglo-Maltese League	18
Mussolini decorating *Capitano Pilota* Mario Rigatti	19
Italian cartoon dropped over Luqa in 1940	19
Italian Junkers 87 Stuka	19
Wellington bomber being prepared for a raid	20
Crash of Wellington at Qormi on 3rd November, 1940	21
PC 347 Carmel Camilleri, George Medal	22
Italian reconnaissance over Hal Far on 27th October, 1940	23
HMS *Gallant* beached beneath Crucifix Hill	24
Widespread destruction at Senglea	26
Damage to Basilica of Our Lady of Victories at Senglea	27
HMS *Illustrious* under attack on 19th January, 1941	28
Villa Navillus at Attard	29
Victory Street, Senglea, in ruins	30
Demolished blocks of buildings at Senglea	31
Oberleutnant Joachim Müncheberg	32
The Borg Brothers	33
The Asphar Brothers	34
Recruitment poster, Royal Malta Artillery	34

Dockyard Defence Battery at Floriana	35
Sunderland L5807 ablaze at Kalafrana	36
Air Vice-Marshal Hugh Pughe Lloyd	36
Pilots of No 126 Squadron	37
Hurricane crash-landed at Hal Far	37
Mobile 90cm searchlight	38
Mooring Vessel *Moor*	39
Night raid on Valletta	40
Ration card for milk powder	40
Family ration card	40
E-Boat (*barchino*)	41
Two-man human-torpedo *(maiale)*	42
Maggiore Teseo Tesei	42
MAS 452 at Fort St Angelo after capture	43
Wrecked outer span of breakwater viaduct	43
6-pounder twin gun at Fort St Elmo	44
Major Henry Ferro RMA	44
Italian underwater breathing apparata	45
Sottotenente Roberto Frassetto	46
Monument in Sicily commemorating assault on Malta	47
Italian 'Whitehead' torpedo at a Sicilian airfield	48
Rearming an Italian Macchi 202	49
Italian yellow container and message to RAF Malta	50
Bombs on Fort Manoel	51
Submarine base at Lazaretto Creek	52
Exploding bombs on Lazaretto	52
Lieut-Cdr Malcolm David Wanklyn VC	53
Marble plaque commemorating ties between the Maltese and allied submariners	54
Dive-bombing attack on Senglea	55
Beach defence trials	56
Buildings in Kingsway, Valletta, destroyed by aerial mine	57
Salvaged furniture from bombed homes	57
The Spirit of Malta	58
Business as usual	58
Destruction in Kingsway, Valletta	59
Selection of I.O.U. vouchers	60
Two-shilling note overprinted one shilling	60
Blitzed houses	61
Regent Cinema bombed on 15th February, 1942	62
Palazzo Parisio in Merchants Street, Valletta	62
St. John's Co-Cathedral	62
Air Raid Warden Miss Mary Ellul of Sliema	63
Damage to Kingsgate, Valletta	64
Breconshire beached at Marsaxlokk	65
Talabot ablaze	66
Pampas ablaze	66
Viscount Cranborne's letter to PC Carmel Cassar	68
Air raid shelter in South Street, Valletta	68
Religious poster	69
Hoisting Red Flag on Palace Tower	70
Life goes on	70
Award of Bronze Cross to Boy Scouts Association	71
Award of Bronze Cross to Girl Guides Movement	72

Letter from Yugoslav partisans to Miss Jane Gauci	73
Maltese VADs on return from Italy	73
Queuing for kerosene	74
Queuing for bread	75
Queuing for milk	75
Distribution of water	76
Queuing for meals from Victory Kitchen	77
Valletta hidden by dust from exploding bombs	78
Tignè under attack	78
Wartime religious poster	79
German aerial photograph of Luqa and Safi	80
Aerial view of Ta' Qali airfield	80
Hurricane in 'sand-bag' pen	81
Maryland in 'stone' pen	81
Pens covered with camouflage nets	82
Receiver Mark I Gunlaying Radar	83
Transmitter Mark I Gunlaying Radar	83
Police clearing debris in Valletta	85
Matilda tank 'Griffin'	86
Internment Camp at Fort Salvatore	87
Commandant and Staff of Internment Camp	88
Sir Arturo Mercieca and deportees at Bombo, Uganda	89
Maltese deportees football team	90
Private air raid shelters	91
Ta' Qali airfield	92
Hal Far airfield	93
'Malta. Malta, you vanished' on German bomb	93
Luqa airfield	94
Message on German bomb	95
Ta' Qali airfield under attack	95
Cartoon: Luqa. What again?	96
Graffiti demanding retribution	96
Point de Vue Hotel at Rabat after bombing	97
Hurricane ablaze at Ta' Qali airfield	97
Bomb-damaged *Chateau Bertrand* at Ta' Qali	98
Map showing enemy activity over Malta on 16th March, 1942	99
Heavy anti-aircraft gun position at Marsa	101
Extract from Grp Cpt Jack Satchell's log book	102
Heavy anti-aircraft gun position at St James's Battery	103
Heavy anti-aircraft gun position in action	104
Commander Royal Artillery with RMA and RA officers	105
1st Coast Regiment, Royal Malta Artillery	105
2nd HAA Regiment, Royal Malta Artillery	106
3rd LAA Regiment, Royal Malta Artillery	106
8th Searchlight Battery, Royal Malta Artillery	107
222nd Battery 68th HAA Regiment, Royal Artillery	107
Capt Gerald Amato-Gauci MC RMA(T)	108
4.5-in HAA gun at Spinola Battery	108
Attack on Luqa	109
Tracers, searchlights, shells and flares	110
Royal Opera House bombed	111
Mosta Dome damaged	112

Gaiety Cinema at Sliema	112
Grand Harbour under attack during April 1942	113
HMS *Kingston* hit	114
HMS *Maori* sunk in the Grand Harbour	114
Bomb damage at Floriana, Senglea and Mqabba	115
HMS *Lance* sunk	116
Statue of Christ the King at Floriana near-missed	117
Gun barrel from HMS *Legion* on Senglea rooftop	117
St Anne Street, Floriana	118
George Cross presentation	119
The George Cross and Citation	120
The King's Own Malta Regiment guarding the George Cross	121
Royal Engineers Bomb Disposal Squad	123
Recovery of unexploded bomb	124
Italian E-boat at Manoel Island	125
Floating mine adrift off Sliema	126
Red Cross painted outside St Andrew's Hospital	127
Ambulance caught in air raid	127
Central Hospital at Floriana bombed	128
Emergency ward at St Aloysius College	129
St Andrew's Hospital in ruins	130
King George V Hospital destroyed	130
Wreckage of Me109	133
Macchi 202 wreckage	133
Spitfire on USS *Wasp*	134
Sqd Ldr 'Laddie' Lucas's flight plan to Malta	135
Spitfire being refuelled and rearmed	136
Times of Malta front page, 11th May, 1942	137
HMS *Welshman* being unloaded at the dockyard	138
Aircraft repairs in Gasan, Muscat and Mamo garages	139
Servicing propellers	140
Ju88 crash-landed at Ta' Qali	141
Carmelo Borg, Fascist Party membership card	142
Axis air bases and minefields around Malta	145
Letter about grain usage for livestock	147
Bus travel permit	147
Broken hulk of *Royal Lady* at Mgarr, Gozo	148
Caterpillar air raid shelter	149
Schembri's omnibus	149
Commemorative Holy Picture	150
Whizz-Bangs streamer	151
'The Raffians' programme	151
Joseph Calleia	151
Maltese farmers and British soldiers	152
George F. Beurling, Malta's top fighter ace	153
Self-portrait of Flt Lt Denis Barnham	154
High Speed Launch 107 at St Paul's Bay	155
HSL 128 at speed	156
Flt Lt George R. Crockett on HSL 128	156
HSL landing injured pilot	157
Letter commending Maltese on British pilot's rescue	158
Italian invasion map of Malta	159

Sir Keith R. Park	160
Beaufort and Cant aircrews	161
Ohio leaving USA	163
Eagle's last moments	164
The tow-wire that saved *Port Chalmers*	165
Dorset under attack	166
Port Chalmers entering harbour	166
Burning fuel marks sinking of *Waimarama*	167
Bramham and *Penn* supporting *Ohio*	168
HMS *Rodney* in action	168
Unloading of *Rochester Castle*	169
Cargo labels	171
Message of appreciation from Captain Richard Wren	171
Salvage money awarded for assistance to *Ohio*	172
Lord Gort on front cover of TIME Weekly Newsmagazine	173
Oberleutnant Ernst Neuffer and damaged Ju88	174
German congratulatory certificate for 100th sortie over Malta	175
Celebrating the capture of Tripoli	179
Sketch of 8th Bn The Manchester Regiment on exercise	180
Pantelleria's surrender message	181
Spitfire of 308th Squadron USAAF	182
King George VI saluting Malta	184
The King inspecting RMA guard of honour	185
The King on the Palace balcony	186
The King at Luqa airfield	186
Eisenhower, Gort and Tedder	187
Landing Craft Tank at Ta' Xbiex	188
Landing Craft in No 4 Dock	188
Aircraft carriers in the Grand Harbour	189
German reconnaissance photograph of harbour area	190
Effigy of Mussolini in Kingsway	191
Times of Malta, ITALY SURRENDERS UNCONDITIONALLY	192
Surrender of Italian naval units	193
Ammiraglio Alberto da Zara at Custom House, Valletta	193
Italian submarines in Lazaretto Creek	194
Maresciallo Badoglio aboard HMS *Nelson* in the Grand Harbour	195
American gun crew at St Paul's Bay	196
Churchill giving 'V' sign to dockyard workers	197
Scroll presented by President Roosevelt	198
President Roosevelt inspecting guard of honour	199
Poster displayed locally on capture of Rome	200
American cruiser *Philadelphia* before and after repair at HM Dockyard, Malta	201
Lord Gort holding Sword of Honour	202
Allied Commanders outside St John's Co-Cathedral	203
Roosevelt, Churchill and Hopkins on USS *Quincy*	204
Times of Malta, GERMANY OUT!	204
Times of Malta, PEACE IN EUROPE	205
Times of Malta, VICTORY AND PEACE ON EARTH	205
Lights of Victory illuminate the harbour area	205
Gen Sir Charles Bonham-Carter	251
Lieut-Gen Sir William Dobbie	251
Field-Marshal Viscount Gort	251
Lieut-Gen Sir Edmond Schreiber	251

War Memorial 261
Commonwealth Air Forces Memorial 262

MAPS

The Mediterranean Sea xix
Allied air power over the Mediterranean, September 1942 178

The Mediterranean Sea

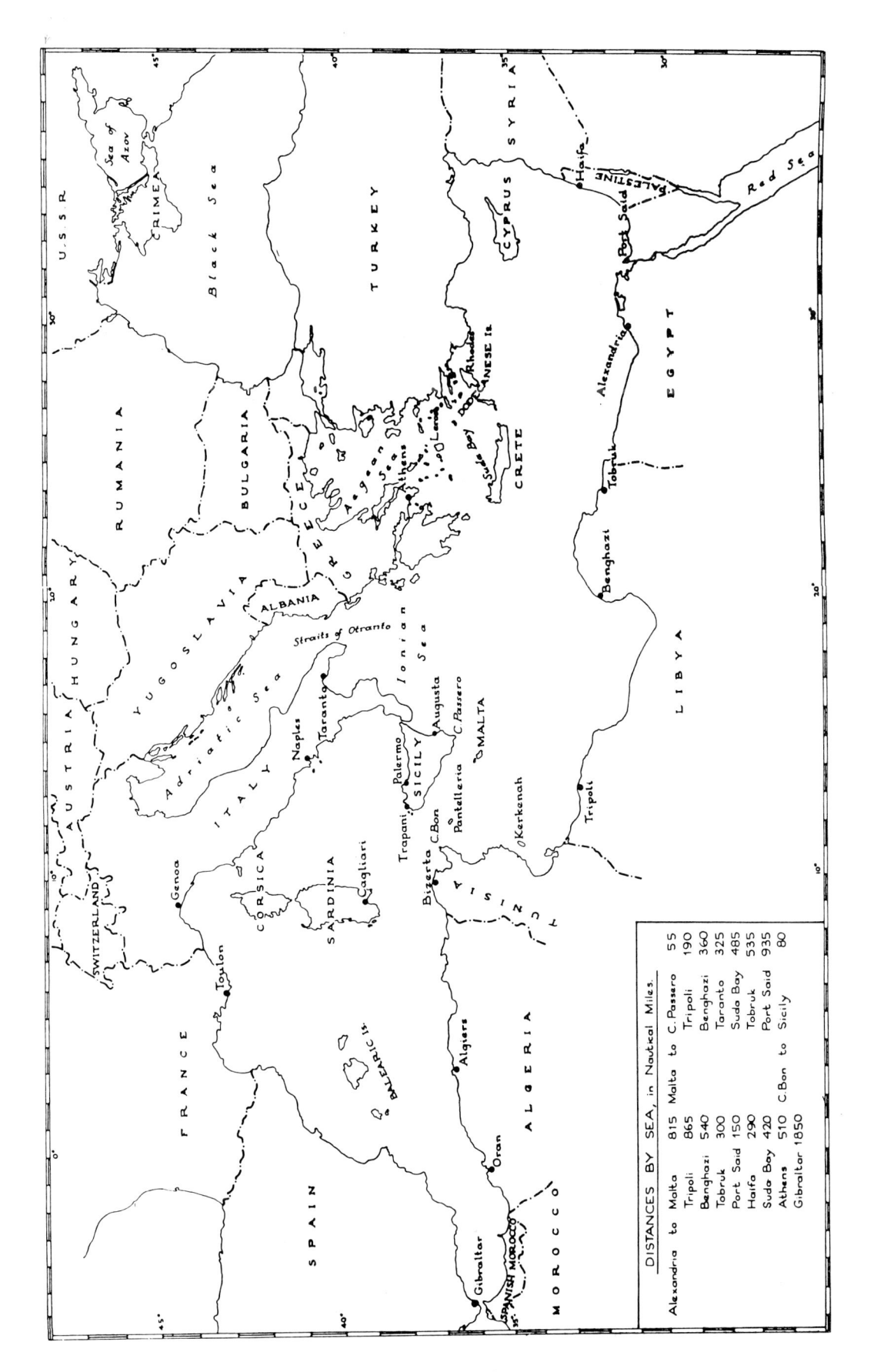

The Maltese Islands.

(via British Legion, Malta Branch)

Chapter One

Declaration of war by Italy — Inadequacy of local defences — First air attacks and casualties — Civil Defence — First convoy to Malta — Hurricane reinforcements — Luftwaffe's arrival in Sicily

The voice over Rome Radio rang loud and clear from *Piazza Venezia* at seven in the evening on Monday, 10th June, 1940, when, interrupted by frenzied cheers, Benito Mussolini addressed the crowd, the country and the world: "We are going to war against the plutocratic and reactionary democracies of the West, who have hindered the advance, and often threatened even the existence of the Italian People. The die is cast and we have, of our free will, well burned the bridges behind us."

In his peculiar, boisterous manner, the Italian dictator had finally taken the crucial decision. The crowd stood there, under the hypnotic power of the *Duce*, waving placards clamouring for Italy's occupation of Gibraltar, Suez, Tunisia and Malta. With France on the verge of defeat and Britain still dazed by the nightmare-turned-miracle of Dunkirk, Mussolini reckoned the time was ripe to throw in his lot with his fellow-dictator, Adolf Hitler, so as to share the fruits of an early victory; he declared war against Britain and France. As from midnight on 10th June, 1940, Malta found herself in the front-line.

The news, though long expected, stunned the Maltese. Mussolini's extra-territorial ambitions were well known and Malta figured prominently in them. The majority accepted the challenge with contempt; those harbouring pro-Italian cultural sympathies deluded themselves into thinking that 'our Italian brethren across the Sea' would never resort to aggression against a friendly country.

(via J.A. Agius)
The crowd at Piazza Venezia *in Rome on 10th June, 1940, waiting to listen to Mussolini declare war on Britain and France. Note placard reading 'Malta' on right.*

An attempt made during the war to excavate three submarine shelters beneath Great Siege Road in Valletta was abandoned.

It was highly debatable to what extent Malta, Britain's stronghold in the Central Mediterranean, was prepared to meet the coming onslaught. Indeed, it is reported that as late as May 1940, in an effort to keep Italy out of the war — which was then considered imminent — the British Foreign Office was actively considering a proposal, made by the French Prime Minister, Paul Reynaud, regarding Mussolini's territorial claims. At the peace conference following the war, Italy would have been given 'belligerent status', without ever having fought, so that her territorial claims would be included in the general settlement of Europe. It was taken for granted that Mussolini would ask for Malta and Gibraltar, as well as Corsica and Nice. However, on 28th May, 1940, the five-man War Cabinet of Britain's National Coalition Government turned down this proposal by a one-vote margin, Prime Minister Winston Churchill, Mr Clement Attlee and Mr Arthur Greenwood voting against, and Mr Neville Chamberlain and Lord Halifax voting in favour.

There were protracted, if not conflicting, discussions amongst the Committee of Imperial Defence about the Island's ability to withstand the effect of modern warfare. In the summer of 1939, the Admiralty advocated the strengthening of Malta as a deterrent to enemy action. This contrasted with the Air Ministry's view that Malta's proximity to Italian airfields rendered the Island too unsafe as a base for the Mediterranean Fleet. The Admiralty probably carried more weight as the Committee of Imperial Defence approved a plan to reinforce the Island, which would have brought the total armament to 122 heavy AA guns, 60 light AA guns and 24 searchlights. The implementation of this plan however, was slow and by June 1940 there were only 34 heavy anti-aircraft guns and 8 Bofors; the number of searchlights was up to strength.

Britain's neglect of Malta's defences had to be paid for and indeed the Maltese and the British, particularly the Royal and Merchant Navies, paid heavily. A case in point was the failure to build submarine shelters. In the mid-1930s, the Navy had urged the digging of such shelters in the rock along Marsamxett Harbour and in fact Captain Guy D'Oyly-Hughes RN had prepared the plans for the project.

This proposal had been approved by the Governor of Malta, General Sir Charles Bonham-Carter,[1] and was also supported by Admiral Sir Dudley Pound, Commander-in-Chief of the Mediterranean Fleet. However, in July 1937, the British Cabinet turned it down on financial grounds.

The whole project was estimated at £340,000, the cost of just one submarine. The loss of many of these submarines was later on severely felt.

2

Likewise, as far back as 1936, plans had been drawn up to construct bomb-proof underground cold stores at *Wied il-Kbir;* these were meant to hold stocks for the Navy and the Army. The cost of £32,000 was considered prohibitive and the project was dropped.[2]

By the time World War Two broke out on Sunday, 3rd September, 1939, it had already been realised that fighter aircraft would have played a vital role in the defence of the Island. It was reckoned that at least four fighter squadrons would have been required for the aerial defence of Malta. Yet not a single fighter had reached the Island by the time Italy declared war.

In March 1940, following prolonged negotiations, Air Commodore Forster H.M. Maynard, Air Officer Commanding Malta, had been authorized to take over six Gloster Sea Gladiators, which were crated and stored at the Fleet Air Arm depot at Kalafrana. They had been left behind by HMS *Glorious* when she left the Mediterranean Station to take part in the Norwegian Campaign. Four of these biplanes, bearing numbers N5519, N5520, N5524 and N5531, were assembled to form a Station Fighter Flight operating from Hal Far. Following a landing accident to one of them, another two, N5523 and N5529, were put into service. This Unit was made up of the following pilots: Squadron Leader Alan C. 'Jock' Martin, Flight Lieutenant George Burges, Flight Lieutenant Peter W. Hartley, Flight Lieutenant Peter G. Keeble, Flying Officer John L. Waters, Flying Officer William J. 'Timber' Woods and Pilot Officer Peter B. Alexander. Like the gunners deployed on coast and anti-aircraft defence, they had no combat experience.

The operational airfields, Hal Far and Ta' Qali, were both grass-surfaced and easily bogged in wet weather. Work on the construction of Luqa Airfield, commenced in October 1939, was completed in April 1940. When war broke out two months later, obstructions were laid along its three tarmaced runways to prevent landings by enemy aircraft. However, the new airfield became operational on 28th June, 1940, when the Fighter Flight was transferred there. Although a skeleton Station Headquarters manned by personnel from Kalafrana and Hal Far had been established in July, Luqa only became an independent station on 18th August, 1940. Ta' Qali was particularly familiar to the Italians, as it had been used

(L.F. Tortell)
The ignition of an explosive charge in an extant fougasse at Salina Bay. The Knights of Malta dug a number of fougasses; these consisted of deep holes in the ground, six feet in diameter. An explosive charge hurled a large quantity of rock over a wide area in the direction of the enemy. The 2nd Bn Royal Irish Fusiliers, who were defending the area, kept this fougasse loaded and primed for use in the event of an invasion.

regularly by *Ala Littoria*, the Italian national civil airline. Italian seaplanes had also used the facilities at Marsaxlokk and St Paul's Bay, whilst Kalafrana was the Royal Air Force's seaplane base.

The coastal defence consisted of seven 9.2" Breech Loading, ten 6" Breech Loading, six 12-pounder Quick Firing and nine 6-pounder twin Quick Firing guns. The 9.2" BL guns were manned by 4th Heavy Regiment Royal Artillery, whilst the Royal Malta Artillery manned the rest; these guns were deployed at Forts Benghajsa, St Leonardo, Madliena, Bingemma, Delimara, St Rocco, Tignè, Campbell, Ricasoli and St Elmo. Six of the 6-pdr QF double-barrelled guns were mounted at Fort St Elmo and the other three at Fort Ricasoli.

Colonel Arthur J. Dunkerley CBE, recalls: "A few years before the outbreak of the Second World War, a programme of rearmament was carried out in our Fixed Defences, replacing some 9.2" guns with 6" long-range guns, and 12-pounders with 6-pounder semi-automatic guns. These were manned by three Coast Regiments, two Maltese and one British, with a strength of approximately 3,000 men. Additional gun positions were erected with a motley collection of guns hauled out of the dockyard; these included old naval guns, two Long Tom field guns of the type used during the Boer War and two Japanese naval guns, all manned by men from 1st Coast Battery, 1st Coast Regiment RMA, which boasted of a strength of approximately 1,200 men." [3]

The need for an early-warning system was felt as far back as the 1930s when a Parabolic Acoustic Mirror was built at Ta' San Pietru, beneath the Victoria Lines, by the Royal Engineers; it was operated by the Royal Signals. Given satisfactory climatic conditions, aircraft over Sicily could be detected. The Mirror, known in Maltese as *Il-Widna* (the ear), was rendered obsolete by the advent of radar.

The infantry defence did not inspire much confidence. There were five infantry battalions: the 1st Devons, 1st Dorsets, 2nd Royal Irish Fusiliers, 2nd Royal West Kents and the 8th Manchesters. Malta had its own infantry regiment, the King's Own Malta Regiment, whose 2nd Battalion 'C' Company was made up of Boy Scouts who retained their distinctive badge. The infantry and artillery strength was eventually augmented as the threat to the Island increased. (See Appendix **A**)

The coastline was ringed with barbed-wire coil and a variety of obstacles and explosive devices. As war progressed, openings were made in the barbed-wire entanglements along several beaches for limited periods to provide

(L.F. Tortell)

The Parabolic Acoustic Mirror fifty years after construction.

(via Ph. Vella)
Officers of The King's Own Malta Regiment. Colonel Edgar Vella sitting at the centre, front row.

access to swimmers, who were warned not to stray away because of booby traps and explosives.

A number of concrete beach-posts, depth-posts and pill-boxes had been constructed during the 1935 Abyssinian crisis. More were built later. Those constructed before the outbreak of war can still be distinguished by their camouflage in the form of natural uncut stone incorporated within their structure. The beach-posts along the coast were intended to prevent the enemy from gaining a foothold on the beaches, whilst the depth-posts were sited inland to engage enemy troops should they have advanced further. These posts were normally manned by six men and a non-commissioned officer who, besides carrying rifles and hand-grenades, were equipped with a Vickers and a Bren gun, as well as a Lyon Light outside the post.

The fact that the Military Authorities could not spare men and equipment to defend Gozo constituted a great risk. There was always the possibility of the Sister Island, a mere five miles away, being occupied, providing the enemy with an accessible stepping-stone for an assault against Malta.

A number of British families, mostly those of naval officers, left Malta on the *Oronsay* on 20th May, 1940, while many others decided to stay on. There was no compulsory evacuation of British families as it was reasoned that such a step would demoralise the local population. British service families moved into St George's Barracks but, eventually, most of them returned to their private residences.

On 31st May, 1940, the Commissioner of Police had issued Police Order No 263, notifying that in the event of an attack by hostile aircraft the alarm for an Air Raid was to be given by the sounding of a warbling note on the sirens or by the firing of maroons. The Raiders Passed signal would have taken the form of a long note on the sirens, while the All Clear was to be signalled by the ringing of church bells. People were instructed to remain indoors or in available shelters until the All Clear signal would be given. Besides other instructions, the notice also carried a list of air raid shelters, namely the Railway Station, NAAFI, St James Cavalier, Upper Barracca, St John's Counterguard, Houlton's Garage, St Andrew's and the Yellow Garage[4] in Valletta, the Argotti and Rundle Gardens and the Parade Ground at Floriana, and the Capuchin Gate and Castile Place at Vittoriosa.

On Tuesday, 11th June, 1940,

(L.F. Tortell)

The Royal Irish Fusiliers erecting barbed-wire fences at Mistra, St Paul's Bay.

Lieutenant-General Sir William Dobbie,[5] Acting Governor and Commander-in-Chief, issued this proclamation: "Whereas I have received information that War has broken out with Italy, I hereby announce to His Majesty's Subjects in the Islands the outbreak of hostilities in humble trust in the guidance and protection of Divine Providence, and in assured confidence of the cordial support and tried fidelity and determination of the people of Malta."

At 6.55 am on that fateful day, while men were travelling to their place of work and housewives were busying themselves with shopping and other chores, the wailing sirens heralded the approach of the first enemy aircraft.

The first bombers to appear over Malta were ten Savoia Marchetti 79s, which crossed the 60-mile channel on their way to their target, Hal Far. These aircraft, belonging to 34⁰ *Stormo* BT based at Catania, were led by *Colonello* Umberto Mazzini. The dust had hardly settled when a second wave of fifteen attacked the dockyard and the two main harbours, to be followed ten minutes later by another ten which attacked the seaplane base at Kalafrana. On each occasion, the S.79s were escorted by Macchi 200s.

During the first raid, a stick of three bombs fell over Upper Fort St Elmo. One of them exploded on the top platform of the *Cavalier*, where men of the Anti-Parachute Squadron 1st Coast Regiment RMA were posted, armed with rifles, to watch out for any landing attempt by the enemy. Bombardier Joseph Galea and Gunners Michael Angelo Saliba, Roger Micallef, Carmel Cordina and Paul Debono were killed. Besides injuring several others, the bomb also killed Boy Philip Busuttil, duty-telephonist at the Harbour Fire Command Post. These Royal Malta Artillerymen, the first victims, are commemorated by a monument on the site where they fell.

The day saw seven bombing sorties and a reconnaissance flight causing negligible damage to military objectives. Although Italian aircrew were ordered to avoid bombing populated areas, several buildings near the dockyard, around Valletta, *Porte-des-Bombes*, Pieta, Guardamangia, Msida, Gzira, Marsa, Zabbar, Tarxien and Sliema were hit; eleven civilians were killed and 130 injured.

The Gladiators and the anti-aircraft batteries, alerted by radar, engaged the high-flying bombers and escorting fighters. The ground batteries were supplemented by gun-fire from HMS *Aphis* and the World War One monitor HMS *Terror* berthed in Lazaretto Creek,

(F.B. Jarvis) *A rubble-wall camouflaged beach-post at St Paul's Bay.*

(via J.C. Saliba) *HMS* Terror *in Lazaretto Creek.*

(via N. Malizia)
A few hours after Italy had declared war, the Italians dropped their first bombs on Hal Far airfield. Photograph taken by crew of a S.79 of 34° Stormo B.T. operating from Catania.

whose 4" guns shook the houses in the vicinity. Neither side lost any aircraft, but one of the Gladiators scored several hits on a S.79 piloted by *Capitano* Rosario Di Blasi. In one of the afternoon raids, six S.79s returned to base with superficial damage from anti-aircraft fire; one of the bombers of 11° *Stormo* BT landed at Comiso with *Sottotenente Pilota Puntatore* Elvio Magrì being the first Italian airman to be wounded over Malta.

Flight Lieutenant (later Group Captain) George Burges recalls the aerial defensive set-up during the first days of the war: "People say there were only three Gladiators in Malta when war started. That is not entirely correct; there were other Gladiators still in crates but certainly the limiting factor to operate was the number of pilots available rather than the number of aircraft. We had four Gladiators but we only flew three whilst the fourth was kept in reserve.

"The day was split into four watches; dawn to 8.00 am, 8.00 am to noon, noon to 4.00 pm, 4.00 pm to 8.00 pm. As there were six pilots, three of us took the first and the third watches, and the other three did the second watch and the fourth. After the first day, we realized that, if instead of sitting in a deckchair until the bell went, we sat in the aircraft, all strapped up and ready to go, it meant a gain of 2,000 feet; that is what we did the following day. That was in June and, besides being very hot, it got extremely uncomfortable sitting for long periods in the cockpit. The Station Medical Officer was against this practice and recommended that we had two days on duty and a day off. So, in fact, except for the first two days of war, one never did see three Gladiators in the air at the same time." [6]

Contrary to general belief, the aircraft were not, at that time, referred to as *Faith, Hope* and *Charity*. Indeed it is not known how or when these came to be so named.

The Island, unprepared for such an early baptism of fire, could not but experience a sense of panic. The first raids brought with them reports of death and destruction. Nearly everyone had somebody in the family employed on work connected with or close to military installations and consequently nobody's mind could be at ease. In the absence of adequate shelters many people took cover under tables, beds and vaults in their home, whilst those caught at their place of work sought protection as best they could. Before darkness fell a large number of families living around the harbour area packed a few essential

(J. Busuttil)
Boy Philip Busuttil RMA. Killed at Fort St Elmo; aged 16.

(Mrs T. Galea)
Josephine Mangion. Killed at Pieta; aged 3.

IN LOVING MEMORY OF

NINU
5 YEARS

NINA FARRUGIA
25 YEARS

JOE
4 YEARS

FIRST AIR RAID VICTIMS AT 6-50 A.M.
WHO LOST THEIR LIVES THROUGH ENEMY ACTION
ON TUESDAY 11th JUNE 1940
AT PIETA.

Heart of Jesus most worthy of al praise, Have mercy on their souls.

(Mrs T. Galea)

Bombed-out families in Floriana leaving the suburb with their belongings on horse-drawn carts.

belongings, loaded them on horse-driven carts and sought refuge in safer parts of the Island.

Apart from the six soldiers at Fort St Elmo, six Maltese naval personnel were also killed, but under different circumstances. In the words of Petty Officer Francis Galea RN, then serving at HMS *St Angelo:* "At 3.00 pm we received a message reporting the presence of an Italian merchant ship some five miles off Malta. When the Italians failed to reply to radio signals, three launches from *St Angelo* were sent out to the ship, already deserted by the crew who had attempted to scuttle her.

"A tug-boat was then detailed to tow the vessel into Marsaxlokk but, on reaching Zonqor Point, we informed *St Angelo* that the ship was sinking; we were accordingly ordered to beach her at Marsascala. At about 7.00 pm our engineer, on sighting Italian aircraft, ordered us back to base.

"On our reaching Xghajra, several bombs were dropped, some of which fell near the launches. Simultaneously, the coastal batteries at Forts Ricasoli and Elmo inadvertently struck at the craft, obviously mistaking them for enemy boats. Two sank outright, whilst the leading one, on which I was, hit by shrapnel from bombs or shells, started taking in water and later sank.

"In spite of injuries to my right hand and leg, I swam towards two minesweepers which rushed to the spot to pick up any survivors; two dockyard workmen, attached to *St Angelo*, were with us on the launches. After a long spell at Mtarfa Hospital, I reported back for duty on HMS *St Angelo*. When I informed the Captain about the shooting incident, I was told to 'keep it dark'. It resulted that the incident had been caused through inexperience on the part of the Jetty Quarter Master who must have failed to report our movements to his relief and to the Military Authorities."[7]

According to Lieutenant-Commander Charles Carnes RNVR, on the staff of Vice

1	Forte S.Leonardo
2	Forte S.Vincenzo
3	Fortino d.Grazia
4	Forte S.Pietro
5	Fortino Rocco
6	Batteria Rinella
7	Forte Ricasoli
8	Ospedale
9	Forte S.Aneglo
10	Arsenale Mil.
11	Arsenale
12	Deposito nafta
13	Magazzini Dogan.
14	Malta Club
15	Forte S.Elmo
16	Polveriera
	...iglia
	Topponi
17	Caserme Florian
18	Dep.torp.siluri
19	Forte Tignè
20	Forte Manoel
21	Fort.Chariddud
22	Forte Spinola
23	Forte S.Luciano
24	Dep.petrolio
25	Off.Calafrana

(via N. Malizia)
An aerial view of the north-eastern part of Malta taken from 6,000 metres on 12th June, 1940. This photograph, showing military targets, was issued to crews of Italian bombers belonging to 59ª Squadriglia, 33º Gruppo, 11º Stormo.

Admiral Malta, this incident led to Vice-Admiral Wilbraham Ford moving a large part of his staff over to Lascaris in order that he could be near the Army and Royal Air Force and have daily consultations with them on movements around the Island.[8]

The pattern of the first aerial bombardment was repeated in varying degrees the following days and the number of families in the harbour area seeking refuge in towns and villages further inland increased from day to day. This exodus brought out the innate qualities of the Maltese, as attested later by the Lieutenant-Governor, Sir Edward St John Jackson, during a Sitting of the Council of Government: "I shall never forget the profound impression that was then made upon me by the charity — by the almost boundless charity — which the poorer classes then displayed in taking their friends and even strangers into their homes, destroying altogether the privacy of their lives, and still more so when in quite a small room as many as 20 and 30 people were accommodated, not only sleeping, but living and eating there as well, and all under conditions of cheerfulness, friendliness and tolerance and give and take. I myself would not have imagined that that was possible either in this country or in any other country."[9]

June 19th was the first raidless day since Italy's declaration of war. On that day, newspapers carried the text of a message from His Majesty King George VI: "I have already heard of the gallant spirit and fine bearing of the Maltese people since they have been brought within the battle zone and I have no doubt that they will be worthy of upholding their great traditions in this struggle in which they are now actively engaged." Two days later, Malta experienced its first night raids. Between 11.50 pm and 3.00 am there were four air attacks, during which bombs were also dropped over Gozo.

When the sirens sounded, people took cover in make-shift shelters but, after a while, many started throwing caution to the wind and watched the intruders engaged by both gunners and fighters. The defenders gained confidence as their performance improved with every raid. The same could be said of the Italians who, on 20th June, hit and sank the 40,000-ton Admiralty floating dock berthed beneath Kordin Heights.

Some forty-five passengers, mostly dockyard workers travelling on a Cospicua bus towards Valletta, were involved in a tragic accident at Marsa Crossroads at about 5.30 pm on 26th June. The bus had stopped to enable the passengers to seek shelter as a raid was on. Almost immediately, it was set ablaze by an incendiary bomb which killed thirty-eight passengers, among whom were eight unidentifiable charred bodies.

One of the survivors, Paul Mizzi, recalls: "Together with three others near the rear foot-board, I alighted and sought shelter in a small shop nearby. I saw at least six corpses and several others injured near the bus. On leaving the scene of disaster, to my astonishment I was told that blood stains were visible on my back. I was taken for treatment with others to Bugeja Hospital at Hamrun. After three weeks, the wound healed and I forgot all about it until 1976 when, on having an X-ray for another complaint, I was told I had a splinter embedded in my back. Although it had been there all that time, I was never conscious of it; as it is not causing any pain, it is still there." [10]

The unexpected arrival of a number of Hurricanes in transit to the Middle East provided a significant boost to the defences and to morale. Air Commodore Maynard convinced Air Chief Marshal Sir Arthur Longmore, AOC-in-C Middle East, to let some of these superior fighters be based here. However, it was a Gladiator that registered the first success over Malta. On 22nd June, Flight Lieutenant Burges and Flying Officer 'Timber' Woods sighted a S.79 over the Island. Woods engaged without success. Burges, in Gladiator N5519, pressed home the attack, shooting the bomber into the sea; the Italian pilot, *Tenente* Francesco Solimena, and another member of the crew became the first prisoners-of-war. The next day, Burges obtained his second success when, in a spectacular and daring dogfight, he shot down a Macchi 200.

The Italians temporarily withdrew the Macchi 200s and replaced them by Fiat CR 42s. On 3rd July, a spirited action took place; during a morning raid, Flying Officer Waters in a Hurricane chased a S.79 which he shot down. No sooner had he set course for base than a CR 42, piloted by *Maggiore* Ernesto Botto of 9⁰ *Gruppo*, pounced on Waters. He crash-landed and the plane was written-off, while Waters escaped injury.

The luck of the Malta pilots did not hold out for long. On July 16th, Flight Lieutenant

(RAF Museum)
An artist's impression of Burges shooting down the first Italian bomber over Malta on 22nd June, 1940.

Burges, in a Gladiator, and Flight Lieutenant Keeble, in a Hurricane, intercepted a numerically superior force of CR 42s. *Tenente* Mario Pinna succeeded in shooting Keeble's plane down. The British pilot crashed to his death barely a hundred yards away from where *Tenente* Mario Benedetti lay in the wreckage of his CR 42.

A few days later, Burges had the distinction of becoming the first Malta pilot to receive the Distinguished Flying Cross. The award was

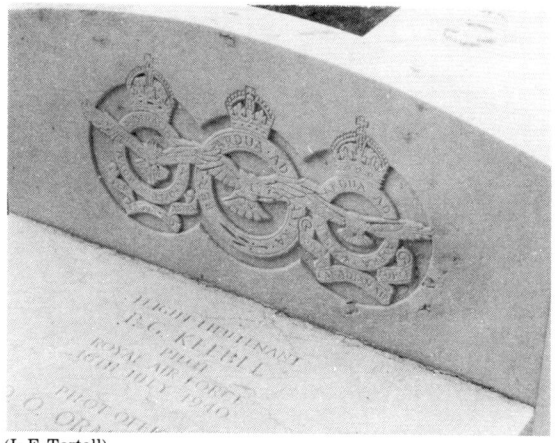

(L.F. Tortell)
Flt Lt Keeble's grave at Capuchins Cemetery, Kalkara.

12

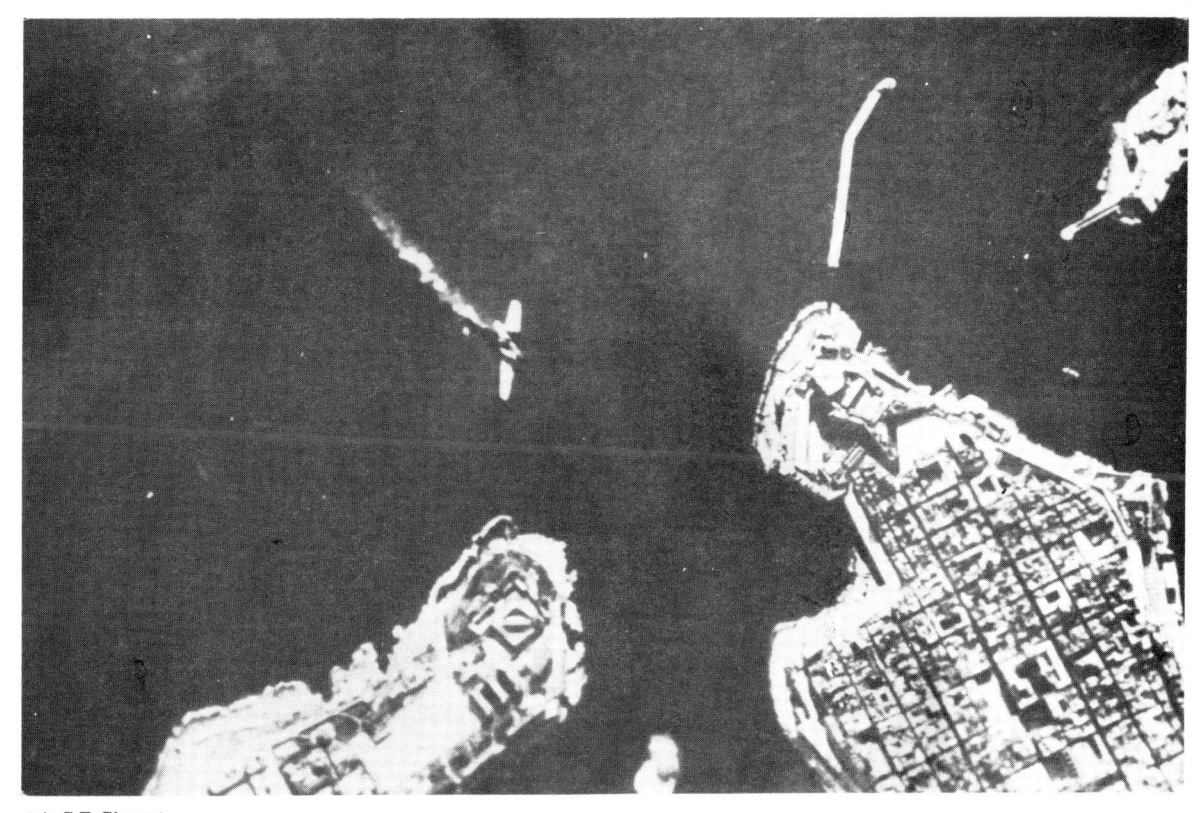

A S.79 trailing smoke over Valletta and Sliema after having been hit by a British fighter on 10th July, 1940.

published in the London Gazette of 19th July; the citation reads as follows: "Although normally a flyingboat pilot, and only transferred to fighter duties since the commencement of war with Italy, Flight Lieutenant Burges has shot down three enemy aircraft and so damaged three more that they probably failed to reach their base. He has shown great tenacity and determination in seeking combat, usually in the face of superior numbers."

The last day of July saw the destruction of the first of Malta's battle-tried Gladiators. A CR 42, piloted by *Capitano* Luigi Filippi, set N5519 ablaze; Flight Lieutenant Peter Hartley, who managed to bale out, was conveyed badly burnt to Mtarfa Military Hospital. *Capitano* Antonio Chiodi, the commander of 75ª *Squadriglia*, did not survive when his CR 42 was in turn shot down by one of the two remaining Gladiators.

In the first six crucial weeks, the Italians, although fighting bravely over Malta, failed to overcome the Island's defences and to weaken civilian morale.

The Passive Defence Corps, commonly referred to as the Air Raid Precautions Organisation, set up before the outbreak of war under Mr C.H. Sansom CMG, now proved its mettle, though in the early stages its role was mostly orientated towards meeting the feared threat of the use of gas. Twelve Centres were established, three at Valletta and the others at Floriana, Marsa, Cospicua, Zabbar, Sliema, Mosta, Tarxien, Msida and Hamrun. In May 1940, the reservists were called up to man their respective Centres by day and night. The Centres housed a first-aid post, a decontamination chamber, sleeping quarters and a canteen, a recreation room and a chapel; these were manned by a superintendent, two doctors, a sergeant major, four sergeants, about thirty-two men, three drivers, a telephone orderly and about ten female wardens. A reconnaissance car and an ambulance were also available at each Centre.

Before the bombs came, the wardens had already instructed people in their district how to use and care for their respirators, commonly known as gas-masks, which were to be carried at all times. Young mothers were also issued with a Siebe-Gorman anti-gas hood for babies. These masks and hoods were made of rubberised fabric and the curved window of cellulose acetate.

As soon as an alert was sounded, a spotter took up his position on the roof to survey any possible 'hits' within the district. On the sounding of the Raiders Passed, the rescue parties hurried to the scene.

The Malta Volunteer Defence Force was formed on 3rd June from among local *kaccaturi* and other game-shooters from the farming community; their main duty was to shoot at parachutists attempting to land. This corps was the forerunner of the Home Guard which increased in strength and efficiency. The men, who at first wore an armband and a steel helmet, were eventually issued with a khaki denim battle-dress and, after being trained by British and Maltese army instructors, attained a high standard of marksmanship.

Another Organisation destined to play a vital role on the Home Front was the Demolition and Clearanace Section of the Public Works Department.[11] Headed by Mr Louis A. Agius BE&A, A&CE, two gangs, each comprising about 40 men, operated from Floriana and Cospicua, whilst a third was kept on call at the Passive Defence Headquarters. Carrying picks, axes, shovels, barrows and ladders, they hurried to the scene of destruction to recover those trapped beneath the debris.

Members of the Special Constabulary, set up on a voluntary basis in May 1940 and comprising about 2,000 members, made sure that people would not loiter in the streets, or assemble at shelter entrances during air raids; as dusk fell, they patrolled the streets to enforce black-out and curfew regulations.[12] A Press Release issued on 4th September, 1940, stated *inter alia* that "... while lighting restrictions in general are being satisfactorily observed, it does not appear to be fully realised that the indiscriminate use of matches or lighters by smokers in the open constitutes a very great danger to public security. This type of light can be discerned from a height of 6,000 feet and at a distance of 6 miles. The Government expects the public to ensure that this practice is stopped forthwith, and the Police have been instructed to take immediate action against offenders."

Smokers were not the only culprits; the *Times of Malta* reported that Felix Zahra of Marsa was fined 10 shillings "for having a light in his house not sufficiently masked and which was visible from outside and from the air", while Moses Darmanin of Hamrun was fined the same amount "for having a torch not covered with blue material and not keeping same facing downwards." Petty offences

(A. Bilocca)
Members of the Tarxien First Aid and Decontamination Centre. Sitting at centre, second row, is Superintendent Anthony Bilocca flanked by Dr Edward Nicholas on the right and Dr Paul Schembri on the left.

(A. Borg)
Members of the Home Guard, Zebbug Group, with trophies won in a marksmanship competition. Company Commander Anthony Borg is seated at centre.

(NWM)
Brigadier C.T. Beckett MC, Commander Royal Artillery Malta, inspecting members of the Home Guard.

indeed, but strict observance of the law was essential. The headlights of all motor vehicles were fitted with metal blinker hoods, while the rear lights were painted dark-blue.

As a precaution against bombing, people were told to use scantlings to reinforce cellars and other spots chosen for shelter, as well as to paint the window-panes in a dark colour as a black-out measure, besides fixing tape across them to minimise the risk of injury from flying glass. Soon enough they realised, to their bitter experience, that these arrangements were totally inadequate; many started seeking shelter in the old railway tunnels in Valletta and Floriana, as well as in the Hypogeum, a prehistoric underground burial place at Pawla, and the Catacombs at Rabat. Some caves were also used by bombed-out families. An Order under the Defence Regulations directed evacuees living at Ghar Dalam, a noted prehistoric cave, to move out by 1st October, 1940, as the Services needed it urgently.

A form of protection against blast and splinters was the erection of blast-walls, made

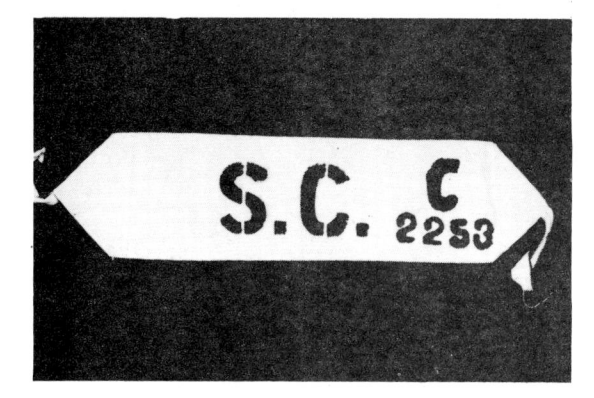

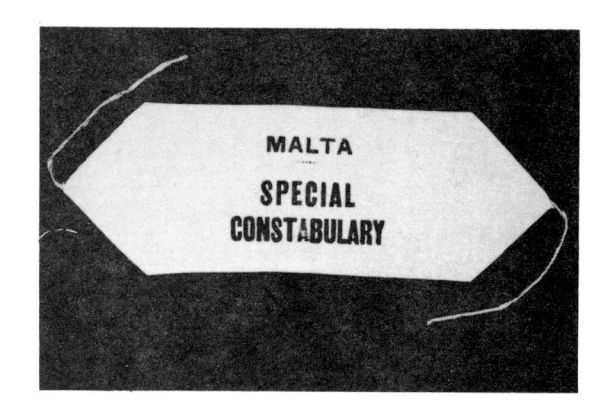

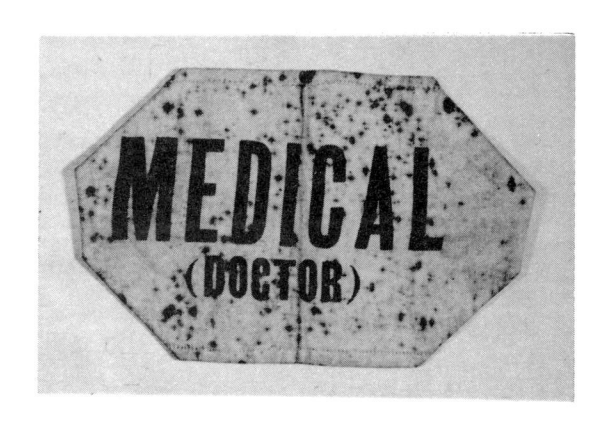

(NWMA)

A selection of armbands.

16

(E. Tonna)
Commissioner of Police Joseph Axisa with members of the Special Constabulary.

of stone or sand-bags, outside historic buildings, monuments and churches. As the bombing showed no sign of relenting and destruction became more wide-spread, paintings and other objects of artistic and historical importance were removed from St John's Co-Cathedral, the Palace, the National Museum and the National Library for storage in safer places; this notwithstanding, several priceless treasures forming part of Malta's heritage were yet to be lost.

A ceremony reminiscent of the early Christians was held at the Yellow Garage, a huge improvised air raid shelter in Valletta, on 8th September, 1940, which date, at that time, marked Malta's National Day. About 36 children, dressed in white and carrying candles, received their First Holy Communion deep down in the rock beneath the bastions guarding the entrance to the capital. The tunnel, temporarily transformed into a chapel illuminated by countless candles, echoed to the chanting of hymns by the children and some 200 shelterers; Canon Joseph Delia, who throughout the war looked after the spiritual needs of the 'Yellow Garagers', delivered a sermon. In the afternoon a modest party, during which the children were given a treat of sweets and souvenirs, brought to an end a happy day.

The face of Malta gradually started taking a new aspect. Destroyed and dilapidated buildings became a common sight; hastily-filled bomb craters added to the deterioration of local roads; barbed-wire fences and other obstacles now appeared all over the Island; private cars, none too numerous those days, decreased even further; owners of motor cycles needed a special permit to use their vehicles. The oddities of war did not even spare the street names, then still written in Italian. They were anglicized. [13]

As week followed week and raid followed raid, the aircraft strength dwindled precariously. The Anglo-Maltese League sponsored by Barclays Bank (DCO) Ltd and Allied Malta Newspapers Ltd, launched the following appeal on 30th July, 1940: "None can have failed to appreciate the great service of the

(E. & V. Cassar)
Presentation Spitfire Malta ...

(E. & V. Cassar)
... *and* Ghawdex *(Gozo)*.

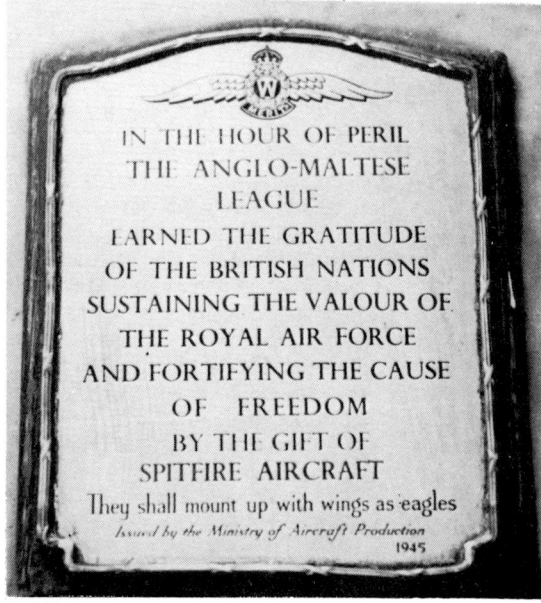

(L.F. Tortell)
Commemorative plaque presented to the Anglo-Maltese League in 1945 by the Ministry of Aircraft Production.

Royal Air Force in the air defence of these Islands against the bombing attacks by Italian aeroplanes, nor can any have failed to observe that other territories of the British Empire have subscribed towards providing additional 'planes for the Royal Air Force. The Anglo-Maltese League, in full conviction that it is fulfilling the earnest desire of all Maltese and English people in these Islands, has consequently undertaken to open a fund, which has been styled "The Fighter 'Plane Fund, Malta" in order that a 'fighter' may be presented to the British Government for service over Malta and as an expression of Malta's admiration for and gratitude to the Royal Air Force."

The sum of £1,968. 19s. 5d was subscribed within the first four days, while the target of £6,000 was reached within twenty days. As contributions kept pouring in, it was decided to keep the fund open to pay for another fighter for a total of £12,000.

Collection boxes were set up in various parts of the Island; the fund was augmented with money derived from film shows, dances, concerts, football matches and other activities. Contributions, ranging from £500 to a farthing, swelled to £12,090 within a period of three months, when the fund was closed on 29th October, 1940. The money was sent in three instalments to the Rt Hon Lord Beaverbrook, Minister for Aircraft Production, with a request that the aircraft be respectively named *Malta* and *Ghawdex*. Credit for the success of this initiative goes to the Hon Ercole Valenzia LP, Mr Algernon Crockford and Mr Joseph Cassar, President, Hon General Secretary and Hon Treasurer respectively of the Anglo-Maltese League.

The two Spitfires, *Malta*, serial number W3210, and *Ghawdex*, W3212, were not sent to Malta. The *Times of Malta* of 15th January, 1941, carried a letter by one of its readers signing himself 'True Patriot': "Some Maltese people are very anxious to know what has become of the money collected in Malta for the Malta fighter planes, namely *Malta* and *Ghawdex*. They were supposed to arrive in Malta by the end of last November. Nothing has been heard about them lately. Will the Government please note this serious matter that concerns every Maltese citizen as it concerns me." (See Appendix **B**)

This fund had in fact been preceded by another one for the purchase by the Maltese people of two Red Cross ambulances for service in London; a multitude of other funds followed: the Malta Relief Fund, Help the Homeless Fund, Naval Comforts (Malta) Fund, Malta Mobile Canteen (London) Fund and Comforts for Wounded Service Personnel Fund. The

(via N. Malizia)
Benito Mussolini decorating Capitano Pilota Mario Rigatti *with the* Medaglia d'Oro al Valore Militare, *Italy's highest military award. Rigatti was injured in action over Malta on 24th August, 1940; the ceremony took place in 1942.*

(via R.H. Barber)
A cartoon showing a CR 42 knocking Hurricanes out of the sky, with British pilots queuing up at the Gate of Heaven, was dropped by means of a small silk parachute from a CR 42 over Luqa in the autumn of 1940.

(via N. Malizia)
An Italian Junkers 87 Stuka (known as Picchiatello) *clearing the cliffs after having bombed Hal Far from 500 metres on 15th September, 1940.*

response to these appeals, and to those launched from time to time, surprised even the organisers as subscriptions poured in from all sections of the population and garrison; donations were also received from Maltese communities in the Commonwealth, the United States and in other countries.

The raising of funds was but a minor facet in Malta's contribution to the war effort. Her strategic position provided the ideal base for a striking force against Italian targets on land and sea. This possibility was assessed from the start by Admiral Sir Andrew B. Cunningham, a great sailor who had much faith in Malta's potential. It was on his initiative that, on 21st June, 1940, twelve Swordfish of No 767 Fleet Air Arm Squadron were posted to Malta for offensive operations. The knowledge that Malta could, and was, striking back inspired confidence at all levels.

The gradual strengthening of the land and aerial defences and the presence of a striking force could not by themselves maintain morale at a high level indefinitely. The replenishment of essential commodities took first priority. Malta, with no natural resources, needed food and fuel to support her high population and increased garrison. It was, therefore, essential to maintain a balance between civil and military supplies; it was no use having bread and no ammunition and *vice-versa*. This led to the setting up of an authority for the Co-ordination of Supplies — COSUP — with the object of assessing and meeting the Island's needs.

The Malta Shipping Committee, established in Egypt some time later, co-operated with COSUP in Malta in ensuring a balanced dispatch of cargo to Malta. But that was only part of the problem. The Mediterranean was no longer the tranquil sea of yesteryear. The Island depended on the Royal and Merchant Navies to deliver the goods. Operation 'Hats', the first of many convoys, set sail from Alexandria towards Malta at about 11.00 pm on 29th August, 1940. (See Appendix **C**)

The three ships in the convoy, *Cornwall, Volo* and *Plumleaf,* had a close escort of four destroyers, *Jervis, Juno, Dainty* and *Diamond,* whilst a heavier force kept its distance to meet any interception by the Italian Navy, which in fact sent a submarine to shadow the convoy. At about mid-day on 31st August, five S.79s launched a determined attack, closely missing *Dainty* and scoring three hits on *Cornwall,* whose crew battled to control the spreading fire and repaired the damaged engines. The listing ship, with many dead on board, rejoined the rest of the convoy at a reduced speed. Malta was sighted at first light on 2nd September when the tugs *Jaunty* and *Ancient* went out to help *Cornwall* into the Grand Harbour. The first convoy had reached the Island. As the three ships and four escorts lay off harbour, an Italian motor torpedo-boat approached the Island but beat a speedy retreat on being engaged by Royal Navy patrol vessels guarding the harbour entrance.

On 1st September, 1940, Flying Officer George Vincent Davies, who had led the first six Hurricanes to Malta on 21st June, 1940, took off from Luqa in his Hudson on a reconnaissance sortie between Cape Bon and Sicily. Three Fulmars from HMS *Illustrious,* mistaking the Hudson for an Italian bomber, attacked it; the badly-damaged plane force-landed in Tunisia, where the crew was imprisoned by the Vichy French. On 3rd November, 1940, Mrs Margory Springs, wife of the American Vice-Consul in Tunis, wrote to Mrs Beatrice Ferguson of Peterhead, whose son, Pilot Officer R.W. Ferguson, had been reported missing: besides giving news about the fate of the British airmen, she also testified to the contribution made by our co-nationals abroad: "There are ten men altogether, the rest (besides your son, Flight Lieutenant Frank Cooper and Flying Officer George Vincent Davies) being non-commissioned, and all really very young. They are interned in an old fort with massive walls on top of a small hill ... As far as their material needs go, you can be quite sure they are being attended to. There is a large Maltese colony here and these people have contributed money, clothes and food, to say nothing of games, in fact everything that can be found here to make them more comfortable than they otherwise would be ... The boys take long walks under guard, play football and have plenty of books, cards and magazines. They have a darts board, a rowing machine, and the Maltese have just brought them each a leather jacket and knitted woollen stockings to keep

(IWM)

A Wellington being prepared for a bombing sortie.

them warm. So there you are, Mrs Ferguson, don't worry about your boy's health or material welfare ..." Mrs Springs requested Mrs Ferguson to pass the comforting news to the wives of the other two officers.[14]

This episode is just one of the many instances showing the assistance extended to allied servicemen by Maltese in foreign territories, such as North Africa, France and Italy. These Maltese, some of whom were subsequently decorated, risked their lives not only in sheltering British servicemen but also in helping them to escape to allied territory.

A change in bombing tactics took place on 5th September, 1940 when five Ju 87 Stukas of the *Regia Aeronautica* carried out the first dive-bombing attack over Malta. Escorted by two fighter squadrons, they attacked Delimara and Marsaxlokk with 500 kg bombs. In that month, Italian-manned Stukas were used in bombing sorties on Luqa, Hal Far and Ta' Qali airfields and on the dockyard; from October to December 1940, most of the attacks were carried out by S.79s escorted by Mc 200s and CR 42s. Several night sorties, generally by single raiders, aimed at lowering the morale of both garrison and civilians alike.

On the evening of 13th October, 1940, a signal was received at RAF Station Kalafrana notifying the arrival of Secretary of State Anthony Eden on a Sunderland. At the time a strong *sirocco* was blowing over Marsaxlokk Bay; heavy swells rendered the laying of a flare path impossible. Warned about the adverse conditions, the pilot signalled that the flyingboat had reached the point of no return and would, therefore, carry on towards Malta. An emergency plan was devised to bring in the Sunderland. A number of launches, dispersed within the bay, opened their searchlights as far as possible into line, together with those from gun positions in the area. The operation was successful, even though the flyingboat ended up dangerously close to Delimara Point. The inclement weather enforced a longer stay which gave Mr Eden time to assess the Island's defences. Travelling with him was Sir John Dill, Chief of the Imperial General Staff.

Towards the end of October, a number of Wellingtons arrived at Malta for operations against Italy and North Africa. Tragedy struck during their second operation when, on the night of 3rd November, two aircraft crashed moments after take-off from Luqa. The first crashed on open ground whilst the other fell on some houses in the outskirts of Qormi, killing two and injuring several civilians. A great part of the burnt-out aircraft remained suspended

(The Times)
Part of the burnt-out skeleton of the Wellington, which crashed at Qormi on 3rd November, 1940; an aeroengine rests on the steel beams at right.

(J. Camilleri)
P.C. 347 Carmel Camilleri, George Medal.

from the steel girders of one of the houses, while furiously burning parts of the plane had fallen into a nearby quarry from the bottom of which rescue workers heard some moaning. Two airmen were sprawled lifeless near the wreckage, whilst a third, though badly injured, managed to move towards the side of the shaft. Efforts to haul him up failed as he was too weak to hold a grip to the rope. Disregarding the risk of exploding bombs, Police Constable 347 Carmel Camilleri volunteered to be lowered into the blazing quarry and succeeded in tying the rope around the airman, Sergeant A.T. Smith, who was then hauled to safety. PC Camilleri was awarded the George Medal on 28th February, 1941, for his bravery.

A number of Glenn Martin 'Marylands' had been operating from Malta in a photo-reconnaissance role since September 1940. In fact, the successful attack by the Fleet Air Arm on Taranto harbour in Southern Italy on 11th November was preceded by several PR sorties, for which all aircrew of No 431 Flight took turns. The photographs showing five battleships, fourteen cruisers and twenty-seven destroyers lying at anchor, were rushed to HMS *Illustrious* (Captain Denis Boyd DSC RN) whose Swordfish launched a torpedo attack. At a single stroke, three of Italy's capital ships were put out of action, whilst a heavy cruiser and a destroyer, moored in the inner basin, were also hit. This daring attack altered the balance of naval power in the Mediterranean. It is unfortunate that some of the aircrew, who had risked so much in gathering such vital information, did not live long enough to read Admiral Cunningham's 1947 despatch on this operation: "In the event, the success of the Fleet Air Arm attack was due in no small degree to the excellent reconnaissance carried out by the Royal Air Force Glenn Martin Flight (No 431) from Malta under very difficult conditions and often in the face of fighter opposition." Following this disastrous blow, the rest of the Italian Fleet withdrew to Naples. Spirits ran high but, inevitably, both the Island and the aircraft-carrier were to pay a dear price.

Nothwithstanding the pressing need for fighter aircraft in Britain, on 2nd August the aircraft-carrier *Argus* flew off twelve Hurricane Mk Is of No 418 Flight; these aircraft joined the remaining Gladiators to form No 261 Squadron. This ferrying operation, code-named 'Hurry', encouraged the Chiefs of Staff to send in another batch of twelve Hurricanes from the same carrier on 17th November. Operation 'White' went awry as only four of the fighters reached Malta while the other eight ran out of fuel *en route*. The blame was attributed to inadequately-trained pilots who were said to have lacked proficiency in assessing the range and endurance of their aircraft. However, the possibility that the Hurricanes were launched from a distance not allowing a sufficient safety margin cannot be ruled out.

Christmas 1940 was by no means a happy one for Malta; yet the Maltese were proud that after six months of hostilities the Fascists had not subdued, much less occupied, the Island. This failure compelled the Italian Chiefs of Staff to seek the intervention of the Germans to solve the 'Malta problem'. In the latter part of December 1940, units of the *Luftwaffe's Fliegerkorps* X, commanded by *Generalleutnant* Hans-Ferdinand Geisler, began to arrive in Sicily to intensify operations against Malta and to give added protection to Axis convoys ferrying men and material to North Africa. The airfields at Còmiso, Catania, Gerbini, Trapani, Gela and Palermo housed an array of aircraft superior to what the Italians possessed: Heinkel 111s, Junkers 52s, 87s and 88s, as well as Messerschmitt 110s. These, together with Italian Savoia Marchettis, Cants, Macchis and Fiat CR 42s, were marshalled against Malta.

The gallant conduct of the civilians was recognised when the awards of the first George Medals were announced on 17th December, 1940. (See Appendix **D**). The honours went to R.H. Lewis and Frank Mallia, Chargemen of Fitters and of Labourers respectively at His Majesty's Dockyard, for 'exceptional, meritorious and devoted service' in the face of enemy air attacks. On 11th June, 1940, a bomb had exploded close to a pom-pom gun at

(via N. Malizia)
A Macchi 200 flying at 5,500 metres on a reconnaissance sortie over Hal Far airfield on 27th October, 1940.

Kordin. The two men volunteered to lead their gangs at erecting splinter plates around the exposed gun position. Their fearless example encouraged others to work even during air raids when bombs were exploding within 100 yards of the site.

Chapter Two

Attack on HMS Illustrious — Recovery of unexploded radio-controlled bomb

Early in January 1941, Operation 'Excess' was mounted in order to send badly-needed supplies to Malta and Greece. On the morning of the 10th, the destroyer *Gallant* shattered her bow on striking a mine, killing 60 men and wounding another 25. Helpless but still afloat, she was towed by HMS *Mohawk* to Malta, where she was beached near the Power Station at Crucifix Hill.

In the meantime Italian S.79 bombers were attacking the heavily-escorted convoy in the vicinity of Malta. These were repulsed by Fulmars from HMS *Illustrious*, the Royal Navy's newest armoured-deck aircraft-carrier. In no time a large formation of German Ju 87s and Ju 88s, making their first appearance in the Central Mediterranean, headed towards the convoy. They singled out *Illustrious* and dropped their bombs over the carrier. The raiders were met with determined resistance from the Fulmars and the Fleet guns but this did not spare *Illustrious* an agonising ten minutes, during which she was hit six times, suffering extensive damage; 126 members of the crew were killed and 91 injured.

Ronald Lucking, who served as a stoker on *Illustrious* between 1939 and 1945, describes the nightmarish scene: "I came off watch from the boiler-room at noon and as Action Stations had already sounded, I proceeded to my damage-control point, the wardroom flat just abaft the keyboard flat. Within minutes, we were hit in the after-lift well. Shortly after, a 500 kg bomb pierced the 4" armoured flight deck, through the hangar-deck and partially into the wardroom flat and ammunition conveyor, approximately 6 feet from where we were assembled. I was fortunate to be blown through the bulkhead door, landing about 30 feet away from the door.

"I went back and saw one of my colleagues, a South African, whom I dragged away, while

(Wm. Rothwell)

HMS Gallant *beached beneath Crucifix Hill.*

petrol from the planes was coming into the wardroom flat. Hit on the back of the head, he instantly succumbed to his wounds. Stoker Hemmings from Bristol and myself survived. Unable to move forward, we made our way to the quarter deck, where we saw many wounded and dead. The two of us rigged up hose pipes and tried to put out the fires in the lift well. The ship was hit again, the bomb splinters hitting the ship's bell while shrapnel damaged the steering gear. We were vulnerable at the stern-end of the ship as the ammunition conveyor was damaged and no shells could reach the aft 4.5" guns. I was literally trapped on the quarter deck until the fires were brought under control.

"I managed to get some sheets from the aft cabins, with which I bandaged as many of the wounded as possible, including some marines. When we were about an hour's distance from Malta, Hemmings and I made our way up to the flight deck and got as far as the citadel, where the doctor covered me with a violet ointment pending my transportation to hospital on arrival in Malta. Hemmings, who was with me all the time, suffered a breakdown and I never met him again. I had burns on my back, arms, shoulders and head, and a couple of slight wounds from shrapnel splinters." [15]

The crippled carrier, on fire and with steering-gear wrecked, headed for Malta with German bombers in pursuit. She limped into the Grand Harbour on 10th January and as she berthed at Parlatorio Wharf, dockyard workers and medical teams mounted a simultaneous operation to save the ship and the wounded. For some reason, possibly adverse climatic conditions, the Germans did not press on with further attacks. Taking advantage of this providential respite, dockyard workers and the ship's crew worked round-the-clock to repair the damage.

The lull lasted till 16th January when, early in the afternoon, seventeen Ju 88s, escorted by twenty Me 110s, and forty-four Ju 87s, escorted by twenty Mc 200s and ten CR 42s, launched their first blitz over Malta with *Illustrious* as their target.

The Authorities had prepared a plan to protect *Illustrious* against this expected attack. The experience gained from previous attacks by Italian-manned Stukas and the advice given by a number of artillery officers, including Captain (later Lieutenant-General Sir) Terence McMeekin, Captain Heath and Brigadier Norman Sadler, resulted in a dense 'box barrage' being put up above the carrier.

The Stukas, fitted with air-driven sirens known as 'Jericho Trumpets' to terrorize the gunners and civilians, dived almost vertically and released their bombs, whilst heavy and light anti-aircraft guns added to the deafening din by firing incessantly at the bombers until the gun barrels wore out. Some of the Ju 87s in their near-suicidal tactics came out of their dive at levels beneath the bastions; this infuriated the Bofors crews around the harbour as they could not engage the enemy until the aircraft had cleared inhabited areas. As the bombers emerged from this curtain of steel, they were pounced upon by a small number of Hurricanes and Fulmars, whose pilots fought with great determination, on some occasions following the raiders right through the barrage.

Bombs rained down on the dockyard and adjacent areas but the plan worked; only one bomb, causing superficial damage, hit *Illustrious*. The brunt of the attack was borne by Senglea, Vittoriosa and Cospicua; Valletta was not spared either. Clouds of dust and smoke shrouded the Three Cities, where many people lost their homes and belongings. Many were killed and hundreds trapped beneath the rubble of their dwellings. This heavy toll was due to the fact that a large number of evacuees had returned to the Three Cities and Valletta after getting over their initial shock, the more so since raids had decreased in number and intensity after July 1940.

Members of the Air Raid Precautions Organisation and the Special Constabulary were joined by policemen, soldiers, sailors, dockyard workers and other volunteers in a frantic search for survivors. Rescue workers had by that time attained a high standard of efficiency and their dedication to duty and disregard for their own safety earned them the admiration and respect of the population. They saved a large number of people. A source of inspiration to the rescue teams in the Three Cities were Superintendent Joseph Storace of the Passive Defence Corps and the District Commissioner, Dr Paul Boffa, who eventually became Malta's first post-war Prime Minister and was subsequently knighted.

Searches went on for so long as people were reported missing; in fact, a group of twelve was rescued after having been entombed for forty-eight hours under forty feet of rubble in a cellar at Two Gates Street in Senglea. Willie Mizzi, one of the survivors, narrates: "When the alert sounded, my son told me to take cover as the raiders were already overhead. I hurried to a neighbour's house, which had a rock shelter hewn in the cellar. On reaching the entrance, the house collapsed under a direct hit, trapping twelve of us, and my dog, inside a cubicle measuring six yards by two.

"For two days we were huddled on top of each other in complete darkness and, as time passed, we suffered from suffocation, and water and food shortage. There was no panic;

Widespread destruction at Senglea.

we just stood there exchanging an occasional word unaware that we were buried under forty feet of rubble. When we had almost given up hope, we felt some gravel filtering into the shelter and shortly afterwards we could see a speck of light through the mound of masonry. The hole was enlarged and we were asked if we were all well, after which Dr Boffa lowered some pills in a bottle and told us to take one each.

"Soon after, we were brought out safe and sound. We owe our lives to my brother-in-law who had organised a rescue party consisting of about fifty dockyard workers and Demolition and Clearance personnel. I lost my home, two shops as well as all my earthly possessions; the merchant in me had not died out, however, and I started selling peanuts to support my wife and two children." [16]

The greatest tragedy perhaps occurred at Vittoriosa where thirty-five people were killed when the crypt at St Lawrence Church, where they were sheltering, received a direct hit. For the people in the blitzed areas, that raid was an unforgettable nightmare; for the Maltese in general, it marked the beginning of a long, harrowing experience.

During the evening of the 11th, the merchant ship *Essex*, loaded with 4,000 tons of ammunition and 3,000 tons of potato seed, in addition to twelve crated Hurricanes as deck-cargo, had berthed in the Grand Harbour. Unloading progressed satisfactorily until the ship was hit during the Illustrious Blitz, when a heavy-calibre bomb struck just forward of the funnel, penetrating 'A' and 'B' Decks before exploding in 'C' Deck. The explosion, causing extensive damage, started a fire which luckily did not reach the hold housing the ammunition. Fifteen members of the crew and seven Maltese stevedores were killed, whilst several others were injured.

Some of the dead stevedores, trapped between plates, could not be extricated before several days. Captain E.J.F. Price DSC RN, the Divisional Sea Transport Officer, Malta, reported: " ... this, no doubt, coupled with the shock the stevedores had received, thoroughly frightened the men who were unwilling to finish the ship. I had no time to organise other labour and, in any case, considered it a good opportunity to show these men, who held an opposite view, that we could unload a ship quite well without them. Sailors were detailed to work the winches, and soldiers worked in the holds and in lighters; we carried on working both by day and by night until 30th January, when the ship was fully unloaded ... All the same, a good deal of damage had been caused to the cargo and a certain amount had been dropped overboard, which had to be subsequently salved by divers ... The dockyard took charge of the ship and pumped out the engine-room and No 3 hold, burning away the plates so that the corpses could be removed ..." [17]. In fairness to the Sea Transport Officer, he did not fail to point out that not only the stevedores were scared: "... The 4th Officer of the ship, Mr Robert George Bush, was the only officer or man who came back to the ship, soon after bombing of the *Essex*, prepared to work ..."[18]

The *Luftwaffe* reappeared on 18th January, when fifty-one Ju 87s, escorted by seventeen Me 110s and nine Mc 200s, attacked Luqa and Hal Far airfields, causing considerable damage. An enveloping barrage, as well as RAF fighters, were ready for the raiders; a handful of FAA Fulmars, operating from local airfields after being flown-off the damaged *Illustrious*, also gave a helping hand. Seven Stukas were shot down by the fighters for the loss of one Fulmar. In this connection the feat of a Maltese sapper, Spiro Zammit, is recorded in the citation accompanying the British Empire Medal (Military Division) he was awarded: "A Fulmar aircraft came down in the sea off Marsascirocco at about 1530 hours on 18th January, 1941, about 40 yards from the shore and in rough weather. No 576 Sapper Spiro Zammit, Royal Engineers (T), immediately dived into the water and, reaching one of the pilots, held him up until rescued by a speedboat. There can be no doubt that Zammit was largely instrumental in saving the life of the pilot, who was in an extremely exhausted condition."

The following day, forty-eight Ju 87s escorted by five Me 110s, ten CR 42s and eight Mc 200s, subjected *Illustrious* to another onslaught but the attack was again repulsed; not a single direct hit was scored, although near-misses caused some damage to her hull below the water-line, thus delaying her departure.

Once again, the areas near the dockyard received a terrible hammering, entire streets being flattened. Rescue workers, who were still searching for victims of the raid on the 16th, had to shift tons of rubble by hand to reach those trapped beneath the debris. Sometimes, when within reach of the victims, their work was hampered by collapsing walls. Undaunted, they removed boulders, fittings, furniture and steel beams until they dropped through sheer exhaustion, their place being promptly taken by other volunteers.

The Basilica of Our Lady of Victories in Senglea, whose belfry clockhands still marked ten minutes to two o'clock, when the church was first hit on the 16th — was completely destroyed on 19th January. The Annunciation Church at Vittoriosa was also severely damaged on the same day. Once more, hundreds of families decided to join those who had already moved inland taking with them the bare necessities on carts. Government utilised

(NWM)

Damage to the Basilica of Our Lady of Victories at Senglea after the attacks on HMS Illustrious.

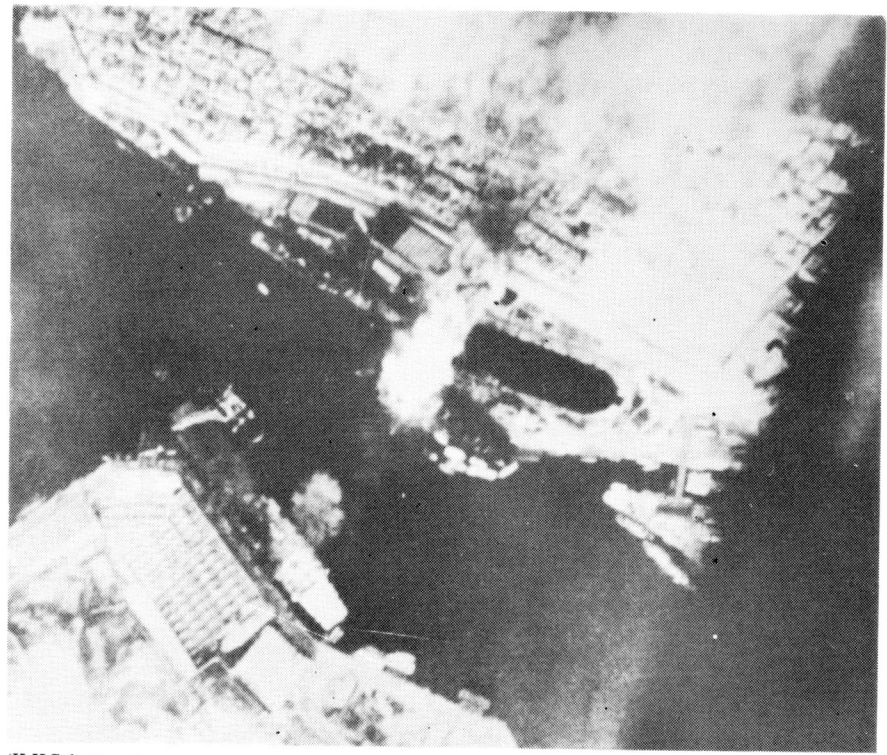

(K-H Schomann)

HMS Illustrious *under attack on 19th January, 1941. The carrier is berthed alongside Parlatorio Wharf.*

its schools to accommodate most of them, whilst several convents were likewise improvised into refugee centres. The proverbial hospitality of the Islanders made it almost natural for families in safer areas to offer accommodation to evacuees or the homeless. Such families were advised to paint one or more Maltese Cross on their front door, indicating the number of families they were prepared to accommodate. Many sought refuge in Gozo and by the middle of 1942 the number of Maltese living in the Sister Island swelled to about 4,000.

Ronald Lucking, one of the seamen who had been wounded on *Illustrious*, recalls his stay at Mtarfa Military Hospital: "I was grateful to be in hospital with all your kind nurses at Mtarfa. I was able to follow the bombing and destruction of Valletta. I made my peace with God, as I had done many times over the last few days, having fixed in my mind the picture of death and destruction under those clouds of dust, little knowing that as a walking-wounded I would be asked to volunteer to rejoin the ship." [19]

Repair work on *Illustrious* went on regardless of raids and bad weather. It was imperative for the carrier to leave Malta. At dusk on 23rd January, she slipped out of the Grand Harbour bound for Alexandria, from where she proceeded to the United States of America for major repairs. According to Admiral Sir Andrew B. Cunningham, Commander-in-Chief Mediterranean Fleet, the *Illustrious* episode stands out as a triumph for British shipbuilders and naval constructors, as well as for the Malta dockyard workers. Major-General C.T. Beckett CB CBE MC paid merited credit to the Maltese and British gunners and attributed the failure of the dive-bombing attacks on the carrier mainly to the special barrage which had been devised. The Royal Air Force and Fleet Air Arm fighters likewise contributed to the overall effort.

The Illustrious Blitz was an exercise in courage; there was courage on the part of the Axis and British airmen; the Maltese, British and naval gunners; the dockyard workers and the civilians. This collective demonstration of courage is perhaps epitomised by the determination of a Maltese dockyard worker. Joseph Gauci, an Admiralty diver, was carrying out an undersea examination of the hull of *HMS Illustrious* when bombs rained down. He carried on with his vital work and, inspired by his example, his attendants remained on the small boat which was tossed about by the wake from bombs exploding all around. The timely completion of this hazardous job enabled the dockyard workers to commence repair work immediately the raiders withdrew. This gallant act earned Mr Gauci the British Empire Medal.

Another episode is worth recording before

(The Times)
The fourteen Maltese Crosses at the entrance of Villa Navillus at Attard indicate the number of families that found refuge there.

closing the *Illustrious* saga. In addition to conventional bombs, the Germans released at least one sophisticated missile, a radio-controlled armour-piercing bomb.

Major Reginald Parker GM, then serving as sergeant with the Royal Engineers Bomb Disposal Unit, recalls in detail the hazardous task of tracing, removing and defusing this new type of bomb, which luckily failed to explode: "The call came to deal with a UXB (unexploded bomb) in Cospicua. On arrival at the reported site, we were under the impression that a bomb had gone off because of the amount of damage. What, as we later found out, had been a nunnery, was now a mountain of stone and rubble. It became obvious to us that something massive had crashed into it; still, initial examination of the area revealed no trace of a bomb or possibly a crashed aircraft.

"We started to dig into the mountain of rubble. This proved very difficult as we had no mechanical equipment; the location, owing to the steps, would have denied us using any heavy equipment even if we had it. After several days we had still found no evidence of an exploded bomb although the excavation had reached a state of a funnel-shaped hole with steep sides, down which large stones would crash occasionally. We gradually enlarged the diameter of the hole and removed several tons of rubble. We then came across pieces of cast light alloy material, some wire and what seemed like pieces of electrical equipment. The possibility of an aircraft crash could now not be ruled out. Still, on reporting to Headquarters, we were told that we had possibly some sort of a new bomb to contend with; we were advised to proceed with caution.

"At last when we got to ground floor level in our enlarged funnel shaped excavation, we discovered that below us there were some cellars and the ground floor was in a dangerous state, broken through in some places and liable to collapse under the mountain of rubble. Having done more clearing, we were confronted by the largest bomb we had met to-date, of such a shape as we had not yet encountered. As the bomb lay, we could not see any fuses. This we reported to Headquarters who confirmed that it was a new type of guided-bomb; we were to do our utmost to recover it intact as none of this type had ever been recovered.

"We propped up the ground floor with timber to prevent further falls and to allow us to work in the cellars in some degree of safety. Our efforts to remove the fuse were abortive as the battered retaining screw ring was damaged.

(IWM)
The statue of Our Lady of Victories stands almost unscathed amidst the debris stretching along Victory Street at Senglea.

The use of brute force, where all else failed, made it possible for us, at least, to get the bomb into the street where we unsuccessfully tried to remove the fuse.

"We had built in our Floriana barracks a heavy wooden sledge so as to carry the bomb down the steps and round the corner. This was achieved by using 'holding back' tackles and pulling ropes, while taking as much cover as possible. It was a relief to get away from the Three Cities and dockyard area, which were constantly being bombed, though to a lesser extent when *Illustrious* departed. In our safer area, we at last managed to remove the damaged fuse. To achieve this, we had to resort to hammer and chisel, ignoring the normal principles of treating fuses gently. We then ceased to call the bomb a 'beast'; we could now admire its excellent finish.

"Later on, Headquarters revealed that the bomb was of an armour-piercing type meant for use against capital ships; it had stub wings and a tail permitting it to glide to some degree; it was capable of guidance by remote control from the aircraft dropping it."[20]

The exact toll of the losses suffered by the *Luftwaffe* and *Regia Aeronautica* cannot be ascertained. The figures released by the British and the Axis vary considerably. Moreover, it is known that many enemy aircraft failed to reach their base in Sicily. Radio stations throughout the world commented about the ferocity of the Illustrious Blitz and the heavy losses sustained by the Axis; Moscow Radio reported the

Entire blocks of buildings in Senglea demolished by bombing.

funeral of 96 German aircrew at Syracuse, whilst a Swiss broadcast told of a mass funeral of 142 at Catania.

With the departure of *Illustrious*, the Germans turned their attention to the airfields. Luqa was attacked repeatedly, sustaining great damage, with hangars and other installations reduced to twisted skeletons; several Wellington bombers were also destroyed on the ground and, following one particularly heavy raid, the airfield was unoperational for forty-eight hours. Due to its proximity to the airfield, Luqa village was not spared. Pilot Officer 'Jock' Barber witnessed one of these attacks: "I remember on one occasion being up at Mtarfa; I had a stand down. I watched a dive-bombing raid on Luqa which went on for what seemed hours until a pall of smoke built up over the airfield, eventually drifting out over the sea. You could not see anything of the airfield; there were so many things burning. Out of this gloom of black smoke, you could see the flashes of the anti-aircraft guns, Bofors in particular. I really took my hat off to these gunners and also, of course, those around the Grand Harbour who did a terrific job."[21]

Chapter Three

Capture of Italian floatplane — First British airborne operation — Conscription — The Luftwaffe *withdraws — Lloyd succeeds Maynard as Air Officer Commanding — Malta Night Fighter Unit — General Dobbie appointed Governor — Rationing — Sinking of M.V. Moor — Heinkel floatplanes at Malta*

On the night of 25th January, 1941, a Cant-Z 501 floatplane, piloted by *Tenente* Aldo Bellenzier, was detailed to search for the crew of another floatplane which had sustained damage on its return to base in Sicily. As the relief plane lost its bearings, the pilot requested base to switch on a searchlight to guide him back. This message was intercepted by the Authorities in Malta who promptly obliged. Pitch darkness prevented the Italian pilot from identifying any landmarks and he touched down near Comino. The Italians were taken prisoners but efforts to tow the floatplane to Malta failed.

Aerial activity on the evening of 10th February, 1941, was heavier than usual but for a change the aircraft were *ours*. What the Maltese and the rest of the world did not know was that an airborne commando raid on the province of Campagna in Italy was about to be launched from Malta. Preparations for the operation, code-named 'Colossus', were carried out in England. On 7th February, eight Whitleys from No 78 Squadron carried the paratroops from East Anglia to Malta. The Force, under the command of Major T.A.G. Pritchard of the Royal Welch Fusiliers, was made up of about forty officers and men. One of the men was an Italian, Fortunato Picchi, who for many years served at the Savoy Hotel in London; he was chosen to act as guide as he knew the proposed landing site quite well, having spent his boyhood in the area.[22] On 9th February, Flying Officer Adrian Warburton DSO DFC, piloting a Glenn Martin, photographed the area around Ginestra, a tributary of the Tragino river. The aqueduct on the eastern part was chosen as the target. On completion of the mission, the parachutists were to be picked up by submarine.

The troops spent two days making last-minute preparations in Malta. The eight Whitleys took off from Luqa at dusk on 10th February; four aircraft carried the men and equipment while the other four attacked the airfield at Foggia to create a diversion. The parachutists landed near their target and the charges were set off at 0030 hours on the 11th. The structure was stronger than expected and the supports, although damaged, did not collapse; a nearby railway bridge was, however, demolished. The men then headed towards the rendezvous at the mouth of the river Sele but the tracks they left in the snow and mud gave them away and they were eventually taken prisoners.

Unknown to them, one of the Whitleys bombing Foggia developed engine trouble and crash-landed in the very area where the troops

(Bundesarchiv)
Oberleutnant *Joachim Müncheberg. By the time this German fighter ace met his death in action in North Africa on 23rd March, 1943, he had been credited with shooting down 135 allied aircraft.*

32

were to board the submarine. On account of this mishap the submarine *Triumph*, which was sailing towards the rendezvous, was ordered to return to Malta as her possible loss and that of her crew would have been too costly. This brought to an end the first wartime British airborne operation.

The *Luftwaffe* in Sicily was reinforced in February 1941 by Me 109Es belonging to 7 *Staffel* of *Jagdgeschwader* 26. This Unit, comprising pilots with considerable combat experience in the Battle of Britain, was led by *Oberleutnant* Joachim Müncheberg, a fighter ace with 23 victories to his credit. Operating from Gela, this Unit achieved great success; Müncheberg excelled himself and, during the four months of operations over Malta, he shot down nineteen Hurricanes. His daring and skill eventually made him one of Germany's top fighter aces, earning him the Oak Leaves with Swords to the Knight's Cross of the Iron Cross, as well as Italy's highest honour, the Gold Medal for Military Valour.

Although many Maltese had already enrolled in the different branches of the Three Services, conscription was introduced on 3rd March, 1941. The Compulsory Service Regulation laid down that all men between the ages of 16 and 56 were liable to National Service. The first to be called up were those who were 20 and 21 years old, residing in the Birkirkara area. Others from various districts and of different age groups were subsequently conscripted.

A unit deserving special mention is the Dockyard Defence Battery. Established in 1939, it had double the strength of a normal battery, so that, when hostilities started, the men alternated between manning the guns and working at the dockyard; this arrangement functioned well and the men excelled themselves in both roles. For some time the Dockyard Defence Battery formed part of the Royal Artillery. It was later integrated with 3rd Light Anti-Aircraft Regiment, Royal Malta Artillery, and was re-designated 30th LAA Battery.

From the start Maltese soldiers, mostly inexperienced, rose to the occasion. Lieutenant Bernard Amato-Gauci, who commanded a detachment of fifty men from 3 Bn KOMR manning twenty-three sangers deployed around Hal Far airfield, recalls: "A formation of

(I. Borg)
The Borg brothers enlisted in the Royal Army Service Corps Expeditionary Force Institute; from left: John, Joseph, Vincent, Walter, Hector and Anthony.

(F. Asphar)
The Asphar brothers: Lieut John Asphar RNVR, 2/Lt Alfred Asphar KOMR, Cpl Frank Asphar RAF and David Asphar of the Merchant Navy.

CR 42s attacked the airfield on 18th January, 1941, and Corporal Arthur Kitney, a Maltese from Pawla, engaged the low-flying aircraft from his sangar atop a roof. A couple of the Italian aircraft attacked the building, severely damaging it, but Corporal Kitney continued firing his Twin Lewis Gun even though injured with a bullet in his shoulder. His courage earned him the Military Medal."[23] Corporal Kitney was promoted sergeant and presented with the medal by General Dobbie on 22nd March, 1941.

A Recruit Training Centre, set up at Fort Ricasoli, aimed at turning a motley crowd of clerks and farmers, shop assistants and masons, intellectuals and illiterates, into soldiers. After a course of basic training these men formed new artillery batteries and infantry battalions. On 30th April, 1941, a raider sneaked in undetected, dropping a stick of bombs into the Grand Harbour. At that time, several *dghajsas* were ferrying RMA personnel towards Ricasoli Barracks. One of the boats carrying twelve men, mostly recruits, capsized as a result of a near explosion some 200 yards off shore. Witnessing the incident from the barracks, Lieutenant Joseph E. Agius, who received the Military Cross for bravery on a subsequent occasion, dived into the sea and, together with two recruits, rescued eleven men encumbered by greatcoats. The drama was repeated two days later when these same men, together with other RMA soldiers, dived into the mine-infested seas off Ricasoli to save personnel from HMS *Jersey*, when the destroyer sank after striking a mine at the harbour entrance; several naval boats took part in this rescue operation.

From 18 air attacks in December 1940, the number rose to 57, 107 and 105 in the first three months of 1941. From the start of hostilities till the appearance of the *Luftwaffe* in January 1941, the heavy anti-aircraft guns and the Bofors had fired 9,546 and 1,098 rounds respectively. The corresponding figures for the following three months rose to 21,176 and 18,660; this sharp increase reflected German participation, specializing in low-level attacks.[24]

The Island was crying out for reinforcements

(NWMA)
A recruitment poster launched as far back as 1939. During Mass, Parish Priests read out a notice stating that recruits were urgently required for the Royal Malta Artillery.

Members of the Dockyard Defence Battery manning a Bofors at the King George V Recreational Ground at Floriana overlooking the Grand Harbour. This photograph, taken on 3rd April, 1941, when the Battery still formed part of the Royal Artillery, shows (front row, left to right) Sgt John Attard, L/Cpl Fred Cassar, Pte Tony Bugeja, Pte Joe Farrugia; (back row, from left) Privates Alphonse M. Borg, Paul Fabri, John Grech and Emanuel Mallia.

and, although another convoy could not be run at the time, an attempt was made towards the end of April to send an unescorted vessel carrying twenty-one Hurricanes and other essential cargo. *Parracombe* suitably disguised, sailed from the west hugging territorial waters. She escaped attention but, unfortunately, struck a mine off Cape Bon. The crew were interned by the French, and Malta lost her promised supplies.

Stories of near-misses, lucky escapes and averted tragedies were recorded nearly every day. Monsignor Michael Azzopardi vividly recalls a perculiar incident: "When war broke out, about 160 elderly people, invalids and handicapped from the Three Cities, were housed at the Government School at Qormi, having failed to find refuge with families in safer areas. The Home, run by the Education Department, had Dr Irene Condachi as Medical Superintendent, helped by twenty-one Religious Sisters acting as nurses, besides the teachers, maids, charwomen and washerwomen from the schools that had closed down; I was appointed Spiritual Director. We occupied the ground floor, while the top floor was still used as a school for about 240 children attending on the 'half-time' system.

"As the siren was not audible from the school, there was a standing arrangement whereby, when a raid materialised, the Police would phone our caretaker who, in turn, would sound a bell sending inmates and students into the rock shelter beneath the school.

"On 8th May, 1941, the feast of Our Lady of Pompeii, I conducted a Service in the chapel; as if having a premonition of an impending disaster, I urged everyone to pray devoutly. Five days later, the bell rang at 2.15 pm and our folk took cover; the students left their classes, descended the stairs and went underground. The caretaker rushed to me saying he had not rung the bell as he had not received the customary call from the Police. At that very instant, a terrific explosion rocked the building, shrouding it in a thick cloud of dust; almost immediately, the alert was given.

"One of the bombs, which landed squarely on the Tabernacle, containing about 400 consecrated Hosts, destroyed the chapel as well as the stairs which the children had used a few

(G.E. Livock)
Sunderland L 5807 shot up by two Me 109s at the camber at Kalafrana on 27th April, 1941, after having led a number of Hurricanes flown to Malta from HMS Ark Royal.

(H.P. Lloyd)
Air Vice-Marshal Hugh Pughe Lloyd.

minutes before. The headmistress, who had remained upstairs, lost her spectacles on account of the blast. She tried to grope her way downstairs amidst the flying dust and fell down to the ground floor. She was unhurt, as were about five charwomen who were hanging the washing on the roof, when the bombs landed; only one caretaker sustained injuries.

"This truly miraculous deliverance, which could have resulted in one of the worst tragedies to befall Malta throughout the war, is shrouded in the mystery as to who had rung the bell before the siren was sounded. Apart from the premises, the only victim was Christ in the Tabernacle who, under the form of the Holy Eucharist, had drawn the bomb towards Him saving us all." [25]

Towards the end of May 1941, preparatory to the launching of Operation 'Barbarossa', the invasion of Russia, the *Luftwaffe* withdrew from Sicily, giving Malta a welcome respite. The *Regia Aeronautica* maintained a reduced pattern of attacks against Malta, meeting strong opposition from the ground batteries and the Royal Air Force which, between 3rd April and 12th November 1941, was reinforced by a large number of Hurricanes delivered in batches by the carriers *Ark Royal*, *Furious*, *Victorious* and *Argus*.

On 12th May, No 185 Squadron re-formed as a fighter squadron at Hal Far. This was the second squadron to be raised on the Island, this time from No 261 Squadron 'C' Flight and No 1430 Flight. Initially equipped with Hurricane Mk Is, the squadron was later provided with the newer Mk IIs which were superior in performance. The squadron's motto was unique for RAF squadrons on the Island in that it was written in Maltese: *Ara fejn hi*. [26]

On 28th June, a third fighter unit, No 126 Squadron, was formed on the Island and operated from Ta' Qali with No 249, which had arrived from Britain on 21st May.

Air Vice-Marshal Hugh Pughe Lloyd took over from Air Vice-Marshal Maynard on 1st June, 1941. The brief of the new Air Officer Commanding was clear enough: "Your main task in Malta is to sink Axis shipping sailing from Europe to Africa. You will be on the Island for six months as a minimum and nine months as a maximum as by that time you will be worn out." [27] Air Vice-Marshal Lloyd remained here for thirteen months, during which period RAF and FAA aircraft intensified bombing operations against harbours in Italy and North

(E.A. Lindsell)
Pilots of No 126 Squadron, relaxing near their dispersal hut, ready for the next scramble.

Africa. They also harassed Axis convoys delivering supplies to the *Afrika Korps*; in this undertaking, they were joined by locally-based British and allied submarines, which included the Polish *Sokol* and the Greek *Glaucos*. Another submarine that operated from Malta for a short period only was the Free French *Narval*, which had arrived here shortly after the capitulation of France. She was, in fact, the only French submarine in the Mediterranean to join the allied cause. Unfortunately, *Narval* was sunk off Derna on 7th January, 1941, by the Italian torpedo-boat *Clio*, during her second patrol.

The Italians made several nocturnal sorties over Malta, usually employing a small number of bombers which, though causing negligible damage, were of considerable nuisance. It was therefore decided late in July, to form the Malta Night Fighter Unit under the command of Squadron Leader George Powell-Sheddon. It consisted of twelve Hurricane Mk IIs based at Ta' Qali, operating in close liaison with the searchlights.

(via Wm. Floyd)
Pilot climbing out of the cockpit of his Hurricane which crash-landed at Hal Far airfield; ambulance and fire tender rush to the scene.

As soon as an intruder was picked up by radar, the Hurricanes would take off and gain height, slyly waiting in darkness close to the fringes of the searching beams. Once an enemy bomber was caught in the cone of the searchlights, a pair of Hurricanes would pounce on the intruder from either direction. This effective and spectacular manoeuvre became quite an attraction for civilians who lingered outside shelter entrances, watching many a bomber come down like a ball of fire.

A mobile 90cm anti-aircraft searchlight. The small wheel on the extreme right was used to alter both the traversing and elevation of the beam.

However, the high rate of success was not due exclusively to the combined efforts of searchlights and night fighters. According to Air Marshal Sir Hugh Pughe Lloyd, "there was one closely guarded secret which arose from some imperfection in the Italian technical arrangements. As soon as the bomb-release trigger had been operated to drop a new type of incendiary bomb, the aircraft would burst into flames. It was important that the Italians should not become apprehensive and as our claims were always published in the Press and given out over the radio in Britain, we had to say that the aircraft was, in fact, shot down. Colonel John Nelson, who commanded the searchlights, knew the secret, as did a few others; but, in order to keep it, the MNFU had to be given an entirely bogus credit of five victories."[28]

It appears that the Italians, unaware of this mechanical fault, attributed their lack of success to the Island's defensive plan. *Generale* Corrado Ricci gives the Italian version: "From a friend of mine, himself a member of a bomber group who had trained at CAI (*Corpo aereo italiano*) on the English Channel, I came to know about the heavy losses suffered by the crews of the same group. These had baptised Malta as the 'Luna Park' because of the great number of searchlights installed on the Island making it look more like a place of entertainment than the deadly trap it actually was. Our BR 20s, purposely painted black as they flew only on night missions, turning silver-like on entering that illuminated vertical colossal cylinder, apart from having to face the anti-aircraft gunners, innocently fell an easy prey to the British night fighters. Within six months, the group was decimated to such an extent that it had to be withdrawn from the battle-front, to be reconstituted in Northern Italy. Nello Brambilla, the flight commander, had himself been shot down.

"The bombers attacked one by one at a few minutes' interval; in the light provided by the searchlights, the crew could see in their wake the red trail of the preceding plane going down in flames. Twelve was the average number of flights before a pilot would normally be shot down; still no pilot was ever withdrawn, while a few had in fact well exceeded this number. The British night fighters, besides waiting for the bombers over Malta, pursued them as far as their base itself, as was the case with *Tenente* Pezzi. The Authorities would not admit such heavy losses, holding that, when a bomber did not return to base and had not been seen falling over the Island, the crew were blamed for

Mooring Vessel Moor *in the Grand Harbour.*

straying off-course and missing Sicily through a navigational error."[29]

On 19th May, 1941, Lieutenant-General Sir William George Sheddon Dobbie KCB CMG DSO, who had been acting as Officer Administering the Government since 24th May, 1940, was appointed Governor and Commander-in-Chief. In the words of Mr Churchill, General Dobbie was "a Cromwellian figure at the key point". The Governor, though past his prime, faced efficiently the many problems besetting Malta. His concern for people, hit by the tragedy of war, endeared him to the whole population.

At this time the enemy laid many mines off shore whilst others were dropped by parachute at night. Several were cleared, some fell on Valletta with disastrous effects, whilst others went undetected. On April 8th, 1941, the Admiralty Mooring Vessel *Moor* was carrying out maintenance work on the boom-defence nets protecting the entrance to the Grand Harbour. Shortly after 5.00 pm, as the vessel started its engine to return to the dockyard, a deafening explosion shook the harbour area. People were perplexed as no alert had been sounded, but news soon spread that *Moor* had struck a floating mine and disappeared in the waters of the Grand Harbour. Of the twenty-nine Maltese crew members and riggers aboard, only one survived. Anthony Mercieca, a rigger/diver, was blown into the air inside the ship's cabin, before plunging about twenty feet under water. He struggled to force open the jammed cabin door and succeeded in surfacing, with debris from the vessel still flying about. He was picked up by a boat from the Boom Defence Vessel *Westgate* and conveyed to Bighi Royal Naval Hospital. The minor facial injuries sustained when forcing open the cabin door did not prevent him from walking out of hospital after a medical check-up.[30] A marble tablet at the Upper Barracca Gardens in Valletta commemorates the twenty-eight Maltese workers who went down with their ship.[31]

With the passage of time, the acute shortage of essential commodities was causing concern. In February 1941, Government had adopted a scheme, drawn up by the Director of the Food Distribution Office, Marquis Barbaro of St George, to ensure an equitable distribution. The rationing scheme, which became operative on 7th April, was at first restricted to sugar, coffee, soap and matches. More items were however gradually added to the list as supplies diminished. The distribution of milk, and later milk powder, was restricted to infants up to the age of two and to invalids. Small portions of frozen meat were distributed twice weekly and, towards the latter part of the year, edible oil, butter, margarine, lard, corned beef and tinned fish joined the list. Kerosene rationing became necessary in May, when a progressive reduction in petrol consumption also took place. In fact, by the end of September 1941, the only unrationed items were bread, paste, cheese, rice and tea. The food situation, bad enough already, became critical as the siege progressed.

(R. Ellis)
The night raid on 28th/29th April, 1941, as seen from Rabat. On right, the explosion from an aerial mine which fell in Kingsway, Valletta.

On the night of Monday, 23rd June 1941, a Heinkel 115 floatplane — BV 185 — flown by Norwegian Lieutenant Haakon Offerdal, arrived in Malta and was hurriedly parked in a hangar at Kalafrana seaplane base, where it was kept under strict security.[32] Engine trouble and bad weather kept the floatplane out of action; it was extensively damaged when Italian bombs hit the hangar on the night of 8th/9th July.

The floatplane was repaired in September and on the night of the 18th carried out a daring but unsuccessful sortie along the North African coast. In the second attempt on the night of the 21st/22nd September, the floatplane crashed into the sea soon after take-off, 20 miles south of Malta. Several search parties were mounted and in the afternoon a Swordfish, piloted by Lieutenant More, sighted the wreckage.

Lieutenant Offerdal was yet to return to Malta when on 27th October, 1941, he took off from Southampton in BV 187. It is understood that he flew several missions to North Africa, later described as of great importance to war operations in the area. The plane was destroyed at its moorings at Kalafrana by a German fighter on 5th February, 1942.

(L.F. Tortell)
The slaughter of goats to feed the population resulted in such an acute shortage of milk that even newly-born infants were fed on milk powder.

(Ph. Vella)
A Ration Card for a family of six.

40

Chapter Four

E-boat attack: radar detection, engagement by coastal batteries, mopping up by Hurricanes, capture of assaultmen

The gunners manning the coastal batteries had the nerve-wracking duty of being in a constant state of preparedness for a possible seaborne assault. Unlike their comrades manning the anti-aircraft batteries, they had not, till then, had the chance to prove their mettle. Their moment of test came at dawn on 26th July, 1941, when the Italian Navy carried out a daring attempt to penetrate into the Grand Harbour and Marsamxett. Their mission was to destroy a convoy that had reached Malta two days earlier and to paralyse the submarine base at Manoel Island.

The expedition left Augusta in Sicily at sunset on 25th July; it consisted of the dispatch boat *Diana* (*Capitano di Fregata* Mario Di Muro), two large motor torpedo-boats (M.A.S. — *Motoscafo Anti Sommergibili*) 451 and 452, two baby submarines (S.L.C. — *Siluro a Lenta Corsa*), one baby submarine carrier (M.T.L. — *Motoscafo Turismo Lento*), one flotilla leader (M.T.S. — *Motoscafo Turismo Silurante*) and nine E-boats (M.T.M. — *Motoscafo Turismo Modificato*). The members of the Tenth Light Flotilla (*La Decima Flottiglia MAS*) included the commanding officer, *Capitano di Fregata* Vittorio Moccagatta, and *Maggiore* Teseo Tesei who had been the brain of the Unit responsible for designing the human-torpedo; even the medical officer, *Capitano Medico* Bruno Falcomatà, had volunteered to participate.

This flotilla, the *élite* of the Italian Navy, had performed with credit when, on 25th March, 1941, it penetrated the harbour defences at Suda Bay, Crete, crippling the cruiser HMS *York*. Its prime target, however, was meant to be Malta as revealed by *Principe* Valerio Borghese, who, for some time after the Malta assault, took temporary command of the Unit: "The idea of forcing *La Valletta*, the harbour of Malta, the chief stronghold of the British Navy in the Mediterranean, the possession of which

(E.D. Woolley)

Motoscafo Turismo Modificato, *commonly known as E-Boat or* barchino.

41

(NWMA)
A Siluro a Lenta Corsa. This two-man human-torpedo was nicknamed Maiale for its proneness to breaking down at crucial moments. The SLC manned by Costa and Barla was found scuttled in shallow water and recovered.

by foreigners is a constant threat to Italy, had been considered as long ago as 1935, when the human-torpedo was taking shape; Malta was the objective for which this weapon had been planned and built." [33]

The assault on Malta was preceded by several reconnaissance sorties, followed by attempts which proved abortive either on account of inclement weather or technical difficulties encountered by the assault craft. The plan had been well prepared but when the assault was finally activated, the Italians relied on outdated information secured through aerial reconnaissance. Valerio Borghese admitted that the Axis did not have an agent at Malta who could provide them with intelligence reports. [34] In spite of some mechanical and navigational difficulties, the assault was launched at 4.44 am; the proposed simultaneous air attack, besides being understrength, was mistimed and misdirected. *Maggiore* Teseo Tesei and *Secondo Capo Palombaro* Alcide Pedretti headed their S.L.C. towards the breakwater viaduct, never to be seen again. *Capitano di Corvetta* Giorgio Giobbe hesitated for some time before ordering *Sottotenente di Vascello* Roberto Frassetto to move in. Having directed his craft towards the viaduct, Frassetto ejected into the sea and a second or two later the

(NWMA)
Maggiore *Teseo Tesei*.

(via S. Ward)

MAS 452 berthed at Fort St Angelo after capture.

explosive-laden craft hit the net but failed to go off. With his blue-lit torch, Frassetto signalled the next boat to move in. *Sottotenente* Aristide Carabelli, picking up the signal, sped for the objective, dashing to his death against the centre pylon. This explosion also set off Frassetto's craft which got entangled in the net and the double detonation brought down the outer span of the bridge which, coming to rest between the pylons, effectively blocked access into the Grand Harbour. The craft had been detected by radar and the gunners had taken up Action Stations. Immediately after the explosion, searchlights illuminated a vast stretch of sea covering the approaches to the Grand Harbour, exposing the assault craft speeding towards the viaduct.[35] This bad start was an ill-omen for the Italians.

Six-pounder guns from Forts St Elmo and Ricasoli, in unison with the other posts guarding the harbour approaches, came into action. Some of the guns at Fort St Elmo could not depress sufficiently to engage, but 'G' Gun, under Sergeant V. Zammit, managed to fire and, with the first round, destroyed the leading E-boat travelling at speed some 300 yards away. Most of the other craft met the same fate at the hands of the coastal batteries; one was sunk by

(The Times)

The outer span of the breakwater viaduct was wrecked during the assault on the Grand Harbour on 26th July, 1941. The steel nets, blocking access into harbour, are clearly visible beneath the inner span; these extended to the seabed.

(RMA)

One of the 6-pounder twin guns at Fort St Elmo.

machine-gunners of the Cheshire Regiment in the Ricasoli area, while a few others were damaged by RMA-manned six-pounders and, abandoned by the crew, drifted out to sea. The attack lasted six short hectic minutes.

The guns went silent as the action died out; two abandoned E-boats, drifting in the Illuminated Area, were unexpectedly reboarded by Italian assaultmen who tried to rendezvous with the larger MAS 451 and MAS 452, which throughout the action had stood outside the range of Malta's coastal batteries. This move provoked a spectacular scene; the late Colonel Henry Ferro recorded: "Sergeant Barbara was the first to call his detachment into action and engage with 'F' Gun. Others joined in and soon there were 'E', 'F', 'G' and 'D' Guns, Elmo; 'A', 'B' and 'C' Ricasoli, the Bofors anti-aircraft guns at Ricasoli, Elmo and Tignè Forts and infantry machine-gun posts within range, all in action. These equipments all had tracers to their ammunition. The resulting fireworks display, as they ricochetted off the surface of the sea and formed interweaving patterns of dark red, green and light red, was a sight witnessed by the crowds, which surprisingly enough for the hour of the morning had gathered along Valletta bastions and Sliema Front, especially at Ghar-id-Dud. The two MTMs jinked, zig-zagged, turned about and manoeuvred in every possible way, as they tried to escape punishment. They were

(J. Sammut)

Major Henry Ferro RMA

44

hemmed in to an area of about 200 yards square. Fire direction was no longer possible with so many guns engaging the same targets. Sergeant Barbara, having stopped firing 'F' Gun, noticed the leading MTM following a fixed pattern of movement. He laid his gun to where the MTM would move next and fired. The MTM ran into his fire and exploded. The pilot of the second MTM jettisoned himself into the sea and swam away. His craft was hit as it rose out of the water. The pilot was too close to survive the explosion.

"At 0600 hours L/Sgt Bates drew my attention to the outline of a MAS that was just visible in the dawning light. Its range, taken on the Depression Range Finder, was 5,500 yards. We decided to test the accuracy of that figure. One round was fired. The shell landed short and, as far as we could estimate, it was just about 500 yards short. What we did not know at the time was that the shell had ricochetted off the water and, by a chance in a million, had bounced about 500 yards to enter the cabin of the MAS. It exploded inside, killing *Capitano* Moccagatta and the crew of MAS 452.

"We learnt about this unexpected event when Vice Admiral Malta (Vice-Admiral Ford) came to Fort St Elmo about a week later and presented me, as OC 3rd Battery RMA, with a shield on which was mounted the *fascio* (Fascist crest) taken off MAS 452. The Admiral said that nine dead officers and men had been found in the MAS cabin and that his Fleet Gunnery Officer had informed him that the hole in the cabin structure could only have been made by a 6-pounder shell, the measurements of which coincided exactly."[36]

At first light Macchi 200s took off to protect any of the surviving units on their return to Sicily, whilst Hurricanes were sent up from Malta to finish off any craft trying to escape. In the ensuing dog-fight, three Italian fighters were shot down for the loss of one British aircraft. The two remaining Hurricanes, spotting MAS 451 and two smaller boats, disabled them with cannon fire, besides strafing MAS 452, unaware of its fate; the rout was now complete.

After taking part in the action from the Harbour Fire Command Post at Fort St Elmo, Lt Bernard J. Portelli RMA led a platoon for rifle-firing practice at St Andrew's Ranges. On arrival, some of the men rushed down to the foreshore; when Lt Portelli joined them, he saw two Italians, shivering and scared, on a wooden raft clinging to the rocks. While some soldiers covered them with rifles, others brought them ashore. The Maltese officer then ordered a sergeant to go to St Andrew's Barracks to inform the Military Police. These eventually arrived, took over *Tenente di Vascello* Francesco Costa and *Sergente Palombaro* Luigi Barla, and handed him a receipt for the men and material taken over. These two Italians were, in fact, the crew of the second S.L.C.

The pilot of the downed Hurricane, Pilot Officer Denis Winton of No 185 Squadron, baled out thirty miles north of Malta. Sighting an immobilised boat, he swam towards it and,

(NWM)

Two sets of underwater breathing apparata, abandoned by Costa and Barla, at St Andrews.

on boarding, was confronted with the corpses of nine Italians; it was MAS 452. The late Group Captain Edward Hardie CBE, M. Mar., at the time a Flight Lieutenant with Air-Sea Rescue, narrated that Winton tried to attract the attention of a civilian-manned RASC launch by waving the Italian flag which he had hauled down. The crew, radioing base that one of the Italian boats was still adopting an aggressive attitude, sailed past, leaving a frustrated Winton to his energetic flag-waving. Six hours after having been shot down, Winton, still clutching the tricolour, was picked up by a Swordfish floatplane sent out to his rescue; the motor torpedo-boat and one of the E-boats were later towed into harbour. The Battle of Valletta was over.

Fifteen corpses were recovered and eighteen men were taken prisoners. Warrant Officer Carmel Blackman RMA, Electrical Light Officer in charge of the Illuminated Area, who witnessed the whole action from No 3 Searchlight Emplacement, the nearest post to the breakwater, recalls: "As soon as the excitement of the initial phase had died down, I noticed one of the survivors on the foreshore. I went down for him and, mistaking him for a German, I ordered him in English to raise his hands, which he did. Identifying himself as *Sottotenente* Roberto Frassetto, an Italian, he asked for a cigarette which I gave him. In return he handed me, as a souvenir, his autographed photo embossed with the official Italian Navy seal as well as his rank rings which he removed from his uniform. I then marched him towards the Fort, to a mixed choir of cheers and jeers from soldiers and civilians on the bastions, where I handed him over to Major Henry Ferro, my Commanding Officer. Frassetto, exhausted but uninjured, was a very courageous and smart young officer." [37]

The Italians regarded this mission very highly; Marc'Antonio Bragadin, the Italian naval historian records: "So ended the Malta failure, the cruellest and bloodiest of all the operations ever undertaken by the crews of the assault craft, but also the focal point of circumstances so extraordinary as to render it without doubt the most glorious of failures; so glorious that any navy in the world would be proud of it." [38] Malta was just as proud of her gunners.

The eighteen survivors were detained at Corradino Military Prison until their departure from Malta on 2nd August, 1941. According to Tullio Marcon, another Italian writer, the prisoners were stoned by a group of workers as they were being taken to the dockyard for embarkation on HMS *Manxman*, which was to take them to Skye in Scotland. The angry crowd, incited by a ring-leader, then surrounded the bus carrying them to the quayside and, were it not for the protection given by an officer brandishing a pistol and soldiers with fixed bayonets, the Italian seamen would have risked lynching. [39]

(via C. Blackman)
Sottotenente *Roberto Frassetto*.

When *Comandante* Pietro Zaniboni visited the National War Museum on the fortieth anniversary of the Battle of Valletta, he recounted that it was only when leaving Malta on *Manxman* that he was able to see the extent of the damage caused to the breakwater viaduct. This retired naval officer, then a *Sotto Ufficiale Capo Nocchiere 3ª classe*, piloted one of the E-boats during the assault and was taken prisoner.

The lifting of certain restrictions under the Official Secrets Act in recent years has revealed an intriguing prologue to this ill-fated operation. Lieutenant-Commander Carnes relates: "We in Malta were receiving very brief terse messages from a source unknown to me, regarding titbits of most useful information about the movement of enemy ships, convoys, submarines and aircraft, and also hints of possible attacks on islands in the Mediterranean. One must bear in mind that in England they were decyphering a portion of enemy traffic and from this decyphering and re-translation of this traffic, information concerning the Mediterranean was evident. This information was passed to Vice Admiral Malta who selected me to do the decyphering; the contents of these messages were passed to the Governor, the Air Officer Commanding, the Staff Officer Intelligence on the staff of the Vice Admiral and to a major of the Royal Marines. But I did not know that these were intercepts of enemy messages; I was told that this was in fact information from an enemy spy in Naples ... We did get two or three messages through this source suggesting there were going to be raids. For example, when Crete was invaded we got a message through 'Ultra' sources that an island was about to be invaded. Nobody knew which island it was. Consequently Malta was put on alert but, fortunately for the Island, it proved to be Crete. We also got a hint sometime in July 1941 that there was going to be another raid which we assumed was going to be on Malta, more so as a convoy was due in the middle of the month and the Admiral said, 'Well, if there is a convoy coming in here, we've got to be prepared to protect it by all means at our disposal'. He ordered all coastal gunners, including the Royal Malta Artillery, to stand-by, sleeping at their guns, ready at a moment's notice to open fire to repulse any possible raid on the Grand Harbour. Of course, this raid could have taken place anywhere around the Island and as a landing and commando raid could have resulted, the British troops, who were guarding the various possible landing beaches, were also put on alert and given extra support." [40]

(T. Marcon)
Monument at Augusta, Sicily, commemorating the assault on Malta. The frontal inscription reads: From here, on 25th July, 1941, towards Malta, the gallant men of X Flotilla Mas, for the Enterprise, unlucky and glorious, sailed.

Dott. Ing. Tullio Marcon, who designed and erected the memorial, provides the following information regarding the three inspired concepts of the memorial:

(a) *The headstone represents simultaneously a rudder and Fort St Elmo;*

(b) *The chain, broken at the extreme end, represents the partly-destroyed bridge providing an unsurmountable obstacle to the assaultmen;*

(c) *the nine bent steel rods, held by the chain, opening out like a flower, simultaneously represent the unity of purpose of the nine recipients of the* Medaglia d'Oro, *and the bursting explosion.*

On the opposite side, there is reproduced an extract from the assaultmen's prayer by Gabriele d'Annunzio: I pray for both, the Victory and the Return; but if Thou, Oh God, should give only one, concede Victory.

Chapter Five

Supplies to Malta by convoys, submarines and unescorted vessels — Offensive operations — Loss of HMS Upholder

The revictualling of the Island posed serious problems. Although the provisions and armaments delivered by the two convoys in July and September 1941, code-named Operations 'Substance' and 'Halberd' respectively, temporarily relieved the critical situation, it was imperative to keep Malta regularly supplied. Submarines helped in this task. Besides interrupting enemy convoys to Libya, submarines of the 1st Flotilla based at Alexandria operated what came to be known as the 'Magic Carpet Service to Malta'. Large submarines and other minelaying ones were used to carry vital supplies to the beleaguered Island. The first run was made by the submarine *Porpoise* which embarked a cargo of petrol and mines, and carried out a minelaying operation *en route* to Malta. *Porpoise* made another eight trips to Malta as an underwater freighter. On one occasion, while berthed near No 6 Shed at Alexandria, she was being loaded with aviation fuel and ammunition. Leading Steward Anthony Buhagiar, a Maltese crew member, recalls: "A seaman accidentally dropped one of the ammunition cases. On bursting open we noticed that this contained waste material instead of shells. The captain immediately suspended loading until each case was examined; six others were found to contain similar material. This was a case of sabotage."[41]

Other submarines utilised in this role included *Rorqual, Parthian, Regent, Cachalot, Clyde, Osiris* and *Otus*.

During July 1941 alone, the 'Magic Carpet Service' brought to Malta 126 passengers, 84,280 gallons of petrol, 83,000 gallons of kerosene, 12 tons of mail, 30 tons of general

(via N. Malizia)
Armourers on a Sicilian airfield setting an Italian 'Whitehead' torpedo before loading for use against a convoy bound for Malta. These torpedoes, constructed at Pola, were the best the Italians had at their disposal.

stores and 6 tons of munitions, including torpedoes for submarines and aircraft operating from this Island.[42]

The supplies delivered, however, were hardly sufficient to meet requirements; it was estimated that the fuel brought in at great risk by a submarine could last three days. It was indeed fortunate that the *Luftwaffe's* absence from Sicily had eased the demand made on fuel and ammunition.

Besides submarines, heavier units of the Royal Navy ran the gauntlet to break the blockade. On 31st July, 1941, the cruisers *Arethusa* and *Hermione*, the minelaying cruiser *Manxman* and two destroyers embarked 1,750 officers and men and 130 tons of stores at Gibraltar. Operation 'Style', primarily aimed at providing additional personnel for the increasing commitments of the garrison, was successfully concluded with the arrival of the ships at Malta on 2nd August.

These reinforcements, together with those ferried during Operations 'Substance' and 'Halberd', augmented the fighting strength of the Fortress, which now exceeded 22,000, including ten British infantry battalions besides the King's Own Malta Regiment.[43]

There was also a marked improvement in anti-aircraft artillery which at the time consisted of 112 heavy and 118 light guns. The total light, field and mobile armaments stood at 104. The aerial defence was also strengthened; by August 1941, the Royal Air Force could count on 15 Hurricane Mk Is and 60 Hurricane Mk IIs.

The Italian Air Force was still a force to be reckoned with. Torpedo-bombers were used to intercept ships sailing towards the Island, whilst the Macchi 202 *Folgore* made its *début*, over Malta on October 1st, 1941. In a spirited dog-fight, *Capitano* Mario Pluda, of the 4⁰ *Stormo* 9⁰ *Gruppo*, shot down a Hurricane piloted by Squadron Leader Peter W.O. Mould DFC and Bar, Commanding Officer No 185 Squadron; the 24-year-old pilot, with nine victories to his credit, was killed. As fate would have it, on 8th November, during an attack on ships of Force 'K' anchored in the Grand Harbour, it was the turn of *Capitano* Pluda to fall victim to the Malta Hurricanes.

The Admiralty again resorted to using unescorted ships sailing singly from Gibraltar in the hope of escaping attention. *Empire Guillemot* used every form of disguise to

(via N. Malizia)
The re-loading of a 12.7mm Breda SAFAT machine gun on a Macchi 202 for a sortie on Malta.

(NWMA)
A yellow-painted metal container, dropped by an Italian aircraft on a local airfield in November 1941, contained the following message:

TO THE COMMAND OF THE ROYAL AIR FORCE — MALTA —

During the attack on one of our fields, at november 12th, Lieutenant Colonel Henry Brown crshed fighting and was burried with the highest military honour.

Sergeant Peter Shabbah Simpson went down on the sea, with parachute. He was taken a little after; he is in perfect health, not even blessed.

Other pilots of yours went down on the sea, fighting, but we were not able to find them.

Will you please, give us notices of two pilots that we lost on Malta, november 8th: Capitano Pilota Mario Pluda and Sergente Maggiore Pilota Luigi Taroni.

Address, please, the answer to the Comando Aviazione da Caccia della Sicilia.

Thank you very much.

According to Giulio Lazzati, an Italian historian, a few days later a British aircraft dropped the following message near Modica in Sicily:

RAF. "Your message received and appreciated. In reply: Capitano Pilota Mauro Pluda was killed in action. His body was found and buried with all honours in a military cemetery. With regret we have no other news about Sergente Maggiore Pilota Luigi Taroni. Probably he fell in the sea but could not be traced notwithstanding several searches."

confound the enemy. She flew Spanish, French and Italian flags while sailing along the North African coast and finally reached Malta on 19th September, 1941. The ship, although sighted by enemy aircraft on more than one occasion, managed to complete her journey unmolested. Her luck ran out on her outward trip in ballast when she was sunk by a torpedo-bomber piloted by *Tenente* Guido Focacci of 283ª *Squadriglia Aerosilurante*; the survivors were landed at Algiers.

The enemy, now aware of this ruse, sank two Malta-bound vessels flying foreign colours: *Empire Pelican* off the Tunisian coast on 14th November by *Tenente* Camillo Barioglio in a S.79 of 130° *Gruppo Aerosilurante* and *Empire Defender* a day later at the hands of *Maggiore* Arduino Buri flying a Savoia S.84 of 36⁰ *Stormo Aerosilurante*. This double disaster led to the cancellation of the sailing of other similarly-disguised merchant ships. The need for these solitary runs persisted until the middle of 1942, the burden falling on submarines, air-freighters and the armed merchant ship *Breconshire* commanded by Captain G.A.G. Hutchinson RN.

Towards the latter part of 1941, aerial offensive operations from Malta gained momentum. Wellingtons, Blenheims, Swordfish, Marylands and Beaufighters attacked ports in Italy and North Africa, bombed and torpedoed Axis shipping in the Mediterranean, and laid mines off Tripoli and elsewhere. The versatile Wellingtons were given curious names by airmen stationed here. A bomb-laden Wellington was called a 'Bombington'; those carrying torpedoes were 'Fishington'; those dropping flares to illuminate the target were known as 'Flashingtons' while those equipped with special apparata to jam enemy radar were referred to as 'Goofingtons'.

Naval operations too escalated in the summer and autumn of 1941. Ships from 14th Destroyer Flotilla, Force 'K' and Force 'B' attacked enemy convoys plying between Italy and North Africa. This alleviated the pressure on the British Army engaged in a fierce battle in the Western Desert. An action worthy of mention took place on the 8th and 9th November, 1941. In response to Rommel's desperate demands for armoured vehicles, ammunition and fuel, a heavily escorted convoy comprising five merchant ships and two tankers was urgently despatched. The British got to know of this convoy before it sailed; as already stated, German 'Ultra' messages, giving precise details of shipping movements, were intercepted and relayed to the Authorities here. In order to

(via N. Malizia)
Bombs exploding on Fort Manoel and in the sea. Photograph taken by 1° Aviere Fotografo Ghezzi of 30° Stormo B.T. on a S.79.

(IWM)

The Submarine Base at Lazaretto Creek

(NWMA)

Dust and sea spray from exploding bombs, shrouding submarines berthed off Lazaretto.

cover up this secret source of information, the British made it appear as if the convoy had been spotted by a reconnoitring Maryland.

Force 'K', made up of the cruisers *Aurora* and *Penelope* and the destroyers *Lance* and *Lively*, set out from Malta and sank the seven enemy cargo vessels. One of the escorting destroyers met the same fate; three others were damaged, one of which was subsequently finished off by the submarine *Upholder*. The four ships of Force 'K' returned to the Grand Harbour shortly after mid-day on the 9th, without a single casualty. *Conte* Galeazzo Ciano, Italian Foreign Minister and Mussolini's son-in-law is reported to have commented: "An engagement occurred, the results of which are inexplicable. All, I mean all, our ships were sunk and one or maybe two or three destroyers. The British returned to base having slaughtered us. Naturally, today our various headquarters are pushing out their usual inevitable and imaginary sinking of a British cruiser by a torpedo plane; nobody believes it." [44]

The effectiveness of such sorties by surface vessels was equalled by that of the submarines. Operating from their base at HMS *Talbot* in Lazaretto Creek, Malta Force Submarines, which in September 1941 was officially organised as 10th Submarine Flotilla under Captain G.W.G. 'Shrimp' Simpson, wrought havoc and destruction among enemy shipping in the Mediterranean. Between January 1941 and May 1942, fifteen Malta-based submarines sent to the bottom about 400,000 tons of supplies, mostly intended for Rommel's *Afrika Korps*. (See Appendix **E**) The enemy could not afford these losses and convoys were consequently re-routed further away from Malta, with inevitable delay and higher fuel consumption.

This significant success was not achieved without cost. A large number of these gallant submariners perished on patrol or were killed when their base was subjected to heavy bombing. An ace, who towered high above this skilled band of seamen, was Lieutenant-Commander Malcolm David Wanklyn of *Upholder* who, on 11th December, 1941, became the first submarine officer to receive the Victoria Cross in the Second World War. By 14th April, 1942, when *Upholder* was lost on her twenty-fifth patrol that was meant to be the last one before returning to Britain, she had sunk 21 vessels with a total tonnage of 128,353.

In November 1941 German U-boats, which until then had operated with a high rate of success in the Atlantic and elsewhere, entered

(The Times)
Lieut-Cdr Malcolm David Wanklyn near the entrance to Upper Barracca Gardens soon after his award of the Victoria Cross.

the Mediterranean. On 10th November, Force 'H' left Gibraltar on an aircraft-ferrying trip to Malta. Two days later, thirty-seven Hurricanes were flown off the aircraft-carrier HMS *Ark Royal* and thirty-four of them, accompanied by seven Blenheims from Gibraltar, reached Malta. As Force 'H' was returning to Gibraltar on the 13th, German submarine U-81, commanded by *Leutnant* Friedrich Guggenberger, successfully torpedoed *Ark Royal*. The carrier, though listing badly, sailed on assisted by a destroyer which was later joined by two tugs from Gibraltar. The list got worse and, at 6.00 am on 14th November, *Ark Royal* sank when only twenty-five miles off Gibraltar with the loss of only one member of the crew, Able Seaman E. Mitchell. The sinking of *Ark Royal* was a particularly severe blow to Malta for, at that time, there was no other carrier readily available to deliver fighter reinforcements and escort convoys to the Island.

(J.A. Agius)
Marble plaque set in the west wall of the spire of St Paul's Anglican Cathedral at Valletta, overlooking the former Submarine Base. The plaque was unveiled on 17th November, 1974, by Vice-Admiral Sir Arthur Hezlet KBE CB DSO DSC.

Chapter Six

Resumption of attacks by Luftwaffe — Threat of invasion — Widespread destruction — Regent Cinema tragedy — Arrival of first Spitfires

Italian aircraft continued bombing the Island until November 1941 when, with the onset of winter, *General Feldmarschall* Albert Kesselring's *Fliegerkorps* II moved from Central Russia to Sicily. Air raids rose from 76 in November to 169 and 263 in December 1941 and January 1942 respectively. The Germans, however, sustained considerable losses and, with Kesselring's approval, *Oberst* Paul Deichmann, the II Air Corps Chief of Staff, devised new tactics. Pin-point bombing, which had clearly failed to achieve the desired results, was discontinued. Instead, bombers started attacking particular targets in force.

This new offensive aimed at annihilating the Island's offensive power and weakening her defensive capacity; this was interpreted as a prelude to an invasion. When Mr Geoffrey N. Nunn, Assistant to the Lieutenant-Governor, spoke over the Rediffusion Relay System on 1st January, 1942, he did not merely convey to the Maltese the seasonal greetings but explained the contents of a leaflet, entitled 'What to do in an Invasion', which Government was issuing. He strongly advised that in the event of an invasion everyone was to remain in his town or village and take cover. He emphasized the importance of keeping the roads clear to facilitate the movement of troop reinforcements, guns, ammunition and supplies to the men in the front-line. Besides, civilians on the road could be used like those in Holland, Belgium and the North of France, where the German forces had marched the refugees in front of their invading columns, preventing Allied troops from engaging them.

The population, unaware of the plans drawn up by the Military Authorities to meet the threat, could not but see the red light in the stricter security measures and the laying of

(The Times)
In spite of its poor quality, this photograph shows a faintly-visible Stuka diving over smoke-and-dust-shrouded Senglea.

55

(F.B. Jarvis)

Submerged mines exploded from a beach-post during trials.

additional obstacles on the sea-bed and along the coast and country roads. Most bays and accessible landing sites were mined so that, in the event of enemy boats succeeding in forcing an entry, the pressing of a button from a nearby beach-post would explode the mines. The many milestones scattered throughout the Island were defaced; many were those who wondered whether this would have confounded the Germans and Italians were they to secure a foothold on the Island. The Maltese took all this in their stride; they were naturally conscious of the possibility, and probability, of an invasion, but they were more concerned with such realities as a meagre meal, the snatching of a few hours' sleep, hitching a lift to work and avoiding the bombs.

Mussolini and several members of the Italian and German High Commands favoured the implementation of Operation *Herkules*, the invasion of Malta, during early 1942. Hitler kept putting off the operation, allegedly due to his distrust of Italian co-participation. He also maintained that the sustained attacks by the *Luftwaffe* would cause the Island to surrender or at least subdue her offensive operations against Axis convoys ferrying men and material to reinforce Rommel's *Afrika Korps*. The German dictator obviously gave priority to the North African campaign over the capture of Malta.

Disagreement was evident among the German commanders as Kesselring himself remarks: "Over and over again, sometimes with the support of the *Comando Supremo*, I urged Goering and Hitler to stabilise our position in the Mediterranean by taking Malta. I even persuaded Rommel to back me up. It was not until February 1942 that I succeeded in getting my plan approved. The occasion was an interview at the Führer's General Headquarters. Tempers ran high. Hitler ended the interview by grasping me by the arm and telling me in his Austrian dialect: 'Keep your shirt on, Field-Marshal Kesselring. I'm going to do it.' — a typical sidelight on the tension at headquarters."[45] Hitler, however, failed to tell Kesselring *when* he proposed to do it!

In compliance with Hitler's directives, aerial pressure over Malta gained momentum. Most attacks were directed against military objectives but populated areas did not escape unscathed. Extensive areas in the Three Cities, Luqa and other parts of the Island were wiped out. Valletta suffered the destruction of a number of historic buildings, including several of the Auberges built by the Knights of Malta. St John's Co-Cathedral escaped with light damage to the Chapel of the German Langue, the vestry, the belfries and the main portico.

56

(NWM)
Buildings adjacent to the Law Courts in Kingsway, Valletta, destroyed by an aerial mine during the night of 28th/29th April, 1941.

The Maltese, on the whole, accepted the loss of their homes and belongings with composure. The unlucky ones, surveying the desolate scene, searched amidst the rubble for items of utility. This was a heart-and-back-breaking operation in which neighbours and strangers lent a hand. The Demolition and Clearance Squads, numerous as they were, could not cope with the demands made on them. The local stone resisted fire, blast and nearby explosions but could not withstand direct hits. Crumbling buildings collapsed into heaps of masonry which was very heavy to remove by hand. There were no other means of doing the job, as the limited mechanical equipment available had priority at the airfields and the dockyard. It was inspiring to see men, women and children removing debris. True Christian charity helped to mitigate the burden of loss; the bombed-out found moral support and material help from the more fortunate neighbours. Their comradeship and generosity were spontaneous; people realised they could find themselves in the same desperate situation the next day, or after the next raid.

British sailors, who had their own cupful of hardship overflowing to the brim, remarked: "They (the Maltese) seemed to be extremely cheerful under the circumstances. It is true that comparatively few of them were killed, but they bore the loss of their homes and possessions with a more than English composure."[46] The

(The Times)
Women and children waiting in a Valletta street for transport to carry furniture salvaged from their bombed homes.

57

(Mrs I. Goddard)

The spirit of Malta. The bar is wrecked but open, the children hungry but cheerful.

(The Times)

Business as usual, or nearly.

Maltese, of course, had no cause to be cheerful but any other reaction would have added misery to their plight.

The same defiant determination was displayed by shop owners. Those whose premises were damaged, worked without respite to clean up the mess, carried out temporary repairs and opened up the following day with a prominently displayed sign: 'Business As Usual'. Some, who had their shops completely destroyed, defied reason and built small cubicles from where they transacted their business; 'V' signs and the slogan 'Blitzed But Not Beaten' on the facades were commonplace. A few enterprising bombed-out grocers erected makeshift stalls in the ditches near shelter entrances. These merchants had little to sell, but their spirit symbolised Malta's determination not to be subdued.

Even the shortage of coins did not disrupt their slack business.[47] Shopkeepers, hawkers and bus owners beat the shortage by introducing a system of IOUs; these chits, extensively used throughout the Island as small change, were invariably honoured. This shortage had worsened as some people had started hoarding silver coins. At one stage, two-shilling currency notes issued in 1918 were over-printed to the value of one shilling and put into circulation to meet the increasing shortage. These were subsequently replaced by new paper-currency notes of various denominations, but the IOUs survived for a long time in the case of smaller denominations.

None suffered more than those residents of Senglea who ignored all appeals to leave the blitzed city. When the City Gate was destroyed, Senglea became an isolated city within a beleaguered Island. The plight of the Sengleans in those grim days is hard to imagine. Ex-Police Sergeant Salvatore Fava, who remained in the city to maintain some form of order under desperate conditions, recalls: "Dr Boffa, a remarkable person, took me to see Mr Andrew Cohen (Assistant to the Lieutenant-Governor) who entrusted me with the task of distributing

(IWM)

Widespread destruction in Kingsway, Valletta, leading to Queen's Square.

(NWMA)

A selection of I.O.Us.

(NWMA)

A two-shilling note overprinted to the value of a shilling.

60

(The Times)

Recovering useful items from blitzed houses.

bread and other supplies, as these became available, to the 300 or 400 people who lived mostly in two shelters amongst the ruins of their homes. To do this, I found a few volunteers who used to take me to Valletta in their *dghajsas* to fetch bread from the Prison Bakery at Kordin; this I distributed at Senglea Point on my return. I know of others who used to row to Valletta to get tankfuls of water. As we were cut off from the rest of the Island, even corpses had to be taken away on the Water Police launch. Despite our precarious existence, morale was high; there was no panic and discipline was maintained. Amongst those who rendered great service were Dr Paul Boffa, Dr Carmel Jaccarini, Archpriest Emanuel Brincat and Rev Anton Galea, Provost of St Philip's Church; I have personally seen the last-named encouraging the soldiers manning the Pom-Pom at Senglea Point during air raids; it is regrettable that his courage has never been mentioned." [48] This was no isolated instance; in Senglea and elsewhere, courage and vital work went unnoticed, much less rewarded.

Although practically every day had its own story, the 15th of February, 1942, stands out in particular, as on that day the Island was under alert for 19 hours 59 minutes. There were four raids lasting respectively from 2.00 am to 7.35 am, 7.59 am to 6.36 pm, 7.25 pm to 7.34 pm, and 7.57 pm to 11.35 pm. During the second raid, at 5.54 pm, a solitary German aircraft flying over Valletta dropped a stick of three bombs along Kingsway (now Republic Street); one hit the Palace, the other the *Casino Maltese* (now Casino 1852), killing six members and two of the staff besides passers-by, while the third landed squarely on the Regent Cinema (now Regency House), where 'The North-West Mounted Police' starring Gary Cooper and Paulette Goddard was being screened.

The picture-house, luckily a small one, was almost full, mostly with servicemen on short leave. The building collapsed, burying the audience beneath a mass of masonry and twisted steel. Soon the site was teeming with servicemen and civilians who arrived on the

(IWM)
The Regent Cinema, teeming with helpers, soon after being hit on 15th February, 1942.

(IWM)
A boy at a shelter entrance watching a man being helped over the rubble of Palazzo Parisio in Merchants Street, Valletta.

(The Times)
A side view of St John's Co-Cathedral; the magnificent church escaped with slight damage.

spot before the Police, ARP squads and medical teams. But ARP Sergeant-Major John Mifsud comments: "These well-meaning people, who lacked the necessary training, stepped over victims buried beneath the debris; they did not do much harm because the majority were already dead. As soon as we arrived a few minutes after the incident, we saw a harrowing scene, with limp and moving limbs entangled between the debris. We searched for the injured to whom we administered first-aid before rushing them to hospital; our timely intervention saved a few lives."[49] Francis Cutajar, from Hamrun, was with his fiancée in the cinema; on hearing the explosion they made for the exit while, instinctively, he shielded her under his arms. A shrapnel severed his arm and killed his fiancée on the spot. He remained conscious but was unable to move as he was wedged among debris.[50] Fifteen civilians and twenty-six servicemen were killed.

Notwithstanding all this hammering, Valletta had up till then still been the seat of Government and the centre of business activity; however, as more debris from bombed buildings rendered streets impassable and as the transport situation worsened, Government was forced to transfer most of its Departments to outlying districts. (See Appendix **F**)

The Council of Government, presided over by the Governor and Commander-in-Chief, continued to meet at the Tapestry Chamber even after the Palace had received a direct hit on 15th February, 1942. But finally even the Island's highest Institution had to move out of Valletta. As recorded on pages 471 to 489 of Volume 6 of the Debates, the last Sitting of the Council at the Palace took place on the afternoon of 25th March, 1942: "A heavy raid being in progress, the Committee adjourned to the shelter under the Palace where discussion on the 'Appropriation Bill 1942' was continued .... The sitting was suspended at 4.55 pm and resumed at 5.10 pm after the Chairman has said 'The Committee may wish to adjourn for a breather. We have no tea today'... The air raid being over, the Committee adjourned to the Tapestry Chamber ... Another heavy air raid being in progress, the Committee adjourned to the shelter under the Palace ... Sitting adjourned at 7.05 pm until Tuesday, 28th April, 1942 at 3.00 pm."

(IWM)
Air Raid Warden Miss Mary Ellul of Sliema, affectionately known as 'Mary Man', clearing rubble after a stick of bombs had fallen in Prince of Wales Road, (now Manwel Dimech Street) Sliema, on 6th March, 1942.

(The Times)
The statues of Grand Masters L'Isle Adam and La Valette at Kingsgate, as well as the bridge leading to the Capital, were damaged by bombs. In 1964, this gate was demolished and replaced by a modern one, renamed City Gate.

When the Council met on the appointed day, the Sitting was held at Government Headquarters, St Venera, because extensive damage to the marble staircase and dining hall was caused when the Palace was hit again on 4th April, 1942. Sittings at the Tapestry Chamber were resumed on 12th January, 1943.

For many months the Authorities had been clamouring for Spitfires. Civilians, too, expressed their confidence that the situation would improve if Spitfires were to be flown out to Malta to match the Messerschmitt 109F. Nearly two years had passed since the start of hostilities and the Royal Air Force in Malta was not only outnumbered but also outclassed by German aircraft.

At the time there was no shortage of Spitfires in Britain and it is maintained that up to 200 of them could have been sent to Malta in July 1941, leaving in the United Kingdom double the number of fighters that had fought during the Battle of Britain. [51] However, it seems that there were a number of reasons for not flying Spitfires out to Malta then, particularly the fear of renewed massive air attacks against Britain, the need of tropicalising the aircraft before dispatch and problems relating to their delivery.

Eventually, on 7th March, 1942, fifteen Spitfire Mk VBs, led by Squadron Leader Edward J. (Jumbo) Gracie DFC, a veteran of the Battle of Britain, were flown off *Eagle* and *Argus*. These were the first to be based at a station outside Britain. The Germans, intent on destroying these reinforcements, sent several Messerschmitts from JG53 'Pik As', commanded by *Major* Gunther Freiherr von Maltzahn, only to be beaten off by Hurricanes from Nos 126, 185 and 249 Squadrons. *Eagle* flew off two more batches of 9 and 7 machines on 21st and 29th March respectively but these were far from sufficient to contain the mounting German offensive. Unfortunately the sustained reinforcement of fighter aircraft received a major setback when *Eagle* had to withdraw for repairs for about a month.

Chapter Seven

Scuttling of Talabot — *Evacuation of parts of Floriana — Life in the shelters — The red flag — The role of Boy Scouts, Girl Guides, Women's Auxiliary Reserve and VADs — Victory Kitchens — Aircraft protective pens*

Malta's needs had to be met to ensure her survival. A convoy, code-named Operation 'MW10', sailed from Alexandria on 20th March, 1942, to replenish the dwindling supplies. It consisted of the freighters *Clan Campbell, Pampas, Talabot* and *Breconshire*. Escorted by a sizeable force of cruisers and destroyers, the convoy was unmolested until the 22nd, when the Italian battleship *Littorio* and the cruisers *Gorizia* and *Trento* engaged the escorts. Through skilful manoeuvring and dispersal of the freighters, Rear-Admiral Philip Vian beat back the incursion. An attack by Italian torpedo-bombers likewise did not cause any damage but as the ships approached Malta they came under heavy attack from the *Luftwaffe*. *Talabot* and *Pampas* managed to enter the Grand Harbour on the morning of 23rd March, whereas *Clan Campbell* was sunk twenty miles off Malta, and *Breconshire* was subjected to three agonizing days of bombing. Crippled by a spreading fire, *Breconshire*, protected by three destroyers, had to lay anchor eight miles off shore. Battling against heavy seas and a determined enemy, she was towed on the 25th into Marsaxlokk Bay. The Germans were bent on destroying her and on the 27th the battered ship finally tilted over. Since April 1941 she had made seven trips to Malta. Even as she lay capsized in the bay, she made her final contribution to the Island when some hundreds of tons of oil were pumped from her hull.

The hopes raised by the arrival of *Talabot* and *Pampas* were short-lived; the tragedy was recorded by Captain E.J.F. Price in his report dated 12th April, 1942, to Vice Admiral Malta: "... When m.v. *Talabot* and m.v. *Pampas* arrived on 23rd March, every possible endeavour was made to commence discharging the ships as soon as possible.

(IWM)

The smouldering Breconshire *beached at Marsaxlokk.*

(The Times)

Talabot *ablaze*.

(IWM)

Pampas *ablaze*.

Lieutenant-Commander R.J. Knott RNR took charge of operations in *Talabot* and Lieutenant J. Dixon RNR in *Pampas*. Owing to strong winds and continual air attacks, great difficulty was experienced in securing the ships and connecting them to the shore by lighters. The crews of both ships were exhausted after their strenuous sea trip with its continual air attacks and it was difficult to get a lot of work out of the crew.

"All derrick gear on *Pampas* was found to have been more or less damaged by splinters while on passage from Alexandria. Arrangements were at once put in hand to discharge this vessel by hand, while repairs were being effected to the derrick gear. The deck cargo was discharged, hatches were taken off, ramps were constructed, and the cargo was carried out of the holds.

"By the evening of 25th March, all derricks were in operation but, from the time of the vessel's arrival, it was not possible to discharge with great speed owing to the determined efforts on the part of the enemy to bomb the vessel in frequent raids, the stevedores leaving the vessel immediately the red flag was hoisted... At about 1400 hours on 26th March, a stick of bombs fell close and around the vessel. At 1430 hours on the 26th, a heavy calibre bomb fell down the funnel and exploded. The engine-room flooded immediately and the vessel was found to be sinking rapidly by the stern. This bomb also started a fire in the amidship accommodation...

"Lieutenant Dixon behaved in a most exemplary manner throughout. By his example and courage during the very heavy raids throughout the unloading, he did his utmost to inspire the stevedores, and he worked whole-heartedly and gallantly to put out the fire...

"The unloading of *Talabot* continued without undue incident until about 1230 hours on 26th March when the ship was hit by a heavy calibre bomb which entered the engine-room and exploded there. The double bottoms were pierced and water with oil on top started to fill up the engine-room... Captain Stokes-Roberts RAOC came on board about this time and this officer and Lieutenant-Commander Knott got a large mobile foamite extinguisher along and poured the foam down the bomb hole. This made no difference whatever to the fire... Shortly after, *Ancient* and two fire floats arrived with parties of men from HMS *Penelope* and other ships. The fire floats commenced to pump foam, and the tug, water, into the engine-room. By this time also the Fire Brigade had got a pump along on the quayside and hoses were run over the barges. The heat from the engine-room was then making the forward bulkhead of No 4 hold red-hot and water was played on this, as well as into the engine-room, by the shore pumps. There was another very determined attack on both ships and bombs fell all round *Talabot* but whether she was hit again or not, I could not be certain. *Ancient* was damaged by a hit or near miss and that tug as well as both fire floats were put out of action. The fire pumps ashore were stopped and the crews went to shelter. Several members of the crew of *Ancient* and the fire floats were either blown overboard or jumped into the sea. Mr Pio Muscat Azzopardi, a locally-entered member of my staff, and myself, had the greatest difficulty in pulling these men out of the water over the lighters and, in one case, Mr Muscat Azzopardi had to give a man artificial respiration on a lighter to bring him to. I should like to place on record the fact that Mr Muscat Azzopardi was most helpful throughout. He went down with me to the ship as soon as we discovered she was hit. He organised some of the stevedores to help the fire party ashore to run the hoses and to lead them to the engine-room casing and to the forward bulkhead of No 4 hold. This he did in spite of the fact that there were continual explosions of the AA ammunition in the mid-ship superstructures throughout. He remained on board during the 1400 hours blitz when nearly all the shore fire party went ashore, guiding one of the hoses until the pump was stopped. He remained on board the ship until the cries for help caused him to go down to the bridge of lighters to pull the men from the water.

"... The ammunition in the top of No 3 hold was now beginning to go off. The ship's sides by the engine-room were red-hot and fire was obviously spreading to No 4. The Master of the ship explained to me that there was a considerable quantity of ammunition in No 4 hold within a few feet of the foremost bulkhead and he advised that, unless we wished to take the risk of a tremendous explosion, it was advisable to scuttle the ship. After consultation with you, I gave orders to *Penelope's* party to carry out this work. This was done and although the ammunition was thus rendered safe, the fire continued to burn for two days..."[52]

Talabot was scuttled by seamen from HM Ships *Penelope* and *Aurora*, led by Lieutenant Dennis Arthur Copperwheat RN, who volunteered for this hazardous operation. With complete disregard for his safety this naval officer placed the depth-charges beneath the hull and detonated them from ashore. Even after scuttling, the ship's upper-deck, which remained above water, continued to belch fire and smoke. For his skill and daring Lieutenant Copperwheat was awarded the George Cross. Police Constables 648 Carmel Cassar and 509 Emanuel Fenech, who, whilst fighting the fire

```
                    Colonial Office,
                    Downing Street, S.W.1.
                    12th June, 1942.

Dear Constable Cassar,
    It gave me great pleasure to be able to ask the
Prime Minister to submit your name to His Majesty
for the award of the British Empire Medal. Please
accept my heartiest congratulations on this award
in recognition of your gallant conduct on March the
26th. Your action on that day in the face of such
great danger was one worthily upholding the standard
of courage which you and all in Malta are setting to
the British Empire.
                    Yours sincerely,
                    Cranborne

Constable Carmel Cassar.
```

(C. Cassar)
Letter from Viscount Cranborne, Secretary of State for the Colonies, to Police Constable Carmel Cassar.

on *Talabot*, rescued a crew member of a tug engaged on the same duty, were awarded the British Empire Medal.

The blazing vessel had been a nightmare to the people of Floriana. Dense smoke enveloped the suburb and, as darkness fell, the flames threw an awesome crimson reflection over the entire area. As the risk of an explosion increased, families residing in the area between St Anne Street and the bastions overlooking the Grand Harbour were evacuated. Hundreds of people made their way to the railway tunnel shelter or sought temporary refuge with friends on the other side of the suburb.

Although the stevedores took cover during the actual bombing, they resumed work immediately the attacks abated. The frequency of the raids made their task more difficult and perilous, as attested by Harry Grossett who, during 1950 and 1951, worked as Assistant to the Chief Salvage Officer of a private company awarded the contract for clearing the *Pampas* wreckage: "We had learnt that there had been an interval between the two bombings and that after the first bomb had fallen (on *Pampas*) Maltese dock-labourers went into the hold to try to retrieve as much of the cargo as they could. Eight of them were down in No 4 hold when the second bomb fell, and their bodies were never recovered. When our divers reached No 4 hold, after clearing the mud away with hoses, they found shattered boxes of incendiary bombs. They sent them up and as they were unloaded we found among the debris the bones of eight men. I had the bones put in a special box and sent them ashore for burial." [53]

Attempts to recover as much cargo as possible from the two ships continued throughout April 1942 and finally 3,970 tons were discharged from *Pampas* out of a total of 7,462, and 1,052 tons from *Talabot* out of a total of 8,956.

Besides depriving the civilians and the garrison of the long-awaited and badly-needed replenishments, this tragedy inevitably dampened the Island's morale. A feeling of despondency overtook the Maltese, the seamen who sailed in the convoy, the gunners who put up a relentless barrage over the Grand Harbour, and the pilots who protected the ships on their coming within range of Malta's fighters.

The loss of these supplies aggravated an already serious situation. Early in 1942, the Maltese faced heavy bombing, starvation and the threat of invasion. Food, ammunition, fuel and other essential commodities were getting scarcer. General Sir William Dobbie, who had gained the admiration and confidence of the population by his bearing and forthright broadcasts, appealed to the Maltese to make further sacrifices. They did; but the intensive bombing and the near-starvation diet were adversely affecting the health of the population. It was not uncommon to see people, including teenagers, being carried on stretchers or on shoulders to the shelters.

People were forced to spend long hours and sleepless nights underground. The spacious railway tunnel in Floriana, the largest on the

(IWM)
People entering a shelter in South Street, Valletta.

Island, enabled many of the 3,000 people seeking refuge there to take down their beds, using sheets or curtains as partitions to gain some privacy. However, only a few shelters offered enough space even for a deckchair, much less for a hammock or a bunk in tiers. A wife would generally sacrifice her turn to use the family deckchair in favour of her husband who had to report for work on the morrow; she passed the night sitting on a stool, resting her head against the moist rock, firmly clutching the small box containing the family's savings, ranging from cash to gold trinkets.

Sanitary facilities were primitive and, except for the large shelters, which enjoyed the benefit of electricity, the others had to rely on a few paraffin lamps and an assortment of small tins with a cotton wick which emitted a minimum of light and a maximum of unpleasant smell. In this limbo one could just make out pictures of Our Lady, Victory signs and cuttings from newspapers showing pilots and gunners, battleships and sloops, Mr Churchill and the King. Young and old, poor and rich alike, lived in such seemingly prehistoric conditions.

It was providential that at such a crucial stage there was no outbreak of an epidemic. However rickets, scabies and boils were rife and took a long time to heal. Lice and bugs likewise inevitably thrived, despite all the precautions taken, as there was no disinfectant to combat these insects. In such unhygienic conditions, people of all ages, huddled together in the suffocating shelters, were thrown about by the blast from exploding aerial mines and bombs. On the other hand this grim existence engendered a *camaraderie* so essential under such trying circumstances. Beneath the safety of the rocks, the Maltese lived, gave birth and breathed their last.

As intervals between one alert and the next got progressively shorter, many people did not bother to rush to a shelter every time the siren sounded. In so doing they were taking too many risks as apart from the dangers from explosions, falling masonry and red-hot shrapnel, they also ran the risk of being strafed by low-flying enemy fighters. Moreover last-minute panicky rushes into shelter entrances added to the hazards.

People within sight of the towers at the Palace and the *Auberge de Castille* had a slight advantage over the rest of the population. From mid-January 1942, once an alert was sounded, an observer at the Palace Tower kept constant watch over the movement of enemy aircraft. When it became apparent that bombers were heading towards the two main harbours a red flag was hoisted to indicate the likelihood of an attack on the area. This was immediately followed by the hoisting of another red flag over *Castille*. It became customary with certain people only to seek shelter once the red flag was up. Those living in ditches relied on youngsters who, on the giving of the official warning, hoisted their own red flags atop their improvised outposts and scattered in all directions shouting 'the red flag is up'. These boys proved most reliable. Subsequently the red flag warning system was extended to Sliema, but it was not found possible to introduce it to other parts of the Island. This warning also helped in the unloading of convoys, as the stevedores sought shelter during 'red flag' periods only.

The homeless had no alternative but to resign themselves to a new way of life. The shelter became their home. Outside the entrance they cooked their meagre meals, consisting of Soup Kitchen fare supplemented by vegetables

(M. Ellul)
A religious poster, invoking Our Lady of Mount Carmel to deliver Malta from danger and for the attainment of peace; these were found in most shelters.

(NWM)
Sailors hoisting the Red Flag on the Palace Tower.

(The Times)
Life goes on.

THE BOY SCOUTS ASSOCIATION

This is to certify that I have awarded to The Boy Scouts of Malta and Gozo the Bronze Cross in recognition of their courage, heroic endurance and devotion to duty in the face of continuous enemy action in the War for Freedom

Date: St. George's Day, 1943.

(L.F. Tortell)

Award of Bronze Cross to the Boy Scouts Association.

secured through friends or on the black market, besides airing the bedding and blankets, and doing their washing.

School life was unavoidably disrupted; children had the time of their life playing amidst the ruins and building their own outposts with masonry. They played at soldiers and when they were dragged in during air raids, many of them kept sneaking out and in again to give a colourful account of what was going on in the sky above; to them war was a live adventure packed with action and drama. Yet they did not understand that a blockade enforced a lack of daily necessities, nor appreciate that their bread and cheese, coffee and milk powder had to be cut down because the long-awaited convoy had failed to arrive. When the pangs of hunger struck, they yelled for what could not be offered them. These children had to mature early in life.

The qualification and efficiency badges on the sleeves of Boy Scouts were no ornament; when their services were needed, these disciplined youths administered first-aid to the injured, helped the Passive Defence Corps and participated in all activities relating to the civil defence of the Island. As mentioned earlier, a company of the King's Own Malta Regiment, formed entirely of Scouts, Rovers and Old Scouts, ranked among the best infantrymen.

Speaking over Rediffusion in October 1942, Vice-Admiral Sir Ralph Leatham KCB, Vice Admiral Malta, referred to another aspect of the work these Boys carried out: "... Naval ratings also man several lookout and signal stations

THE GUIDES OF MALTA AWARD OF THE BRONZE CROSS

In recognition of the courage and endurance displayed by the Members of the Movement in Malta during the war of 1939–1945, especially during the period of intense enemy activity.

The fortitude and cheerfulness shown has been an example to the entire Movement, and is a source of special pride to their fellow Guides in the British Empire.

Finola Somers
Chairman Awards Committee.

(L.F. Tortell)

Award of Bronze Cross to the Girl Guides Movement.

throughout the day and night around the coast, and to augment them we have taken in from the Boy Scouts Groups a number of 'Special Coast Watchers'. Apart from communicating with ships, their duty is to spot and report anything of interest or unusual that may happen around them — and it is really remarkable what naturally sharp eyes the Maltese lads have. They are often the first to see anything. They are of the greatest help in air raids when they add to the information required for the control of the fighters. During the heavy blitzing, the bravery of men in these posts was outstanding — nothing but the open sky above their heads, nothing to hit back at the enemy with, and bombs raining down and exploding all round them... During a very severe raid, the officer-in-charge at one station ordered a lad of sixteen to go down the spiral staircase for protection. He at once disappeared below. A moment or two later the officer saw him again on the top of the tower. 'Why haven't you done what I told you?' the officer asked. 'I went down the steps as far as I thought was necessary to obey your order, Sir, and have now returned to my duty', the boy replied..." [54]

The devotion to duty displayed by these youngsters did not go unrewarded. On Sunday, 2nd May, 1943, Lord Gort, on behalf of Lord Somers, the Chief Scout, presented the Bronze Cross to the Scouts of Malta and Gozo; the coveted award, bestowed only 'for special heroism and extraordinary risk', was received on their behalf by Scout Joseph Panzavecchia BEM.

The Girl Guides too contributed to the war effort. The majority undertook knitting for the Forces, whilst several grown-ups took up clerical work with the Services or joined the St John's Ambulance Brigade, the Communal Feeding Department or the Passive Defence

Corps. In the early stages, they also helped in assembling anti-gas respirators. After the war, the Maltese Girl Guide Movement was awarded the Bronze Cross.

The willingness of Maltese women to play their part was manifest as far back as September 1938 when 3,000 volunteers enrolled in the Women's Auxiliary Reserve set up by Lady Bonham-Carter, the wife of the then Governor of Malta, General Sir Charles Bonham-Carter. They trained several hundred Air Raid Wardens and Decontaminators; did sewing and knitting for the Forces and refugees; and when war broke out supplied the Three Services, the Civil Government and the Dockyard with trained personnel, thus releasing many men for active service.

Members of the St John's Ambulance Brigade worked among the wounded and the sick at the various hospitals. About fifty of them joined the Voluntary Aid Detachment, performing sterling work at Mtarfa Military Hospital, at several Advanced Dressing Stations and at the dockyard. When war eventually receded from our shores, twenty-two young ladies crossed over to Italy to work in Field Hospitals in the Taranto area. Their dedication and devotion to duty earned them high praise from the Supreme Allied Commander Mediterranean, Field-Marshal Sir Harold Alexander, in a message dated 17th August, 1945, addressed to the Governor of Malta:

> H Q Base Jugoslav Army
> Medical Section
>
> V.A.D. Gauchi
>
> 45 General Hospital
>
> The war is over and you also will be probably leaving very soon. Before you do so we would like to express all our recognition for what you have done for our Jugoslav wounded and patients
>
> We may assure you that all the Jugoslavs who have known you will keep you in their memories. With your unstinted work you made many friends in Jugoslavia and at the same time you have helped towards a better understanding between our two countries. Thus you have done your part in cementing a lasting peace.
>
> Will you, please, accept as a visible sign of our recognition the "Titov lik".
>
> COMMISAR OF MEDICAL SECTION   CHIEF OF MEDICAL SECTION
> (Captain FAJFER)   (Lt Col Dr NEUBAUER)

(Miss J. Gauci)
A letter from Yugoslav partisans to Miss Jane Gauci, expressing their appreciation for her work.

(Miss J. Gauci)
Maltese VADs on return from service in Italy. Standing extreme left is Miss J. Gauci, who was awarded the Titov Lik.

"The devotion to duty and outstanding work of the Volunteer Aid Detachment of Members of the St John's Ambulance Brigade, Malta, who are now about to leave this Command, will long be remembered by all those with whom they came in contact.

"These ladies first came to Italy during the busy period when large numbers of Yugoslav sick and wounded, men, women and children, were arriving daily.

"In spite of language difficulties and the severe and unusual nature of many of the wounds, these volunteers carried out their duties with unfailing cheerfulness and efficiency; their labours undoubtedly mitigated to a very great extent the suffering to which their patients had been submitted.

"More recently they have shown the same high standard of efficiency in their care of British sick and wounded after the evacuation of most of the Yugoslavs to their own country.

"The people of Malta may well be proud of these ladies who, not content with having worked throughout the long months during which their homeland was subjected to constant attack, then volunteered to come overseas to nurse sick and wounded British and Allied personnel, thus adding a most valuable contribution to the war effort of the Empire and United Nations as a whole.

"Please accept on their behalf my most grateful thanks for their services in this theatre of war."

Two of the Maltese VADs, Miss Jane Amy Gauci and Miss Lily Pether, were honoured with the Yugoslav decoration *Titov Lik*.

The dwindling stocks, which threatened a famine, continued to cause anxiety to the

Authorities. On 5th May, 1942, Government took the drastic decision to ration bread, Malta's staple food, to the extremely low level of 10½ ozs per head daily. This decision was taken with reluctance as it was feared it would deal a staggering blow to morale. But people accepted it as yet a further sacrifice, the like of which they had already confronted and surmounted. They seemed to realise the helplessness of the situation and that the only alternative to the dreaded capitulation lay in accepting further sacrifices. In April, pasta, rice and tomato paste were rationed, as was tinned milk for as long as stocks lasted; reductions were made in the entitlement of sugar, oil, coffee, soap and kerosene and, shortly afterwards, supplies of frozen meat and rice were exhausted. To keep the precarious situation under some measure of control, the Communal Feeding Department had been set up in January 1942 under the directorship of Mr R. Wingrave Tench OBE. The Soup Kitchens, originally set up by Government to provide meals to those whose homes had been demolished and consequently had no means of cooking, were replaced by Victory Kitchens to cater for a larger section of the population as well as to economise on food and kerosene.

Families were urged to register voluntarily at the Kitchens, bartering in turn a percentage of their ration. The first Victory Kitchen was opened at Lija on 3rd January, 1942.

Through necessity rather than choice, Victory Kitchens mushroomed throughout the Island. In June 1942, forty-two were functioning in the following localities: Lija, Balzan, Attard, Qormi, Birkirkara, Rabat, Zabbar, Marsa, Mdina, Kalkara, St Paul's Bay, Hamrun, Zejtun, Pietà, Zebbug, Valletta, Kirkop, Floriana, Msida, Sliema, Dingli, Mosta, Siggiewi, Gzira and St Julians. The recruitment of staff, including supervisors, storekeepers, sales assistants, cooks, assistant cooks and labourers, was not so easy as most men and the majority of women were already engaged on other vital work. Housewives and other willing but inexperienced young ladies filled this pressing gap. Through the intervention of Archbishop Mgr Dom Maurus Caruana OSB, a number of Sisters from various Religious Orders were asked to lend a helping hand and by July 1942 they were running fourteen Victory Kitchens. The number of persons drawing meals from the Kitchens rose to over 100,000 in October 1942 and up to 175,536 in the first week of January 1943 when the stock of food and paraffin fell. At the peak of the siege, 200 Kitchens served registered subscribers with their portion at mid-day or in the evening, against payment of sixpence a portion. The number of subscribers dropped to 20,500 by the end of January 1943 as a result of a sudden improvement in the food and fuel situation.[55]

The weekly menu consisted of:

Monday and Saturday:	Maccaroni with tomato sauce.
Tuesday:	*Balbuljata* (scrambled eggs and tomatoes)
Wednesday and Friday:	Vegetable soup or herrings.
Sunday and Thursday:	Stewed meat or corned beef with tomatoes and baked beans.

The extent of malnutrition prevalent in Malta at the time is perhaps best realised when actual

(The Times)

Queuing for kerosene at Castille Square, Valletta.

(The Times)
Queuing for bread in Merchants Street, Valletta.

(The Times)
Queuing for milk in Merchants Street, Valletta.

Policemen supervising the distribution of water inside Kingsgate, Valletta. (The Times)

figures of nutrients taken are compared to the daily amount recommended by the medical authorities as shown in the following table [56]:

Type of Work	Calories		
	Men	Women	Children
Sedentary	2,250	2,000	0-1 year — 1,000
Light	2,750	2,250	2-6 years — 1,500
Medium	3,000	2,500	7-10 years — 2,000
Heavy	3,500	3,000	11-14 years — 2,750
Very heavy	4,250	3,750	15-19 years — 2,500 Girls
			15-19 years — 3,500 Boys

In fact, during the summer of 1942, the daily calorie intake in Malta per adult was never more than 1,500 but more often as little as 1,100; children received less. Rations to servicemen worked out at about 2,300 calories; sailors, soldiers and airmen were subjected to unmitigated physical and mental strain, though no more so than many civilian workers. [57] (See Appendices **G** and **H**) By way of comparison, throughout the war the calorific value of daily rations in the United Kingdom never fell below 2,800.

Although subscribers to the Victory Kitchens were told that they were being offered goat meat, it did not take a statistician to realize that there were not all those goats on the island. Contributions to the *Times of Malta*, some of which are reproduced hereunder, reflected the feelings of the people:

10th August, 1942 — E.A. from Rabat:

"Imagine our big 'Oh'! of surprise when the portions of three persons offered in one plate consisted of a piece of skin with a good layer of fat and a shadow of meat on top, six tablespoonfuls of sauce and five peas."

14th August, 1942 — Worried housewife from Sliema:

"Some days there is quite enough meat, some other days very scanty portions are served wallowing in water, masqueraded red, and a few peas, at the rate of two half-peas per head.

Queuing for meals outside a Victory Kitchen.

So far so good. But what about the *minestra* (vegetable soup)? The vegetables are cut in big chunks, half a turnip, big pieces of long-marrow with skin, turnip leaves and stalks in quantity, a shadow of pumpkin and tomatoes, just to give a hectic colour, a few *zibeg* (type of pasta) swimming in water ... pure water. Not very inviting."

1st September, 1942 — Spectator from Valletta:

"The mid-day meals supplied from the Victory Kitchens of Valletta and of several other districts had to be thrown away *en masse* today. The meal was composed chiefly of liver in a sort of stew. It was hard and had a bitter taste, which made it unpalatable and uneatable. This suggests that the gall had not been removed from the liver either before it was put in cold storage or before it was cooked. To this negligence may be due the fact that valuable food had to be thrown away. A slice of corned beef was passed round hours later."

To allay any fear of food poisoning, the following Notice was issued from the Lieutenant-Governor's Office about the complaint mentioned in the last extract:

"The Government wishes to inform the public that the liver which was issued to the Communal Feeding Department for service in Victory Kitchens yesterday had previously been inspected and passed as being wholly fit for human consumption though somewhat bitter in taste. It is usual for all frozen liver, especially that kept long in storage, to have this bitter flavour. A large number of the customers of the Kitchen found the meal unpalatable and were not prepared to accept the meal provided. The Government deeply regrets that this situation should have arisen. Arrangements were made immediately by the Communal Feeding Department to ensure that all those who had received an unsatisfactory lunch were given a portion of corned beef either at once or later in the day." There is no doubt that the food supplied by these Kitchens was exceedingly poor and at times hardly edible, yet there can equally be no doubt that the Kitchens and their staff, even though occasionally subjected to verbal abuse, played a significant part in overcoming what could have been a catastrophic situation.

The role of the Institution was objectively assessed in the editorial of the *Times of Malta* (30.12.42): "...They have in fact been 'Siege Kitchens' providing a meagre daily sustenance masquerading under the title of a 'meal' for either lunch or supper, and this at a time when other meals were unobtainable for the thousands who had had their homes, and with them their store cupboards, wiped out, or who had long since exhausted any food reserve ... So the fact is that Victory Kitchens have been catering for a hard-tried public existing under siege conditions of acute severity, when not only food but fuel was short... The Siege Kitchens of Malta provided the means by which all were hungry together and nobody starved outright. The majority knew hunger not as a Lenten fast but as a daily occurrence and the meaning of the Lord's Prayer 'Give us this day our daily bread' took on a living significance. Parents of young children were the real heroes and heroines. They fasted to the limit so that the children should not cry. For the first time since British rule, deaths in Malta outnumbered births..."

Improvisation helped to make life a little more bearable; men found fig and vine leaves a substitute, albeit a distasteful one, for tobacco — they also kept the butt-ends of their fags, and others they found in the streets, to roll into cigarettes; women made coats from blankets, and dresses from curtains and from silk recovered from parachutes; worn-out tyres were turned into shoes and sandals; the bottom parts of bottles were cut off to serve as cups. Yet the population never gave in to defeatism or despair. They showed infinite trust in their stamina and that of their defenders, deriving additional strength from their Faith.

As Allied fighters chased Axis bombers, the blue skies turned black with an umbrella of flak puffs from anti-aircraft shells; towns and villages disappeared behind a curtain of dust and smoke; the air vibrated with the deafening noise of siren-screeching Stukas, exploding bombs, thundering guns and crumbling buildings. No doubt many cursed the enemy; the majority, however, resorted to prayer. Such improvisation became part of our war-time pleadings to the Almighty:

(IWM)
Valletta hidden behind a thick curtain of dust from exploding bombs. The prominent feature to the left is the Phoenicia Hotel and that to the right is St Publius Church at Floriana.

(via J.E. Hall)
Tignè under attack.

Qalb imqaddsa ta' Gesu u ta' Marija
Ghamlu l-bombi jaqghu fil-hamrija.

Regina tal-Vittorji,
Regina tas-Sema w l-Art,
Ilqa' l-bombi fil-mantell tieghek
U ehlisna minn dan l-attakk.

Sacred Heart of Jesus and Mary
Make the bombs fall into the soil.

Queen of Victories,
Queen of Heaven and Earth
Gather the bombs in Thy mantle
And deliver us from this attack.

The gunners, pilots, wardens and firemen were not forgotten in this prayer in English written soon after the Illustrious Blitz:

Bless this shelter, Lord we pray,
During air raids night and day;
Bless the people here within,
Keep them safe and free from sin.

Bless the gunners as they work,
The searchlights guide when dangers lurk;
Bless each chasing aircraft crew,
Lend Thine aid to all they do.

Bless the members of Thy flock,
Keep them free from air raid shock;
Bless the light and keep it bright
And away from alien sight.

Bless our wardens one and all
Answering their Country's call;
Our gallant firemen, help them Lord
Let Thy grace be their reward.

Bless all those who work for peace
That hostilities may cease.

A look at the airfields could easily convince one that the enemy had by no means given up. These and the newly-constructed airstrips at Safi and Qrendi were often put out of action temporarily through bombing and it took an army of servicemen, policemen and civilians to fill the many craters along the runways. An observer was detailed to mark bomb craters along the runways and dispersal areas with red flags; no sooner was an air raid over than lorries and carts would hurry towards the scene and dump their loads of gravel and rubble into the gaping holes, while an almost obsolescent steam-roller trundled back and forth levelling the material to enable the incoming fighters to land, refuel and rearm in readiness for the next scramble. Servicemen and civilians walked abreast along runways and dispersal areas collecting shrapnel and splinters which were a menace to aircraft landing or taking off.

Most of the recovery equipment at the airfields had been destroyed through bombing. Trucks, Bren gun carriers and even tanks were employed to drag crash-landed aircraft away into the workshops or scrap-yard, depending on the extent of the damage. When an extensively damaged aircraft was considered a write-off, all salvageable parts were removed for spares.

As attacks increased both in frequency and ferocity a large number of pens was constructed to protect the aircraft from further destruction. At first sand-bags were used but these soon gave way to 4-gallon petrol cans and oil drums filled with earth. Stone from destroyed buildings proved even stronger and was never in short supply. As soon as the

CRUSADE OF PRAYERS TO
OUR LADY OF VICTORIES
FOR MALTA AND ENGLAND.

O Marija, Ghajnuna ta' l-Insara, ehles lill-Imperu Ngliz u bierek l-Isqfijiet, il-Qassisin u r-Religjuzi taghna; bierek ukoll 'l Mexxejja taghna, 'l Irgiel taghna, 'l Hbiebna u lil Niesna kullimkien.
(40 ... Ind. Cell. ...)

Mary, Help of Christians, save the British Empire and bless our Bishops, Priests and Religious; our Leaders, our Men, our Friends and our Peoples everywhere.
(40 days Ind. each time).

ISSIEHBU fdis-Xirka
Mbierka mill-
E. T. Mons. Arcisqof.

Ikthu lill-
BROTHER PRESIDENT,
De La Salle College,
GZIRA.

JOIN THIS CRUSADE
Blessed by
H. G. the Archbishop.

Apply to:

Salesian Press, Sliema

(via Ph. Vella) *A wartime religious poster.*

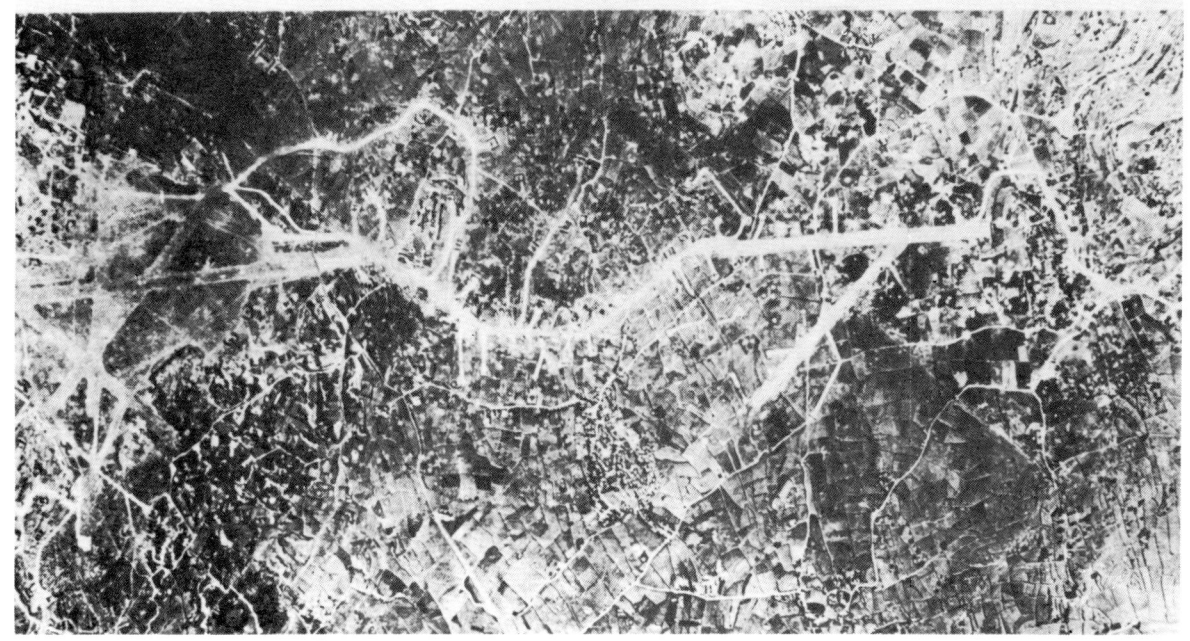

German photograph showing taxiways joining Luqa airfield to Safi airstrip.

Aerial view of Ta' Qali airfield in 1944, showing runway, dispersal areas, pens and bomb craters.

(NWMA)

Hurricane in 'sand-bag' pen.

(T. Mullins)

Maryland in 'stone' pen.

material was delivered on the few available trucks and numerous horse-drawn carts, all hands set about building the walls. This was no easy task since a pen for a Wellington, for instance, needed about 3,500 tons of stone to enclose an area ninety-by-ninety feet. Other pens were also erected as decoys to house written-off aircraft; the extra effort put in was amply justified, as these were given due attention by the Germans who dropped their bombs on these dummy targets.

To provide access to these pens, scattered over a wide area, it was necessary to construct twenty-seven miles of dispersal runways. This job was again undertaken by servicemen and civilians who were untrained for such work.

Air Vice-Marshal Hugh P. Lloyd, Air Officer Commanding Malta, stresses the importance of these enclosures: "Pens and nothing else had saved us from vital damage. Pens, pens and pens — we had pens for everything. By the end of April our pens totalled three hundred and fifty-eight. There were twenty-seven for the Wellingtons, two hundred and five for the fighters, sixty-seven for the Marylands, Beaufighters and Blenheims, and thirty-four for the Swordfish and Albacores; for the steam-rollers and the petrol bowsers there were twenty-five. No, the Spitfires did not save Malta; Malta saved herself by the combined efforts of everyone on the Island. Malta stood four-square: the civilians, the navy, the army and the air force. The battle for Malta was not in the air alone; there was every bit as fierce a battle on the ground, even if it was not so dangerous. The soldiers made by far the greater proportion of the pens. In early 1942 there were fifteen hundred of them working on the aerodromes and sometimes, during the really bad periods of the combined offensive by Kesselring and the weather, there were as many as three thousand. We wanted all the help we could get in addition to that provided by the civilians. Everybody made pens ... No one had to wait long to see the effectiveness of their work, and some parties became so interested in it that their pens appeared like long narrow boxes, open at one end. The deeper the pens, with the aeroplane against the back wall, the less the danger from splinters. It was a simple matter with the fighters as they could be manhandled on the ground with ease. So one of the side walls would be extended and then built partly across the entrance, leaving only a narrow entry, so that a bomb could only damage the fighter by falling inside the pen or by blowing down its walls. With the Blenheims and the Wellingtons, on the other hand, there was no such easy solution because the surface of the ground was not sufficiently level for man-handling these heavier aircraft. As some of the Germans would take an individual aeroplane inside a pen for their aiming mark, we tried camouflaging some of the pens with netting, but there was not sufficient material for more than a dozen."[58]

Work had to go on round-the-clock, come rain, come bombs. It was only when enemy aircraft attacked a particular area that the men scrambled to the nearest slit trench for limited protection. Acting Petty Officer Anthony Debattista RN, who had been awarded the Distinguished Service Medal for gallantry whilst serving on the corvette *Lanner* during the evacuation of Crete in 1941, was detailed to supervise such work on his return to Malta on 25th January, 1942: "Another Maltese Killick, four Petty Officers from HMS *Aurora* and I were in charge of Maltese civilians building pens at Ta' Qali; my group numbered between sixty and seventy workers. During the mid-day break on 17th March, 1942, we were playing football when a German dive-bomber planted four bombs in our area. To my order, the men jumped into the nearest slit trench. Noticing that Joseph Petroni was lying on the ledge, I dragged him towards me only to find myself covered in blood sprouting from his gaping back. Another victim was George Debono, a former Hamrun Spartans player, whilst a third was slightly injured. On the morrow, on being informed that a worker was unaccounted for, I searched the area and recovered his mangled body, which I placed in an empty petrol tin for eventual burial; he was an elderly man who had served at Salonika during the First World War."[59]

Axis aircraft devised an ingenious way to strafe the airfields. Macchi 202s, Reggiane 2001s, and Messerschmitt 109s would approach the aerodrome at a very low level with undercarriages lowered to deceive the gunners, RAF personnel and infantrymen manning sangars into mistaking them for friendly aircraft coming in to land. This proved to be a short-lived deception.

(L. Davies)
Pens, covered with camouflage nets, to minimize the risk of detection from the air.

Chapter Eight

Radar — Ancillary and Service Corps — Royal Tank Regiment — Malta Police Force

Radar, along with so many other factors, is regarded as one of the main contributors to Malta's defeat of the enemy. Radar (then known as RDF, Radio Direction Finding) was first brought to Malta in March 1939 when Air Ministry Experimental Station 242 was set up at Dingli Cliffs, one of the highest spots on the Island. This was the first 'transportable' radar station installed outside the United Kingdom. By the middle of July 1941, the number of stations was increased by three — 501 AMES at Tas-Silg, 502 at Madliena, and 504 also on the cliff-tops at Dingli. These three were COL (Chain Overseas Low) stations and plotted medium to low-flying aircraft, whereas 242 was a COH (Chain Overseas High) station capable of plotting high-flying aircraft.

The information received by the stations, consisting of the approximate number of aircraft and their respective height, was passed to the Filter Room at War Headquarters housed in a labyrinth deep down Lascaris bastion in Valletta. Incorporated therein were the vital Operations Rooms which were constructed by the Royal Engineers, under the command of Major Styles, to plans prepared by Flying Officer J. Max Surman.[60]

The plotters in the Operations Room, both RAF personnel and a number of British and Maltese young ladies, sat around a table on which was a large map of the Central Mediterranean with the Maltese Islands in the centre. Counters placed on the grid references, on receipt of instructions from the Filterer, gave an accurate picture of aerial activity over and around Malta. The tracks on the Filter Table were identified by the letters 'F', 'B', and 'C' for 'Fighter', 'Bomber' or 'Coastal' respectively. Information about aircraft movements was also received from other sources. The Observer Corps, composed of about 50 British and Maltese airmen scattered at various vantage points along the Island, passed visual reports to the Fighter Operations Room at Lascaris.

The radar stations registered the presence of all aircraft, Axis and Allied. A device called IFF — Identification Friend or Foe — fitted to British aircraft, was activated when hit by radar beams, sending back a specially-coded blip on the radar screen. On receipt of an IFF track, the Plotters placed a counter on the Filter Table against the relevant plot. For more accurate control of British fighters intercepting hostile aircraft a GCI (Ground Control Interception) station was also set up near Salina Bay.

(J. Fleming)
Receiver for Mark I Gunlaying radar.

(J. Fleming)
Transmitter for Mark I Gunlaying radar.

Radar was so successful that other stations were subsequently set up at Ghar Lapsi, Qawra, Wardija and at Gozo. These stations, which also fed information to the gunners, were of invaluable help in containing to some extent the German onslaught. However, at one stage in 1942, the benefit of the early-warning system was almost lost. This was due to jamming by the Germans.

This blow was only averted through ingenuity. Professor Reginald V. Jones, Britain's wartime Assistant Director of Intelligence (Science), only a few years ago revealed that the Germans had installed some powerful jammers in Sicily to neutralize the radar stations in Malta. These achieved the intended effect and the Authorities in Malta had to seek the assistance of the Air Ministry. The local stations were advised to keep on scanning so as to give the impression that the jamming had not been successful. The ruse paid off, as after a few days the Germans switched off their jammers.

At the end of the war, Professor Jones spoke at length to *General* Wolfgang Martini, the Director General of Signals and Radar of the *Luftwaffe*, then a prisoner-of-war. At one point, the General mentioned Malta in particular, as he had been quite surprised that his powerful jammers had not been effective. Professor Jones writes that *General* Martini laughed ruefully when told of the ruse.[61]

Less complex but of great importance was the work carried out by the Ancillary and Service Corps: the Royal Engineers, Royal Army Ordnance Corps, Royal Army Service Corps and, later, the Royal Electrical and Mechanical Engineers. With understrength complements, over-stretched duties and sparse stores, they worked without respite to keep the Fortress battle-worthy. They had to meet the needs of a garrison which, from 4,000 before the war, by early 1942 had risen to about 30,000, a third of whom were Maltese.[62] In the drama of Malta, these men did not steal the show nor make the headlines; their back-stage work, however, was essential. Although their difficulties were at times overpowering, they accomplished their respective tasks with admirable organisation and planning. The Royal Army Ordnance Corps (later REME) had the responsibility of keeping anti-aircraft batteries and gun positions, scattered throughout the Island, supplied with ammunition and spare gun barrels. The shells were stored underground at Mosta Fort and other bomb-proof localities, whilst other equipment, stores and spares were housed at the Ospizio in Floriana, and at Marina Pinto, Marsa; when these depots were very severely damaged early in 1942, most of the material was transferred to a rock sub-depot at Gharghur, whilst the capacity at Mosta was increased by the construction of 6-inch concrete roofs to the moats around the fort and at the disused Targa Battery. Repairs and maintenance of equipment were carried out at Mamo's Garage at Gzira.

The intensification of enemy action necessitated the dispersal of the sub-depots even further. St Edward's College in Cottonera was one of the places utilized for this purpose. The existence of these sub-depots and over one hundred dispersed store-houses for ammunition, gun barrels and other material, served a double purpose: the cutting down of losses in the event of a depot being hit, and reasonable accessibility to the guns, which was essential in the absence of mechanised transport. The ammunition stock fluctuated with the high expenditure of shells during the blitz, the difficulty of replenishment and, at a later stage, the stockpiling in connection with the Sicilian campaign. The following figures reflect the situation [63]:

June 1940	— 1,750 tons
June 1941	— 8,000 tons
December 1941	— 13,000 tons
June 1942	— 6,000 tons
April 1943	— 16,000 tons
June/November 1943	— 25,000 tons to 26,000 tons

Wastage in any form was not tolerated; men from the Corps recovered a large amount of small arms ammunition from ships sunk in the harbours or off the coast, about half of which was serviceable. Spares for the guns were also in short supply, resulting in considerable improvisation locally, mostly at the dockyard. Fuel shortage led to kerosene being added to petrol to make supplies of this vital commodity last longer. Moreover, about 10,000 bicycles were used by the Services.

The Royal Army Service Corps, severely handicapped through lack of adequate transport, requisitioned about 1,000 cars and lorries. Some buses were converted into ambulances to cope with the number of casualties.

Yet these vehicles were not sufficient and, at one time in 1941, no fewer than 500 mule-driven carts were hired from farmers and stone-masons each for £5 a week. In 1942, a Malta Section of the RASC was formed and designated as the Army Service Corps, Malta Territorial Force. The Official History of The Royal Army Service Corps records: "A special tribute must be paid not only to the civilian drivers and men of the MTF but also to those Maltese civilian employees who were permanently employed by the RASC before and during the war. Men in all categories gave loyal service."[64]

In May 1943, Nos 32 and 651 Companies RASC (GT) were reinforced with the arrival of Nos 178 and 468 Companies (Palestinian GT). The last-named General Transport Company was, however, decimated *en route* to Malta. Sholmo Tamir, at the time serving in the Israeli Transport Units of the British Army at Alexandria, records this tragedy in his book *Pirkei Shelihut* ('From the Life of an Emissary'): "On the first of May they gathered on board ship, out at sea, to celebrate the Workers' Festival. Suddenly a wave of German planes swept down over the ship and launched a heavy bombardment. One of the bombs struck midship, penetrated into the vaults and pierced the vessel which sank immediately. Our lads leapt into the sea, struggled with the waves, clung to beams and planks, showed great courage and exemplary team spirit, but few were lucky enough to survive. 140 of them perished in the depths of the sea."[65]

The Malta Auxiliary Corps was set up before the outbreak of war and provided the various artillery and infantry regiments with cooks, telephonists, drivers, motor-cyclists and other general dutymen. The members wore no uniform except for an arm-band, but were nonetheless subject to military discipline. The history of 7th Heavy Anti-Aircraft Regiment Royal Artillery records: "The Regiment was fortunate in having an excellent team of Auxiliaries attached to it, men and boys — some were not more than sixteen years old — who did their duties and a great deal more. Kitchen boys helped to replenish ammunition, dining-room orderlies became stretcher-bearers ... The Regiment would have been hard pressed without this faithful and reliable band who seldom received the recognition their services so richly merited ... Our twenty-two Maltese per battery were a godsend."[66]

Although the smallness of the Island limits the use of tanks, there was a small detachment from the Royal Tank Regiment. No 1 Independent Troop Royal Tank Regiment, comprising three officers and sixty-five NCOs and men under the command of A/Major R.E.H. Drury from 1st Army Tank Brigade, sailed from the Clyde in October 1940 on the troop ship *Louis Pasteur*. On reaching Gibraltar, the men transferred to destroyers which brought them to Malta on 10th November, 1940. The tanks, four Infantry Mk IIs (Matildas) and two Mk VI Bs, which had been loaded on a fast merchantman, arrived a week later. These were soon repainted in 'rubble wall' camouflage and,

(IWM)

Policemen clearing debris from opposite the Royal Opera House in Valletta.

Matilda tank 'GRIFFIN'.

to recall the dash across the Mediterranean, the four Matildas were named after the destroyer escort, *Faulknor, Greyhound, Gallant* and *Griffin*.

The detachment was a self-contained unit, having its own motor transport, stores and fitter staff. Maintenance and minor repairs to tanks and vehicles were made wherever the detachment was stationed, while overhauls and engine changes were carried out at Mamo's Garage in Gzira. The unit, initially deployed on the outskirts of Birkirkara, was subsequently stationed at Floriana, Bubaqra, Safi and near Verdala Palace.

Early in 1942, the 6th Royal Tank Regiment was ordered to reinforce this troop. 'A' Squadron, equipped with A 9 and A 13 Cruiser-type tanks armed with 2-pounder guns, sailed from Alexandria. The convoy suffered considerably from enemy attacks and, in fact, only eighty-five officers and men, and eight tanks reached the Island on 19th January, 1942, moving to Verdala on the following day. In the spring of 1942, A/Major S.D.G. Longworth took over command and led the troop until its departure to Egypt in July 1943.[67]

The civilian contribution to the defence of the Motherland was as important as one could expect. The Police were in the forefront; their role underwent drastic changes and the men soon adapted themselves to their new duties. Besides their work at the airfields, they helped with the unloading of convoys, escorted supplies to safe storage to avoid pilfering, took part in rescue operations and the clearing of rubble, and distributed water in bowsers to blitzed areas besides performing a multitude of other duties. A portion of their normal work and responsibility was shouldered by the Special Constabulary. The Regular Police were often commended for their services. Besides Constable 347 Carmel Camilleri, who was awarded the George Medal for gallantry on 4th November, 1940, and Constables 648 Carmel Cassar and 509 Emanuel Fenech, awarded the British Empire Medal for bravery during the *Talabot* tragedy, similar cases of exemplary conduct are recorded. On 12th February, 1942 Police Constables J. Meli and V. Gili volunteered to take in a Police motor-boat the Captain of HMS *Maori*, who wanted to reboard his ship, ablaze in French Creek. Amidst falling bombs and exploding ammunition from the destroyer, they accomplished their mission, after which they rescued some members of the ship's crew who were struggling along the burning ship. Inspector Charles Coppola, Sergeant M. Buttigieg and Special Constable J. Sammut likewise risked their life when, on 3rd July, 1942, they entered Villa Apap in Hamrun to rescue an elderly invalid lady, despite the presence of a heavy unexploded bomb which, in fact, completely demolished the building soon after the rescue operation was over.

Ten regular members of the Malta Police Force lost their life through enemy action; the Special Constabulary too had its roll of honour.

Chapter Nine

*Internment of enemy aliens and a number of Maltese —
Deportation to Uganda — Repatriation to Malta*

With the outbreak of war on 3rd September, 1939, a number of persons, regarded as a risk to the internal security of the Island, were taken into custody.

The Reformatory at Fort Salvatore in the Cottoner Lines was converted into an Internment Camp and Lieutenant-Colonel Victor Micallef was appointed Commandant, with Major Edgar Amato-Gauci as his Second-in-Command and Captain (later Major) Walter Bonello as Adjutant. The number of internees was about ten, two of whom were Maltese, the others being of German and Austrian nationality. In view of this small number of internees, the two first-named officers returned to their former posts, while Captain Bonello assumed command of the camp. The guards were originally members of the Royal Navy and Royal Marines but were later replaced by Maltese personnel.

About fifteen to twenty female artistes, mostly Austrians, employed at the 'Rexford' Cabaret in Strait Street and other night clubs, were also interned at Villa Portelli in Sliema under the charge of Lady Vera Bernard.

In May 1940, the number of internees at Fort Salvatore rose to about a hundred as several Maltese, known or alleged pro-Italian sympathisers, most of them supporters or members of the Nationalist Party, were rounded up. These included Dr Enrico Mizzi, Leader of the Party and Editor of *Malta*; Dr Herbert Ganado, Editor of *Lehen is-Sewwa*, several professionals, businessmen and dockyard workers.

Amadeo D'Agostino, an engine fitter at HM Dockyard, recalls his experience: "... On 31st May, 1940, while at work, several of us were suddenly ordered to board an open bus. Instead of leaving by the nearest gate, we were paraded around the dockyard, probably as a warning to others, before being taken to Fort Salvatore. ..."[68] D'Agostino was released after a six-month detention; he lost his job at the dockyard.

The internees were not served with a formal charge, much less did they undergo a trial. A number of them had been rounded up on mere suspicions. Indeed, besides D'Agostino several others were released when it was realised that they were harmless or had, in fact, been innocent victims of malicious accusations.

On 10th June, 1940, Sir Arturo Mercieca, the Chief Justice and President of the Court of Appeal, was summoned before General Dobbie who informed him that he had received instructions from the Secretary of State to ask him to tender his resignation or he would have been removed from Office. After protesting about this unprecedented step, Sir Arturo chose the former course. Three days later, Sir Arturo and Lady Mercieca, as well as two of

(The Times)
The Internment Camp at Fort Salvatore.

(W. Bonello)
The Commandant and Staff of the Internment Camp. Standing, from left: Mr Robert Magri, Mr Gerald Randon and Mr Vincent Tanti. Seated: Rev Can Joseph Agius-Mizzi, Capt Harry Briffa, Major Walter Bonello (Commandant), Lt Robert Nunns and Mr Tabone.

their children, were issued with a warrant decreeing their internment at their residence at San Pawl tat-Targa, near Naxxar. A small number of clergymen were likewise confined to their place of residence.

As soon as Italy entered the war, the Italian community in Malta, numbering between 700 and 800, had to be taken into custody. As there was no room at Fort Salvatore for this additional influx, the Authorities decided to repatriate them on a captured Italian ship. Another ninety-nine foreign internees are reported to have been deported to Palestine on 9th July, 1940.

On 7th July, 1940, a stick of bombs hit the camp, claiming no casualties but causing such extensive damage that it had to be evacuated. After being given some brandy to recover from shock, the internees were assembled in the yard where the Commandant ordered them to pack their belongings after which they were transferred to the Juvenile Section of the Civil Prison at Kordin. This move led to protests and, at Dr Ganado's request, Archbishop Dom Maurus Caruana offered to place St Agatha's Convent at Rabat at the disposal of the Authorities. The new camp offered better accommodation and security from air attack. The internees, now numbering fifty-seven, were generally well-treated during their confinement.

Early in 1942, the threat of an invasion made the Authorities take the drastic measure of ordering the deportation of forty-seven internees. The duty of conveying the decision fell on Major Bonello, who recalls: "I went to their dormitory and, after ordering a roll-call, I addressed them in English as there were two Englishmen: 'Gentlemen, some of you will have to be deported.' I then pinned the list on the notice-board."[69] This took place on 31st January, 1942.

On 3rd February, thirty-eight of the internees who were to be deported filed a law suit against Major Bonello, Camp Commandant, and Sir Edward St John Jackson, Lieutenant-Governor, praying the Civil Court to declare that Government could not order their deportation. They also asked that the case be heard with urgency.

On Saturday 7th February, His Honour Mr Justice Anthony Montanaro Gauci found for plaintiffs, as the Court held that the Malta Defence Regulations did not give the Governor the right to deport British Subjects from Malta.

The Council of Government debated a new Bill on Monday, 9th February, empowering the Governor to deport British Subjects from Malta and have them interned in another colony of the British Empire. The Bill was passed through all stages and became law that same day. During the debate, Sir Ugo Mifsud, one of the two Nationalist Party members, criticised the proposed law so strongly that he suffered a heart attack and died two days later.

The internees filed a fresh law suit on the morrow, requesting the Civil Court to declare the new Ordinance invalid. The Court, presided once more by His Honour Mr Justice Montanaro Gauci, passed judgement on 12th February, this time finding against plaintiffs. Although the internees filed an appeal on the same day, forty-two of them were deported the following day.

The Deportation Order (See Appendix I), dated 12th February, 1942, did not include the names of Salvatore Bartolo, William Borg, Albert Laferla and Albert Stilon, who were exempted on medical grounds. Another internee, who was listed among the deportees, remained in Malta as he was an inmate at the Hospital for Mental Diseases. Lady Mercieca and Miss Lilian Mercieca, the wife and daughter of the Chief Justice, chose to accompany Sir Arturo into exile.

The deportees were taken to Parlatorio Wharf and were ordered into the holds of *Breconshire*. Before the ship set sail, the Number One went down the holds and arrogantly addressed the deportees: "We have no sympathy for you, I am sure you realise that; but you can be sure that the Navy will see you through. There are no boats for you and if anything happens and you take to the boats, you will be shot." A sailor, armed with a rifle with fixed bayonet, stood guard by the hatchway. Dr Ganado recalls that when he mentioned this episode to a British Naval Commander-in-Chief, whom he was hosting after the war, the Admiral remarked: "I apologise in the name of the Royal Navy."[70]

The ship left harbour at dusk on Friday, 13th February, 1942. After the first night at sea, the deportees were provided with a good breakfast by the Maltese messmen. That day, *Breconshire* was attacked and the deportees had a terrifying time down the dark holds. After three days the ship reached Alexandria and the deportees, although praised by the Captain on their behaviour, were jeered at by some sailors as they disembarked. Following a brief stay at Alexandria, they were driven to Cairo and on 10th March, 1942, started the long train and sea journey to Uganda, their final destination.[71]

Dr Ganado recounts another episode bringing out a positive human element in unusual circumstances. Lieutenant Duce, one of the British officers forming the escort party, treated the Maltese extremely well. During the journey, however, he did not permit the group to listen to the wireless; the Maltese reacted in

(A. Gauci)
Sir Arturo Mercieca (standing) with his wife, daughter and other Maltese deportees outside his bungalow at Bombo.

(H. Ganado)
A team of Maltese deportees, wearing the Maltese Cross, prior to a football match at Bombo. Back row, from left: Giovanni Casabene, Carmelo Lateo, Carmelo Chetcuti, Orazio Laudi, Edgar Soler, Dott Enrico Mizzi, Albert Bajona, Dott Scata (Italian medical officer), Carmelo Farrugia, Emanuel Cossai and Henry Gatt. Front row, from left: Ladislau Klein, Umberto Pirrone, Antonio Farrugia and Joseph Scicluna.

the only way they could, ostracizing him. On arrival at their destination, he told them they could use the radio and added: "I did not allow you to listen to the radio for your own good because there have been some fierce air attacks over Malta and the Italian news bulletins were stating that Malta was in flames; that would have driven you mad." Dr Ganado describes Lieutenant Duce's action as 'heroic'.[72]

Meanwhile, on 4th May, 1942, the Court of Appeal, composed of His Honour Chief Justice George Borg and Judges Luigi Camilleri and William Harding, reversed the judgement of the First Hall of the Civil Court and declared the deportation of the internees illegal. The news reached the internees in Bombo, Uganda, in mid-May. They hoped that they would soon be repatriated, but another two years, and for some of them three years, had to elapse before they were able to see their homeland again.

After a comfortable spell at Bombo, the group was sent to Soroti, even though it was considered unhealthy for Europeans due to rampant malaria. In fact, after a visit by a Red Cross delegation, the camp was closed down and the Maltese were moved to Entebbe. Despite the hazardous journey on *Breconshire* and the unfavourable conditions at Soroti, all the deportees survived; ironically enough, Albert Laferla and Albert Stilon, who had remained in Malta for health reasons, were killed on 21st March, 1942, when a bomb hit St Agatha Camp.

At the time of Italy's surrender in September 1943, the Maltese deportees were still in exile. Following a motion tabled in the Council of Government by Dr George Borg Olivier of the Nationalist Party on 4th March, 1944, the Lieutenant-Governor announced that the repatriation of a number of deportees had been approved; in fact, eighteen of them returned to Malta in April 1944. The other group, including Sir Arturo and Lady Mercieca, Miss Lilian Mercieca, Dr Herbert Ganado and Monsignor Albert Pantalleresco, returned to Malta *via* Italy on 8th May, 1945.

While the deportees were still *en route* to Malta, the Security Officer, Major Paradise, handed each one of them the warrant decreeing their release, which had been signed in advance by the Governor, General Schreiber, but purposely left undated. The British officer was not a little worried when the Maltese told him that the warrant, like their deportation, was null. The date on the official warrants of release had just been inserted by Major Paradise and could not, therefore, have been signed by the Governor at the Palace in Valletta on that day as stated in the warrants.[73]

Chapter Ten

Digging of more shelters — Tragedies in shelters — Massive attacks on Ta' Qali

Nature's greatest gift to Malta, its rocky structure, was never put to better use than during the war years. Were it not for the strength of the Malta stone that minimised the effect of bombing and blast, besides rendering ineffective the use of incendiaries, the alarming tonnage of bombs dropped would have wiped out the Island. The abundance of rock also provided improvised housing accommodation to the inhabitants, who in their underground shelters found refuge from death. Yet, the number of such shelters was inadequate and the Maltese Representatives in the Council of Government kept stressing the importance of such places of refuge. Eventually the number of employees from the Public Works Department, already engaged on such work in the target areas, was augmented by more workers, under Mr Charles Cyril Mavity, to construct shelters in the refugee-receiving areas. Mr Mavity, seconded from the Civil Engineer's Department at HM Dockyard, was appointed Supervisor Shelter Construction on 21st September, 1941. Shelters constructed by the Authorities and private persons amounted to about 2,000; these provided no more than two square feet of space for each person. As war dragged on, families dug private cubicles to enjoy some degree of comfort and privacy; one can still come across the entrances to some of these private shelters in various parts of the Island, including the rock-face beneath the bastions near *Porte-des-Bombes* outside Floriana. Tunnelling Companies from the Royal Engineers assisted by local labour, excavated tunnels at the dockyard and other Service Establishments housing workshops thus ensuring that essential work could proceed even during air raids. An auxiliary power station was installed underground at the Barracca Ditch.

The rocky nature of the Island, which had

(The Times)

Private shelters hewn beneath the bastions.

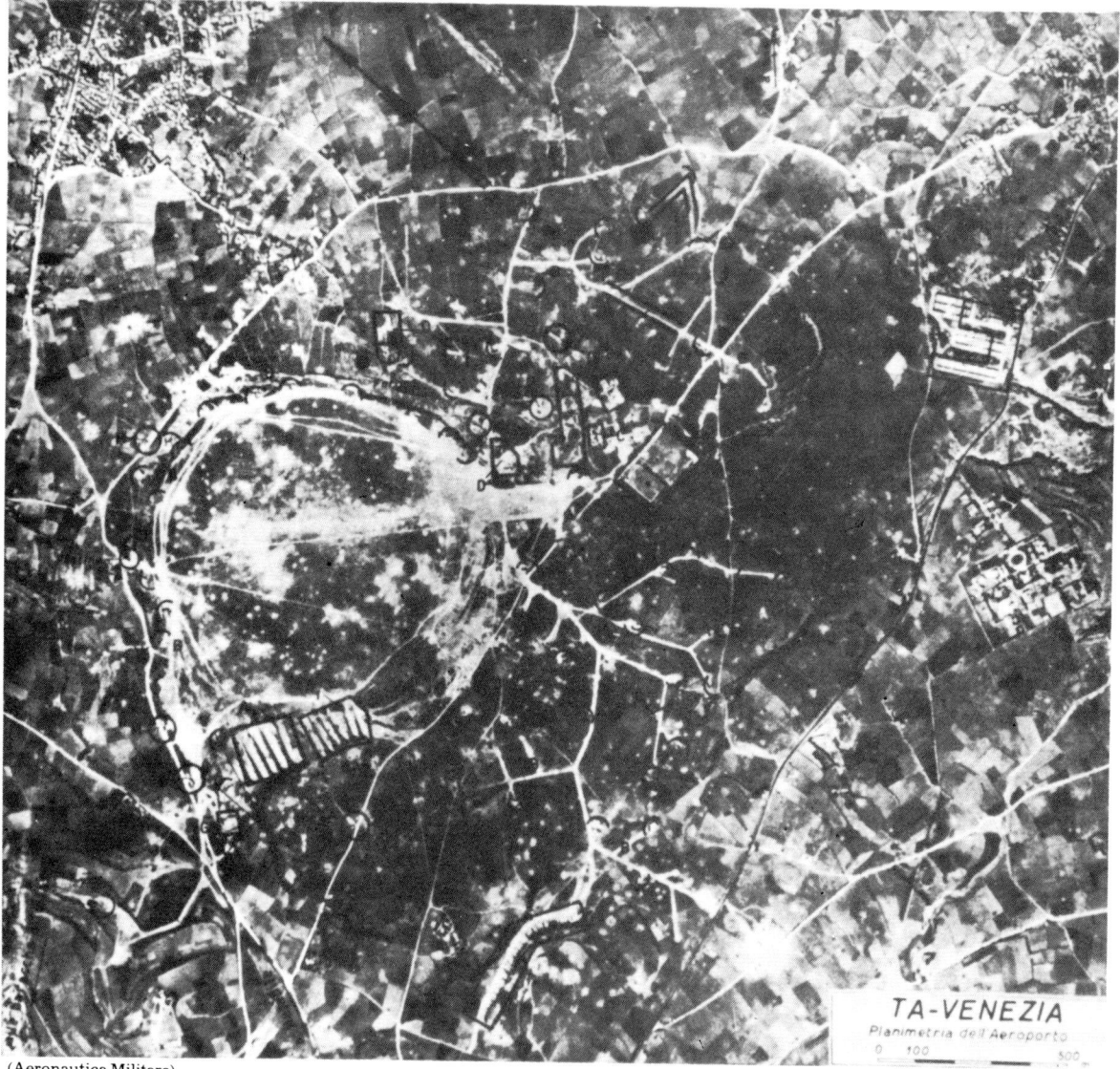

(Aeronautica Militare)

Ta' Qali airfield.

often elicited uncomplimentary remarks from some pre-war visitors, turned out to be one of Malta's main assets. *Feldmarschall* Kesselring recorded: "Several factors made the battle against the Island Fortress difficult. There were natural shelters hewn out of the rock on the perimeter of the airfields and around the harbour where aircraft and stores could be safe-guarded, and against which even the heaviest delayed-action bombs could not have a really devastating effect. Even an attempt to blow up the entrance with *Jabo* bombs was unsuccessful. Only searching and sweeping attacks with small calibre bombs (contact-fuses) offered reasonable prospects of success."[74]

These newly-hewn shelters, old caverns, cisterns, tunnels and catacombs were, in the main, impregnable; yet some of them turned out to be death-traps. This was due either to faults in the rock formation or to sheer misfortune. It is appropriate to record a few of these incidents:

21st March, 1942: At about 2.45 pm two bombs hit the entrance and the emergency exit of a shelter in Gafà Street, Mosta, which besides the normal twenty families using it, was crowded with a number of workmen who had taken shelter therein on their way back home from Mellieha. Mrs Giovanna Vella, who used the shelter regularly together with her husband and six children, recalls: "At the simultaneous explosion of the bombs, I heard a sound resembling the dragging of big chains down the shelter steps, besides other terrifying noises. I also saw a streak of fire flashing across the

(Aeronautica Militare)

Hal Far airfield.

(Bundesarchiv)
"Malta, Malta, you vanished and took with you my happiness". In this quotation from Act III from the opera 'Martha', the name 'Martha' is substituted by 'Malta'.

Luqa airfield.

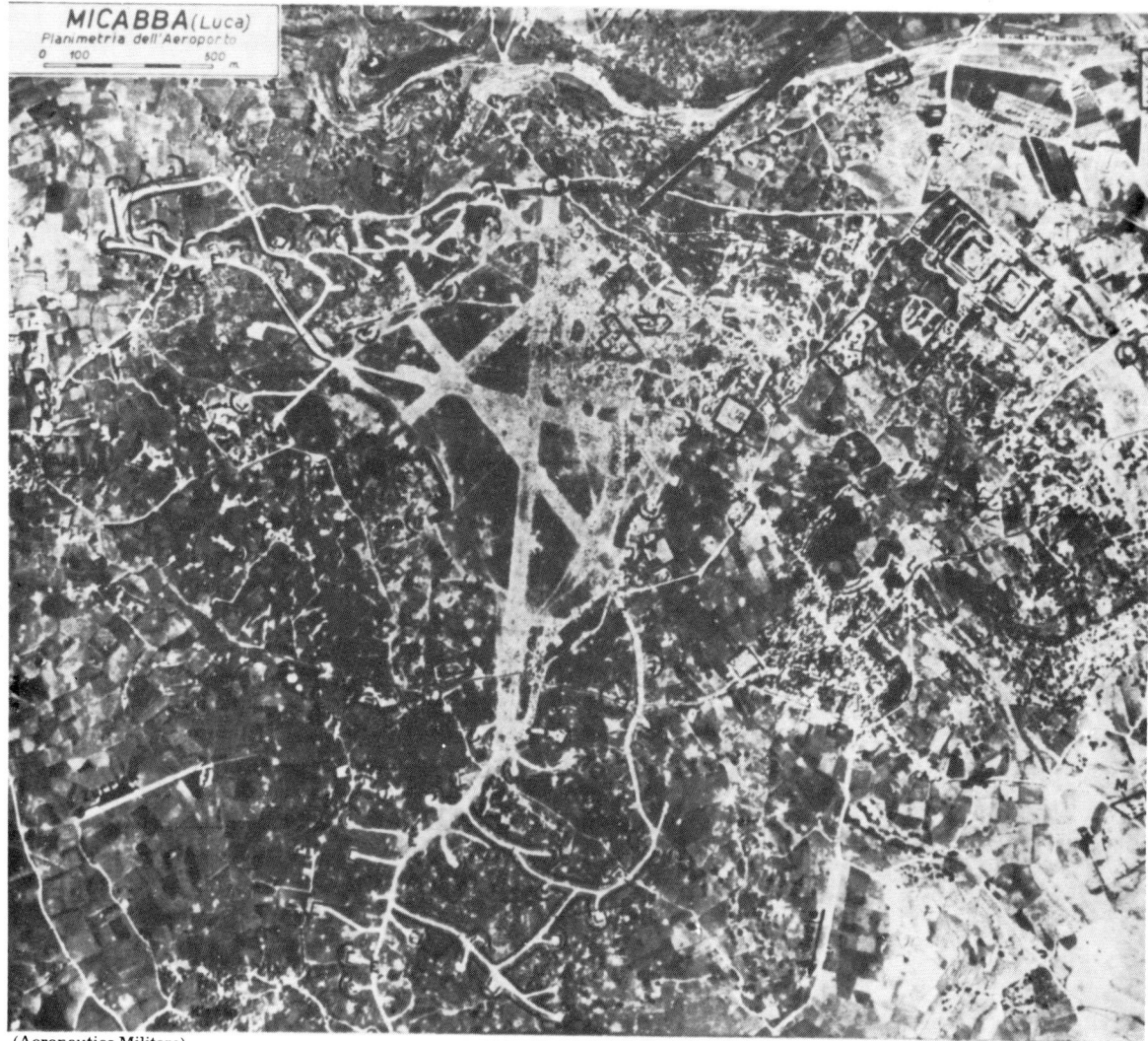

whole length of the shelter, killing or injuring those in its wake. Grown-ups and children yelled and moaned; suddenly complete silence and darkness overtook us. I was surrounded by corpses, including that of my son Joe; his body seemed to have shrunk by the blast. My husband, Bartholomew, and another son, Charles, were killed at the entrance. After about an hour, RAF and ARP personnel and other volunteers forced an opening, taking out the survivors and victims."[75]

A former Observer in the *Luftwaffe*, who held the rank of *Oberfeldwebel* (Flight Sergeant), while visiting the National War Museum related how on 21st March, 1942, he flew with a number of Ju 88s belonging to *Geschwader* 1 which took off from Catania at 1434 hours with specific orders to bomb Mosta, as it was presumed that flying personnel and dock workers were billetted there. He contended that, on approaching Mosta, the crew noticed that most of the bombs dropped by the preceding formation had fallen outside the village. He claimed that they likewise released their bombs on the periphery to avoid killing defenceless civilians.[76] However, some bombs did find their target; it is recorded that of the forty-eight civilians killed through bombing on that day, thirty-one resided at Mosta.

24th March, 1942: Kalkara was subjected to heavy bombing; about fifteen people sought refuge in a store, reinforced by a concrete roof, used as a shelter for the residents of Rinella Street. At 4.25 pm the store received a direct hit. ARP workers, Maltese soldiers and others from the Cheshire Regiment searched amidst the rubble but found no survivors. When they had almost given up hope of finding anyone alive, one of them noticed a leg protruding out of the rubble; it was seven-year-old Victor Hili, who (via N. Malizia) *The message on the bomb in the foreground reads: 'Iron greetings for Malta'.*

(NWMA) *Ta' Qali under attack, viewed from Mdina.*

recalls: "When the building collapsed, I was wedged between two stones and, luckily, a mattress landed on my chest, breaking the impact of more falling debris. I regained consciousness after about one or two hours but I felt as if I had been caught in a vice; I was losing breath and getting weaker as time passed, but I did not give up hope. After what seemed an eternity, on hearing some voices, I started yelling my name. Suddenly there was digging around me and, in fact, I was hit on the head with a pickaxe. I was taken out and conveyed to hospital. My mother, two sisters and my younger brother were not so lucky."[77]

Tragedy struck again in the same street during the same attack. Four members of the Coster family went down to their private shelter when the raiders were overhead; there was a loud explosion and the house crumbled on top of them. Thomas Coster takes up the story: "My brother, watching the bombing from a distance, rushed home and entered the shelter to see what had happened to our mother, my other brother, grandmother and an aunt. When my brother failed to come out, a cousin of ours went in and he too did not emerge; the same thing happened to a neighbour and the fourth man fainted at the entrance. It was then realised that a gas pipe had burst and the fumes added to the tragedy; it is likely that those inside had been overcome by these fumes, as the emergency exit was not blocked."[78]

24th March, 1942: Hal Far was subjected to a heavy attack. A deluge of bombs fell all over the airfield; two shelter chambers opposite the NAAFI Canteen and the Pilots' Shed, where about 28 servicemen and civilians were seeking refuge, were hit. The thick concrete roof-slabs collapsed on top of the chambers, trapping all inside. Moans and groans could be heard. Not even with the use of a Bren gun carrier could the rescue party dislodge the massive blocks of concrete; the shelter became their grave. The corpses were recovered some months later by soldiers from the King's Own Malta Regiment.

9th April, 1942: At about noon, Luqa village received another hammering but this time the damage and loss of life staggered even the hardened villagers. Stukas dropped several bombs, destroying many houses and severely damaging the Parish Church. The focal point in the village, however, was the shelter in Pope Innocent Street which was hit and 23 of the 32 people inside lost their life. The villagers were reluctant to use this shelter, a small one designed to house about 30 people, as they considered it unsafe because water from nearby cisterns seeped in. Still, most of the people in the vicinity used it when raids were frequent as it was impracticable for them to seek shelter elsewhere. A bomb fell on a nearby house and exploded in its empty well. Barely a foot of rock separated the well from the shelter, which caved in. Huge boulders were thrown into the refuge while water from an adjacent well seeped through the cracks. Two men clambered up the emergency exit to seek help

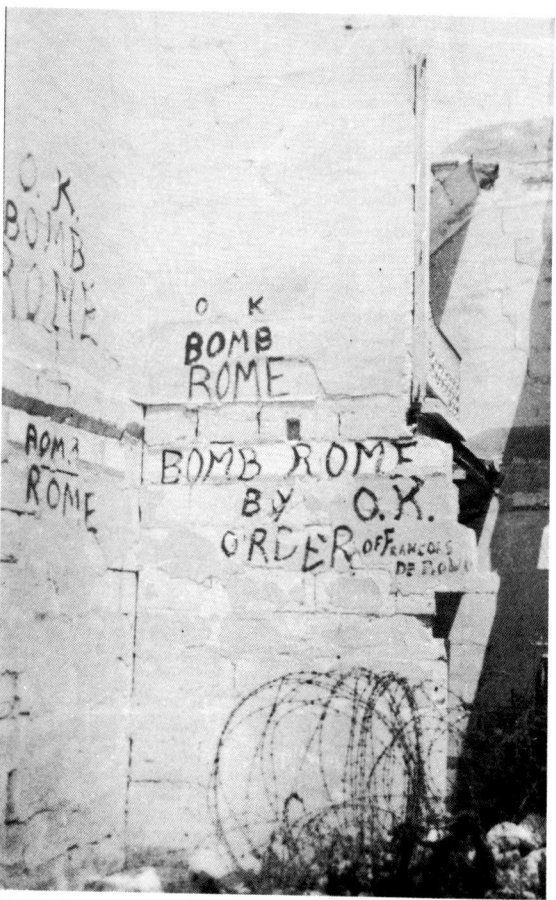

(NWMA)
Luqa. What again?

(S. Ward)
Graffiti, demanding retribution, appeared throughout the Island as the scale of bombing increased.

96

(NWMA)
On 21st March, 1942, five pilots and another officer were killed at the Point de Vue Hotel, at Rabat, requisitioned to billet RAF officers stationed at nearby Ta' Qali airfield.

(N.E. Sciberras)
A Hurricane ablaze at Ta' Qali. In the background is the Military Hospital at Mtarfa.

(NWMA)
Chateau Bertrand at Ta' Qali, known as the Mad House due to its unorthodox design, housed RAF Other Ranks. Extensively damaged by bombing, it was subsequently demolished as it was a hazard to flying.

as, besides a number of dead, the injured were in danger of drowning in the rising water. Having rescued two children, two villagers were joined by an Englishman, who by using a rope, lowered himself into the shelter and brought five injured persons to the gaping hole, through which they were hauled to safety. On being told of the tragedy, General Dobbie rushed to the scene and ordered that two servicemen be sent down at a time to make a thorough search; the third pair of rescuers brought up a soldier's shirt and a dismembered body. One of the soldiers, on coming out of the shelter, told an onlooker: "They are all torn to pieces."[79]

The mounting casualties and damage to inhabited areas told on the population. Voices were raised that the Royal Air Force should retaliate by bombing Italian cities, including Rome; slogans to this affect were painted over walls throughout the Island. These sentiments may have prompted Dr Henry Sacco MD (Constitutional Party) to table a Question in the Council of Government during the Sitting of 10th March, 1942: "Whether the attention of the Imperial Government is regularly drawn to the indiscriminate bombing of civilians by the enemy, and whether stress is made on the insistent demands of the suffering public to bomb Italian cities in retaliation." Sir Edward St John Jackson, the Lieutenant-Governor, replied on behalf of Government: "The Secretary of State for the Colonies and, through him, His Majesty's Government, are regularly informed of the effects on civilian personnel and property of bombing attacks on Malta. Targets for bombing attacks from Malta must be determined by the military needs of the Middle East campaign in which Malta has an honourable part."

The blitz went on and for some time the Germans' wrath was focused on Ta' Qali. At sunset on 20th March, 1942, about sixty Ju 88s escorted by Me 110s and other night-fighters approached the airfield and wave after wave dropped their bombs on the same target. Cajus Bekker, a German historian, states that stereo photographs had shown a ramp on the airfield's boundary, besides which there was a huge heap of earth and rock, leading the Germans to believe in the existence of an underground hangar. To cope with such a target, a number of Ju 88s dropped 2,000-lb armour-piercing rocket bombs which could penetrate the rock up to forty-five feet. Incendiary bombs were also dropped on the ramp itself in the hope that the burning oil would set on fire the fighters supposedly parked inside. When the attack on Ta' Qali was repeated the next morning, the Germans claimed they encountered no fighter opposition. Over two hundred German aircraft covered the sky above Ta' Qali; the bombers came from *Kampfgruppen* 606 and 806 from

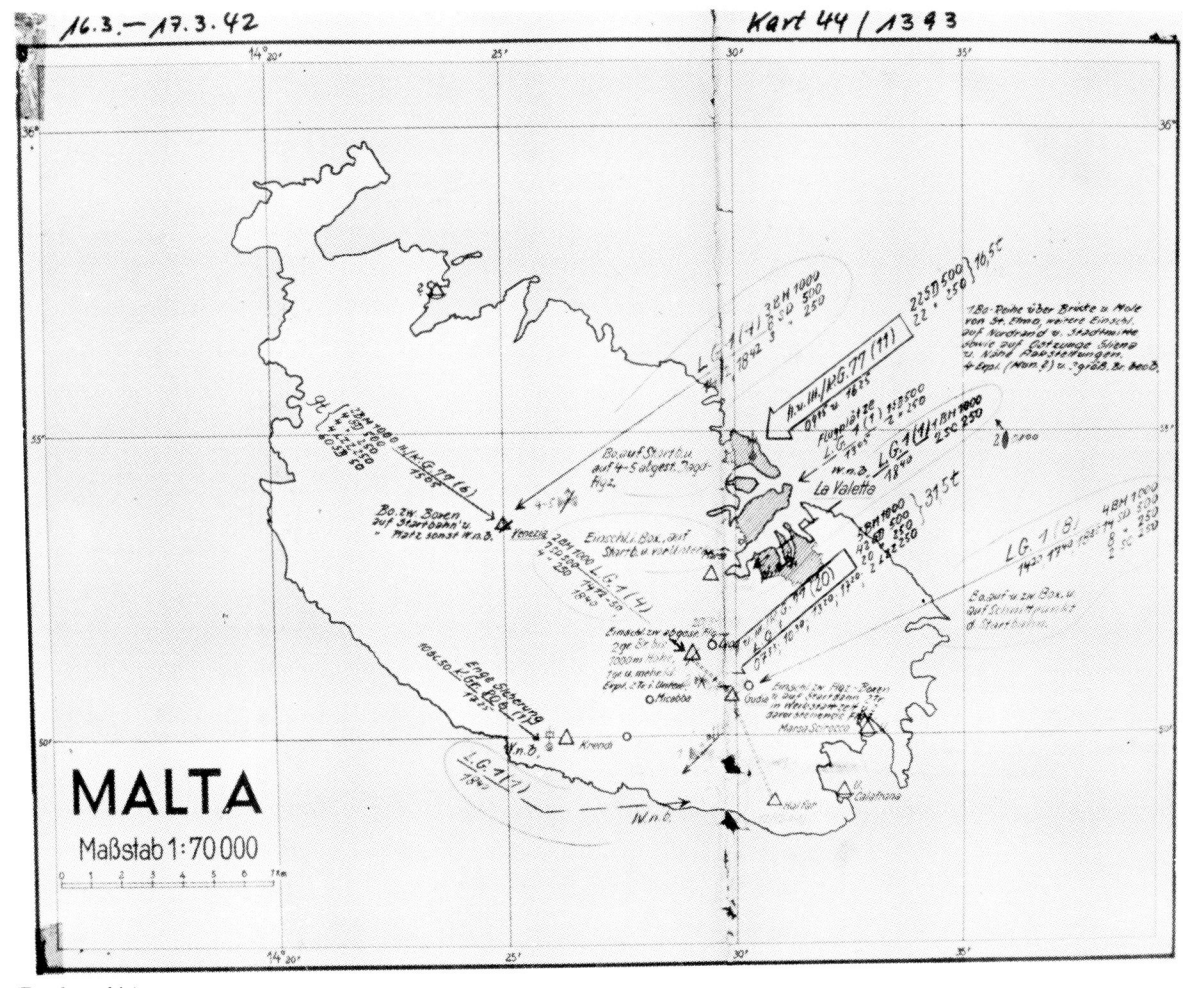

(Bundesarchiv)
Map showing enemy activity and claims over Malta on 16th March, 1942; all sorties being flown before midnight.

(a) Venezia (Ta' Qali) attacked by 6 aircraft of II Gruppe/KG 77 at 1505 hours.

Bombs dropped:	2	BM	1,000
	4	SD	500
	4	SD	250
	4	LZZ	250
	60	SD	50

Result: Bombs between pens, on runway and other airfield installations.

(b) Ta' Qali attacked by 4 aircraft of LG 1 at 1402 and 1842 hours.

Bombs dropped:	3	BM	1,000
	8	SD	500
	3	SD	250

Result: Bombs on runway and 4 to 5 parked fighter aircraft.

(c) Sliema attacked by 11 aircraft of II and III Gruppe/KG 77 at 0915 and 1625 hours.

Bombs dropped:	22	SD	500
	22	SD	250

(d) Valletta attacked by 1 aircraft of LG 1 at 1305 hours

Bombs dropped:	1	SD	500
	2	SD	250

(e) Pawla-Vittoriosa area attacked by 1 aircraft of LG 1 at 1840 hours.

Bombs dropped:	1	BM	1,000
	2	SC	250

Result of attacks (c), (d) and (e): One bomb hit bridge and mole near St Elmo, other hits in northern edge and centre of town; others on east-cape of Sliema and near anti-aircraft battery. Four heavy explosions and three fires registered.

(f) *Luqa airfield attacked by 20 aircraft of I and III Gruppe/KG 77 at 0733, 1030, 1320 and 1720 hours.*

Bombs dropped:	5	BM	1,000
	42	SD	500
	20	SD	250
	2	LZZ	250

(g) *Luqa airfield attacked by 4 aircraft of LG 1 from 1412 to 1450 hours and at 1840 hours.*

Bombs dropped:	2	BM	1,000
	7	SD	500
	4	SD	250

Result of attacks (f) and (g): Hits between parked aircraft, two big fires with smoke up to 1,000 metres, one big and a row of smaller explosions. Two hits on quarters. Other hits on runway.

(h) *Gudja airfield (Safi airstrip) attacked by 8 aircraft of LG 1 at 1420, 1740 and 1835 hours.*

Bombs dropped:	4	BM	1,000
	14	SD	500
	8	SD	250
	2	SC	250

Result: Hits between pens and on runway. Two hits on workshop and on 2 aircraft parked in front of it.

(i) *Heavy anti-aircraft battery at Hagar Qim attacked by 1 aircraft of K.Gr.806 at 1725 hours.*

Bombs dropped:	10	SC	50

Description of bombs:

BM 1,000 = aerial mine of 1,000 kg
SD 500 = thick-walled fragmentation bomb of 500 kg
SD 250 = thick-walled fragmentation bomb of 250 kg
LZZ 250 = thick-walled fragmentation bomb of 250 kg with delayed-action fuse
SD 50 = thick-walled fragmentation bomb of 50 kg
SC 250 = thin-walled mine bomb of 250 kg
SC 50 = thin-walled mine bomb of 50 kg

Catania, I/KG 54 from Gerbini and two *Gruppen* of KG 77 from Còmiso. These were escorted by fighters of JG 53 and 11/JG3 (*Udet*) and the Me 110s of 111/ZG 26. Bekker claims that this was the first time in the war that the Germans resorted to 'carpet bombing' — a principle propounded in the inter-war years by the Italian General Giulio Douhet — and by sunset Ta' Qali looked like an erupting volcano.[80]

Wing Commander (later Group Captain) Jack Satchell, the airfield's Station Commander, explains: "We encouraged the Germans into believing in the existence of an underground hangar. What happened was that we tried to cleave the rock, which caved in. On realizing the impracticability of the project, we painted half-open hangar doors and put in the openings all our broken down Hurricanes and Spitfires, mocked up with pieces of wood and sacking. The Huns plastered hell out of them; we did not mind!"[81]

The blasting of Ta' Qali reached unprecedented proportions; hundreds of armour-piercing, incendiary and high explosive bombs were dropped. The airfield and adjacent dispersal areas, littered with bomb craters, were ablaze with burning fighters, stores and equipment. In spite of this devastation, Ta' Qali was again operational within a few hours; servicemen and civilians filled in the craters and removed the wreckage.

Chapter Eleven

Start of Spring Blitz — Anti-Aircraft defence — King George VI assumes Colonelcy-in-Chief of Royal Malta Artillery

The blitz resumed in March 1942. Hordes of German aircraft seemed intent on wiping Malta off the map. These attacked the dockyard, the harbour installations, the airfields, the seaplane base, anti-aircraft batteries, barracks, stores, towns, villages, ferry and fishing-boats. This battering went on day after day, week after week; a prelude to an intended finale. The fighter defence was decimated; the task of intercepting the swarms of aircraft, flying at will and at all levels, fell on a few remaining Hurricanes and Spitfires.

In answer to the 200-240 daily Axis sorties, Malta could seldom muster more than six fighters at one time. Whilst these engaged the enemy, their bases at Ta' Qali, Hal Far and Luqa were systematically plastered with bombs and cannon fire. Dense columns of smoke shrouded the airfields.

The gunners likewise faced an awesome task, firing as fast as their guns allowed and as long as ammunition lasted. Some of their guns were silenced by direct hits whilst others, engulfed in dust from near-misses, kept up a steady barrage. They were joined by Maltese and British infantry troops manning Twin Lewis Guns and Bren Guns in sangars surrounding the perimeter of the airfields. Every available gun was used in a desperate effort to repel each attack.

Royal Air Force ground crew, using .303" armour-piercing and incendiary bullets, fired their rifles at low-flying aircraft. Wing Commander Satchell devised his own way of having a go at the Germans: "We were still being machine-gunned on the ground, so I set up a pair of .5" Vickers 'K' guns in a bomb crater. To fire them, I made use of a pair of motorcycle

(G. Coney)

A heavy anti-aircraft gun position at Marsa Racecourse.

(J. Satchell)
Extract from Wing Commander Jack Satchell's log book. The signature confirming the entry belongs to Group Captain A.B. 'Woody' Woodhall, who distinguished himself as Fighter Controller during the Battle of Britain and later at Malta.

handle-bars, complete with twist clips, which gave me 'elevation', while the handle-bar provided 'traversy'; the two triggers were fixed to fire the guns. I used this frequently and, on one occasion, Squadron Leader Lord David Douglas-Hamilton (Commanding Officer No 603 City of Edinburgh Squadron) was coming in to land, with flaps and wheels already down, when I spotted a 109 sitting on his tail pumping lead into him. I aimed the gun directly at Lord David's aircraft; the deflection of the speed was just right and I hit the German aircraft which went straight up into the air before plunging down at the far side of the airfield. It was very spectacular indeed. The pilot, who baled out just before the plane crashed, was taken prisoner." [82]

For long periods during April, which registered 282 alerts, the brunt of beating back the savage assault fell squarely on the gunners, almost continuously in action. Such was the intensity of the attacks that in April the heavy and light guns fired 72,053 and 88,176 rounds respectively, resulting in the destruction of 102 enemy aircraft. (See Appendices **J** and **K**). It is worthwhile recalling that in the three months following the Illustrious Blitz in January 1941, the ammunition expenditure was of 21,176 and 18,660 rounds by the heavy and light guns respectively.

It is to the credit of RAOC workshop staff and mobile teams of armament artificers that it was only on very rare occasions that the unserviceability of the anti-aircraft artillery exceeded five per cent. [83]

A detachment of Royal Marines was stationed at HMS *St Angelo*. It was commanded by Captain (later Lieutenant-Colonel) Franklin F. Clark, who describes the evolution and role of this Unit. During the early stages, the Marines manned Lewis gun positions at Fort St Angelo, the Dockyard Power Station and Corradino Heights, besides a 4-inch field gun sited at the Armament Depot to cover the entrance to the Grand Harbour. The Marines' request for heavier guns was met by the Authorities. On 11th November, 1940, they commenced training on a Bofors mounted near the oil fuel tanks at Corradino manned by the Dockyard Defence Battery. The first Bofors was delivered to *St Angelo* on 25th January, 1941; with the assistance of men from 10th LAA Battery RMA, it was dragged up to the Upper Parade Ground level and then to its site on the Fort's Upper Barracca. The second gun arrived on 27th January and was manoeuvred to the same site that very day; both guns became operational within a couple of days. The Royal Marine Light Anti-Aircraft Battery was to a large extent independent; discipline and internal organisation were the responsibility of the Senior Officer Royal Marines. The guns, stores and equipment were successively held on charge from 10th LAA Battery RMA (Major E.R. Amato), 59th LAA Battery RA (Major R.J.W. King) and 30th LAA Dockyard Defence Battery (Major L.G. Bolton MC). The third Bofors, mounted in the Ward Room garden opposite the Customs House, was manned in turns by the RMA, the Buffs and the RA, before being moved out of the Fort.

The two Bofors went into action for the first time on 4th February, 1941; their first success was claimed on the 28th of the month when a mine-laying aircraft was last seen diving towards the sea, a few feet from the breakwater. In the following months, the Marines performed with skill and on 27th March, 1942, were commended by the AOC Malta for their active participation in the defence of the harbour area.

Like all the other gun positions scattered over the Island, the Marines at *St Angelo* got their

Heavy anti-aircraft gun position at St James's Battery, between the villages of Tarxien and Luqa, equipped with Height-and-Range Finder and Predictor. The former instrument supplied information for the Predictor calculations, while the Predictor forecast the likely position of the aircraft.

share of bombs; over sixty fell within the precinct of the Fort. Only two failed to explode.

The last engagement by the Marines was on Sunday, 10th May, 1942, when the *Luftwaffe* received its greatest beating over Malta. For tactical reasons, the LAA positions in the harbour area were then re-sited. The two Bofors manned by the Marines were dismantled on May 18th and moved to either side of the Great Bell on the Fort's Upper Barracca. Five days later the guns were formally handed over to 3 LAA Regiment RMA (Lieutenant-Colonel E.J. Salomone OBE RMA).

Their contribution was given official recognition; Lieutenant-Colonel Clark was awarded the Distinguished Service Cross and Bar, while four Marines received the Distinguished Service Medal and five others were Mentioned in Despatches.[84]

Lieutenant-Colonel Joseph A. Sammut OBE, who, while still a Temporary Major, commanded the 7th Battery 2nd Heavy Anti-Aircraft Regiment Royal Malta Artillery deployed at Tal-Bizbizija, Targa, limits of Mosta, explains the composition and role of the heavy artillery at the time: "By 1942, the heavy anti-aircraft defence had expanded to five regiments: two RMA, the 2nd and 11th; three RA, the 4th, 7th and 10th. These made up the 10th Heavy Anti-Aircraft Brigade, with 112 guns of 3", 3.7" and 4.5" calibre, deployed in 29 troop positions of four guns each, except for two 3" troop positions which had two guns each; a battery consisted of two troop positions.

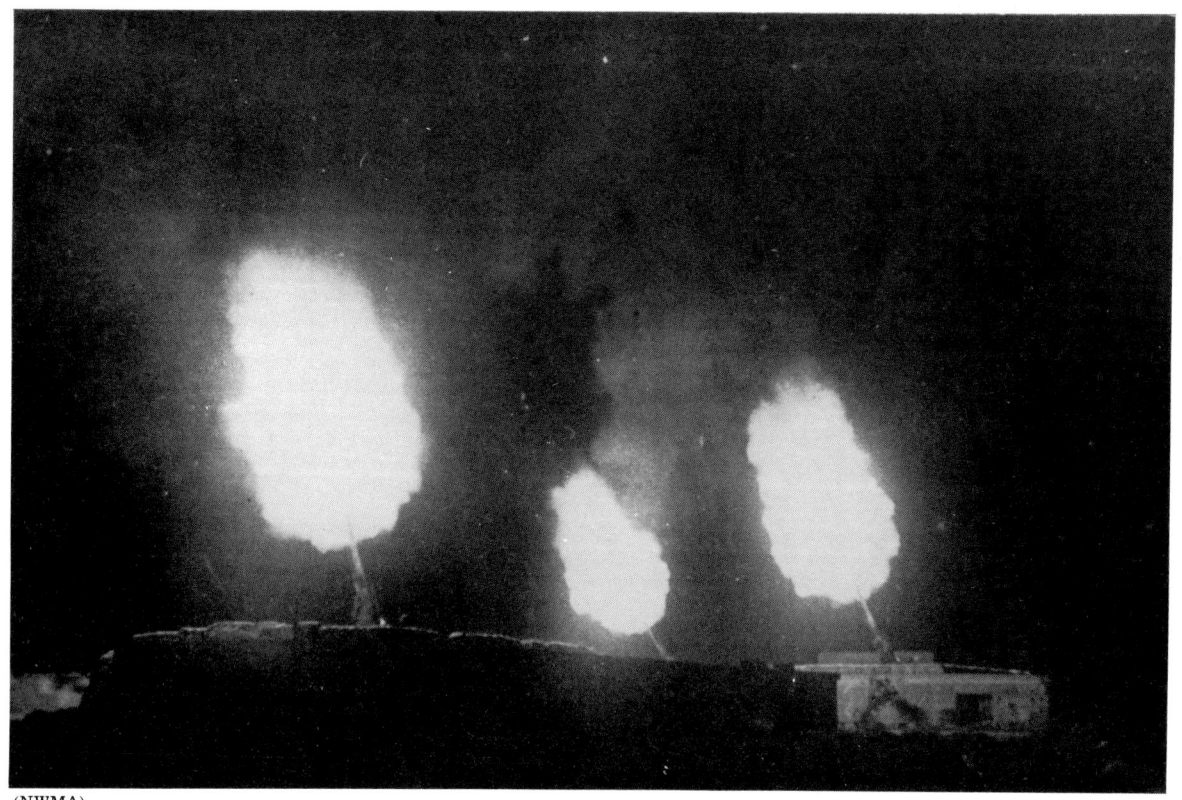

(NWMA)
A heavy anti-aircraft gun position in action. The equal jets of smoke from each gun indicate that they are firing under instrument control.

"The RMA and RA were one and the same team under the Commander Royal Artillery. The defensive plan was the usual anti-aircraft one: engaging the enemy before reaching his line of bomb-release. We endeavoured to hit him, bombs and all, before he could have had the chance of releasing them or, at worse, through harassment, spoil his aim. Broadly speaking we had two methods of action. The first was pure gunnery; the guns, under control of the Island's Early-Warning System and their own radars and Fire Control Instruments, clamped on to their target endeavouring to destroy it. The second was the 'barrage' method used to repel heavy and concerted attacks by low-level Ju 88 bombers and Ju 87 dive-bombers on a vulnerable point. This entailed that all available guns would fire on predetermined lines in order to build up over the vulnerable point a defensive umbrella, actually box-shaped, through which the enemy had inevitably to fly. This method worked with great success during the heavy attacks on HMS *Illustrious* and on ships unloading in the Grand Harbour.

"The co-ordination of both methods, often resorted to, implied that gun positions initially engaged by instrument control and then turned on to 'barrage'; while some gun positions would concentrate on instrument control, others would simultaneously put on to 'barrage'. The tactical situation of the moment determined the course best to be adopted. Co-ordination between Royal Air Force and Anti-Aircraft Artillery was essential and we maintained it to a paramount degree."[85]

The valour in action of Maltese gunners is recorded by Major Gerald Amato-Gauci, Troop Commander 23rd Battery 11th Heavy Anti-Aircraft Regiment Royal Malta Artillery (Territorial), who was stationed at St Peter HAA Position. He recalls: "Our battery, armed with 4.5" guns standing on high ground, was the first to sight and engage the incoming raiders on their sorties over the Grand Harbour and Luqa airfield. The Germans, who had come to expect a hot welcome from us, tried to wipe us out. For a period we were singled out for two attacks, one at dawn under a blinding sun and another at dusk. We were also attacked on full moon nights when they could see us whilst we could not; it was a frightening experience but we always stood up to them and managed to beat them back...

"In the spring of 1942, the ammunition stock was so low that we were ordered to fire only two

(J. Sammut)
The Commander Royal Artillery with Royal Malta Artillery Commanding Officers and Royal Artillery Senior Officers at Tignè Officers Mess in 1944. Seated, left to right: Major 'Jock' Campbell RA, Lt Col Edgar J. Salomone OBE RMA, Colonel Arthur J. Dunkerley CBE RMA, Brigadier Samuel Clarke CBE (CRA Malta), Lt Col Joseph T. Terreni OBE RMA, Lt Col Henry A. Ferro RMA and Major Denis Bromilow RA. Standing, left to right: Major Leslie T. Cocks MC RA, Lt Col Harold R. Micallef MBE RMA, Major Frederick Peck MBE DCM RA, Lt Col Godfrey L. Rampling OBE RA, Lt Col Joseph A. Sammut OBE RMA and Lt Col George Bell RA.

(RMA Collection)
1st Coast Regiment, Royal Malta Artillery, June 1943. Commanding Officer, Lt Col Arthur J. Dunkerley OBE RMA.

(RMA Collection)
2nd HAA Regiment, Royal Malta Artillery, December 1944. Commanding Officer, Lt Col Joseph A. Sammut OBE RMA.

(G. Saliba)
3rd Light Anti-Aircraft Regiment, Royal Malta Artillery, 1941-45. Commanding Officer, Lt Col Edgar J. Salomone OBE RMA.

(RMA Collection)
8th Searchlight Battery, Royal Malta Artillery, October 1943. Commanding Officer, Major Harold R. Micallef MBE RMA.

(T. Mullins)
222nd Battery 68th HAA Regiment Royal Artillery at Tignè Barracks, 1944. At centre, Lt Col George Bell.

of our four guns; in May, the position deteriorated to such an extent that we were restricted to six rounds per gun a day ... During one of the attacks, a house near the battery used as a magazine was hit and caught fire. Sergeant Joseph Camilleri, one of our best Number Ones, entering the room through a hole in the wall, tried to put out the blaze with a piece of sacking and started throwing the shells out of the window. He was soon joined by others, while a group of men smothered the shells in soil and sand bags; in this way, we averted a major explosion and saved the badly-needed shells ...

"On 27th April, 1942, seven Ju 87s dive-bombed the battery, totally destroying No 3 Gun which, luckily, was unmanned due to the shortage of ammunition. During another attack by five Stukas on 9th May, a stick of bombs fell on the battery; one, exploding in front of No 4 Gun, killed four men and wounded five others... From our vantage point, we could claim a captivating view which made us witness some terrifying explosions over Valletta and the Three Cities; many of these were caused by mines which threw into the sky an awesome cloud of white dust ... The long alerts, sometimes almost round-the-clock, were aimed at lowering our morale and tiring us out; although getting tired, all the men stuck to their guns.

"Our men, all conscripts, became so efficient that the Territorials of the 11th Regiment were

(G. Amato-Gauci)
Captain Gerald Amato-Gauci MC RMA (T) standing near the 4.5-in anti-aircraft gun hit on 27th April, 1942, when five Stukas attacked St Peter's HAA Position. Four Maltese gunners were killed and another five wounded.

(J. France)
The 4.5-in HAA gun at Spinola Battery hit by bombs on 25th April, 1942. Twelve British gunners and Signalman Richard Mifsud of the Royal Corps of Signals lost their life.

(G.E. Livock)
An attack on Luqa as seen from Kalafrana. The sky is mottled with flak puffs, while a dense curtain of smoke stretches across the airfield and surrounding areas.

rated as the best in Malta's anti-aircraft defence set-up. We at St Peter's shot down about twenty aircraft with many others trailing smoke only to fall into the sea out of our sight. Our battery lost eight men while about twenty-eight sustained injuries. Sergeant-Major Carmel Caruana was awarded the George Medal; Sergeant Joseph Camilleri the Military Medal and Sergeant S. Azzopardi was 'Mentioned in Despatches'."[86] For his exemplary devotion to duty when injured in action on 11th January, 1942, Major Amato-Gauci, then a 2nd Lieutenant, was awarded the Military Cross on 26th February, 1943.

Besides St Peter's other heavy anti-aircraft batteries at Ta' Giorni, Tal-Qroqq, St Rocco, Salina, Ta' Cejlu, Hompesch, Spinola, Marsa, Marnisi, Ta' Karac, San Leonardo, Manoel Island and elsewhere were often bombed and strafed, resulting in loss of life. What is perhaps not commonly known is the fact that a number of gunners were killed or injured as a result of the premature burst of anti-aircraft shells overhead. In one instance a gun crew at Marsa sustained casualties when a premature burst killed a gunner and injured two others. The remainder of the gun detachment had a miraculous escape when a piece of shell splinter struck a round on the primer and the whole recess of ammunition was blown up.[87]

Light anti-aircraft gun emplacements deployed around the Island, particularly those close to vulnerable points, were likewise subjected to merciless beating; the gunners expected no mercy and they dispensed none.

On 28th June, 1942, a bomb just missed a Bofors manned by 10th Battery 3rd LAA Regiment Royal Malta Artillery on the Kalafrana road. With resolute determination and disregard to safety, Lance Sergeant Fedele Zarb and his men moved the gun to a new position and re-engaged the enemy. Awarded the Military Medal for conspicuous bravery, leadership and skill, Lance Sergeant Zarb was later killed, together with five gunners, when his gun position, guarding Kalafrana seaplane base and Hal Far airfield, received a direct hit on 20th July, 1942.

Fr Harry Born OP, a Maltese army chaplain attached to 2nd Heavy Anti-Aircraft Regiment Royal Malta Artillery, speaks in glowing terms about the gunners. He recalls that one Sunday he was celebrating Mass at Tignè Point Battery when an attack materialised. With his steel helmet on, he continued with the Service while splinters were falling all around. As the guns blazed away he could hear the shrill voice of Bombadier Ellul, a gunner from Birkirkara, exhorting his crew: 'Keep firing lads, God is

(The Times)

Tracers, searchlights, shells and flares light up the sky over Malta.

with us'. On another occasion, Fr Raymond Formosa, of the 3rd Light Anti-Aircraft Regiment, was saying Mass on a gun position during an air raid. Lieutenant-Colonel Edgar J.Salomone, the Commanding Officer, spontaneously covered the Hosts in the paten with his steel helmet.[88]

All the gunners must have appreciated the gesture of King George VI who, on 3rd April, 1942, assumed the Colonelcy-in-Chief of the Regiment. In conferring this signal honour, the King sent the following message to General Dobbie:

"I have been watching with admiration the stout-hearted resistance of all in Malta, Service personnel and civilians alike, to the fierce and constant air attacks of the enemy in recent weeks.

"In the active defence of the Island, the Royal Air Force have been ably supported by the Royal Malta Artillery, and it therefore gives me special pleasure, in recognition of their skill and resolution, to assume the Colonelcy-in-Chief of the Regiment. Please convey my best wishes to all ranks of my new Regiment, and assure them of the added pride with which I shall follow future activities."

Chapter Twelve

Blitz intensified — Royal Opera House destroyed — Mosta Dome bomb episode — Submarines withdraw from Malta — Award of George Cross to Malta

During April 1942, death and destruction gained a new dimension. Stories of tragedies and miraculous escapes overlapped each other and people bore successive calamities with admirable composure. This, however, did not diminish the immensity of the suffering to which the Islanders were subjected. In the words of historian Alan Moorehead: "It was a siege of annihilation. One after another all the other great sieges were eclipsed — England and Odessa, Sebastopol and Tobruk. Malta became the most bombed place on earth." [89]

Two of the Island's architectural gems suffered different fates. In the evening of 7th April, 1942, the Royal Opera House was demolished along with several other buildings in Valletta; two days later, the closest thing to a miracle occurred when, during a heavy raid on Ta' Qali, a stick of bombs fell around Mosta Church. Rev Salvatore Magro, who was inside the church, remembers: "At about 4.40 pm one of the bombs went through the dome, bounced twice off the wall, skidded the whole length of the church and finally came to rest without exploding. At the time there were about 300 people attending a Service and, while the majority sought refuge in the side chapels, some remained kneeling. The dome was damaged but inexplicably no one was injured." [90] The bomb and another two, which failed to explode outside the church, were quickly removed.

(NWM)

The Royal Opera House in ruins.

111

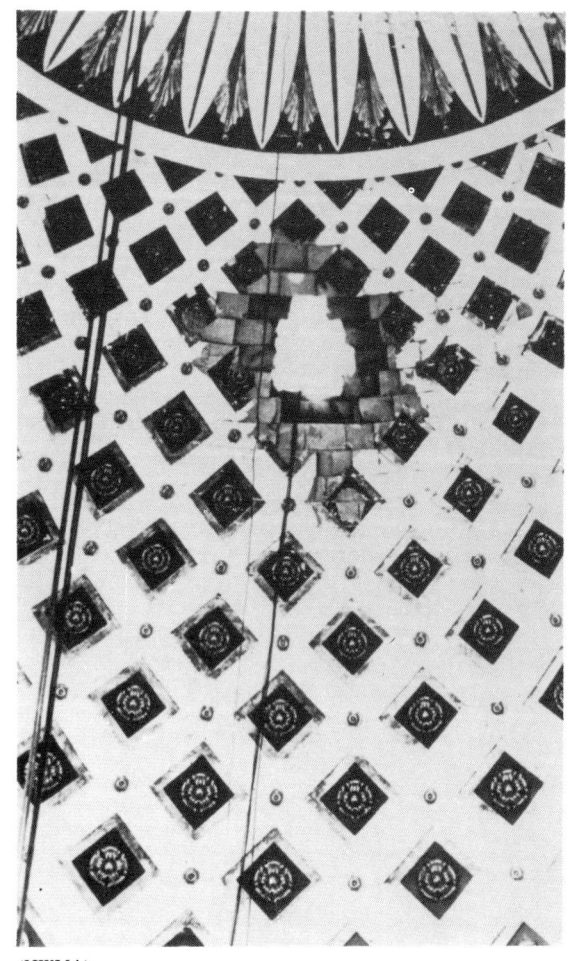

(NWMA)
Mosta Dome pierced by a bomb on 9th April, 1942.

The agony lingered and April proved to be the worst month. The blitz increased in intensity and the population and the garrison suffered more misery. During the month, Malta was under alert for a total of 12 days, 10 hours and 20 minutes. The Germans seemed to have an inexhaustible reserve of aircraft as more machines were utilized day after day. Records show the daily number of bombers, excluding night raiders or escorting fighters, over Malta in the week ending 25th April, 1942[91]:

	Ju 88s	Ju 87s	Total
19th April	120	71	191
20th April	235	62	297
21st April	100	40	140
22nd April	136	43	179
23rd April	106	30	136
24th April	124	33	157
25th April	220	39	259
Grand total			1,359

It is calculated that the tonnage of bombs dropped during the month amounted to 6,727, distributed as follows[92]:

Ta' Qali	841 tons
Hal Far	750 tons
Luqa	804 tons
Kalafrana	196 tons
Dockyard	3,156 tons
Elsewhere	980 tons

This exceeded any monthly tonnage of bombs dropped over the United Kingdom during the height of the Battle of Britain. Another unenviable local record was that of casualties; in April 1942, 339 civilians and 208 servicemen were killed through enemy action.

The Germans felt elated at the sustained tempo of this offensive. In the words of Cajus Bekker: "By the end of the month the Germans hardly knew where to drop their bombs. So far as could be judged from the air, every military target had been either destroyed or badly damaged. In an Order of the Day, II Air Corps summarised its successes: 'During the period March 20th till April 28th, 1942, the naval and air bases of Malta were put completely out of action ... In the course of 5,807 sorties by bombers, 5,667 by fighters and 345 by reconnaissance aircraft, 6,557,231 kilograms of bombs were dropped ...'"[93]

(F. De Domenico)
Sliema: Gaiety Cinema in High Street.

(NWMA)
The Grand Harbour under attack during April 1942, photographed from the cockpit of a Junkers 88.

The destruction wrought by the April Blitz was almost catastrophic. At the dockyard everything above ground was either destroyed or badly damaged; only one of the drydocks remained serviceable. Two destroyers, three submarines, three minesweepers, a Royal Fleet Auxiliary oiler, five tug-boats and the floating crane had been sunk. (See Appendix **L**) What work could be done was carried out in underground workshops. The crater-littered airfields looked like a moonscape; wreckage from aircraft, equipment and workshops added to the grisly scene.

The Germans, however, did not reckon with the stubborn resistance of the defenders and the resolution of the civilian population. Malta was down but not out.

Amidst the shambles at the dockyard lay HMS *Penelope*. Her survival is an eloquent tribute to her crew, under Captain A.D. Nicholl, and to the dockyard shipwrights and artificers. The cruiser, whose crew included eleven Maltese ratings, had docked for the repair of damage sustained on 26th March. She was a major target during the blitz and it was a unique opportunity for the Germans to settle accounts with one of the ships that had been molesting their supply line to North Africa.

They bombed the dock on more than one occasion; on 4th April she was hit and repair

(NWM)

HMS Kingston *hit by bombs in No 4 Dock on 11th April, 1942.*

(IWM)

HMS Maori, *one of several units sunk in the Grand Harbour.*

(NWM)
Floriana: Gunlayer Square corner with St Thomas Street.

(IWM)
Senglea: Victory Street.

(NWM)
Mqabba: Vincenti Tower

(D. Armour)
A bomb lands squarely on one of the granaries at Floriana. St Publius Church, in the background, was extensively damaged on 28th April, 1942.

HMS Lance *sunk at the Dockyard on 9th April, 1942.*

work had to be suspended as water leaked into the dock through the damaged caisson. The dock pump, itself damaged by bombing, was repaired thus enabling the resumption of work. On the following day, the cruiser was attacked again and near-misses littered her deck with boulders. More bombs exploded close by but her luck held out. This was due mostly to the unrelenting efforts and skill of the ship's gunners who distinguished themselves. Together with the gunners in the harbour area, they put up a protective umbrella of steel.

At nightfall on 8th April, the ship stole out of harbour, bearing the scars of battle; her side platings, riddled with bomb splinters, were plugged with wood, earning her the nickname 'Pepperpot'. The battle-weary crew left to the shouts of 'Well done, Penelope' from Maltese dockyard workmen and seamen from other ships, and to a single-word-message from Churchill — 'Bravo'.

Although the Maltese did not lose their nerve as they saw the Island crumbling around them, they condemned the enemy's indiscriminate bombing. Grief was tempered with anger as they witnessed the destruction of the Island's palaces, public buildings and churches. (See Appendices **M** and **N**) At 7.50 am on 28th April, 1942, St Publius Church at Floriana was hit by several bombs which wrecked the dome and portico, besides blasting the entire edifice. The roof of the crypt, used as a public shelter, collapsed under the weight of fallen masonry. Luckily, many of the people sheltering there had already left the crypt to go to work or back to their homes, but those still inside were buried beneath the rubble. ARP workers and other volunteers rushed to the scene and rescued the terrified survivors, many of whom were taken to hospital suffering from wounds of varying degrees. Thirteen corpses were later recovered.

One of the most frightening aspects of bombing was the blast effect produced by heavy-calibre bombs and aerial mines. When HMS *Legion* received a direct hit at the dockyard on 26th March, 1942, the barrel of one of the forward turret guns was dislodged from its mounting and hurled a distance of 760 feet, landing on the roof of a destroyed building in Two Gates Street, corner with St Peter Paul Street, in Senglea. The same effect occurred when a direct hit destroyed the market at

(The Times)
A heavy-calibre bomb fell near the statue of Christ the King, opposite the Phoenicia Hotel at Floriana. The explosion brought down part of the roof of the Railway Tunnel shelter, underneath, injuring several people.

(NWM)
The gun barrel from HMS Legion *resting on a demolished house at Senglea.*

Merchant Street, Valletta; one of the enormous steel girders was hurled over the rooftops, coming to rest near Fort St Elmo. Much smaller but no less dangerous were the numerous 'butterfly' and similar types of anti-personnel bombs in the form of thermos flasks and fountain pens, showered over Malta. Despite repeated warnings, children and even adults were killed or mutilated on handling these lethal objects.

On 7th April, 180,000 cubic feet of town gas were lost by fire during an air raid; this resulted in the supply of the commodity being cut off as from 24th June. Between the 6th and 15th April, all six flour-mills were put out of action by bombing. Repair work on the mills was given priority and those aware of the alarming situation sighed with relief when St Joseph's, Gatt's and Chapelle's mills resumed work on 18th April, whilst Pisani's, St George's and St Publius's did so on the 20th April, 24th April and 1st May respectively. The power station was rendered unserviceable for 72 hours during the last few days in April and, as from 26th May, electricity supply was restricted to essential services.

The thoroughness of the blitz dealt yet another blow to Malta's minimal offensive operations when the 10th Submarine Flotilla

St Anne Street, Floriana.

was withdrawn from Malta. For quite some time, submarines had to lie submerged at their base in Marsamxett harbour during the day as they had been selected as prime targets by German bombers, which could bomb almost at will due to lack of allied fighter availability. Moreover, without fighter cover, the minesweepers could not remove the large number of mines laid by Italian E-boats or dropped by German aircraft in the harbour approaches; these mines constituted an added hazard to submarines. The Commander-in-Chief, the Vice Admiral Malta and the Flotilla's Commanding Officer tried to hold on at Malta as long as possible as withdrawal would have deprived the Allies of any means of intercepting Axis shipping in the Central Mediterranean and along the Italian coast.

Captain Simpson, however, was preoccupied with the mounting losses and, as it became evident to him that the RAF could not provide the necessary protection, he advised Admiral Leatham that the drastic decision could not be postponed any longer. The Vice Admiral Malta agreed and informed the C-in-C accordingly. Late in April and during the first ten days of May 1942, the surviving submarines sneaked out of Marsamxett harbour bound for Alexandria. In his report about the circumstances leading to the withdrawal of the flotilla, Captain Simpson remarked that the Maltese ratings and workmen had shown great spirit and that he had never had a complaint. [94]

It was not until the end of July 1942 that Admiral Sir Henry H. Harwood, who on 20th May, 1942, succeeded Admiral Cunningham as Commander-in-Chief Mediterranean, authorised the flotilla's return to Malta. This was possible because the raids had by then abated and a large number of mines had been cleared from the harbour approaches. Vice Admiral Malta reported: "In recent weeks 206 mines have been swept up chiefly by four hastily-repaired local minesweepers manned mostly by Maltese naval ratings, who have faced up to this dangerous and most difficult task with indomitable spirit." [95]

At the height of the battle, General Dobbie received the following message, dated 15th April, 1942, from His Majesty King George VI:

> "To honour her brave people
> I award the George Cross
> to the Island Fortress of Malta
> to bear witness to a heroism
> and devotion that will long
> be famous in history."

In the evening, the Governor spoke to the people over the Rediffusion Relay System. Pointing out that this was the first time that an honour of this kind had been bestowed by a British Sovereign on a community[96], General Dobbie continued: "The safety and well-being of this fortress rests, under God, on four supports. These are the three Services and the civil population. Each of them is essential to the well-being of the others, and each one depends on the other three and cannot do without them."

Congratulatory messages poured in from all quarters, including the harassed defenders of Sebastopol, Kronstadt, and the Philippines.

The award made front-page news in most British and Allied newspapers. The significance of the award is clearly shown in an editorial in *The Times* (of London) of Saturday, 18th April, 1942, under the headline 'Malta Makes History': "Honour has come to Malta in a form which is unique in British history. Other nations have been in the habit of conferring decorations on composite bodies — a regiment or a city which has given gallant service — but it had been the essence of the British method that awards should be to individuals. Even when a regiment or detachment has been honoured, it has been the leader, or a selected member, who has received the award.

"But now Malta — the first part of the British Commonwealth to be so decorated — has received the George Cross, 'to bear witness' as His Majesty said in his telegram to the Governor, 'to a heroism and devotion that will long be famous in history'. No one, least of all our enemies, will deny that an honour had never been more richly deserved. Nor will there be doubt that the Islanders, much as they have borne and have yet to bear, will fulfil the

(NWMA)
Viscount Gort VC and Sir George Borg during the presentation ceremony on 13th September, 1942. Commissioner of Police Joseph Axisa is seen, on left, holding the case containing the George Cross and the Citation.

BUCKINGHAM PALACE

The Governor
    Malta.

   To honour her brave people I award the George Cross to the Island Fortress of Malta to bear witness to a heroism and devotion that will long be famous in history.

George R.I.

April 15th 1942.

Men of The King's Own Malta Regiment guarding the George Cross.

determination expressed in the Governor's reply, 'that by God's help Malta will not weaken but will endure until victory is won.'"

The bestowal of this prestigious award, highly appreciated by the Maltese, helped to boost the morale of the people and the defenders at a time when the 'Target Date' for surrender had already been fixed.

Conditions prevailing in Malta at the time were such that a public ceremony could only be held on Sunday, 13th September, 1942, and, even then, it was felt necessary, for security reasons, not to allow any news of the ceremony to reach the outside world before it had actually taken place. The texts of the speeches were sent to the Secretary of State in London and to the Minister of State in Cairo by secret telegram, for distribution to the Press not before Monday, 14th September, 1942.

The presentation ceremony took place at the Palace Square, still partly stacked with masonry from destroyed buildings. Detachments from the Navy, Army, Royal Air Force, Police, Special Constabulary and Passive Defence Organisations lined the square. The case containing the George Cross and the citation was brought out from the Palace by Police Commissioner Joseph Axisa who handed it to Viscount Gort VC, who had in the meantime replaced General Dobbie as Governor and Commander-in-Chief. Addressing the gathering, Lord Gort said: "On my appointment as Governor of Malta, I was entrusted to carry the George Cross to this Island Fortress.

"By the command of the King, I now present to the People of Malta and her Dependencies the decoration which His Majesty has awarded to them in recognition of the gallant service which they have already rendered in the fight for freedom.

"How you have withstood for many months the most concentrated bombing attacks in the history of the world is the admiration of all civilized peoples. Your homes and your historic buildings have been destroyed and only their ruins remain as monuments to the hate of a barbarous foe. The Axis Powers have tried again and again to break your spirit but your confidence in the final triumph of the United Nations remains undimmed.

"What Malta has withstood in the past, without flinching, Malta is determined to endure until the day when the second siege is raised.

"Battle-scarred George Cross Malta, the sentinel of Empire in the Mediterranean, meanwhile stands firm undaunted and undismayed awaiting the time when she can call 'Pass Friend, all is well in the Island Fortress'.

"Now it is my proud duty to hand over the George Cross to the People of Malta for safe-keeping." Lord Gort closed his address by reading the citation.

His Honour Sir George Borg, the Chief Justice, received the case from the Governor and delivered an address, after which the case was placed on a plinth in the centre of the Square, where men from the 1st Battalion The King's Own Malta Regiment mounted guard as the crowd filed past to see the insignia and document.

Chapter Thirteen

Bomb Disposal — Hospitals and Dressing Stations — Bombing of hospitals

It is estimated that the enemy dropped 17,000 tons of bombs over Malta, some of which failed to explode. Bomb Disposal Squads — formed from the Royal Army Ordnance Corps and British and Maltese soldiers of No 24 Company Royal Engineers — were set up to remove the menace of these unexploded bombs. Together with similar units from the Royal Air Force and the Royal Navy, they defused or blew up about 2,500 tons of bombs.

Major Reginald Parker GM recalls how the Army Bomb Disposal Squad was formed and how it worked: "Two RAOC officers, Captain Robert L. Jephson-Jones and Lieutenant (later Brigadier) William M. Eastman — the first recipients of the George Cross on 28th December, 1940 for outstanding bravery in Malta — led a group of men and formed the Bomb Disposal Squad soon after the first Italian bombs fell over Malta. We continued with the job alone until November 1940 when the Royal Engineers, under Lieutenant R.E. Talbot GC, joined us...I think we dealt with more bombs than any such squad in the United Kingdom; we seldom had to dig for them. We could, and often did, deal with a bomb in a matter of minutes whereas in Britain it often took days of digging to reach a bomb.

"In fact, at the back of Lintorn Barracks (now Beltissebh) at Floriana there were so many UXBs stocked that we had to dispose of them through deep-sea dumping. Once we were being towed out to the 5-mile buoy by a minesweeper when we were attacked by a

(The Times)
Members of the Royal Engineers Bomb Disposal Squad standing near some of the bombs defused by them. Lt George D. Carroll is on left.

German aircraft; we were set adrift, floating about in the rough sea on a flat-bottomed barge with bombs rolling about.

"Following this experience, we started dumping the bombs over a cliff beyond Hal Far. On one occasion, we had to remove a long-delayed-action type fuse bomb at Hal Far aerodrome. The clock had stopped but we used an electro-clock stopper in case it would restart; we did not want to defuse it for fear of an anti-withdrawal device which the Germans often used. We loaded it, plus clock stopper, onto a lorry, drove to the cliff, disconnected the clock stopper, and rolled it over. We thought, and hoped, that the clock was faulty or jammed; about four hours later, it went off among all the bombs we had been dumping in that spot. It was the biggest bang we had heard, knocking shutters off windows miles away...

"The first 'butterfly' bombs were collected and stored at Police Stations for 'safety'. We eventually took over and dealt with them by remote-control method. We dealt with so many of these, particularly at Luqa airfield, that every sapper worked individually. A tricky situation arose when we had to deal with one that stopped under a Swordfish loaded with a torpedo...

"We broke many rules — we had to — to get the job done. We were a well-trained group of sappers, experienced down to the lowest rank. The squad was extremely loyal; I often had to force them off while the ticklish defusing was being done. Even so, they sometimes watched, in a way gaining experience to cope with the rushes of work as in the case of the 'butterfly' bombs."[97]

Major Parker was awarded the George Medal on 27th May, 1941. Several of his colleagues in the Three Services were similarly rewarded for acts of bravery, selflessness and devotion to duty. Lieutenant Thomas W.T. Blackwell MBE was awarded the George Medal on 6th November, 1942; his citation reads: "About 10 o'clock on the night of 30th July, 1942, a number of delayed-action bombs were dropped in Birkirkara, Malta. One of these bombs partly demolished a house in a very built-up area, thereby burying a number of civilians. The bomb remained partially exposed. Lieutenant Blackwell, on arrival at the site, discovered that the bomb contained two delayed-action fuses, the clocks of which were both working. He decided that the proper course was to remove the bomb as soon as possible to a less vulnerable area, so that efforts could be made to rescue entombed people. As no lifting tackle was available, Lieutenant Blackwell decided that the bomb had to be towed away. It was necessary first to clear a passage for the bomb, and in this he was ably assisted by PC John

(IWM)
An unexploded bomb being hoisted onto a recovery vehicle.

Bayliss, a local police constable. Lieutenant Blackwell then tried to haul the bomb clear by means of a truck and a towing rope. The layout of the street permitted a towing rope only twelve feet in length. The first attempt failed owing to the bomb becoming stuck in the debris. It was then obvious that two persons were required, one to drive the truck, the other to guide the bomb. PC Bayliss volunteered to drive the truck, which he did, and with Lieutenant Blackwell guiding the bomb, the operation was completed. During the process of removal, another bomb of the same stick exploded. The fact that people buried under the debris of the house on which this bomb had fallen were, when extricated, found to be dead, does not detract from the gallantry of the action of Lieutenant Blackwell and PC Bayliss."[98] For his part in this dangerous undertaking, the Maltese policeman was awarded the British Empire Medal.

A naval officer who distinguished himself in bomb disposal was Lieutenant Cyril Rowlands RNVR who, between January 1941 and July 1942, tackled more than 70 UXBs, mostly around the dockyard and harbour area. Several of the unexploded bombs which he managed to render harmless were of 750 kg calibre and the 1,000 kg PC bomb, later christened 'ESAU', which was an entirely new type, unknown even then in the United Kingdom.

Awarded the George Medal on 2nd September, 1941, Lieutenant Rowlands received a Bar to the medal on 7th November, 1942. This outstanding Bomb Safety Officer (as designated in the Royal Navy) did odd jobs even whilst off-duty. His report shows that on 18th April, 1942, he defused a 50 kg bomb at No

(E.D. Woolley)
The only E-boat to survive the assault on the Grand Harbour on 26th July, 1941, was found abandoned about seven miles off shore. Lieut Woolley towed and beached her on Manoel Island and later dismantled her. This type of craft, essentially meant for attacking ships, powered by an Alfa Romeo racing engine, could reach a speed of about 40 knots. Lieut Woolley is seen at the controls.

13 St Margaret Street, Sliema: "This bomb was lying in the drawing room of a house opposite my residence and was dropped by a fighter-bomber. As several people would have had to evacuate the area, I removed the bomb within ten minutes of dropping, during the raid. Military informed." [99]

The work carried out by bomb disposal personnel was not restricted to dealing with unexploded bombs. Mention should be made of an episode connected with the dismantling and rendering safe of an Italian MTM captured after the attack on the Grand Harbour on 26th July, 1941. Lieutenant Edward D. Woolley GM RNVR was in charge of this operation; he was voluntarily assisted by Chief Petty Officer Motor Mechanic Leslie Hanlon RN.

The craft, fitted with a complicated firing device of a type till then unknown to the allies, contained 500 lbs of high explosive and had two clock mechanisms, each of which was capable of initiating the explosive. The removal of these clocks, with their attached detonators and primers, called for extreme care and skill.

The successful completion of this hazardous operation enabled the British to learn all about the mechanism and thus devise defensive plans against the use of these craft.

This risky undertaking earned Lieut Woolley a Bar to his George Medal and Petty Officer Hanlon the British Empire Medal. Later, Hanlon received the George Medal for other

(E.D. Woolley)
This E-boat was sunk during an air raid on Manoel Island. After salvage, Petty Officer Chief Motor Mechanics Hanlon and Packenham-Walsh stripped the engine and rebuilt it. The craft was shipped to Britain in September 1943. Photograph shows Woolley flanked by Hanlon and Packenham-Walsh at Manoel Island.

A floating mine adrift off Qui-Si-Sana, Sliema.

dangerous work carried out in conjunction with Lieut Woolley.[100]

The Royal Air Force too had its Bomb Disposal Unit. Unfortunately very little is known about its role except for what Air Marshal Sir Hugh Lloyd recorded in his memoirs: "The most startling feature of those attacks was the high proportion of delayed action bombs, which were so numerous that the few men in the bomb-disposal parties could not possibly dispose of them. One of the volunteers was Squadron Leader Dickinson[101], who had never before seen the inside of a bomb. He had so much practice in a few days that he became the established expert. Fortunately fate was kind to him, and to Squadron Leader Hardeman, too, as no bomb exploded in their hands. The sight of those two men unscrewing a fuse at the bottom of their respective bomb holes used to frighten me to death; yet they dealt with hundreds of bombs with apparent non-chalance, and I know for a fact that they worked sixteen hours a day — they had to." [102]

Besides unexploded bombs, several sea mines which drifted towards the coast had to be exploded or rendered harmless. One of the men who dealt with a large number of these mines was Lieutenant (Acting Lieutenant-Commander) William Ewart Hiscock RN, based at HMS *St Angelo*. This retired naval officer, who had rejoined the Service when war broke out, faced death on several occasions as waves tossed him about while handling the bobbing mines; his efficiency and courage earned him the Distinguished Service Cross. He was killed with his wife on 15th February, 1942, when their home at St George's Barracks received a direct hit. Hiscock was posthumously awarded the George Cross for 'great gallantry and undaunted devotion to duty.' His successor, Chief Petty Officer le Bargy, carried on with the same dedication and skill, earning for himself the Distinguished Service Medal and later the George Medal, besides being promoted.

From information supplied by the Explosive Ordnance Disposal Technical Information Centre at Kent, it emerges that the Germans used several new types of bombs over Malta; an official report dated 16th February, 1942, states: "Six bombs of a new type were dropped on Malta on the night of 1st January, 1942. The bombs were apparently fitted with 'rocket-type accelerators'. This fact is confirmed by witnesses who saw the bomb fall and by subsequent reconstruction of recovered fragments. These fragments included the *venturi* unit. From the position of individual fragments it would appear that at least one of the bombs, which had failed to detonate, had

(W. Ager) *A Red Cross painted in the grounds of St Andrew's Hospital.*

(IWM) *An Austin K2 ambulance caught in an air raid whilst going up Old Bakery Street, Valletta.*

The Central Hospital at Floriana extensively damaged through bombing.

bounced off a water-pipe and had broken up. The accelerator consists of six candles, which discharge through the *venturi*. From the noise generated during its fall, it is assumed that all six candles burn simultaneously. The dimensions of the bomb are not stated..."[103]

In the first eighteen weeks of 1942, the number of unexploded bombs from heavy daylight raids by German aircraft rose from 6 to 143 per week. The majority were 50 kg and 250 kg high explosives, but some 1,000 kg (Hermann) and 1,800 kg (Satan) bombs were also recovered. During the next four weeks, when the raids were mainly carried out by Italian aircraft, UXBs increased to 364 in one week; they were mostly of small calibre. The following five weeks, when Italian and German aircraft raided Malta, a large number of anti-personnel bombs were dropped. In one week alone 584 UXBs were reported.[104]

The majority of bombs, however, did go off and the consequent devastation kept rescue parties and medical teams working incessantly to render assistance to the stricken. For lack of sufficient stretchers, doors, unhinged by blast, were used to carry the dead and wounded to waiting ambulances and buses whose seats had been removed. The hospitals were too congested to retain all but the seriously injured; many were given first-aid and sent home or to nearby shelters. The hospitals themselves were by no means safe places, despite the fact that these were clearly marked with the Red Cross.

The increasing number of civilian casualties necessitated the setting up of several emergency hospitals. The newly-built St Luke's Hospital at Guardamangia was not yet fully operational when war broke out and, although hit during the first raids, it received patients evacuated from the Quarantine Hospital at Lazaretto as this was being used as a submarine base. The problem got worse when the Central Hospital at Floriana (now Police Headquarters) was extensively damaged on 14th February and 3rd May, 1941. St Vincent de Paule Hospital, situated between Marsa and Luqa, was also hit and about 600 elderly inmates were evacuated to Gozo on 20th March, 1941; this building was later used for billets by the Royal Air Force. On 19th April, 1942, St Paul's Home for the Elderly, run by the Little Sisters of the Poor at Hamrun, was bombed and thirty-four inmates and Sisters were killed. The Mental Diseases Hospital at Attard was hit on 18th July, 1941, 20th March, 9th May and 28th June, 1942, causing the death of six patients, in addition to a religious nursing sister and two female employees who were posthumously commended by the Governor. The Blue Sisters Hospital at St Julian's and *Santo Spirito* and

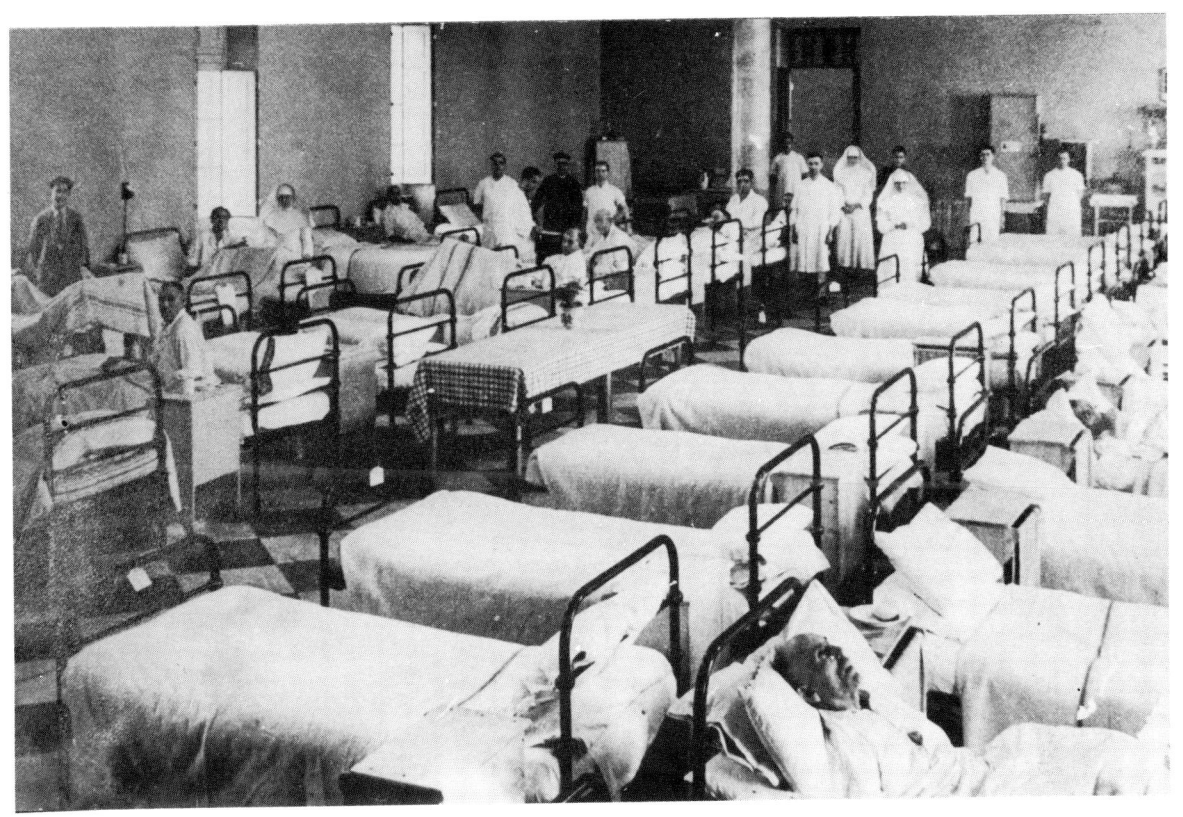

(NWMA)
One of the main halls at St Aloysius College at Birkirkara converted into an emergency ward. The Rector of the College, Fr Joseph Delia SJ, is in the background.

Sawra Hospitals at Rabat were not bombed.

This alarming situation was foreseen by the Medical and Health Authorities, headed by Professor Albert V. Bernard OBE MD. Several schools and other buildings were converted into hospitals; among these were the *Istituto Tecnico* Vincenzo Bugeja and the Adelaide Cini Orphanage at Hamrun, St Aloysius College and the Primary School at Birkirkara, the *Mater Boni Consilii* School at Pawla, the Jesus of Nazareth Orphanage at Zejtun and the Sacred Heart Convent at St Julian's.

The number of patients swelled when typhoid broke out in July 1942 and again in July 1943. On the latter occasion, the Ta' Qali reservoir, cracked by bombing, was contaminated by sewage; out of 1,275 cases reported, 135 died. Moreover, an outbreak of Polio in November 1942 crippled 415 persons and killed another 17.

The 90th British General Hospital at Mtarfa was the main military hospital. Mounting service casualties necessitated the opening of further hospitals: in August 1941, the 45th British General Hospital became operational at St Patrick's, while the 39th British General Hospital at St Andrew's was opened the following month; further equipment for this hospital had been lost at sea while being shipped to Malta. All the three hospitals were not spared. On 13th April, 1941, 36 bombs were dropped on the 90th at Mtarfa, causing serious damage. The following day, the Italian radio claimed that the attack was in retaliation for the bombing of an Italian field hospital in Libya. A worse fate awaited the 39th at St Andrew's when, on 23rd April, 1942, it was subjected to a ruthless attack by German bombers, resulting in extensive damage and considerable casualties; the patients and staff were transferred to the 45th at St Patrick's. The 39th was subsequently housed in a new hutted site accommodating 300 beds at Ghadira Bay. During the Siege, an estimated 100 bombs fell within Service hospital areas, destroying accommodation for 400 patients.

Another two hospitals which were extensively damaged were the Royal Naval Hospital at Bighi and the King George V Hospital for Merchant Seamen (now Sir Paul Boffa Hospital) at Floriana; the latter was totally destroyed on 26th April, 1942.

To cater for minor injuries and ailments, the Services set up several Dressing Stations scattered throughout the Island. The Army had Main Dressing Stations at Hamrun and Gharghur, Advanced Dressing Stations at

St Andrew's Hospital in ruins.

Rabat, Mgarr, Wardija, Naxxar, St. Andrew's, Floriana, Zabbar, Zejtun and Tignè, and Regimental Aid Posts at Gudja, Tarxien, Qrendi, Siggiewi, Marsa, Birkirkara, Attard, Mgarr, St. Paul's Bay, Mellieha and Buskett. The Royal Air Force had an Advanced Dressing Station at Luqa and two other Dressing Stations whilst the Royal Navy had another Dressing Station. The staff manning the main hospitals and these stations were mainly British and Maltese personnel from the Royal Army Medical Corps, besides members of the Voluntary Aid Detachment and of the Queen Alexandra's Imperial Military Nursing Service.

Not all the patients in the Service hospitals and dressing stations were victims of direct enemy action. The official history of the British Army Medical Services states: "The conditions in Malta in 1941 and 1942 were such as to expose even the most stout-hearted among its garrison to the risk of a breakdown. Violence continually descended from the skies and, save for the gunners and the fighter pilots, there was no means of retaliation. It had to be endured. To the endurance and to resilience of everyone there is a limit; no wonder then that anxiety neurosis, though not labelled as such, came to figure largely among the causes of sickness.

The King George V Hospital, Floriana, situated near the Power Station, destroyed by bombing.

"In March 1942, when the bombing was at its peak, a notice reading as follows was posted at all gun sites:

* Fear is the weapon which the enemy employs to sabotage morale.
* Anxiety neurosis is the term used by the medical profession to commercialise fear.
* Anxiety neurosis is a misnomer which makes 'cold feet' appear respectable.
* To give way to fear is to surrender to the enemy attack on your morale.
* To admit to anxiety neurosis is to admit a state of fear which is either unreasonable or has no origin in your conception of duty as a soldier.
* If you are a man, you will not permit your self-respect to admit to anxiety neurosis or to show fear.
* Do not confuse fear with prudence or impulsive action with bravery.
* Safety first is the worst of principles.
* In civil life, anxiety neurosis will put you 'on the club'. In battle it brings you a bayonet in the bottom and a billet in a prisoner-of-war camp." [105]

Chapter Fourteen

Lord Gort relieves General Dobbie — Aerial defence reaches a nadir — USS Wasp *ferries Spitfires — The Glorious 10th of May*

Lord Gort VC arrived on 7th May, 1942, to take over from General Dobbie, who was relieved for health reasons. The handing-over and swearing-in ceremony was carried out without any pomp and with minimal formality. The new Governor and Commander-in-Chief arrived on a Sunderland from Gibraltar at about 9.00 pm, while a raid was in progress. As he was being driven from the quay, a bomb fell near the battered Station Commander's house on the outskirts of Kalafrana, where Sir William and Lady Dobbie were waiting, together with a number of Service and Civil high officials. After a lengthy private conversation, General Dobbie introduced Lord Gort to the officials but then an unexpected hitch cropped up: "When it came to the Chief Justice to administer the Oath of Office to Lord Gort, Mr Peter Paul Decesare, Clerk to the Council of Government, discovered, to his and to everyone's consternation, that he had forgotten to bring along a Bible. General Dobbie eased the tension by taking out a pocket Holy Book from his uniform jacket and the ceremony proceeded without further mishap." [106] To set the seal to this occasion, Chief Justice George Borg, whilst appending his signature, stained the document with blood from a slight cut to his finger, which he had suffered during the explosion. General and Lady Dobbie and their daughter, Sybil, then left Malta on the same flyingboat that had brought the new Governor.

Reports appearing in a section of the British Press held that, before coming to Malta, Lord Gort had been told that the Island would be unlikely to hold out for more than six weeks and that his task would probably be one of final capitulation. The Governor, who had commanded the British Expeditionary Force until its evacuation from Dunkirk, was reputed to have answered that should things reach that stage, rather than surrender, he would lead what men he could muster and fight it out in Sicily.

At the time that Lord Gort took over the Governorship, Malta was facing an acute shortage of all essentials. Fighter strength had diminished considerably and no striking force was available. The Island lay as a helpless target for the Axis Air Forces. Worried by this alarming situation, which was rendered worse by reports of an imminent invasion, Lord Gort made representations that the Service Commanders be placed under his direct command instead of their respective Commanders-in-Chief in the Middle East. This was approved and on 15th May, 1942, Lord Gort assumed the office of Supreme Commander of the Fighting Services and of the Civil Administration. He held this unique appointment until 1st December, 1942, when, in view of the improved situation at Malta, the Commanders-in-Chief Middle East reassumed responsibility for offensive operations from the Island.

The absence of fighter opposition enabled the German fighters to indulge in strafing sorties almost at leisure, their confidence bordering almost on impudence. ARP Superintendent Anthony Bilocca recalls: "On 1st April, 1942, a flight of Messerschmitts attacked St James's Battery, protecting Luqa airfield. One of the fighters swooping low, hit its tail-wheel against a rubble wall and had to force-land in a nearby field. The virtually undamaged aircraft was guarded by the military until aviation experts were flown out from Britain. We took the uninjured pilot, Franz Pilz, to our Centre at Pawla till we escorted him in a Service ambulance to St Andrew's. An attack was in progress and, on reaching the *Chalet* on the Sliema seafront, we stopped the vehicle and took him out to watch the barrage; impressed by the intensity of the flak, he exclaimed: 'This is hell Island'." [107]

Not all the German pilots could claim such luck. On a Sunday afternoon in April 1942, a Junkers 88 was shot down into the sea by ack-ack fire, approximately two miles from St Julian's Tower. "Two crew members swam towards the shore from the sinking aircraft. People along the Sliema Front, from the Tower to Ghar-id-Dud, watched with perplexity as two Me 109s skimmed low over the water, acting as if offering protection to the two men; this prevented RAF High Speed Launches from attempting to rescue them in fear of being attacked by the Messerschmitts. One of the men did not make it, while the other reached the shore near Sliema Point Battery; the angry crowd made it difficult for a patrol from the Lancashire Fusiliers, with fixed bayonets, to escort him into the Fortress. When the German airman was later transferred to an internment

(IWM)

An RAF officer inspecting the wreckage of an Me 109.

(via N. Malizia)

A Macchi 202, belonging to 360ª Squadriglia, 155º Gruppo, 51º Stormo C.T. extensively damaged at Gela after a sortie over Malta.

camp on a truck, the onlookers booed and stoned the vehicle."[108]

Quite a different scene occurred on Sunday, 23rd March, 1941: "A white parachute appeared high up, just above Zebbug Parish Church. People on roof-tops pointed at the black figure dangling under the canopy and wondered whether he was British or German. I followed the crowd running towards Wied Qirda on the outskirts of the village; members of the local Home Guard, armed with rifles, joined the crowd ... To everyone's delight we saw a large group of people coming towards us carrying a British pilot shoulder high on a stretcher. The joyous throng carried the airman through the streets of the village, whilst women came out to offer him drinks. The *défile* moved on, flanked by the Home Guard. More people came out of the Parish Church, where the Bishop was conducting Confirmation. The pilot, with tears in his eyes, waved with one arm, resting the other on the stretcher. He was taken to the Police Station, waiting for an RAF ambulance."[109]

Wing Commander P.B. 'Laddie' Lucas CBE DSO DFC then a squadron leader commanding No 249 Squadron, recounts his personal experience: "I recall, soon after the second lot of reinforcements had landed from *Eagle*, being hit ignominiously in the glycol tank by a cannon shell from a 109 in circumstances which are best left unsaid. Aided by fortune rather than skill, I contrived to coax the Spitfire back across the coast, and with a dead stick and a fair quantity of smoke emerging from the coolant tank, landed the aircraft wheels up, in a small cornfield in the south-west of the Island. Three old Maltese women, in long dresses with black scarves over their heads, were working in the field. As I climbed out of the cockpit into the dusty heat of the day, one of them came stumbling over the rough ground towards me. She stared anxiously into my face. Tears, not words, spelled out her relief. With simple dignity, she laid her hand first on the wing of the aircraft and then on my arm. As she made the sign of the cross, devoutly and deliberately, across her chest, a smile of benign tranquillity spread over

(US National Archives)
Crewmen aboard USS Wasp *hold back a tropicalised Spitfire against the pre-take off run-up.*

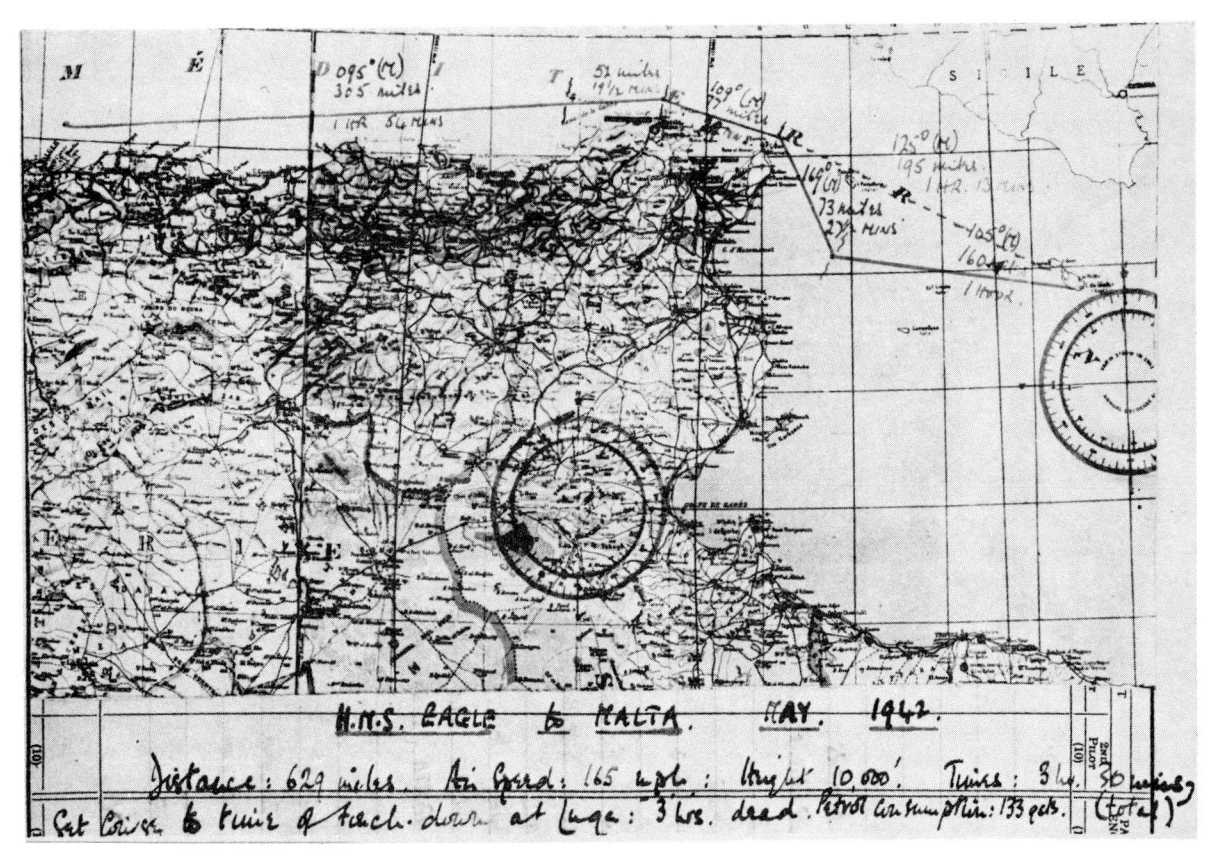

Squadron Leader 'Laddie' Lucas's flight plan from HMS Eagle to Malta for 18th May, 1942.

that kindly, ageing face. For a moment, in a blessed Malta field, the Roman and the Anglican Churches were as one."[110]

Further fighter deliveries were essential but, at such a crucial stage, HMS *Eagle* was laid up for a month with steering gear defects. As no other suitable British aircraft-carrier was available, Mr Churchill convinced President Roosevelt to allow the USS *Wasp* to undertake one of these trips.

On the morning of April 20th, at a point some 55 miles to the north of Algiers, the carrier *Wasp* (Captain J.W. Reeves, Jr. USN) turned into the wind and launched 47 Spitfire Mk VCs on their 660-mile flight towards Malta; only one aircraft failed to reach the Island.

Although the American carrier had stayed safely out of range of enemy bases in Sicily, the Germans followed every step of the operation. Their radio monitoring station supplied the *Luftwaffe's* II Air Corps with last-minute information, enabling them to estimate the time when the Spitfires were to land at Malta. In fact, within twenty minutes of the Spitfires' arrival, the Germans bombed Hal Far and Ta' Qali, destroying twenty and damaging twelve of the newly-arrived fighters. Subsequent aerial combat with Messerschmitts from *Jagdeshwader* 53 took its toll and after three days only six or seven Spitfires were still left serviceable.[111]

This setback prompted the Air Officer Commanding Malta to send a strongly-worded message to the Air Ministry on 25th April: "Regret that the quality of the pilots from Operation 'Calendar' is not up to that of previous operations. In No 601 Squadron, seven pilots out of 23 have had no operational experience, and a further four have less than 25 hours flying on Spitfires; 12 pilots of the 23 have never fired their guns in action. The Commanding Officer of No 601 Squadron (Squadron Leader John D. Bisdee) also reports that seven of his experienced pilots were posted away from the squadron just before they left. Only fully-experienced operational pilots must come here. It is no place for beginners. Casualties up till now have been the beginners."[112]

It is worth going back to the one Spitfire that never reached the Island. Tony Holland, one of the pilots who flew off *Wasp*, tells the story: "...The 47th, Sergeant Walcott, was a disappointment. He was a new man who had only been with the squadron a very short time, not long enough to share the *esprit de corps* of

A Spitfire being refuelled and rearmed.

the squadron. We only came to know later that this young American had shared a cabin with a Canadian flight sergeant to whom he had confided that he had no intention of ever reaching Malta. Later, when I was in Halton RAF Hospital in England, my next-bed mate, then just a young Flying Officer but now an Air Marshal, told me that he had heard that the American pilot had crash-landed his Spitfire on the other side of the Atlas Mountains, managing to reach the nearest United States Consulate where, on claiming to be a lost civil pilot, he was repatriated to the United States..."[113]

The sky over Malta was still wide open for the German and Italian Air Forces. Besides exposing the garrison and civilians to constant harassment this also prevented the sailing of convoys to the Island. This predicament worried the British Prime Minister who appealed to President Roosevelt to allow *Wasp* to deliver another batch of Spitfires to Malta. Mr Churchill expressed his fear that without the desired reinforcements Malta would be 'pounded to bits'. Mr Roosevelt, aware of the importance of strengthening the Island, agreed to make the aircraft-carrier available for a second trip. On 9th May, sixty-four Spitfires were flown off USS *Wasp* and HMS *Eagle*: this prompted Churchill to send the now-famous signal to the American carrier: "Who said a wasp couldn't sting twice?"

The lesson learnt during the previous delivery did not go unheeded. Elaborate preparations were made to ensure the safety of the new reinforcements by having them airborne again within the shortest possible time. As this was by far the largest number of aircraft delivered to Malta in one batch it was essential to have them dispersed and, accordingly, they were split up in groups which were to land at Luqa, Ta' Qali and Hal Far. On touch-down, each aircraft was met by a resident pilot who guided his charge to a pre-allotted pen stocked with aviation fuel and ammunition. As soon as the engine was switched off, the Malta pilot climbed into the cockpit while ground crews hurriedly removed the long-range tank and refuelled and rearmed the aircraft. This concerted effort enabled the aircraft to take to the air in under fifteen minutes from landing; a highly creditable performance by Malta's 'erks'.

The arrival of these Spitfires was well timed. The 2,650-ton 40-knot HMS *Welshman* sailed from Gibraltar on 8th May carrying powdered milk, canned meat, dehydrated foodstuff, ammunition, smoke-making canisters, aero-engines as well as over 100 RAF technicians to service the Island's fighter force. *Welshman* had minor modifications made to her superstructure, mainly the addition of cinder screens to her three funnels so as to resemble a French *Léopard*-class destroyer. Flying French colours, Captain W.H.D.

982nd DAY OF WAR AGAINST NAZISM

H.M. KING GEORGE VI
AWARDED TO MALTA
The "GEORGE CROSS"
ON THE 966th DAY
OF THE WAR
APRIL 15th 1942

TIMES OF MALTA

No. 2,094   PRICE 2d.   MONDAY, MAY 11, 1942

BATTLE OF MALTA : AXIS HEAVY LOSSES

'SPITFIRES' SLAUGHTER 'STUKAS'

BRILLIANT TEAM WORK OF A.A. GUNNERS AND R.A.F.

63 Enemy Aircraft Destroyed Or Damaged Over Malta Yesterday

THE total number of enemy losses over Malta today (Sunday) is
Destroyed 22 — probably destroyed 20 — damaged 21

The specification of these is as follows:

DESTROYED	Probably Destroyed	Damaged
R.A.F. — 12 bombers	11 bombers	11 bombers
4 fighters	9 fighters	10 fighters
ANTI-AIRCRAFT ARTILLERY		
5 bombers	(Several more enemy aircraft were damaged by	
1 fighter	Anti-Aircraft Artillery that were probably later	
	destroyed by our fighters).	

The last two days have seen a metamorphosis in the Battle of Malta. After two days of the fiercest aerial combat that has ever taken place over the Island the Luftwaffe, with its Italian lackeys, has taken the most formidable beating that has been known since the Battle of Britain two and a half years ago. Indeed, in proportion to the numbers of aircraft involved, this trouncing is even greater than the Germans suffered at this time.

It has always been known that man for man, and machine for machine, the R.A.F. were infinitely superior to the Hun, and everybody looked forward to the day when he could be met on terms of parity, for they looked upon the outcome as a certainty. That day has arrived. The R.A.F., even had numerical superiority over its fighter opponents for the first time, and the results have excelled the most optimistic expectations. Our fighters have formed, with the A.A. Artillery, a team which has dealt out appalling destruction on the enemy.

COURAGE OF MALTA'S GUNNERS

Teamwork has been the watchword during all these weary months of taking pounding, with very little else to do but grin and bear it. And if during the last couple of days the R.A.F. have been more in the limelight than the gunners, over the whole period of Malta's affliction they must be looked upon as a brilliant forward line, supported by equally magnificent backs, who have never once let anyone down. For months on end these gunners have hurled steel and defiance at the enemy, no matter what the circumstances. They have been subjected to probably the most diabolical bombing that gunners have ever known; they have been ceaselessly machine-gunned; they have suffered casualties, but others have taken their places, as nobly as those who died or were badly wounded. Yet never once have they faltered, and their total of 101 enemy aircraft destroyed in April alone was a fitting climax to months of magnificent, steady achievement. Above all, their courage, at times under most distressing conditions, has been superb. The people of Malta owe them a debt which is incalculable.

APRIL ORDEAL

Since the beginning of April this Island has endured the saddest phase in her career — until yesterday. She has been pounded without ceasing, and circumstances have prevented much in the way of hitting back on the scale which was desired. But yesterday it was known that the boot was on the other foot. The Hun realized it, too, at the last moment. He set about the problem, as he thought, with the same insolent ease as that to which he has hitherto thought he was entitled. He set out to liquidate our aircraft on their aerodromes, in the same methodical, ponderous way which he has always used. "Little and often" seemed to be his policy, and there were five raids during the day. His bombers, and the Italians who ape him from a prodigious height, came in as usual with their fighter escort in swarms.

SHATTERING SHOCK FOR THE HUN

But he got a shattering shock. Instead of being on the ground our fighters were in the air, waiting for his blood. They chased the fighters and pounced on the bombers before the enemy quite knew what it was all about. For the first time for a great while the R.A.F. met the enemy on equal or better terms, and at the end of the day he retired to lick gaping wounds which he had never anticipated. Thirty of his aircraft, with the help of the gunners, had been badly mauled, and of these 7 had been shot down out of the sky, and a further 7 had little hope of getting home.

SALUTARY LESSON FOR ITALIANS

During the afternoon's raids the sky looked like the outside of some fantastic wasps' nest, with aircraft milling about in a breathless, hectic rough-house. The noise of cannon and mach-ine-gun was all the sweeter for the fact that half at least of them were for once on our side. That being so, nobody on the ground had the slightest qualms about the result. Nor did the R.A.F. fail to take full advantage of the position. They chased their opposite numbers all round the sky, and hauled themselves at the bombers. The Italians especially got a salutary lesson which it is hoped that they will not forget—for their own sakes. Their usual five bombers were seen crossing the sky in their usual tight vic formation, not varying their height as though their pilots had their eyes glued to a spot on an extremely high horizon. But what was not usual was the fact that of this five only two limped back to base. Spitfires had sent the other three hurtling into what they claim to be their own sea, and two of their fighter escort probably followed them.

Today (Sunday) the good work has been carried on even more successfully. This morning German bombers came over to try to cause more havoc in the already stricken dockyard area. Again they met a trick which surprised them, for they were confronted with a pall of smoke and the prospect of a grim game of blind man's buff. Before they reached the curtain R.A.F. fighters had frightened some of them into dropping their bombs into the sea. Those that survived found fighters waiting for them as they pulled out of their dive, and for some minutes there was mad pandemonium, with bombs, heavy and light A.A. guns, cannon and machine-guns forming a hellish cacophony of sound. Most of those that made the attack were dive-bombers.
(Continued on Page 4, Col. 3)

EASTERN FRONT

Strong Russian Attacks
(Reuter's Service)
LONDON, May 10.

Strong Russian attacks supported by tanks and artillery on the northern front in the Lake Ilmen region in one of them the Russian tanks broke through the German lines as reported by a High Command survey given over the German radio.

The break-through occurred south-east of Lake Ilmen when several Russian infantry regiments supported by 46 tanks launched an assault on a four-mile front held by a German infantry division. The report admits that individual tanks broke through.

Fighting on the Kalinin Front is reported in a supplement to Sunday's Soviet communique. Here, in two days, the Germans lost 600 Officers and Men in killed alone. Artillery operating with the Russian garrison on the Smolensk front destroyed 5 German blockhouses and German artillery.

The supplement adds that a German prisoner states that the first German Tank Division lost one half of its effectives in recent fighting on the Eastern Front.

CHURCHILL'S STIRRING BROADCAST

A Tribute To Malta

(Reuter's Service)
LONDON, May 10.

In the course of his world-wide broadcast tonight (Sunday), the Prime Minister Mr. Churchill, paid a tribute to Malta and welcomed back General Dobbie, for nearly two years "the heroic defender of Malta." For the moment it looks as if the terrific air attack on Malta had slackened.

"It looks," said the Prime Minister "as if a lot of enemy aircraft have been moved eastwards. If so, this supreme air battle for Malta, upon which they have concentrated such an immense preponderance of strength and for which they sacrificed so many aircraft, will have been definitely won."

GENERAL DOBBIE AND LORD GORT

Paying a tribute to the leadership of General Dobbie, Mr. Churchill said that after two years of battle the Governor of Malta was taking a well-earned repose. Of the new Governor, the Prime Minister said that he knew of no man in the British Empire to whom he would sooner entrust the combatting and beating down of other perils that may beset Malta.

A STERN WARNING

Germany was warned by Mr. Churchill that if Hitler used poison gas against Russia, Britain would use her growing air superiority to carry gas warfare on the largest possible scale against military objectives in Germany. Such use of poison gas against Russia by Germany would be treated as if it were used against the British Isles and it's thus for Hitler to choose whether he wished to add that additional horror to aerial warfare.

BOMBING OFFENSIVE

The British and American bombing offensive against Germany would be one of the principal features of this year's world war. Now was the time to see Britain's increasingly superior air strength to strike hard and continually at the German home front, which remained the foundation of the whole enormous German invasion of Russia.

MUSSOLINI'S MISCALCULATION

Mr. Churchill delivered his broadcast on the second anniversary of his being entrusted with the office of Prime Minister. He spoke of the past, present and future in this World War, and said how
(Continued at foot of Col. 4)

FAR EAST

Chinese Successes

CHUNGKING, May 10.
THE Japanese retreating in the south-east of Yunnan are suffering heavy casualties with the Chinese fighters hot-on-the-round them, says the communique.

There is nothing to suggest the truth of U.S. Axis reports that British forces in the Chaofang valley are about to be terminated it was stated authoritatively in London on Sunday. The latest information is that the British force is well drawn up the valley in good order.

MIDDLE EAST FRONT
(Reuter's Service)
CAIRO, May 10.

The Middle East communique today (Sunday) says: Some small enemy columns, including tanks and artillery, withdrew on being engaged by our light forces.

Nothing was known in London on Sunday of the claims that the Axis powers had landed airborne troops in the Matmarica desert which forms the eastern end of Cyrenaica, and destroyed petrol and oil dumps.

Twenty-two were killed and forty wounded in an air raid at Alexandria early on Sunday morning, says a Ministry of the Interior communique.

MALTA PROGRAMME FROM AMERICA TODAY

There will be a Special "March of Time" Programme from the United States about Malta on the African Service of the B.B.C. from 5.30 to 6.30 p.m. (local time today, Monday, May 11, 1942).

STOP PRESS

WASHINGTON, May 11.—The attack on Tokyo on April 18. was made by American Army bombers. From low altitude, military, naval and industrial plants were bombed in the vicinity of Tokyo, unmistakably and accurately. Large fires were started which in some instances burned for two days.—Reuter.

CHUNGKING, May 10. Attempting to break through the Chinese cordon by a thrust across the Yunnan border in the Chefang area, the Japanese have lost 3,000 men killed, according to tonight's Chinese communique. (Reuter).

MOSCOW, May 10. Yesterday, says the Soviet midnight communique, 25 Nazi aircraft were destroyed on the Russian Front. The Red Air Force lost 15 planes. (Reuter).

Mussolini had miscalculated the strength of Britain and the Empire, and how Italy's African Empire had been liquidated.

(We shall be publishing the text of Mr. Churchill's stirring broadcast in Tuesday's Times of Malta).

ANGORA, May 10.—A British built submarine, the "Oruce-e" has been handed over to the Turkish naval authorities at Alexandretta. The submarine, which is a vessel of 690 tons, was brought from Britain by a British crew. (Reuter).

(IWM)

HMS Welshman, *disguised as a French cruiser, being unloaded at the dockyard.*

Friedburger steered the ship to Malta, baffling two Ju 88s which hovered hesitantly overhead off the Tunisian coast.[114] The ship reached Malta at 6.00 am on 10th May and was unloaded in less than seven hours.

As expected, the Germans mounted a series of raids to sink *Welshman* in harbour but they did not expect the reception prepared by the Spitfires and the artillery. A belated innovation for Malta was the use of smokescreen, which effectively shrouded the harbour area. *Welshman* left Malta later that evening. This fast minelayer was to make other trips to Malta; in June her cargo consisted of more aero-engines, glycol coolant and 20 mm cannon shells, while in July she delivered flour, edible oil and paravanes.

The newly-arrived Spitfires, a tonic to an Island avid for success, put up a brilliant show as they chased the Stukas and escorting fighters wherever they found them. The enemy was overwhelmed by the superiority of the Spitfires and the skill of their pilots. The Air Officer Commanding Mediterranean was exultant at the turn of events; at 12.20 pm he sent a 'Most Important' message, bearing No OPS 832, to the Fighter Station at Ta' Qali: "My heartiest congratulations to you all on your magnificent performance this morning. Good Work. Kill them all."[115] On Monday, 11th May, the *Times of Malta*, came out with the bold-type banner headline "Battle of Malta: Axis Heavy Losses. Spitfires Slaughter Stukas", giving a glowing account of the brilliant team-work between the anti-aircraft gunners and the Royal Air Force, who, the newspaper claimed, accounted for 22 destroyed enemy aircraft, with a further 20 probably destroyed and 21 damaged. The 'Glorious Tenth of May' was one of Malta's finest days, marking a temporary pause in German supremacy over the Malta skies.

The ferrying of fighter reinforcements to the Island continued. In twenty-five operations undertaken between August 1940 and October 1942, 718 out of the 764 aircraft ferried reached Malta safely. (See Apendix **O**) Philip Dixon, who flew off *Furious* on 17th August, 1942, relates: "The aircraft that were to fly to Malta had been stowed in the hangar deck before being taken up by means of a lift to the flight deck and ranged at the stern in batches of eight. The aircraft engines were started, warmed up

(NWM)
Repairs to aircraft and equipment were carried out at Gasan, Muscat and Mamo Garages at Gzira. These civilian workshops are situated some miles away from the airfields.

Servicing of propellers.

and pilot checked; if anyone had any doubts about the serviceability of their aircraft, they got out and the aircraft would be pushed overboard complete with their kit, which in fact was only a haversack stowed behind the armour-plating in the fuselage.

"Because of the short deck, the engine would have to be opened up against the chocks and brakes so as to get as many revs on as possible before the aircraft would be allowed to move forward. During this revving-up period, the aircraft would be subjected to considerable torque from the engine. In an effort to combat this, the aircraft was not lined on the centre-line of the flight deck but pointed towards the ship's island; in addition to this, some right rudder was applied. Both these measures helped to combat the pull to the left exerted by the engine. Not only was this rather uncomfortable from the point of view of the pilot, who could see the deck on his left where he had to go, but he had to overcome the tendency to correct his line; he was in fact flying down the deck instead of allowing the engine to pull him round. This was probably the cause of the one fatal crash that took place on take-off from the aircraft-carrier.

"As *Furious* had a ramp towards the front of the flight deck, one had to apply slight pressure on the control column to change the angle; this again gave rise to difficulty to the one person who crashed. As far as could be deduced, Sergeant Fleming, who not having flown off a carrier before, tended to put on left rudder to straighten his run and, as he approached the ramp, he pulled hard back on the stick, creating two factors which tended to create a stall: coarse rudder and backward pressure on the control column. It appears that he dropped his left wing which caught a signal lamp just off the edge of the deck and cartwheeled into the water.

"At the time, I was in my aircraft between decks waiting to go onto the lift as the first of the next batch of aircraft to go up, and it was rather disconcerting to hear the engine noise of the aircraft going across the lift and then hearing the Tannoy announce 'Do you hear there, do you hear there, crash on the port side'.

"After take-off, we climbed to 20,000 feet, as instructed, and flew the mapped course. This took us round the north of Cape Bon and down to a point slightly south-west of Pantelleria and then on a more easterly course to Malta. We

A Ju 88 crash-landed at Ta' Qali.

were told that if the weather would be fine, and the weather would normally be fine, from the Island of La Galite we should fly southeast over Tunis to Korba and then join our original track. This was to keep further away from the Italian Island of Pantelleria.

"We had 90-gallon overload tanks on our Spitfires and these were to be dropped somewhere off the coast at Korba. For some reason or other, possibly because I was concentrating on making sure that I had sufficient fuel, I lost my formation and flew most of the way on my own, fortunately without incident. After I had crossed the coast near Korba, I made a very brief transmission calling the base at Malta, giving my call-sign and asking for a homing. It was very reassuring to have an almost immediate response with a course to steer. As I followed this course, eventually a small bank of clouds appeared on the horizon, as it often did with Malta. I approached the Island from the south and landed at Luqa. I got out of the aircraft, which was subjected to the usual very quick rearming and refuelling and it took off with another pilot."[116]

Chapter Fifteen

Borg Pisani lands in Malta; his capture, trial and execution

The local defences often detected the presence of Italian submarines and motor torpedo-boats but it was only on a few occasions, under cover of darkness, that these enemy craft managed to slip into some of the bays. On 18th May, 1942, *Tenente di Vascello* Giuseppe Cosulich guided his torpedo assault craft (MTSM 218) into Marsascala Bay, where *Palombaro* Giuseppe Guglielmo plunged into the sea to observe minor coastal defences such as landing obstacles, barbed wire obstructions, machine-gun and sentry posts. Having escaped detection, Guglielmo ventured further into the bay and even went ashore. When he took to sea again he could not locate the craft; he was later captured ashore in nearby St Thomas Bay.

That same night, Caio Borghi was brought to Malta aboard a torpedo assault craft (MTSM 214) manned by *Sottotenente di Vascello* Ongarillo Ungarelli and *Secondo Capo Motorista Navale* Arnaldo De Angelis. When about 150 yards off shore, Borghi took to the water in a dinghy and headed towards a cave at Ras id-Dawwara, between Dingli and Imtahleb, where he arrived at about 2.00 am. He was carrying four bags with food sufficient for twenty days, a radio transmitter/receiver, lengths of rope, a code booklet and chemicals to enable him to erase code messages, a pistol, a hand grenade and currency notes to the amount of £200 to compensate anyone helping him.

Caio Borghi was the undercover name of Carmelo Borg Pisani, who was born at Senglea on 10th August, 1914. Since childhood he had nurtured pro-Italian sentiments and after attending the Italian school *Umberto Primo*, he enrolled in Fascist organisations in Malta. In October 1936 he was awarded a scholarship by the Italian Government to study Art at the *Regia Accademia di Belle Arti* in Rome where he took some time to establish himself. The impending war crisis tore him between his love for Italy and his motherland.

On 30th May, 1940, he wrote to Mussolini informing him of his decision to stay in Italy and at the same time offered his services to see Malta's annexation with Italy materialize. On 7th June, he enrolled in the Fascist Party and, three days after the declaration of war, volunteered to enlist in the Italian Army but poor eye-sight let him down. In April 1941, with the help of influential persons, he enlisted in the *Milizia Volontaria per la Sicurezza*

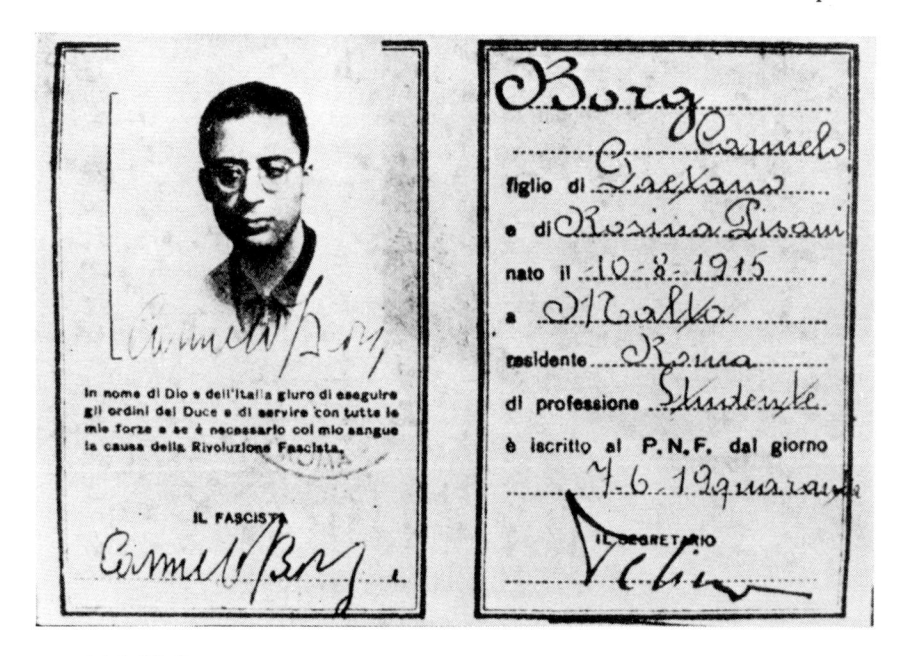

(via L. Mizzi)
Membership card issued at Rome on 7th June, 1940, to Carmelo Borg on joining the Partito Nazionale Fascista *(National Fascist Party). On the card, the year of birth is erroneously given as 1915.*

Nazionale — Comando della 112ª Legione CC NN. After serving in the Greek Campaign between May and September 1941, Borg Pisani resumed his studies in Rome. Later he attended a course at Messina for officers of *Milmart* (*Milizia Artiglieria Marittima*), whose responsibility was the protection of the Italian coast.

At the time, plans were being worked out in Sicily for the invasion of Malta and Borg Pisani was selected to undergo special training preparatory to being sent on a difficult and delicate mission, which was to bring him to Malta in order to report on the food situation and on the morale of the people; he was also to check the state of the defences of Malta, Gozo and Comino, and to find out if there was a radio station on Filfla. Moreover, he was to investigate about the running of the blockade by a British ship which used to anchor at Marsaxlokk. On completion of his mission, Borg Pisani had to be picked up to return to Italy.

The chosen landing site could not have been worse because the cliff above the cave is unscaleable. Within two days the sea had washed away all the items he was carrying, most of which were later retrieved by the British military authorities; the code booklet, however was never found. Realising his helplessness, he waved and shouted for help. His desperate pleas were eventually answered; Robert Apap, an evacuee from Sliema, reported his presence to RMA personnel manning a searchlight post in the vicinity. The soldiers, using binoculars, traced a man wearing black swimming trunks and a beret, and reported to headquarters.

As it was impossible to get down the steep cliffs to rescue him from land, Flight Lieutenant George R. Crockett was detailed to leave Kalafrana on High Speed Launch 128 and head towards the spot. On reaching the site, he spotted the man clinging to the cliffs. When the launch was within a few yards off shore, a deckhand threw the end of a heaving line which the man failed to grasp. Leading Aircraftman C. Martins dived overboard, swam towards the rocks with the line and convinced the man to jump into the water; eventually both were hauled aboard.[117] On the way back to Kalafrana, Borg Pisani told LAC Joseph Pace, the only member of the crew who could speak Italian, that he had been sent from Italy. An awaiting ambulance conveyed the exhausted man to Mtarfa Military Hospital.

In the meantime, Captain (later Colonel) Tommy Warrington RAMC received a telephone call informing him that a civilian, rescued from the Dingli area, was on his way to Mtarfa for medical attention. This came as a surprise to him as it was unusual to send civilians to military hospitals except in emergencies. By the time the ambulance reached Mtarfa an air raid was in progress and Captain Warrington went to see if the man needed medication before sending him on to *Santo Spirito* Hospital at nearby Rabat. When Captain Warrington opened the ambulance door, the light from his torch was sufficient for him to recognise the man as Carmelo Borg Pisani as both had been brought up at Senglea. The doctor asked Borg Pisani, in Maltese, if he recognised him, to which he received a negative answer. Thereupon, Captain Warrington identified himself and Borg Pisani, to his relief, recalled who the doctor was. As Captain Warrington knew that Borg Pisani had remained in Italy to continue his studies when war broke out, he brought this to the attention of his Commanding Officer, who in turn instructed him to report the matter to the Intelligence Branch. Borg Pisani was brought to Captain Warrington's consulting room and given some refreshments. During the course of conversation, Borg Pisani, of his own free will, went into details with the doctor about the nature of his mission. He proved himself co-operative when interrogated by the Intelligence Officer, who arrived the following morning in the company of Commissioner of Police Joseph Axisa.

Borg Pisani was then taken to a house at St Julian's and, three days later, was transferred to 11, Ghar id-Dud Street, Sliema, one of a number of residences where British Intelligence housed allied secret service agents, including Italians, Germans and Yugoslavs. It is claimed that Borg Pisani now started being inconsistent; while at one moment he told members of the Malta Police Criminal Investigation Department that he would be collaborating with them, a little later, in despondency, he would tell them that he did not stand a chance and that he would be executed. On 7th August, 1942, he was transferred from Sliema to Kordin Civil Prison.

On 12th November, his trial commenced before the Criminal Court, composed of the Chief Justice and President of His Majesty's Court of Appeal, Sir George Borg, and two judges, Professor Edgar Ganado and Dr William Harding. The defending counsels were Dr Alberto Magri and Dr Paul Borg Grech, a cousin of the accused.

An amendment under the Malta Defence Regulations 1939 provided for the suspension of the system of trial by jury in similar cases. The trial took place behind closed doors. As it is not possible to consult the records of criminal cases, very little is known of what was actually said in court.

Carmelo Borg (so cited in court) was charged, in Bill of Indictment No 7871, of:

Count One: Conspiring to overthrow His Majesty's Government by helping, in one way or another, His Majesty's enemies.

Count Two: Enlisting in the *San Marco* Regiment, in which he served until September 1941 and during which period he accompanied his regiment to several places occupied by Italy, among them Patras and Athens, at a time when Greece was an ally of Great Britain.

Count Three: Landing in Malta, as a *Sottotenente* in the Italian Armed Forces, on the night of 17th/18th May, 1942, with the intention of transmitting information to the enemy, a mission for which he had volunteered.

The last two counts carried the death penalty.

Witnesses for the Prosecution were Mr Joseph Axisa, the Commissioner of Police, Captain Tommy G. Warrington RAMC, Leading Aircraftman Joseph Pace RAF, the Hon Roger Castillo and George Howard, the diver who had recovered the material from the seabed. Defence counsels produced Superintendent Emanuel Calleja of the Criminal Investigation Department, Superintendent Vivian de Gray, also of the Malta Police, Legal Procurator Augusto German and Lieutenant Lamm.

On Thursday, 19th November, 1942, the court, finding Borg Pisani guilty on the three counts, sentenced him to death. A few days before the hanging was to take place, Captain Joseph Agius, the Director of Prisons, received a letter from the Governor turning down a plea for clemency, which he handed to Borg Pisani through Sergeant-Major Mifsud. Having read it, Borg Pisani burnt it. Hopes of a last-minute reprieve faded on 23rd November when the Director of Prisons, in the presence of witnesses, read out to Borg Pisani the contents of a warrant issued by Lord Gort ordering the hanging to take place between six and ten on the morning of 28th November, 1942.

During the last five days Borg Pisani met members of his family and a few close friends. At three o'clock on the morning of the day of execution he joined the attending priests in meditation and prayer. As the hour drew nearer, in conformity with local custom, hooded members of the Confraternity of the Rosary and the priests accompanied Borg Pisani from his cell to the chapel where Mass was said. The condemned man, fully resigned to his fate, retained his composure throughout. The Mass over, the sombre cortege, with Borg Pisani blind-folded and hands tied, headed towards the gibbet. The condemned mounted the steps and was led towards the spot of execution. As soon as his legs were tied, he was heard reciting the Acts of Contrition and Faith. At 7.34 on the morning of Saturday, 28th November, 1942, Carmelo Borg Pisani paid with his life for his ideals.

News of the execution reached Italy some time later through Reuter's News Agency. The front page of *La Tribuna Illustrata* of 20th December, 1942, carried a full-page coloured drawing showing Borg Pisani falling to his death from bullets of a British military firing squad; the caption stated, among other mistruths, that he shouted *Viva l'Italia* as he fell.

The Fascist Party and Press lauded the heroism of Borg Pisani, who was posthumously awarded *La Medaglia d'Oro al Valore Militare*, Italy's highest award for bravery. The academy where the Maltese student studied was renamed *La Regia Accademia di Belle Arti Borg Pisani*; squares and streets were named after him (these were changed again after the collapse of the Fascist regime) and scholarships were awarded in his memory. Mussolini also referred to him in one of his speeches and Italian schools commemorated his memory. As recently as 25th November, 1979, the *Secolo d'Italia* published an article extolling Borg Pisani's dedication to Italy.

Chapter Sixteen

Efforts to supply Malta — Gozitan contribution — Attacks on seacraft plying between Malta and Gozo — Travel restrictions — Entertainment — Malta's top fighter ace

The running of convoys to Malta was fraught with danger. Losses to ships and men continued to mount but this was a price that had to be paid. It was imperative to keep the Island supplied at all costs. Most material was delivered by sea but aircraft played a small yet important role as well.

British Overseas Airways Corporation (BOAC), then the United Kingdom's national airline, had few aircraft that could carry a reasonable load over what was considered at the time a long distance. An air link was, however, operated during the winter of 1941/42 by five Short S.30 Empire flyingboats between Poole, Lisbon, Gibraltar, Malta and Cairo. The flyingboats were so timed as to arrive at Kalafrana after dark, to refuel and take off before dawn. The risk of this route, combined with delays due to bad weather, made it uneconomical to deliver supplies to the Middle East with the result that this operation had to be terminated on 17th February, 1942.

Yet vital stores still had to be flown to Malta. This service was shared between transport aircraft of the RAF and the merchant air service. The merchantmen flew trips to the Island from east and from west; a night service was flown from Cairo three times a week and another from Britain, sometimes shuttling to Gibraltar, at whatever irregular intervals could be managed.

The service from Britain was flown by a converted military flyingboat which had been used by BOAC on the run to West Africa. She started operations during March, flying from Poole to Malta, *via* Gibraltar, with a load of six passengers and a ton of mail and freight. Then she did one shuttle from Malta to Gibraltar and back before returning to Britain. She operated in that way for several months making a turn-round at Kalafrana in a single night. During May the C.W. 20 land-plane *Saint Louis* also made occasional flights between Gibraltar and Malta, using the airfield at Luqa. She had to be unloaded, refuelled and reloaded in a single night, more often than not during air raids.

On 6th May, Lockheed Lodestars started a thrice-weekly night service from Cairo flying essential aircraft spares and ammunition to the Island, and ferrying out crews of transit aircraft whose machines had been destroyed. The loss of intermediate stops at bases along the North African coast, overtaken by Rommel's *Afrika Korps,* made this service impossible to continue. A further attempt in June and July to fly, *via* Gibraltar, Whitley Vs seconded from the RAF to BOAC and converted into freight-carriers was also discontinued because, apart from a low pay load of 1,000 lbs, local fuel supplies could not be spared for refuelling them on their outward journey.

Royal Air Force Hudsons and, later, Dakotas of No 24 Squadron based at Hendon flew 323 shuttle flights bringing in supplies *via* Cornwall and Gibraltar.

In the twelve months from October 1941 to October 1942, 133,304 lbs of freight and mail as well as 202 passengers were flown into Malta; 29,422 lbs of cargo, the greater part of it mail, and 540 passengers were flown out of the Island.

(Crown)
Map showing Axis air bases and minefields surrounding Malta.

145

The devastating blitz that ravaged Malta between March and May 1942 was not the only threat to the Island's security. The Axis had effectively mined the approaches to Malta to prevent any ships sailing to and from the Island, well aware that sooner or later another convoy would have to be sent if the Island were to hold out.

These dreaded mines were taking their toll. On 8th May, 1942, the submarine *Olympus, en route* from Malta to Gibraltar, with, on board, several crew members of other submarines sunk in Malta during April, struck a mine about five miles off the Grand Harbour; there were only nine survivors.

The local desperate situation called for drastic decisions. In June 1942, the Admiralty despatched simultaneously two convoys comprising seventeen supply ships from Gibraltar and Alexandria. A major naval and air battle raged at either side of the Mediterranean as the ships struggled to reach Malta. The six ships in Operation 'Harpoon', sailing from Gibraltar under heavy escort, were subjected to attacks by the Italian Navy and by the *Luftwaffe*. The convoy went ahead even when several of the ships and escorting vessels met their doom. On 16th June, the two surviving merchant ships, *Troilus* and *Orari*, made harbour, but not before mishap struck again. It was customary for the escorting minesweepers and those locally based to sweep a path of sea to provide a clear and safe passage to the Grand Harbour. Due to a signalling error, the two ships and their escorts passed through an unswept area. The Polish destroyer *Kujawiak* hit a mine and sank, whilst other units, including *Orari*, sustained minor damage. The two ships that made harbour brought 15,000 tons of supplies.

The other convoy sailing from the East, under the code-name Operation 'Vigorous', faced a similar onslaught from aircraft and E-boats, with the Italian Fleet steaming menacingly towards the scene. Loss and damage sustained by the eleven vessels and the escorting units in Bomb Alley, coupled with near-exhaustion of ammunition and the threat of an engagement by the Italian Navy, compelled the Commander-in-Chief to order the surviving vessels to return to Alexandria.

The disappointing outcome of the attempts to relieve Malta by sea brought the imposition of more restrictions and additional cuts in ration entitlements. Since 5th May, 1942, the rationing of bread consisted of 10½ ozs per person per day. The task of controlling the manufacture and delivery of this essential commodity fell on Mr Louis J. Degiorgio, who was appointed Bread Distribution Officer. The quality of bread, which since 22nd July, 1941, had included 20% potatoes, deteriorated further due to the high extraction rate and to the addition of maize. Mr Degiorgio had to face dwindling stocks, transport problems to deliver the commodity to the registered bread-sellers, and mounting complaints from all quarters. Moreover, as the fuel reserves diminished, he had the added responsibility of providing firewood to ensure adequate supplies to bakers.

Meals from Victory Kitchens necessarily became poorer in quality and smaller in quantity. To supplement the tiny portions, housewives scoured farmhouses in search of anything edible. A few odd potatoes or carrots or maybe a bit of pumpkin were commonly bartered for gold or silver trinkets. People living along the coast, lucky enough to own a boat, would wait for the All Clear to row out to sea to net in as many fish floating over the surface as a result of bombs falling into the sea nearby. One had to pay exorbitant prices on the black market for eggs, meat, milk and anything eatable. To some, carobs, normally used as fodder, became part of their diet.

These austere conditions provided the ideal atmosphere for pilferage. Offenders were severely dealt with as shown in the following list, taken at random from official records:

a) Joseph Ellul of Pawla was sentenced to 18 months' imprisonment with hard labour on 28th May, 1941, for stealing 3 cases of milk from premises at Marsa demolished through enemy action.

b) Carmel Abela of Zebbug was fined £20 on 6th June, 1941, for stealing 2 bars of chocolate worth 4d from s.s. *America*.

c) Anthony Saliba of Marsa, aged 12, was fined 10s on 23rd August, 1941, for stealing 2 packets of butter from a lighter.

d) Gerald Vella of Zabbar was sentenced to 10 days' imprisonment on 2nd September, 1941, for stealing 3 bars of chocolate worth 1s from a lighter.

e) Gunner Flynn, RA, was sentenced to 10 days' imprisonment on 2nd September, 1941, for stealing a tin of pears worth 1s 3d from Mifsud Verandah.

f) Pte James Bowler, Cheshire Regiment, was sentenced to 10 days' imprisonment on 1st October, 1941, for stealing 2 tins of milk from Mifsud Verandah.

g) Angelo Tabone of Qormi was sentenced to 29 days' detention on 22nd October, 1941, for stealing 2 tins of beans from s.s. *Deucalion*.

h) Nazzareno Pace of Mqabba was sentenced to 10 days' imprisonment on 14th September, 1942, for stealing 1s 4½d worth of sweets from a lighter.

i) Cpl Phillips and Sappers Hardley and Cliff RE, were sentenced to 20 days' imprisonment each on 13th October, 1942, for stealing 60 bars of chocolate, 25 packets of cigarettes and 3 bars of soap from s.s. *Brisbane Star*.

Fourteen-year-old Anthony Zammit of Marsa was charged with stealing 2½d worth of grain from Marsa Wharf; a benevolent Magistrate let him go with a stiff warning.

Equally stern measures were taken against black-marketeers or similar law-breakers; P. Farrugia, a shop-keeper from Sliema who sold leather at £2.2s.6d per rotolo and shoes for £5 a pair, was fined £800, imprisoned for 10 months and had about 1,000 rotoli of leather confiscated. A 36-year-old female Victory Kitchen Supervisor, Mary Azzopardi, was jailed for 18 months on being found guilty of forging and misusing meal tickets.

On 3rd July, 1942, Lord Gort confided to Mgr Michael Gonzi, Bishop of Gozo, the seriousness of the situation. Mgr Gonzi, who was in Malta helping the ailing Archbishop, promised his full co-operation: "The following evening I returned to Gozo; next morning, Mr George Ransley, the Commissioner for Gozo, and I visited all the farms, one by one, explaining the desperate position. All farmers agreed to hand over their stocks of wheat in an effort to save the country. When I phoned Lord Gort telling him to send two trucks to collect the wheat, he was delighted and thanked me."[118] The wheat reached Malta safely although the narrow stretch of sea dividing the two Islands was a favourite hunting-ground for German aircraft. Me 109s flying at mast-level strafed all types of light vessels ferrying supplies and passengers to and from Malta.

```
                    LIEUTENANT-GOVERNOR'S OFFICE,
                        Hamrun, 20th June, 1942.

Reverend Sir,
        It is the wish of His Excellency the Governor that
the attached notice be read during the Masses on Sunday,
June 21st. It would also be appreciated if the topic is made
the subject of an address. It is felt that many farmers
probably do not appreciate the seriousness of the present
position and will endeavour to keep livestock alive by
feeding grain which must be reserved for human consumption.
It is realised that you can play a big part in bringing the
facts before the farmer and your kind cooperation will be
much appreciated.

                        I have the honour to be,
                                Sir,
                        Your obedient servant,
                                Blahm
                        Assistant to Lieut-Governor.
```

(via J.A. Agius)

The Maltese schooner *Marie Georgette*, with twenty passengers and crew on board, was machine-gunned on 29th December, 1941, while plying to Gozo. When the skipper, Marcel Theuma, beached the burning vessel at St George's Bay, the German fighter made another pass and Theuma, mortally wounded, died at St Patrick's Military Hospital where he had been taken by servicemen and civilians who hurried to the spot to give assistance; two other crew members and a passenger were also killed. Following this tragic episode, the Authorities curtailed the movement of these unarmed vessels and maintained only a restricted passenger and cargo service.

On her arrival at Marfa with 209 passengers on Wednesday 18th March, 1942, the Malta-Gozo ferry *Royal Lady*, skippered by Anthony Gabriele, was machine-gunned by two bombers returning from a sortie over Malta. Only three persons were injured as, on sighting the intruders, the passengers scurried for shelter. *Royal Lady*, hit again on 6th May, 1942, broke in two at Mgarr, Gozo.

The local schooner *Anna Dacoutros* sank on Thursday 2nd April, 1942, on receiving a direct hit on her way to Gozo. The s.s. *Franco* was also rendered temporarily unseaworthy on 10th May, 1942, after incessant attacks.

The sturdy Gozo boats meandered through mine-infested waters; a few were sunk on hitting mines inside the Grand Harbour or between the two Islands. Some of the passenger ferries plying between Marsamxett and Sliema, and between the Customs House and Senglea and Vittoriosa, were sunk, aggravating an already-serious transport service.

The issue of petrol was restricted to route buses, which ran a restricted service lasting about two hours in the morning and three in the

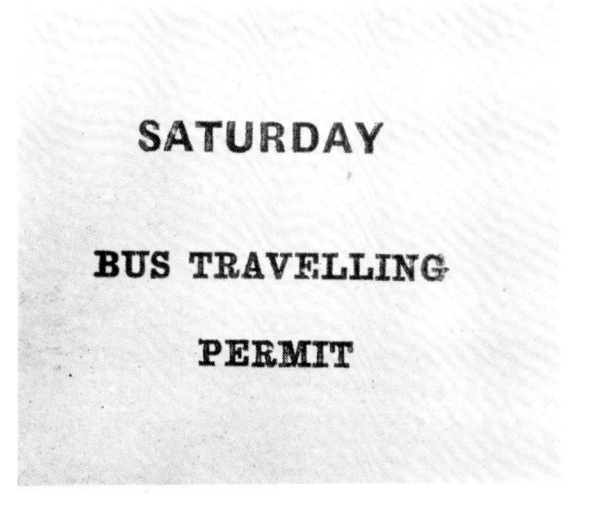

SATURDAY

BUS TRAVELLING

PERMIT

(via Ph. Vella)

(NWMA)

The broken hulk of Royal Lady *at Mgarr Harbour, Gozo, on 6th May, 1942.*

late afternoon, and to a handful of officials engaged on essential duties. Dockyard workers and civilians employed with the Services were given Travel Permits authorising them to use buses during weekends.

An added hazard to a people worn out by prolonged bombing and undernourishment, was the transfer of the bus terminus to the outskirts of the respective town or village; this fuel-economy measure had its dangers. The Valletta terminus was transferred as far out as *Porte-des-Bombes*, whilst that at Rabat was moved down the hill near the Zebbug Road, a stone's throw from the Ta' Qali perimeter. Some passengers were injured at the latter terminus when a bomb destroyed two buses. The Authorities expressed a desire that buses should continue their trips during air raids to prevent late attendance at work. Drivers, advised to use their discretion whether to continue the journey during a raid, were instructed to stop if any passenger wished to alight to take cover in any of the several caterpillar shelters constructed along some of the main roads to provide limited protection.

The curtailed public transport forced several people to take to the roads or hitch lifts from military vehicles and horse-drawn carts. Bicycles now become prized possessions, as these could easily be carried over the debris-covered streets, Lord Gort himself setting the example. Memories of a bygone era were revived with the reappearance of the omnibus on the roads. The enterprising Joseph Schembri of Hamrun refurbished the old horse-drawn carriage, which could carry from twelve to fifteen passengers on a regular shuttle-service between Valletta and Birkirkara. This mode of transport, together with the few surviving cabs, proved to be a blessing to travellers.

Frequent cuts in electricity and water supply were due to damage and economy. Relays over the local Rediffusion network were often interrupted owing to power failure and damaged cables; the voice of the announcer cutting in with "Air Raid Warning, Air Raid Warning; *Sinjal ta' attakk mill-Ajru, Sinjal ta' attakk mill-Ajru*", repeated over and over again in a monotone, had a depressing effect.

As only a few households had a wireless set, the only regular contact with the outside world was through the *Times of Malta*, the *Sunday Times of Malta* and *Il-Berqa*, which never missed an issue; for some time the edges of these newspapers were singed as the warehouse where the newsprint was stored had caught fire through bombing. Another newspaper that maintained regular publication, even if in a reduced format, was

(TheTimes) *A 'caterpillar' shelter at Floriana; Phoenicia Hotel in background.*

(L. Britton) *Schembri's Omnibus.*

O Mary conceived without sin, pray for us, who have recourse to Thee.

The people of Cospicua dispersed throughout the whole island by the cruelties of war celebrating for the first time the feast of THE IMMACULATE CONCEPTION in the Parish Church of Birkirkara humbly pray OUR LADY QUEEN OF PEACE to spread her maternal mantle over MALTA and to grant The British Empire a Victorious Peace.

8/XII/1941.

(via Mrs M. Porsella Flores)

A commemorative Holy Picture.

Lehen is-Sewwa, the official organ of the Malta Catholic Action. The *Malta Chronicle and Imperial Services Gazette*, founded in 1887, ceased publication on 4th July, 1940, 'owing to wartime difficulties of production'. The Government Information Office distributed the *Information Service Bulletin* and *Malta Review* in Maltese and English versions. These newspapers covered the local scene besides giving news from other theatres of war. Their aim was to boost morale and to inspire confidence in final victory.

Social life in Malta had for ages been centred around the parish; parochialism has always played an important part in the culture of the people and the curtailing of the *festa* in honour of the respective patron saint could not but have a disconcerting effect. This does not imply that outdoor celebrations, especially the traditional processions, were completely discontinued. A procession with a Holy Relic was held in Valletta on Monday, 4th August, 1941, on the feast of Saint Dominic. A similar procession took place in Sliema on Sunday, 23rd August, 1942, on the occasion of the feast of Our Lady Star of the Sea.

Likewise, a large number of Maltese were avid cinema-goers, perhaps due to lack of other forms of entertainment. The cinema retained its popularity, even though most of the films were old and screened throughout the Island on a roster basis. To encourage people to attend, a few of the picture-houses boasted the presence of an air raid shelter on the premises. Special shows at reduced prices were organised for servicemen. The wailing sirens and the simultaneous projecting of a notice reading 'Air Raid Warning' often sent some of the audience into the shelters, while others, slumped in their seats, kept on watching Joe E. Brown in 'Flirting with Fate' or Robertson Hare in 'Spot of Bother' or George Formby in 'Trouble Brewing'.

Three concert Parties, 'Whizz-Bangs', 'Raffians' and 'Fly Gang', gave variety shows in theatres, at the main Service halls and at lonely outposts. Except for a few professionals, most of the cast were amateurs; enthusiasm made up for lack of class. Other forms of entertainment for the Forces included boxing at the Command Fair (now the Mediterranean Conference Centre) in Valletta, concerts at the

THE "Whizz"-Bangs"
MALTA'S FRONT LINE CONCERT PARTY

(via Miss C. Ratcliffe)

British Institute in Valletta, and dances in various halls throughout the Island. Officers found relaxation at the Union Clubs in Valletta and Sliema, at Captain Caruana's and Marich's Smoking Divans and the Monico Bar in Valletta. Other ranks frequented such clubs as the Vernon (now the Central Bank), Toc H, Knights of St Columba, Under-Twenty, Connaught Home, Salvation Army and St Andrew's Hostel. Several servicemen did not miss an occasional visit down the Gut, as Strait Street in Valletta was so affectionately known, where young girls and not-so-young matrons vied with each other in entertaining their customers, especially if they happened to have a bar of chocolate, some biscuits or cigarettes.

The Royal Air Force Rest Camp at St Paul's Bay provided a haven to the tired pilots who looked forward to spending a few days of relaxation in a congenial atmosphere; there they could swim in the picturesque bay or ramble across the countryside.

The civilian population too got its restricted share of entertainment besides the cinema. Maestro Joseph Camilleri put up variety shows, comprising ballet, concerts as well as comic

```
Programme
ROYAL AIR FORCE H'QUARTERS
PRESENTS
"THE RAFFIANS"
IN THEIR 100TH PERFORMANCE IN MALTA
OUT OF THE BLUE
A MUSICAL REVUE
Devised & Produced by Sgt. DON NITHSDALE
AT THE
Manoel Theatre

UNDER THE PATRONAGE OF
Air Vice Marshal          Vice Admiral
Sir KEITH R. PARK         A. J. POWERS
K.B.E.,C.B.,M.C.,D.F.C.   C.B.,C.V.O.
Major General W.H. OXLEY, C.B.E.,M.C.

IN AID OF WAR CHARITIES.
```

(via P.G. Hewlett)

(D. Nithsdale)

ENSA (Entertainments National Service Association) eventually brought over several artists, including Noel Coward, George Formby, Gracie Fields, Tommy Trinder and Leslie Henson. Maltese film star Joseph Calleia (pictured above), who visited his native land in 1944, besides entertaining the troops, also made several appearances in local cinemas.

Maltese farmers and British soldiers sharing a happy moment.

entertainment at the Adelphi Theatre in Rabat, while the Malta Lyric Company performed at the Roxy Theatre, Birkirkara, and Levy Wine and his International Variety Revue at the Regal Theatre, Pawla. Dockyard workers improvised their own entertainment at lunch breaks for their mates and seamen from ships undergoing repair at the Yard. Enterprising ARP Superintendents, fully conscious of the need for maintaining good morale amongst the population, encouraged amateur performers in their districts to produce plays in Maltese, besides inviting regimental bands to cheer the people up. A welcome attraction in various towns and villages was the Beat Retreat by the bands of Irish or British infantry battalions, whilst the RMA, RA and KOMR bands played military marches and popular war-time tunes to large crowds.

Several families from every stratum of society extended hospitality to servicemen who, besides being separated from their dear ones, were also deprived of letters from home owing to the mail being held up or lost in transit. Many friendships were formed, quite a number of which eventually led to the altar. In spite of language problems, farmers too welcomed servicemen stationed in the vicinity of their fields and showed their friendliness in a most tangible way, sharing some of their crops, eggs and fruit.

A family that distinguished itself in entertaining the Forces was the Sciclunas. The Marquis and Marchioness opened their palatial residence at Dragonara (now the Casino) where battle-weary officers and men relaxed or refreshed themselves in luxurious reading rooms, played billiards and tennis, swam in the private pool or from the adjacent beach, or strolled along the well-laid gardens. The Marquis chatted informally with his guests, whilst the Marchioness played the piano. They also invited many convalescents from Service hospitals, who enjoyed a change from the drab wards.

As war dragged on, the aerial defence of the Island was strengthened. During June and July 1942, *Eagle* flew off 125 Spitfires of which only five failed to reach Malta. The improved situation was not restricted to numbers but also to quality. The pilots, with considerable combat experience in the Battle of Britain, came from far and wide; there were representatives from Britain, Canada, Australia, New Zealand, Rhodesia, South Africa, Free France, Belgium as well as a few Americans.

One of the pilots flown off *Eagle* on 9th June, 1942, was Sergeant Pilot George Frederick Beurling. This young Canadian, who perfected the art of aerial combat with painstaking training and persistence, brought with him a reputation for a dislike of discipline, formalities and routine. Malta, considered a "fighter pilots' paradise", offered him the ideal setting to prove his mettle. His eagle-eyed perception and exceptional deflection shooting, combined with his obsession to fly fighter aircraft, made him foremost among his fellow pilots.

Three days after joining No 249 Squadron operating from Ta' Qali, Beurling scored his first success by damaging an Me 109. Although aerial activity over Malta had temporarily abated, Beurling, who had acquired the nickname 'Screwball' for his indiscriminate use of this appellation to everyone and everything, continued to demonstrate his skill in the air and whilst on the ground, perfected his aim by shooting at stationary and moving targets. His chance came on 6th July with the reappearance in strength of the *Luftwaffe* and *Regia Aeronautica;* on that day he shot down an Me 109 and two Macchi 202s, besides damaging a Cant Z-1007. As his score mounted, he earned decorations and a commission, but disappointment awaited him at the height of brilliancy in action over Malta.

On 14th October, 1942, aircraft from his squadron took off to intercept a plot of eight Ju 88s escorted by about fifty Me 109s. Displaying skilful airmanship and superb marksmanship, he weaved his way around the intruders. After shooting down a bomber and a fighter, he sustained injuries to his hand and forearm when his cockpit was hit by a burst from one of the bombers. Taking evasive action, Beurling went to the aid of one of his colleagues who was being chased by a Messerschmitt. His enthusiasm and sense of *camaraderie* were to cost him dearly because an unsighted Me 109 riddled his Spitfire with cannon fire. The aircraft went out of control and in spite of additional injuries to his leg, heel and arm, Beurling succeeded in baling out. Picked up by an Air-Sea Rescue launch, he was taken to hospital for treatment, where news soon reached him of the award of the Distinguished Service Order in addition to his Distinguished Flying Cross, and Distinguished Flying Medal and Bar. His score over Malta totalled 26⅓ victories, making him the Island's top fighter ace. (See Appendix **P**) The concluding sentence of the DSO citation is an eloquent tribute to Beurling: "This officer's skill and daring are unexcelled."

During his convalescence at Mtarfa, Beurling reluctantly received the news of the expiration of his tour of duty at Malta. On 1st November, 1942, he was one of a number of Malta veteran pilots who were flown out in a Liberator which later crashed into the sea at Gibraltar. He survived, but several of the other pilots were killed, including Pilot Officer John W. Williams DFC and Flight Lieutenant Eric L.

(IWM)
George F. Beurling, Malta's top fighter ace.

Hetherington DFC, who had been credited with 8 and 5⅓ victories respectively over Malta. On board the aircraft there were also several civilians, including three Maltese and an English woman and two babies. Mrs Isabelle Aston, née De Domenico, one of the Maltese, and her two-year-old son, Simon, were among the fifteen victims.

The men who fought in the sky over Malta were held in high esteem by the local population; they were greeted wherever they went. People prayed for their safety as the vibrating noise of aero-engines penetrated deep down into the shelters. These daring and gallant pilots fought under conditions which taxed their stamina and morale. Notwithstanding the lapse of over forty years, Leo Nomis, an American pilot who belonged to No 71 Eagle Squadron, UK, and who later served with No 229 Squadron operating from Ta' Qali, recalls: "... In my opinion, of all the sieges during the Second World War that of Malta was the most famous and unique. ... The stories of the actions at Malta are seemingly endless and, of all my service with the RAF, the memories of those days remain the sharpest and most haunting. Perhaps it was the conditions and the atmosphere which existed in no other theatre of war. There was an aura of fatality about the Malta of those times, which one had to experience to really know. Every pilot I knew, with the exception of the then Sergeant Pilot George 'Screwball' Beurling, cursed his lot and yearned to return to the comparative luxuries of the United Kingdom. But, in retrospect, it was an experience never to be forgotten and always remembered with a certain sense of belonging to history. In short, looking back across the years, serving at Malta, in spite of the hardships, hunger and the constant presence of danger and death, is curiously one of those parts of one's life, which, if given the chance, one would do all over again." [119]

(D. Barnham)
A self-portrait of Flt Lt Denis Barnham of No 601 Squadron, author of "One Man's Window", which describes life in Malta during the spring of 1942. This pencil sketch is one of a number of illustrations in his book.

Chapter Seventeen

Air-Sea rescue operations — Projected invasion of Malta — Park succeeds Lloyd as Air Officer Commanding — First aerial hijack

Many airmen, Allied and Axis, would have perished had it not been for Malta's Air-Sea Rescue Unit. During the early stages of the war, the Unit operated three High Speed Launches, Nos 107, 124 and 224 from Kalafrana. Regardless of rough seas and enemy fighters, they set out to pick up ditched airmen; a work of mercy which did not discriminate between friend and foe.

On one occasion, Flight Lieutenant William Hardie, who commanded the Unit until October 1941, cast off in search of a British pilot whose aircraft had been shot down about fifty or sixty miles to the south-east of Malta: "Visibility was poor and we went on and on. I saw some wreckage on the horizon and we altered course; it turned out to be from an Italian troop ship. It was then that I saw a fighter pilot swimming like mad. On getting him on board, I asked 'Where are you going?', to which he replied, 'I thought I give you boys a helping hand in getting nearer to Malta.' I told him 'You were heading straight to Benghazi.' On regaining his composure, he told me that before ditching he had shot down an Italian bomber. We looked around and came across one of the plywood wings with the badly-burnt captain on it; when we picked him up, he wanted to shake hands with the boy who had shot him down. It was indeed a nice gesture but it would have done the captain's hand no good. On the way back, some twenty miles from Filfla, I noticed a rubber dinghy from which we recovered two Fleet Air Arm officers whose Swordfish had run out of fuel. I went out for one and came back with four." [120]

Flight Lieutenant Hardie was succeeded by Flight Lieutenant George R. Crockett who had at his disposal two newly-delivered HSLs 128 and 129, the veteran 107, some unarmed

(J.C. Middleton)

High Speed Launch 107 casting off from St Paul's Bay.

HSL 128 at speed. (NWMA)

seaplane tenders and an old pinnace. By the time Hardie handed over in October 1941, twenty-eight British, two German and ten Italian aircrew had already been rescued.

Soon after assuming command, Flight Lieutenant Crockett was made responsible for the combined Marine Craft and Air-Sea Rescue Units. To meet the increasing commitments, on 6th October, 1941, an ASR base was opened at St Paul's Bay, while on 11th August, 1942, a third base was set up at Sliema from where the former RASC launch *Clive* now operated as HSL 100.

The masters and crews of the HSLs were on constant call; they spent hours combing vast areas of water and doing square searches for ditched airmen. Their very existence was a morale-booster to the airmen who knew that a launch would speed to their rescue should they find themselves 'in the drink'. The humane spirit shown by the crews in risking their life to save others was not shared by some trigger-happy enemy pilots. Several of the launches were strafed, culminating in a most vicious attack on 4th February, 1942, when German fighters mauled HSL 129, killing three members of the crew and injuring two others; the skipper, Flight Lieutenant Victor A. Nicholls, succumbed to his injuries at Mtarfa three days later. Whilst the attack was in progress, Flight Lieutenant Crockett steamed out in an unarmed seaplane tender. As he jumped aboard HSL 129, he witnessed "a most sanguinary sight of wanton destruction."[121]

(J. Pritchard)
Flt Lt George R. Crockett on HSL 128. The lifebuoys painted on one of the hatches record the number of rescues.

156

(D. Morgan)

An HSL landing ashore an injured pilot.

Following this incident, Air Headquarters provided the launches with a fighter cover of Hurricanes. This protective measure was doubly welcomed by the crew of HSL 107 as this older launch could only dispose of one set of twin machine guns as against the two sets aboard HSLs 128 and 129.

Flight Lieutenant Crockett kept a detailed account of his several missions. On Monday, 18th May, 1942, he took HSL 128 out of Kalafrana at 1103 hours to look for a Spitfire pilot who had baled out a few miles off Hal Far. Due to the presence of more than thirty Messerschmitts, he had two Hurricanes as escort, with Spitfires close by flying at operational height. Some time later, an Me 109 got on the tail of a Hurricane which cartwheeled and plunged into the sea two miles ahead of the launch. During the fruitless search for the Hurricane pilot, the launch was unsuccessfully attacked by a Messerschmitt. Crockett withheld fire but the Spitfire pilots reacted, shooting down a Messerschmitt about five miles off the launch's course. Crockett had to make a decision: to continue with the search for the Spitfire pilot some miles away, to pick up the German pilot, or to return to base to seek clarification about the location of the Spitfire pilot. On weighing the situation, he decided to rescue the German first since he was closest. Within ten minutes, *Unteroffizier* Johann Lompa was hauled aboard. Though visibly relieved on being rescued so promptly, he wouldn't or couldn't give any information about the Spitfire pilot. He told a German-speaking member of the crew that they should better get back to safety as quickly as possible as he reckoned his fellow-pilots would consider the launch a legitimate target. Crockett was not to be so easily dissuaded, the more so as he reasoned that the Germans would not attempt another attack now that he had one of their pilots on board. Restarting engines, he headed further out and eight miles off Benghajsa Point found the Spitfire pilot, Pilot Officer Norman Fowlow, in his dinghy. Flight Lieutenant Crockett thus recalls what followed: "Lompa helped Fowlow over the side and then acted as mine host, welcoming him aboard with a warm handshake and generally making a fuss; for him the war was over and he bore nobody any ill-will now. In the short twenty-odd minutes it took us to run back to Kalafrana, both our passengers fell asleep, getting over the shock of having been shot out out of the sky, a shock which had affected each one in such a diverse way. HSL 128 returned to base at 1212 hours. The whole operation had taken just a little over an hour, but I am sure it was the most important hour in our Rescue Launches' history. HSL 128 had done her job without fear or favour. More important, she had been seen to do it and by more foes than friends." [122]

After three days of several missions, Crockett left base at 1504 hours on HSL 128 to investigate the report of a rubber dinghy sighted a mile off Benghajsa Point. Seventeen minutes later, the launch picked up *Unteroffizier* Gerhard Beitz who claimed that he had been paddling his dinghy towards Malta for three days. [123]

The Swordfish floatplane, engaged in rescue work since the start of hostilities, was in the early part of 1943 joined by Walrus seaplanes based at Kalafrana. Maltese civilians also put to sea in their small boats to pick up survivors. Flight Lieutenant Crockett recalls one such instance when on Saturday, 13th December, 1941, he was called out for a Blenheim which ditched close to Grand Harbour "but a Maltese *dghajsa* beat us to the rescue." [124]

The contribution and success of Malta's Air-Sea Rescue Unit was exceptionally high as shown by the following table compiled by Flight Lieutenant Crockett: [125]

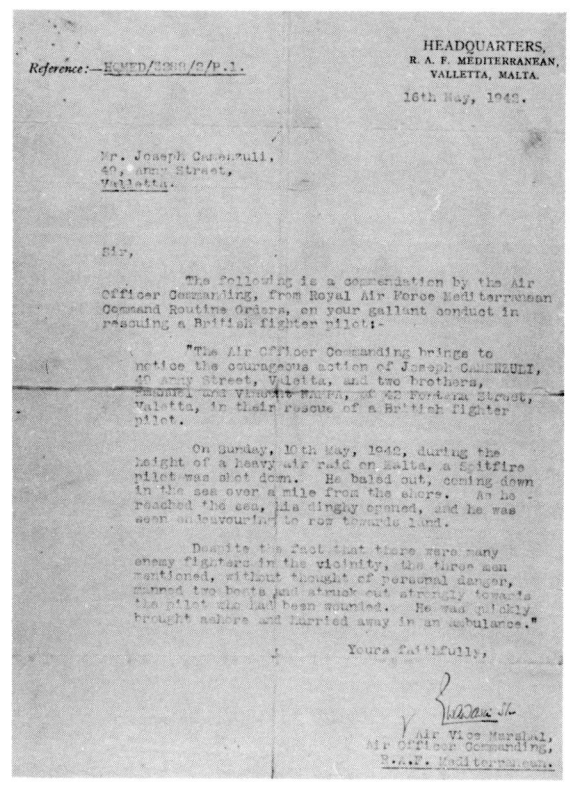

(NWMA)
Letter from Air Headquarters commending Maltese civilians on the rescue of a British pilot on 10th May, 1942.

Number of Aircrew Picked Up					
Period		British	German	Italian	Totals (alive)
Total to Oct	1941	28 (+ 4 dead)	2	10 (+ 3 dead)	40
Nov — Dec	1941	12	—	1	13
Jan — Dec	1942	85 (+ 8 dead)	32	8 (+ 2 dead)	125
Jan — Dec	1943	70 (+ 2 dead)	5 (+ 1 dead)	—	75
TOTALS		195	39	19	253 (+ 20 dead)

The best individual 'scores' for launches to the end of December 1943 were:

High Speed Launch 128: 106 aircrew rescued
High Speed Launch 107: 86 aircrew rescued
High Speed Launch 166: 25 aircrew rescued
Seaplane Tender 338: 25 aircrew rescued

The Air-Sea Rescue Unit included seventeen Maltese airmen while many other Maltese served in the Marine Craft Section seeing to the maintenance of the launches. Crockett attests to their proficiency: "HSL 128 had been knocked about more by the elements than by the enemy and my carpenters had to fit strengthening pieces in several places to keep her in a seaworthy condition. These carpenters were Maltese boat-builders and their workmanship was of the best, with generations of making and repairing their native *dghajsas* behind them. The repairs they made to launches or marine craft lasted for ever." [126]

The savage and unrelenting attacks which marked the return of the *Luftwaffe* to Sicily in December 1941 were part of the plan for the implementation of Operation *Herkules*, referred to by the Italians as *Operazione C 3: Malta*. Plans for the invasion of Malta had been worked out to the minutest detail, leaving nothing to chance; the expert advice of Japanese strategists, with their vast experience of similar operations in the Far East, was also sought. Spitfires operating photo-

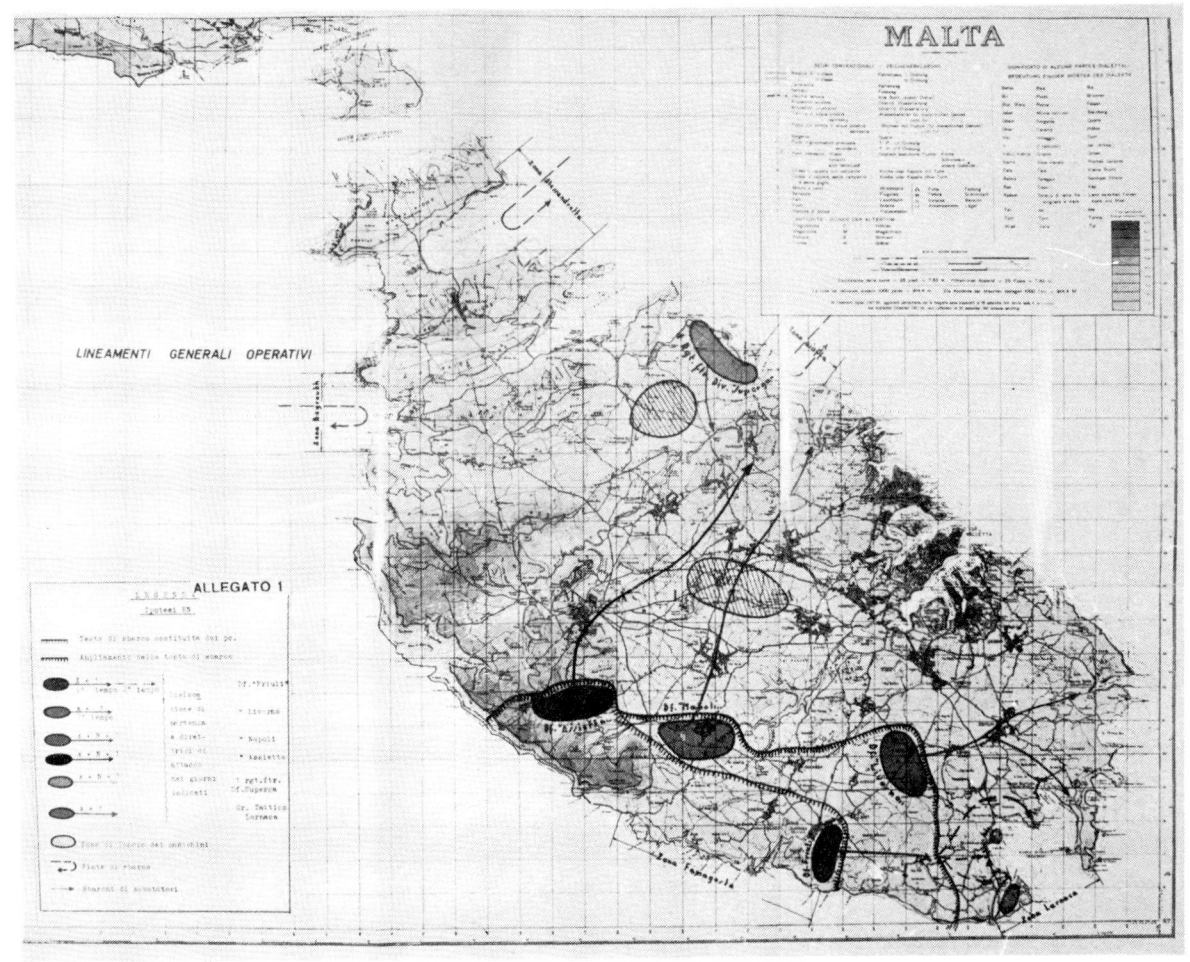

Italian map of Malta showing proposed landing sites.

reconnaissance sorties over Sicily in April 1942 showed that a 1,500-yard long and 400-yard wide airstrip for gliders had been started at Gerbini on the Catania Plain. On the basis of this information, it was assumed that the assault was imminent. By 21st April, the strip was already cut and levelled; likewise, two further strips became fully operational by 10th May. Everything was ready; landing sites were chosen and the men were assigned their roles. All that remained was agreement between Hitler and Mussolini on the date of the assault. The *Führer* continued to have his doubts and fears; distrust of the Italian Navy and the staggering losses suffered in the airborne invasion of Crete made him drag his feet in the hope that Rommel's success in North Africa would render this risky venture unnecessary.

As the two dictators and their advisers argued and counter-argued, the invasion force was kept in a state of alert. A vast concentration of men and material was poised in Italy waiting the order to launch the assault: nearly 100,000 crack Italian and German troops and an impressive array of armour, besides, of course, the Italian Navy and units of the German Navy (See Appendix **Q**). The impending action was postponed further after Rommel's capture of Tobruk on 21st June, 1942. Elated at this success and the prospect of a rapid advance into Egypt, Hitler decided to postpone indefinitely the invasion of Malta; this, however, he did not divulge to the *Duce* or anyone else except to a few of his closest confidants. In fact, in July, *Feldmarschall* Albert Kesselring and *General* Kurt Student advised: *Malta ist sturmrief* (Malta is ripe for the assault). Kesselring, however, soon became aware of Hitler's intentions: "Subsequently Hitler was certainly happy that the victory at Tobruk gave him an excuse to call off the distasteful Malta venture without loss of face. In this he found a loyal yes-man in Goering. Goering was afraid of a second costly 'Crete with gigantic casualties', although the two operations were in no way comparable. I told him Malta could be occupied with a minimum

159

of forces and of losses, and that the effort required, if we postponed the assault till later, would be much greater and more wasteful. Meanwhile on the Italian side the *Comando Supremo* had to contend with the renewed hesitancy of the *Supermarina*. Operation Malta was shelved."[127] Officially, Operation *Herkules* was set aside in August 1942; in fact, it became impracticable when, soon after the fall of Tobruk, some of the men and material earmarked for the assault on Malta were transferred to reinforce Rommel's *Afrika Korps* advancing towards the Nile, only to be stopped at El Alamein by the British Eighth Army. The invasion of Malta failed to materialise. Kesserling laments this in no indisputable terms, attributing it to two main facts: "Italy's missing her chance to occupy Malta at the start of hostilities will go down in history as a fundamental blunder ... and that the deliberate refusal to repair the first mistake was the second fundamental strategic error which placed the Mediterranean Command at a decisive disadvantage."[128]

Malta, however took no chances. A state of alert was maintained and, as late as 26th June, 1943, the Manager of the Telephone Department issued a 'Most Secret' circular entitled "Action Instructions to Operators in the Event of Invasion or Attempted Invasion of the Island by the Enemy." *Inter alia*, this sealed circular, bearing reference number TD 374/41, stated: "This envelope contains lists of certain Civil Officers to be informed of occurrences connected with the above emergency and indicating the action to be taken by Telephone Operators at the Valletta and Central Exchanges.

"The necessary information will be passed by means of the agreed code words ONLY, namely:-

(a) VOLCANO — meaning 'You are to take up the position allotted to you in the Emergency Scheme immediately'. This is passed to subscribers on List 'A'.

(b) CYCLONE — meaning 'Movement of Civil Officers without the permission of the Military Authorities is now to cease'. This is passed to subscribers on List 'B'.

The particular code word to be passed will be notified to the Valletta Exchange by the Lieutenant Governor's Office, probably by the Lieutenant Governor personally. ... Code-word calls will receive priority over all other calls."[129]

It is still highly speculative what would have happened had an invasion been attempted. Kesselring's views have already been recorded. On the British side, opinions vary. Whereas some maintain that Malta would have withstood any assault, others are more guarded

(via J.A. Agius)

Sir Keith R. Park.

in their views. Brigadier Kenneth P. Smith, Commander 1st (Malta) Infantry Brigade at that crucial period, gives a hypothetical assessment. The garrison, in his opinion, was confident of defeating an airborne or paratroop invasion alone, but if this had to be carried out in conjunction with a seaborne assault, the defences of Malta might have been overwhelmed by sheer weight of numbers and equipment.[130]

On 14th July, 1942, Air Vice-Marshal Hugh Pughe Lloyd was succeeded by Air Vice-Marshal Keith Rodney Park, a New Zealander, as Air Officer Commanding. Lloyd was a highly competent commander, admired for his skill and respected for his tact. His brilliant leadership was an inspiration to the pilots and the ground-crews who, as a team, kept the airfields operational despite constant hammering, causing discomfort to the enemy. His successor brought with him the experience gained during the Battle of Britain, in which he distinguished himself as AOC 11 Group. His 'Forward Interception' plan aimed at meeting

(via D. Armour)
The Beaufort and Cant crews posing for a photograph on 29th July, 1942, before going their different way. Left to right: Plt Off W. Dunsmore RAF, Italian corporal, Italian flight engineer, Lt E.T. Strever SAAF, Italian second pilot, Sgt J. Wilkinson RNZAF, Tenente Pilota *Mastrodicasa, Sgt A.R. Brown RNZAF and Italian wireless operator.*

the German bombers before reaching the Island; a plan that was to achieve considerable success. Malta-based aircraft carried out bombing and torpedo-bombing attacks on Axis bases and shipping spread as far afield as Sardinia and Crete. One such sortie took place on 28th July, 1942, when a Beaufort of No 217 Squadron attacked an Italian merchant vessel off the coast of Southern Greece; the mission, one of ordinary routine, had a dramatic sequel. An escorting destroyer hit the British aircraft, which ditched; the crew took to their dinghy. The captain was Lieutenant Edward T. Strever SAAF of Klerksdorp, South Africa; the others were Pilot Officer W.M. Dunsmore RAF of Maghull near Liverpool, Sergeant J.A. Wilkinson RNZAF of Auckland and Sergeant A.R. Brown RNZAF of Timaru. On being picked up by an Italian floatplane, they were taken to Préveza in Greece, where they were detained but given warm hospitality by the Italians. The following morning they were taken aboard Cant-Z 506 B Serial No MM45432, belonging to 139ª *Squadriglia Ricognizione Marittima*, bound for Taranto for interrogation and imprisonment. *Tenente Pilota* Mastrodicasa piloted the floatplane which had

a second pilot, an engineer and a wireless operator/observer, besides a *carabiniere* as an armed escort. The prisoners, not relishing the prospect of confinement 'for the duration' and encouraged by the fact that the escort was airsick, managed to overpower and disarm the Italians. As soon as the Sicilian coast was sighted they changed course towards Malta, without the aid of charts and chancing the fuel situation. On approaching the Island, they were set upon by Spitfires that kept firing despite Dunsmore's waving of his white vest as a sign of surrender. To avoid being shot down, Strever ordered the Italian pilot to touch down off the coast; as the floatplane did so, the engines running out of fuel, cut out.

Flying Officer J.S. Houghton, who at different times commanded Air-Sea Rescue High Speed Launches 100, 107 and 128 at Kalafrana, St Paul's Bay and Sliema, relates: "The Cant, forced down by Spitfires halfway between Sliema and St Paul's Bay, about two miles off shore, was towed by HSL 107 to St Paul's Island. It was then passed over to our Seaplane Tender and taken to a buoy off St Paul's Pier, where the five Italians and four Commonwealth airmen were taken ashore. A very strong army guard was provided to prevent the locals from attacking the Italians. The South African captain, who had led the hijack, brandished his revolver, leaving no doubt as to what he would have done if the Italians had been harmed. After the airmen had been taken away, I went aboard the Cant and found two suitcases full of Italian money. The next day, our Seaplane Tender towed the Cant to the Grand Harbour for examination."[131] It then took off, making a good touch-down at Kalafrana, where, on 31st July, British markings were painted over the Italian ones. The Royal Air Force had intended to use the captured floatplane on air-sea rescue work but its unmistakable design would have caught the attention of Spitfires; it left Malta shortly afterwards.

Chapter Eighteen

The Santa Marija *convoy — Malta Convoy Fund — Malta and the Desert Campaign — Failure of the October Blitz — Shortage of essential commodities — Lifting of the siege*

The deteriorating situation persisted, since the June 1942 convoys failed to replenish the Island's needs. The build-up of German and Italian aircraft in Sardinia and Sicily, added to the hazards from surface craft and submarines, rendered the passage of another convoy a most risky undertaking. But the risk had to be taken, as Malta's loss would have denied the Allies of a staging post to the Middle East, jeopardized the fate of the British Army fighting in North Africa, and turned the Mediterranean into an Axis lake. Operation 'Pedestal' was planned against this dismal background; it was a determined effort to fight a convoy through to the Island which was on the verge of surrender. Fourteen fast vessels, including the American tanker *Ohio*, under a heavy escort provided by warships from the Home Fleet, entered the Mediterranean on the night of 10th August, 1942. The Commodore of the convoy, officially called 'WS 21S', was Commander A.G. Venables RN (Retired) on *Port Chalmers*. The scene was set for one of the most daring and dramatic actions of the Second World War. Protecting the vessels, the Royal Navy had the three aircraft-carriers *Eagle*, *Victorious* and *Indomitable* (with their 72 fighters), *Furious* which flew off 38 Spitfires to Malta and left the convoy, the battleships *Nelson* and *Rodney*, besides seven cruisers, thirty-two destroyers, eight submarines and other units. (See Appendix R)

On reaching the Sicilian Narrows, the main escorting force, under Vice-Admiral Neville Syfret, was to withdraw to Gibraltar, leaving four cruisers and twelve destroyers, under Rear-Admiral Harold Burrough, to accompany the merchant ships to Malta. To meet this formidable force, the Axis had eighteen Italian

(US Coast Guard)

Ohio *leaving the United States of America in January 1942.*

(via F.W. Dawe)

Eagle's last moments.

and two German submarines, nineteen motor torpedo-boats and over 850 aircraft, comprising bombers, torpedo-bombers and fighters. In addition, six cruisers and eleven destroyers were detailed to intercept the convoy, whilst a fresh minefield was laid off Cape Bon across the convoy's path. The first blow was struck on 11th August when *Leutnant* Helmut Rosenbaum on German submarine U-73, skifully avoiding a screen of destroyers escorting *Eagle*, sent four torpedoes into the carrier, sinking her in eight minutes with the loss of 230 of her crew. For the following three days, the ships and escorts were subjected to an onslaught from the air, the sea and underwater; this went on round-the-clock, but the ships sailed on steadily towards Malta. Many of them, however, were not destined to make port as the enemy unleashed a savage assault that sent precious cargo and life down to the sea bottom.

The successful use by the *Luftwaffe* of the He 111s as torpedo-bombers was supplemented by the launching of some new and experimental missiles by the *Regia Aeronautica*. It is recorded that at 1240 hours on 12th August, the convoy was attacked by ten S.84s of 38° *Gruppo* 32° *Stormo* BT, each carrying two *FFF motobombe*. These missiles were equipped with a detachable parachute and a motorised propeller giving them a spiral trajectory; they could reach a speed of 15 km in the water. On the same day, *Maresciallo* Mario Badii, piloting a S.79 carrying 1,000 kg of explosive, took off from Villacidro. On reaching height, he baled out and the aircraft was then radio-controlled towards the British naval formation by a Cant-Z.1007 *bis*, aboard which was *Generale* Ferdinando Raffaelli, the mind behind this type of 'flying bomb'. However, after covering about 200 km, the S.79 developed a fault in the radio-control apparatus; it flew out of control and crashed on the mountains at Khenchela near Constantine in the Algerian hinterland. [132]

Port Chalmers had a lucky escape as related by her master, Captain Henry Pinkney: "We were being attacked by aircraft, submarines and E-boats. A torpedo-bomber came in at us and I saw the track of the torpedo coming straight for and right up to the ship. Then I saw the paravane tow-wire behaving strangely. We hauled it in and as the paravane came out of the water there, entangled in the wire, was a whacking big torpedo. We cut the whole lot adrift, paravane and all. The torpedo went straight to the bottom in about 400 fathoms, and in about half a minute there was a big explosion which shook us pretty badly." [133]

On the 12th at noon, *Deucalion* was damaged by torpedo-bombers and was later sunk; that afternoon Stukas damaged the carrier *Indomitable* and sank the destroyer *Foresight*. With the approach of dusk, Italian submarines joined the fray and *Axum* fired three torpedoes, hitting the cruisers *Nigeria* and *Cairo*, and the tanker *Ohio*. The convoy plodded on and more ships were either hit or sunk; *Empire Hope* and *Clan Ferguson* were lost, whilst bombers hit the

(Cunard)
The tow-wire that saved Port Chalmers. *This photograph, taken by a crew member, shows the 21-inch torpedo and the paravane moments before they were cut loose.*

cruiser *Kenya*, the merchant ship *Brisbane Star* and the tanker *Ohio*.

At dawn on the 13th, the torpedo-bombers, Ju 87s, Ju 88s and the submarines were joined by E-boats from Trapani as the ships approached the Sicilian Straits; the American supply ships *Almeria Lykes* and *Santa Elisa*, and the British *Wairangi* and *Glenorchy* were sunk by torpedoes from these craft. These staggering blows threw the ships into confusion as they strayed to avoid the attacks, some going up in flames and others experiencing a slow, agonizing end. The destroyers were in constant action, one moment protecting the ships and at the next heaving towards stricken vessels to rescue men from the sea, patches of which were ablaze with burning oil. The E-boats caused further punishment with the immobilisation, and eventual loss, of the cruiser *Manchester* and damage to *Rochester Castle*. At 8.00 am, twelve Ju 88s attacked the surviving vessels; *Waimarama* became a mass of fire as bombs hit the hold containing aviation fuel. Burning debris from this ship fell on *Melbourne Star* and the struggling *Ohio*. As *Waimarama* sank, flames from burning fuel spread on the surface and billowed high into the sky. The handful of survivors, who jumped or were thrown overboard by the explosion, were doomed. They could hardly believe their eyes on seeing HMS *Ledbury*, under the intrepid command of Lieutenant-Commander Roger Hill, steaming right through the flames to snatch them from certain death. Admiral Sir Richard Onslow KCB DSO and three Bars, described that action as the bravest he had seen in all his years at sea.[134]

The trials of *Ohio* were by no means over; during an attack by Italian-manned Stukas, one aircraft was shot down by Spitfires and another hit by gunfire; parts of this crashed on the deck of the tanker, starting yet another fire. Still *Ohio* steamed on, stalled and sailed again.

At this stage of unrelenting battle, fate came to the aid of the battered ships. The German and Italian Air Forces, disappointed at their failure to annihilate the entire expedition, were resolved to finish their task with an all-out effort. To achieve this, they needed all the aircraft at their disposal; none could, therefore, be spared to protect the Italian naval squadron.

Deprived of fighter cover, the Italian ships were consequently withdrawn just before engaging the convoy. This decision reflected the lack of trust and co-operation between the Italian Air Force and Navy. The resulting failure of the Italian Navy to deal a death-blow to the remaining ships virtually saved Malta.

To add to the humiliation of the Italian Navy, the Malta-based submarine *Unbroken*, under the command of Lieutenant Alastair Mars, intercepted the retreating squadron. Mars fired four torpedoes which immobilised the cruisers *Bolzano* and *Attendolo*.

More aerial attacks, however, wrought added havoc. *Rochester Castle*, *Port Chalmers*, *Dorset*, *Brisbane Star*, *Melbourne Star* and *Ohio* received further punishment; finally *Dorset* went down following an attack by Stukas — the last ship to be sunk when almost within sight of Malta.

During the afternoon of the 13th, *Port Chalmers*, *Rochester Castle* and *Melbourne Star* appeared on the horizon. People danced and sang in the streets; "some felt like swimming towards the horizon to assist the limping ships into the Grand Harbour."[135] As the battle-scarred vessels slid between the arms of the breakwater, the sound of the band of the Royal Malta Artillery, playing from the ramparts of Fort St Elmo, was drowned by cheering people cramming every vantage point around the harbour area; their delirious welcome exploded into a frenzy of wild excitement as each of the three ships sailed past. The handkerchiefs, brought out to express unbound joy, were used to wipe many a tear.

(IWM)

Dorset, *which survived this attack, later sank.*

(IWM)

Soldiers at Fort St Elmo welcoming Port Chalmers *into harbour.*

(via G.E. Fanthorpe)
Burning fuel marks the spot where Waimarama *went down. At right, a destroyer is seen steaming towards the blaze to pick up survivors.*

Whilst the people celebrated and rejoiced, two other ships, *Brisbane Star* and *Ohio*, were still at the mercy of a foe determined on their destruction. The former arrived to another wild welcome on the 14th, but there was still no sign of *Ohio* carrying vital fuel, oil and kerosene, without which Malta could not survive.

The sturdy American tanker, manned by a British crew, was lying crippled and smouldering some miles off Malta. Throughout the journey, she had been singled out for ferocious attack by all means at the enemy's disposal. She was torpedoed and holed; several fires were started; her boilers blew up and her engines failed. She was twice abandoned and twice reboarded. Repeated attempts to take her in tow failed, but the tanker would not sink as if aware that Malta's survival depended on her. The ship's resistance was equalled by the prowess of British seamen, who, with no time for rest or food, manned the crippled ship, now out of control. As the tanker came within the protection of Malta's fighters and minesweepers, a desperate effort was made to salvage the slowly sinking vessel. The Royal Navy undertook the herculean task of leading the tanker towards Malta. The destroyers *Bramham* and *Penn* were towing alongside, lashed against the hulk of the tanker, whilst *Ledbury* acted as an emergency rudder to prevent *Ohio* going round in circles. These gallant little ships were joined by the minesweeper *Rye* despatched from Malta to tow ahead. The Stukas did not fail to carry out another attack but were beaten off by gunfire from the destroyers. Three more minesweepers, *Speedy*, *Hebe* and *Hythe*, were sent out from Malta to shield the other units as *Ohio* inched her way towards Malta.

A hidden obstacle, in the form of a minefield, lay ahead. Lieutenant-Commander Hill of *Ledbury* distinguished himself again when he averted a catastrophe by edging the tanker clear of the danger zone.

Early on the morning of 15th August, *Ohio*, with decks almost awash, was literally carried into the Grand Harbour. A scene of mass hysteria, as the Maltese thronged the bastions, rooftops and the Barraccas shouting themselves hoarse and weeping with joy, greeted the gallant ship as she was slowly manoeuvred alongside the sunken hulk of the Royal Fleet Auxiliary *Plumleaf* at Parlatorio Wharf in French Creek.[136]

(IWM)

The destroyers Bramham *(right) and* Penn *supporting* Ohio *inside the Grand Harbour.*

(NWMA)

HMS Rodney *engaging enemy aircraft with her 16-inch guns at 1242 hours on 12th August, 1942.*

Unloading Rochester Castle.

The *Ohio* saga has become a legend. It is recorded that the crew had been taken off the ship by the destroyers *Bramham* and *Penn* as, at one stage, it looked as if the tanker was about to sink. She was then reboarded by Royal Navy personnel and by some of her own crew led by Captain Mason. The presence of naval personnel on board the tanker is confirmed by Admiral of the Fleet the Earl Mountbatten of Burma, who later wrote that his nephew, David, Third Marquess of Milford Haven, then serving as a lieutenant on HMS *Bramham*, was actually on board the *Ohio* at the moment of bringing her into Malta Harbour.[137]

The seamen who sailed in 'Pedestal' will never forget the convoy experience. The horrifying scenes depicted in films, books and in the Press give some indication of the five-day drama in the Central Mediterranean. Frederick Treves, a Junior Apprentice on *Waimarama*, recounts: "I was then very young and extremely frightened. The attacks were terrifying; I cannot think of another word. The worst for me were the Stukas; their sirens made a most appalling noise. The sky was absolutely mottled with flak from the ships; *Rodney* and *Nelson*, for the first time in history, fired their 16-inch guns at their highest angle possible, but they were really bombardment guns, not anti-aircraft, and nothing had ever been seen like it. The destroyers too were simply remarkable. To me, the worst sight of all was seeing *Eagle* go down, because you could see both planes and men sliding into the sea; you could actually hear the screams and yells ... At night, the E-boats started up and blew up a number of ships ... It was extremely frightening; no, it was not frightening, it was terror, absolute terror. Four bombs hit *Waimarama* at 8 o'clock on the 13th; I was blown, quite miraculously, onto some bags of lime while another man fell on top of me. I thought I was actually dying but I kept remarkably peaceful ... I saw all the smoke and decided to dive over the side. The ship, with smoke about 6,000 feet high, sank in about two minutes. Half of the crew of the vessel behind us abandoned ship because they thought they had been hit. The aircraft following the Ju 88 that bombed us blew up in mid-air from our ship's explosion. I think about nineteen crew members were saved and maybe over a hundred died ... Commissioned Gunner C. Musham from the destroyer *Ledbury*, an extremely brave man, came out in a wooden boat and I was picked up in the second round. He came back and picked a lot of us, despite the flames. The Germans were by then machine-gunning us and dropping mines all round *Ledbury* to try to get her away or hit her. They did not succeed and that's how we were picked up. I suppose I was in the water for about an hour..."[138]

Malta could breathe again; although 53,000 of the 85,000 tons of supplies loaded at the Clyde in Scotland finished at the bottom of the Mediterranean, the remaining 32,000 tons enabled Malta to stave off the dreaded Harvest Day, commonly referred to as Target Date. Troops and policemen were once again roped in to assist the stevedores in Operation 'Ceres', involving the quick unloading and safe-storage of the cargo, an operation completed by 22nd August.

Frank S. Hewlett, a crew member of *Ledbury*, recounts a simple story bringing out the human element and highlighting the bonds of friendship between the Royal Navy and the Maltese: "... We remained in Malta, anchored off Senglea, for about ten days. I happened to come into the Mess one afternoon for the usual mug of tea and was surprised to see two members of the Royal Malta Artillery sitting at the Mess table. I was hailed by one of the shipmates with 'Here is Lofty the pipe-smoker'. Although the two gunners had already been supplied with a quantity of cigarettes, one of them yearned for some decent pipe tobacco; I handed him my pouch. Remembering I had made up a perique approximately two months previously, I went to my locker and cut the perique in half and handed it to him saying 'Here you are, Tommy, there's about six ounces of good leaf tobacco there and, if you go carefully, it should last until the siege is lifted'. He wanted to pay for it but as leaf tobacco was only 1s 6d a pound, I would not accept a penny. I felt rather embarrassed on seeing him almost in tears; after all, we had only been under intensive attack for five days or so, whilst the inhabitants of Malta had been sticking it out for two years. Before we sailed from Malta, *Ledbury*, *Bramham* and *Penn* landed their stores of food, with the exception of two days' rations, and all their NAAFI supplies, and delivered them to Fort St Angelo. Just a drop of water in the ocean, but a token of the respect the Navy felt for those they would leave behind on the Island Fortress of Malta."[139]

The masters and ships that reached Malta have earned themselves a place in maritime history: Captain Richard Wren of *Rochester Castle*, Captain David Macfarlane of *Melbourne Star*, Captain Henry Pinkney of *Port Chalmers*, Captain Frederick Riley of *Brisbane Star* and Captain Dudley Mason of *Ohio*, who was awarded the George Cross. Operation 'Pedestal' was concluded on 15th August, the feast of the Assumption. Ever since, the magnificent saga has been known in Malta as *Il-Convoy ta' Santa Marija*, since the feast of the Assumption is locally known as *Santa Marija*. Churchill sums up the operation: "Thus in the end five gallant merchant ships out of fourteen got through with their precious cargoes. The loss of three hundred and fifty officers and men and of so many of the finest ships in the Merchant Navy and in the escorting fleet of the Royal Navy was grievous. The reward justified the price exacted. Revictualled and replenished with ammunition and vital stores, the strength of Malta revived."[140]

The arrival of the five ships was hailed as a triumph. The British Press praised the Merchant and Royal Navies on their achievement, even though the losses were high. The Maltese rose to the occasion. The masters and the crews found warm hospitality from the population. Lord Gort received them at San Anton Palace, whilst they were entertained by several clubs, institutions and private families. The masters and officers of the five ships were invited to a luncheon at the *Casino Maltese* on 4th September and, five days later, the Business and Mercantile Community of Malta held a function at the Roxy Theatre in Birkirkara, during which the masters were presented with a silver model of a Gozo boat and a silver watch inscribed "For Valour and Devotion to Duty, Malta Convoy, August 1942". The officers were offered temporary membership of the exclusive Union Clubs in Valletta and Sliema, while the Vernon, Toc H, the Knights of St Columba Hostel, Under Twenty, Connaught Home and Salvation Army placed all facilities at the disposal of the ratings. The "Raffians" gave a special performance in their honour at the Manoel Theatre in Valletta, let free by Captain Godfrey Caruana. The Management of the theatre and nearly all cinemas on the Island offered them a large number of complimentary tickets. A simple gesture of appreciation, which drew the admiration of the Command Welfare Officer, was that made by G.M. Bonello, a barber from St Julian's who gave his services free to all the men accommodated at the Toc H and in the vicinity.

Labels fixed on cargo delivered by convoys.
(via Ph. Vella)

The sense of generosity and appreciation was, however, best shown when on 21st August, 1942, the *Times of Malta* launched the 'Malta Convoy Fund', for the dependants of seamen who had lost their life in Operation 'Pedestal'. Subscriptions, big and small, poured in from every town and village, regiment and platoon. When the Fund closed on 12th October, the sum of £7,525.15s had been received by Mr Joseph Cassar, Honorary Treasurer of the Anglo-Maltese League. Following consultations between the sponsors and the British Sailors' Society, it was agreed to allot £1,000 to the Society's Samaritan Fund, with the balance being invested in the Prince of Wales Sea Training Hostel for the sons of seamen lost in the August convoy.

A few days before the Fund closed, Major-General C.T. Beckett, Commander Royal Artillery Malta, wrote to draw the sponsors' attention "to the presence on board these valiant ships, and sailing under the Masters' orders, of detachments of the Maritime Regiment of the Royal Regiment of Artillery. These detachments man the Light Anti-Aircraft guns and by their presence did much to drive away and bring to disaster the enemy air attack. Of the gallant Company that sailed with the Malta Convoy there were many who, with their ships and with the ship's company besides whom they fought, made the supreme sacrifice. They should not be forgotten, nor should their dependants be forgotten, in the midst of Malta's generosity." This justified appeal necessitated the re-allotment of the Fund as under:

To Prince of Wales Sea Training Hostel	£5,525.15s
To Samaritan Fund	£1,000
To Royal Artillery Benevolent Fund	£1,000

When the enthusiasm had abated, Operation 'Pedestal' caused some boat-rocking of a different nature. Frederick Treves kept a diary from the time he had joined *Waimarama* at Birkenhead; he noted that the packing cases marked MALTA, lying on the quay before loading, were visible to one and all. On his return to Britain, he remarked on this lapse of basic security and Admiral of the Fleet The Earl of Cork and Orrery, and Admiral Lord Chatfield took the matter up. It was on the evidence of Mr Treves' diary that Mr Justice Tucker held an inquiry on behalf of the British Government which resulted in the alteration of the coding of material shipped by convoys.[141]

Besides delivering badly-needed supplies, the arrival of the convoy was a morale booster, as the civilians and garrison realised that they were not cut off from the rest of the Allied world; however, this did not mark the end of the siege. The period of most stringent rationing was August to November 1942; at this time it

Message of appreciation from Captain Richard Wren of Rochester Castle *to Customs and Excise Officer Oreste Vella.*
(Ph. Vella)

Explanation of Amount of the accompanying Payable Order in favour of Messrs. John P. Kippin

If any enquiry respecting this payment is necessary, please quote the No. and Date of the Payable Order and return this form to the Director of Navy Accounts, ADMIRALTY, BATH.

	£	s.	d.	
P/JX. 182272. O/Sea.	2	12	6	Award for assistance rendered to SS "Ohio" by HMS "Bramham" on 13-15/8/42. S.1586A is returned herewith.

(J.P. Kippin)

Seamen on destroyers that towed Ohio to Malta were subsequently awarded salvage money.

was practically impossible to obtain anything but a few vegetables in addition to the rationed commodities.[142]

Cigarette-smokers took a deep breath when, on 30th October, 1942, after many months of enforced abstinence, an issue of 30 cigarettes a week was introduced on a ration basis, to be increased to 50 with effect from 15th January, 1943.

The aviation fuel delivered by 'Pedestal' enabled the Royal Air Force to intensify operations. During July and August 1942, one hundred and twenty-five Spitfires reached Malta, to be followed by Beaufighters and Wellingtons. Together with locally-based submarines, they launched a fierce offensive, hitting the enemy at its sorest spot, the supply of Rommel's *Afrika Korps*.

The North African campaign was very closely related to Malta's fate throughout its entire course. During April and May 1942, Mr Churchill and General Claude Auchinleck, then C-in-C Middle East, held conflicting views about military strategy involving Malta. The British Prime Minister insisted on launching an offensive in the Desert, aimed at regaining possession of airfields in Western Cyrenaica so as to provide fighter cover to another Malta convoy; Auchinleck was more intent upon making a defensive stand in the Desert and sending considerable reinforcements to India. After consulting the Chiefs of Staff, the Defence Committee and the War Cabinet, Mr Churchill informed General Auchinleck that "the loss of Malta would be a disaster of the first magnitude, and probably fatal in the long run to the defence of the Nile Valley. ... We are determined that Malta shall not be allowed to fall without a battle being fought by your whole army for its retention." He, therefore, pressed for action and even threatened Auchinleck with being relieved of his command unless an offensive was launched to provide a distraction, facilitating the passage of a convoy to Malta in the dark of the moon period in mid-June. In his memoirs, Churchill remarked that this attitude towards a high military commander was most unusual.

The heroic resistance of the Maltese people was given wide publicity in the overseas Press. On 5th April, 1942, *London Calling*, under the heading 'Gallant Malta', reprinted a tribute to the Island which naval commentator Commander Anthony Kimmins RN had broadcast some time previously on the Home Service of the British Broadcasting Corporation: "... Never before in history have human beings endured or survived such attack. Yet life goes on; schools are open, bands play amidst the rubble and people listen in the sun; makeshift shops appear from the ruins. The daily papers make their regular appearances, but nowadays there's little gossip or difference of opinion to swell the columns; the people are too united in one thought. And through it all, no sign of panic disfigures the dignity of Malta. I have heard people say 'Poor Malta'. I never heard such insulting nonsense. 'Precarious Malta', possibly. 'Proud Malta', yes. 'Gallant Malta', every time. But 'Poor Malta', never."

Across the ocean, a merited tribute to dockyard workers appeared in the 4th May, 1942 issue of *Life* magazine: " ... Generally, Malta's morale appears good. Maltese dockyard workers, for instance, know that the harbor area is the hottest spot on the Island, but they come to work day after day. They prudently retire to nearby shelters when raiders are

(Reprinted by permission from TIME, The Weekly Newsmagazine; Copyright Time Inc. 1942)

overhead, but they make up most of the lost time by fast work between bombing. Malta may fall, but it has already done its job. It has written one of the great unsung epics of this war ..." Furthermore, the cover and main feature in *Time* Newsmagazine of 26th October, 1942, were dedicated to Malta: "... This week Malta still stood, battered and bloody, with guns and planes ready for the next Axis raid. No spot in the wide world has taken such sustained and savage bombing. To defend it, the British have paid dearly. But they still cling. If the world wonders, the British have a twofold answer. Malta is worth the price for strategic reasons. Sixty miles from Sicily, the Island is a constant menace to Axis supply routes in the Mediterranean. She is a base for British submarines. She is a potential base for an attack on southern Europe. And deeper than practical reasons, she has become Britain's symbol of resistance, as Stalingrad and Bataan became symbols of valor to Britain's allies ... The native Royal Malta Artillery and the Royal Artillery raised a curtain of flame that was fearful to behold. Even Moscow never lifted such an ack-ack barrage. Captured German pilots admitted that they had been unnerved by it. It probably saved the Island from devastation, saved many a British warship and transport as she lay in the harbors or squatted helplessly in drydock. ... Remarkable was the stoicism of the civilians. In the most perilous areas near dockyards and airdromes, families took up permanent dwelling in the rock shelters. Between attacks, between clearing the rubble and recovering bodies after the raids, the Islanders excavated more holes in which they could crawl. But Malta's peril is not ended; rather it has been enhanced. The stronger she becomes, the more the Axis is determined to flatten her into the sea. Today the center of Valletta is a ruin. ... Stoically the Maltese burrowed into their ancient Island. Grimly, for the power and the glory and for Christendom, the Island of the Knights fought on."

In the autumn of 1942, the *Afrika Korps* and the Eighth Army were building up their respective strength for the offensive; Malta's main role remained the harassment of sea and air transport destined for North Africa. The Eighth Army broke out of El Alamein on 23rd October, 1942, and *Feldmarschall* Erwin Rommel had to leave hospital in Germany to take personal command in an effort to contain the British offensive. The Axis received another blow on 8th November, when Allied armies landed in French North Africa, waging a fierce battle simultaneously on two fronts. Now more than ever before, the Axis regretted their blunder in not having invaded Malta. The tide had turned and such an undertaking was now unfeasible. Instead, a final attempt was made in October to subdue Malta's striking power.

The Italo-German offensive started on the 10th of the month with a sharp increase in the number of raids, mainly aimed at the airfields. The Island was now armed to its teeth, with morale at its highest. The fighters and gunners mauled the Junkers, Cants, Messerschmitts, Macchis and Reggianes that hurled themselves in a desperate bid to obliterate Malta's airfields. They failed and *Generale* Giuseppe Santoro admits that no airfield was put out of action for more than half an hour, and that, at the height of the October Blitz, it was only for one single night that aircraft from Malta could not attack Italian naval traffic. *Feldmarschall* Kesselring too had confided to *Maresciallo* Ugo Cavallero, Chief of the Italian General Staff, that any German airman, daily engaged in more than one risky sortie over Malta, developed a state of tension defined as 'Maltese sickness'. However, these raids caused additional damage to populated areas and serious loss of life. The Axis Air Force fared no better and, although at first the Germans were sending in as many as eighty Ju 88s escorted by nearly double that number of fighters, after a week they were forced into having 100 fighters escorting just fourteen bombers. The Spitfires met the intruders out at sea and the ones that managed

(E. Neuffer)
Oberleutnant *Ernst Neuffer* near his Ju 88 which crash-landed at Catania after having been damaged by ground artillery and Spitfires over Malta on 15th October, 1942.

to get through had to face more Spitfires and the fury of a concentrated anti-aircraft artillery not restricted to a rationed number of rounds.

A German pilot belonging to KG 51, who flew about 100 missions over Malta between March and October 1942, recounts: "...We returned to Sicily from Crete towards the end of September, when the defence of Malta was very strong. At dusk on 10th October we approached the Island at 7,000 metres and, while heading towards the harbour area, my radio operator cried out 'Fighters, fighters'. Three Spitfires, flying at a higher altitude, dived and opened fire on my aircraft, killing the observer in his seat on my right and wounding the radio operator. As the engines were running rough, I did an emergency dive, released the bombs and turned back towards Sicily with one of the engines on fire. When some 300 metres away from Catania airfield the gunner, who was uninjured, jumped out of the aircraft. I stopped the engine to prevent the fire from spreading and crash-landed in a field. Luckily I escaped with injuries to my head and legs only. Italian civilians took the radio operator and me out of the aircraft and we were driven to a hospital at Catania; my radio operator died whilst being operated upon. I was the sole survivor. ..."[143]

Another *Luftwaffe* pilot serving with 2 LG 1 recalls that on 15th October, 1942, his Ju 88 was hit by 4 anti-aircraft, 24 cannon and 150 machine gun shells whilst flying over Malta. Although the port aileron, steering controls, landing gear and other mechanisms had been destroyed, he managed to reach Sicily, where he crash-landed at Catania.

Four days later, when returning from another sortie to Malta, he was forced to ditch his

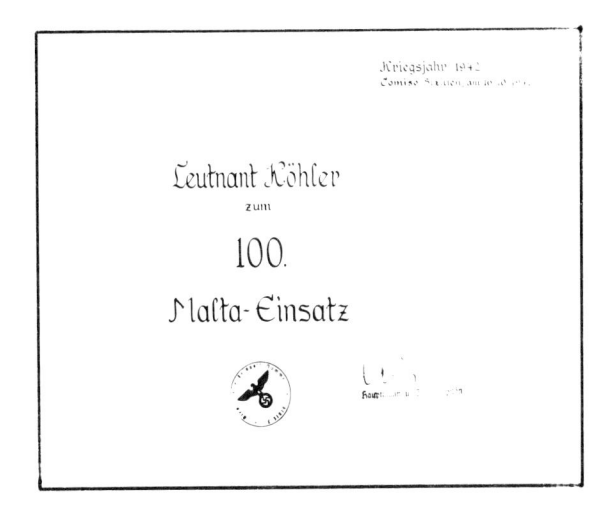

(A. Kohler)
Congratulatory certificate presented to Leutnant Armin Köhler on completion of his 100th sortie over Malta on 10th October, 1942. This Luftwaffe fighter pilot, credited with 69 victories during the Second World War, was subsequently promoted Major and awarded the Knight's Cross of the Iron Cross.

aircraft in the channel. The crew, rescued by a British destroyer after four days in a rubber dinghy, was brought to Malta and hospitalized.[144]

During the ten-day battle, the enemy flew approximately 2,400 sorties, dropping about 440 tons of bombs. This comparatively low figure reflected the enemy's reluctance to risk losing more bombers over Malta; instead, for some time, Me 109 fighter-bombers flew over the Maltese skies. The insignificant results achieved did not justify the mounting losses and the new blitz came to an abrupt end on 20th October, 1942, when nearly all the German aircraft were transferred to North Africa. The Axis conceded defeat; the Air Battle of Malta had been won.

Credit for the successful outcome of the Air Battle of Malta deservedly goes to the Royal Air Force and to the gunners. However, the part played by a branch of the Royal Navy should not pass unrecorded. In a report dated 20th August, 1943, Thomas L. Justice, Inspector of Fitters at the Royal Naval Torpedo Depot at Kalafrana, refers to the supply of breathing oxygen without which the Royal Air Force could not have operated at all: "... The only source of supply of the Royal Air Force, a mobile unit, was destroyed by enemy action on 30th December, 1941. There remained only two oxygen plants on the Island, the dockyard plant which was fully occupied to meet Admiralty requirements, and the plant at the Torpedo Depot, Kalafrana. This plant was adapted to supply breathing oxygen for the Royal Air Force and has since that time supplied practically the whole of the breathing oxygen used by the RAF in defensive and offensive operations. Because the supply exceeded in quality the RAF specifications and on no occasion failed to meet the very heavy demands for the quality of oxygen required, attention was not focussed on the plant, and its vital contribution to the defence of the Island was not appreciated.

"Nevertheless, it is no exaggeration to say that without the oxygen produced by this plant, the RAF could not have defeated the *Luftwaffe* in May and October 1942, and in justice to those responsible for running the plant, this fact should be officially recorded. In this connection should be cited N. Attard and A. Carabott, Fitters, and A. Caruana and H. Roberts, Skilled Labourers."[145]

Although the Gozitans, and a considerable number of Maltese who had moved to the Sister Island, were living under war conditions, they were not subjected to the same dangers and austerity prevailing in Malta. Enemy aircraft flew unmolested over Gozo and on rare occasions engaged in strafing. On 24th December, 1941, bombs fell at Victoria, destroying two houses and killing 24-year-old Carmela Borg. Several other bombs were dropped later but the most serious incident occurred on 10th October, 1942, when two Ju 88s, chased by Spitfires, released their bombs over Sannat village, causing considerable damage and the death of eighteen civilians, besides badly injuring 35 others. These were by no means the only Gozitans to lose their life in wartime. Many others died whilst working or serving with the Forces in Malta, or on the high seas with the Royal and Merchant Navies.

The marked decline in aerial activity over Malta after the October Blitz relieved some of the strain both on the garrison and the population. However, the problem of commodity shortages of every kind persisted; although aircraft from Malta operated regularly, fuel supplies as well as other vital stores were again running short. No supplies in appreciable quantity had been received since August and there was again the need for another convoy. Before this could be despatched, alternative steps were taken to send in supplies. In October, the submarines *Parthian* and *Clyde* made a trip each from Gibraltar while *Rorqual* came twice from Beirut, bringing in aviation spirit, diesel and lubricating oils, torpedoes and foodstuffs. More aviation spirit and torpedoes were delivered by *Parthian* and *Clyde* in November. Also in November, an attempt was made to send three unescorted and disguised merchant ships. *Empire Patrol* sailed from Alexandria with a cargo of aviation spirit and benzine. She was spotted by a German aircraft whilst near Cyprus where she put to port due to engine trouble. Two other ships, *Ardeola* and *Tadorna*, entered the Mediterranean bound for Malta with foodstuffs. At first they formed part of the Algiers assault convoy but soon, having detached themselves from the convoy on 9th November, they were engaged by shore batteries; both ships were stopped and boarded, the crew being interned by the French.

These setbacks did not deter the Chiefs of Staff from their efforts to keep Malta supplied. *Manxman* and *Welshman* were again utilized; on 12th November the former reached Malta from Alexandria with 350 tons of foodstuffs, whilst the latter arrived from Gibraltar six days later. These supplies, delivered in small quantities at regular intervals, were meant to keep Malta on her feet until the arrival of the next convoy. In fact, the four ships comprising Operation 'Stoneage' sailed from Alexandria on 15th November, 1942, having loaded at Port Sudan to avoid suspicion. Torpedo-bombers carried out a single attack on the four merchant ships, escorted by five cruisers and seventeen destroyers, causing damage to one of the cruisers. The British *Denbighshire*, the Dutch *Bantam* and the American *Mormacmoon* and *Robin Locksley* entered the Grand Harbour at three o'clock in the morning on 20th November and, as dawn broke and news of the arrival of the convoy spread, the harbour area became congested with people watching the unloading of the ships. The jubilant crowd had every reason to celebrate — the Siege had finally been raised.

Aerial pressure against Malta continued to ease. In December 1942, there were 35 alerts compared to 169 in the same month the previous year. This augured well for the festive season. If the traditional turkey was still only a nostalgic dream, the population was reminded that Christmas comes but once a year. On 8th December, Mr Charles Nalder, who in September 1942 had succeeded Marquis Barbaro of St George as Food Distribution and Enforcement Officer, announced a slight increase in rations for Christmas, with beans as a luxury, besides another special item: "... In general to brighten the proceedings during Christmas week, we will make an issue of candles; four candles and eight night-lights for every family." Some were not amused; the Maltese regarded this as the 'Joke of the War'.

Chapter Nineteen

Offensive operations — Royal Air Force claims 1,000th victim — Invasion of Pantelleria and smaller islands — Preparations for invasion of Sicily — Construction of airstrips at Gozo

The relief of Malta was followed by the victorious offensive of the Allied armies in North Africa, in support of which Malta-based aircraft threw their full weight. To the outside world and to many in Malta, it appeared that retribution was beyond the Island's capability. Newspapers and news bulletins occasionally reported that an Axis convoy or targets in Sicily, Italy or North Africa had been attacked. The Authorities did not want to give details of the offensive capability of the Island as they feared that this would provoke a new series of attacks. When weather permitted, Wellingtons, Blenheims, Swordfish, Beaufighters, Beauforts and Albacores pounded enemy positions in North Africa and in Sicily, helping to a significant extent Montgomery's advance into Cyrenaica and Tripolitania. They also inflicted enormous losses on Axis shipping and, following the Desert Victory, turned their might against harbours, airfields, marshalling yards and other military installations in Sicily and Southern Italy.

During November 1942, Spitfires from No 185 Squadron based at Malta assumed for the first time a fighter-bomber role. Air Vice-Marshal Sandy Johnstone, who joined a Spitfire Wing at Malta in September 1942 as a junior officer, recalls that two 500-lb bombs were fitted under the wings of locally-based Spitfires, just as had been done to Hurricanes in the Western Desert. Following several successful trials, a chemical factory at Pachino in Sicily was chosen as target for the first bombing attack. Twelve such Spitfires took off from Malta, escorted by twelve others, flying northwards and keeping close to sea level to avoid detection by enemy radar and defences. [146]

That same month, on the 24th, three Beaufighters of No 272 Squadron took off on an early afternoon hunting spree. Flying Officer E.E. Coate, spotting a six-engined Blohm und Voss Bv 222 flyingboat 30 miles north of Linosa, attacked it from the beam, coming out of the sun. Coate's first burst blew large pieces off the fuselage, while a second long one hit the three port engines and fuel tank which burst into flames. The giant aircraft lost height and hit the sea, bounced back into the air before dropping its left wing and finally blowing up as it plunged into the sea. The aircraft, Bv 222V-6, belonging to a special Unit, *Lufttransportstaffel See 222*, was the first of its type to be lost in action. [147]

The end of 1942 saw a considerable strengthening of the Royal Air Force's offensive arm in Malta. More Wellingtons, Albacores and Beaufighters flew in from the Middle East, whilst Mosquito Mk IIs from No 23 Squadron were based here, the first aircraft of its type to operate from a station outside the United Kingdom. Although the first operational sortie by this squadron was carried out on the night of 29th/30th December, 1942, the first Mosquito to land in Malta was W4055, a PR1. This was on a long-range flight from Benson and reached Malta in 4¾ hours on 4th November, 1941.

The pendulum in Tripolitania was now swinging the Allies' way. Following the capture of Benghazi on 20th November, 1942, General Montgomery's Eighth Army pressed onwards towards Tripoli. At this stage, the Allies carried out a series of operations aimed at preventing the Germans from blocking the entrance to the harbour at Tripoli and from demolishing the port facilities before falling into Allied hands. Besides the intervention of bombers from Malta and the Middle East, at least two naval operations were carried out from Malta. On the night of 18th/19th January, 1943, the submarine *Thunderbolt* launched two chariots aimed at destroying any potential blockships. One of the chariots managed to reach the harbour entrance but the blockships were scuttled before it could intervene; the crew were taken prisoners. The other craft, having developed mechanical trouble, had to be destroyed; her crew, likewise taken prisoners, later escaped and joined the advancing Eighth Army. The second attempt was made by motor torpedo-boats from Malta; on the night of 20th/21st January, they attacked the breakwater at Tripoli harbour. During this sortie, the MTBs torpedoed the Italian submarine *Santarosa* which was being towed by tugs. As the Eighth Army was on the outskirts of Tripoli, several craft, attempting to escape to other Tripolitanian and Tunisian ports, were sunk by British naval ships sweeping the coast.

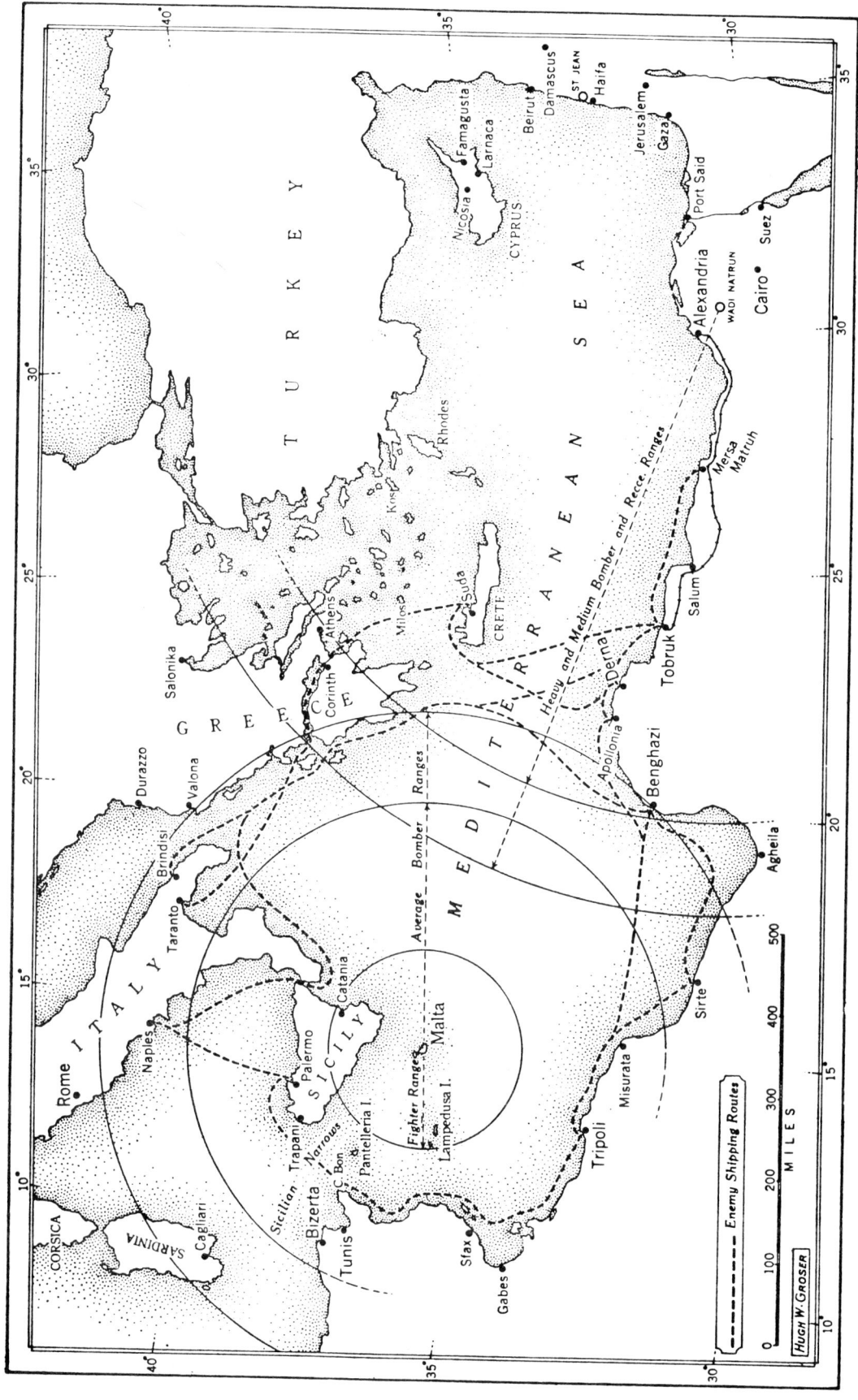

Allied air power over the Mediterranean, September 1942.

Children at the Palace Square, Valletta, celebrating the capture of Tripoli.

British and Commonwealth troops converged on Tripoli, fighting a determined enemy and a cruel desert. For two-and-a-half years, the capture of the Tripolitanian capital had been the goal against which the Allied army had thrown its full weight. Rommel made a final stand but, as it became evident that he could not hold the city, he withdrew his troops towards the Mareth Line. The Highlanders marched into Tripoli with pipes shrilling; it was a joyful occasion for the battle-weary infantrymen who had suffered so much in the long and torturous campaign. One of them was 193897 Lieutenant Albert Joseph Dimech, a Maltese serving with The Seaforth Highlanders (Ross-Shire Buffs, The Duke of Albany's), who distinguished himself to earn the Military Cross. This award was thus recommended by the Commander-in-Chief Middle East: "On the morning of the 21st January, 1943, Lt Dimech showed great gallantry in leading his Company after his Company Commander had been wounded, although he, himself, had already been twice wounded during the morning.

"On the first occasion, although wounded, he went out alone to round up a party of enemy who came forward with their hands up. The enemy, however, fired on him instead of surrendering, wounding him a second time. He still carried on, encouraging his men until the majority of the forward Platoons were either killed or wounded. He was then taken prisoner along with some other wounded, but managed to effect his escape.

"Lieutenant Dimech showed great gallantry and determination and his example was a source of great encouragement to the men of his Company."[148]

The capture of Tripoli on 23rd January, 1943, marked the beginning of the end for the Axis forces in North Africa. Malta went *en fête*; flags were brought out, people thronged into Valletta where the two City bands, preceded by groups of children carrying club banners, paraded down Kingsway, playing popular marches.

Life in Malta took a new turn with the allied advance in North Africa. While the number of alerts in October 1942 was as high as 153, this dropped to a mere 5 in February 1943. No less than thirteen ships, including two tankers, reached Malta unmolested between 5th December, 1942, and 2nd January, 1943.

Although war had receded from the shores of Malta, the Maltese continued following with keen interest the fate of ships previously engaged on the Malta run. On 1st December, 1942, whilst laying mines off Bizerta, HMS

BATTLE INOCULATION
GHAIN TUFFIEHA FEB/43.

(The King's Regiment)
Sketch showing the 8th Bn The Manchester Regiment undergoing field exercises. This is one of 93 sketches drawn by Colour-Sergeant John Whitehouse depicting the battalion's tour of duty at Malta.

Manxman was torpedoed by German submarine U-375 and had to be taken into Gibraltar for repairs. HMS *Welshman*, steaming to Alexandria on 1st February, 1943, was torpedoed by U-617 and, after three gruelling hours, sank, taking down with her 152 naval officers and men, in addition to a number of soldiers and airmen.

Early in January 1943, a handful of members of COPP3 (Combined Operations Pilotage Parties) arrived from Britain on a Dakota; they were joined by another small party from the Middle East. On 27th February and in the first days of March, after trying out their canoes and equipment at Ghajn Tuffieha Bay, they left Malta in three groups on the submarines *Unbending*, *United* and *Unrivalled*. Joined by COPP4 on the submarine *Safari* from Algiers, they headed towards Sicily. Operating in pairs, they faced continuous risks both from the heavy seas and the enemy; as they paddled and waded ashore, they took soundings and notes of the beaches. During these lightning operations, five Coppists, on venturing further ashore, were taken prisoner, whilst five others, including their leader, Lieutenant-Commander Norman Teacher DSO RN remained unaccounted for. Lieutenant Bob Smith and his paddler, David Brand, missed their rendezvous with the submarine *United*; their options were most unenviable: either paddling inshore to surrender at Gela or paddling out to the open sea, hopefully to reach Malta. Notwithstanding a menacingly choppy swell, which soon turned into a storm, they decided on the latter course. When one of the blades of the paddle snapped, they had to take turns, one paddling with one blade and the other baling water out of the canoe. All day and night they fought the sea and exhaustion, making very slow progress as their craft was continuously tossed by the waves. At the break of dawn, they came within sight of Malta, having defiantly paddled a distance of about seventy-five miles in their fragile canvas canoe. The incursions into enemy waters and territory by members of this little-known Organisation provided information considered invaluable in the preparation for the large-scale seaborne landing which was to follow.

The British infantry battalions started attack-orientated training; the local terrain proved ideal for field exercises. A select Unit, the Malta Special Service Troops, was set up and practised commando tactics at Manoel Island. On 4th April, 1943, ten officers and 86 men from the Buffs, Cheshire, Royal West Kents, Royal Irish Fusiliers, Durham Light Infantry and the Royal Corps of Signals, in absolute secrecy, embarked on naval craft at Marsamxett Harbour, to capture the Kerkenna Islands near Sousse. After spending a few days at Tripoli, checking their equipment and carrying out final preparations, they reached the two Kerkenna Islands, Rhabi and Chergui, where they landed without opposition since the Italian garrison had been evacuated two days earlier. The Force returned to Malta on April 19th.

This minor operation showed that the Malta garrison had shed its defensive role. However, it was not all plain sailing. Men from 234 (Malta) Infantry Brigade were to suffer heavily in the Aegean Islands during the latter part of the year. The 231 Infantry Brigade, known also as the 1st (Malta) Infantry Brigade, composed of the 2 Bn Devons, 1 Bn Hampshires and 1 Bn Dorsets, left Malta on 30th March, 1943, for Alexandria, where they underwent further combat training.

At the end of the war, all the infantry battalions that had served at Malta during the siege were authorised to add 'Malta' to their battle honours, which honour went also to the King's Own Malta Regiment.

In the air, Malta's striking force claimed other victories. On Wednesday, 28th April, 1943, Squadron Leader John Joseph Lynch of Alhambra, California, and Pilot Officer A.F. Osborne of Reading took off in Spitfires and headed for Sicily; off the coast, Lynch spotted a Ju 52 which he attacked. The Junkers, hit in the starboard side of the fuselage, trailed smoke and crashed into the sea; it was the one-thousandth victim.

Meanwhile, the North African campaign was coming to a victorious end. On 12th May, 1943, the Allied armies joined hands in Tunisia. Whilst *Feldmarschall* Erwin Rommel and six hundred and sixty-three officers and men escaped, *General* Alexander von Arnim and a quarter of a million troops were captured; so ended the legend of Rommel's *Afrika Korps*.

Malta's role was now of a different nature; the Island became a veritable gigantic aircraft-carrier right on the enemy's doorstep. Ships crammed every inlet in Malta's harbours; stores, vehicles and ammunition were dispersed in the countryside, covered by camouflage nets. The Royal Air Force arrived in strength, aircraft being parked wing-tip to wing-tip at the various airfields. This massive build-up in Malta for the invasion of Sicily worried the Axis who launched a series of attacks on Malta. On the few occasions when the raiders managed to penetrate the defensive screen, the bombs dropped caused only a few casualties and negligible damage.

The proposed invasion of Sicily was preceded by that of Pantelleria, Lampedusa, Linosa and Lampione. Pantelleria, the largest of the Islands and once a major threat to convoys sailing towards Malta, was subjected to a naval and aerial bombardment. The 11,000-strong Italian garrison laid down arms on 11th June, 1943, even before Allied troops had disembarked from the assault craft. Showing a large white cross on the airfield, *Ammiraglio* Gino Pavesi, commanding the Island, radioed to Malta the surrender of Pantelleria on the pretext that water had been exhausted, although sufficient supplies of the commodity are said to have been found when the Allies landed.

Lampedusa's surrender bordered almost on the farcical. On 12th June, Sergeant Pilot Sydney Cohen took off from Malta in a Swordfish on an air-sea rescue mission. The aircraft developed some fault and force-landed on the nearest Island which turned out to be Lampedusa, where a number of Italians, waving odd pieces of white cloth converged on the aircraft. The bewildered pilot was offered the Island's surrender by the men; he asked to see the Commandant, who confirmed the decision, asking him to deliver a written message to this effect to the Authorities in Malta. The Swordfish took off while Allied bombers, still unaware of the Island's surrender, were attacking the harbour. Cohen flew to Tunisia where he handed the Island's surrender document to the Americans.

The 140-strong garrison of Linosa raised the white flag on 13th June on sighting HMS *Nubian*, whilst Lampione was occupied the following day.

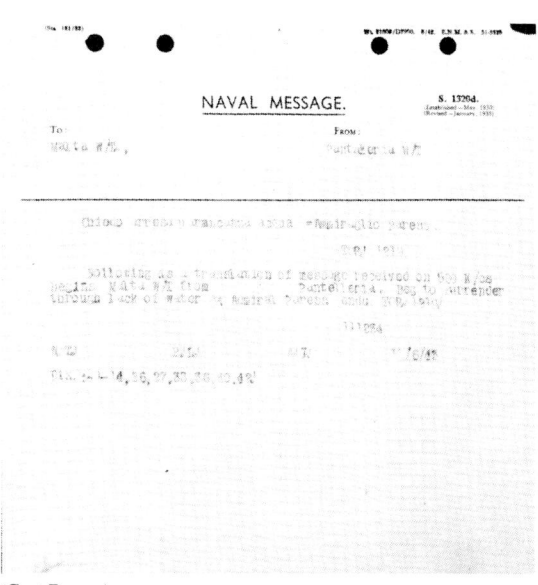

(Gort Papers)
Pantelleria's surrender message as received at Malta.

(Wm. White)
Spitfire of 308th Squadron 31st Fighter Group USAAF operating from Gozo during Operation 'Husky'.

Plans for the invasion of Sicily were now at an advanced stage. In his memoirs, General Dwight D. Eisenhower, the Supreme Commander Allied Forces Mediterranean, testifies: "Because of the existence of splendid naval communications at Malta, that place was chosen as our headquarters for the initial stages of the operation. ... Malta then presented a picture far different from the one of a few months earlier, when it was still the target for a hostile air force that had little effective opposition. Malta had taken a fearful beating but the spirit of the defenders had never been shaken. As Allied air and naval support approached them through the conquest of North Africa, they rose magnificently to the occasion. By the time we found need for Malta's facilities, its airfields were in excellent condition and its garrison was burning to get into the fight." [149]

The underground War Headquarters at Lascaris was a bee-hive of activity as British and American officials worked on the plans for the operation, code-named 'Husky'. Aerial support was of paramount importance and the need was felt for further reinforcements to General George Patton's Seventh Army during and after the initial stages of the assault.

Since airfields and dispersal areas in Malta could not take the additional Spitfires required for this purpose, it was decided to build an airfield at Gozo. A strip of cultivated land skirting the villages of Xewkija, Ghajnsielem, Nadur and Xaghra was chosen. Lord Gort requested Bishop Gonzi to approach the farmers, who agreed to cede their fertile fields against adequate compensation.

Construction was assigned to the Americans. Company 'E', 2nd Battalion, 21st Engineer Aviation Regiment left Sousse in Tunisia on 1st June, 1943, on nine Landing Craft Tanks. The convoy, carrying six officers and one hundred ninety-seven men, and their equipment, reached Marsalforn Bay on 6th June. Work on an East-West runway started two days later. Tractors, scrapers and mechanical shovels levelled the area; the historic Gourgion Tower, which stood in the way, had to be demolished. The American servicemen and Gozitan labourers worked in earnest with two shifts operating from 0500 to 2100 hours.

When Sir Keith Park visited the site some days later, he ordered the construction of an additional runway as well as revetments or blast pens. Additional equipment and seventy thousand sand bags were shipped from Malta; this required the setting up of three shifts working twenty-four hours a day. Work on the second runway started on 15th June with about 300 Gozitans constructing revetments of stone and sand bags.

Both runways, each measuring 150 feet by 4,000 feet, were completed on 20th June, while work continued on the construction of taxiways, hardstandings and revetments. The new dispersal facilities provided accommodation for seventy-eight aircraft.

The airstrips became operational on 22nd June, 1943, and the first American-piloted Spitfires of 31st Fighter Group landed on the following day.

Work on the airfield was completed on 25th June and five days later Company 'E' returned to North Africa. The British Authorities had doubts whether the work could be completed in time; in fact it was ready one week ahead of schedule. This was made possible by the efficiency of American engineers, who had at their disposal the most modern mechanical equipment existing at the time, the labour of Gozitan workers and the persuasive manner of Mgr Gonzi who, soon afterwards, became Malta's Archbishop and was subsequently created a Knight of the British Empire in recognition of his services to the Allied cause.

Chapter Twenty

King George VI visits Malta: welcome by population, tour of the Island, presentation of Field Marshal's baton to Lord Gort

June 20th, 1943, was a memorable day. At five in the morning, a completely unexpected announcement over the Rediffusion Relay System sent the people scurrying into Valletta; His Majesty King George VI was arriving by sea on a brief visit to the Island.

In no time at all vantage points around the Grand Harbour were crammed with people, some perilously perched on bastion edges and bomb-damaged buildings. The Maltese Flag, alongside the Union Flag, went up everywhere while portraits of the King and the Royal Family appeared all over the Island. The people were thrilled at the prospect of even catching a glimpse of the Monarch. As they waited, they could hardly believe that the King would be sailing through a hostile sea, with enemy air bases a mere 60 miles away. They waited and looked out towards the horizon as they had done a few months earlier when the battered survivors of the *Santa Marija* convoy had struggled to reach the beleaguered Island. Although circumstances had changed, their excitement was not without concern for the King's safety. The tense atmosphere suddenly erupted into a tumultuous roar as HMS *Aurora*,

(IWM)

King George VI saluting Malta from the bridge of HMS Aurora.

184

(The Times)
The King, accompanied by Major Harold R. Micallef, inspecting an RMA guard of honour at the Customs House.

escorted by four destroyers, neared the beckoning arms of the breakwater. The King, in his white naval uniform, stood erect on a specially-erected platform on the bridge saluting the George Cross Island; there he remained until the ship dropped anchor in Dockyard Creek. As the crowd roared a vociferous welcome, for a moment Malta forgot the ugly reality of war. This was an occasion to be cherished and nothing, in any way, was to be allowed to mar it. For twelve hours on that beautiful, hot summer day, the King and the Maltese shared joy and risk.

The spontaneity and the warmth of the welcome, against a background of devastation, impressed His Majesty, who in his diary recorded this historic visit: "On Sunday at 8.15 a.m. I was on the bridge as we came in to the Grand Harbour. A lovely sunny morning. A wonderful sight. Every bastion and every view point lined with people who cheered as we entered. It was a very moving moment for me. I had made up my mind that I would take a risk to get to Malta and I had got there and by sea. Mussolini called the Mediterranean Sea his Italian Lake a short time ago. Lord Gort the Governor came on board as we secured, and I landed at 9.30 am. I drove through cheering crowds to the Palace in Valletta and met the Council. I presented Gort with his Field Marshal's baton in their presence. I saw the George Cross I gave Malta on April 15th, 1942.

Then I went on to the Balcony overlooking the Square and received a great ovation from the people below. I then went to the Naval Dockyard and was shown round it by Rear-Admiral Kenneth Mackenzie (the Admiral Superintendent) who had been there for 4½ years. There is nothing left above ground but all the workshops, electric light plant etc. are now in tunnels underground hewn out mostly by manual labour, under Mackenzie's direction. The parish of Senglea just above the dockyard is a mere shell and I met the R.C. priest (Canon Emanuel Brincat) who did all he could for his parishioners. Most of his flock are now evacuated, as they cannot live there. Only 80 killed. Gort then took me for a drive round part of the Island to show me some of the devastation of the 6 month 'Blitz' which the Island endured. November 1941 to April 1942. We arrived at the Verdala Palace where Gort is now living and had lunch there. I met the R.C. Archbishop of Malta and the R.C. Bishop of Gozo, besides the Lieutenant-Governor Mr Campbell. I rested after lunch and then after tea where I met the military staff officers about 20, Gort took me to see the other side of the Island. I saw the runways of the RAF airfields made by Maltese labour and the aircraft dispersal points. Air Marshal Sir K. Park, whom I knighted, is in command and has done a great deal in extending the aerodromes in the last year. In each village the population gave me a great reception and I found the profusion of flowers

(L.F. Tortell)
The King acknowledging the crowd's welcome from the Palace balcony.

(L.C. Lyons)
The King leaving the Control Tower at Luqa airfield.

which they threw into the car was quite detrimental to my white uniform. I dined with Gort and later when it was dark I reembarked in the *Aurora* and left Malta by night. A very strenuous day but a very interesting one to have spent." [150]

Covering the Royal Visit, which the King described as 'the real gem of my tour', was a small army of service and civilian reporters and photographers. They followed every move and nothing escaped their attention. Alfred Wagg, an American naval commentator, records a small but significant episode: "... Laughter and gaiety, restrained for a long time, had its fling that day. I stood at one side of the Customs House steps as the King alighted from the brass-funnelled, antiquated barge. Lord Gort greeted him. The Royal Malta Artillery band played the National Anthem. Then the King stepped forward to inspect the guard of honour. Steel-helmeted artillerymen, under the command of Major H.R. Micallef, presented arms. The King did not return Major Micallef's snappy salute, but — instead — put forth his hand." [151]

Mr David Campbell [152] bade His Majesty farewell: "You have made the people of Malta very happy today, Sir", to which the King answered: "But I have been the happiest man in Malta today." [153]

Chapter Twenty-One

Allied Commanders arrive for invasion of Sicily — General Eisenhower's message to Malta — Last civilian victim through aerial bombardment — Mussolini's downfall

The impending assault on Sicily brought to the Island more British and American warships besides a large number of landing craft of all shapes and sizes; infantry battalions were billeted in barracks, under canvas along the countryside, and on troopships anchored off the coast. With the men and the material came the commanders; General Bernard Law Montgomery moved his headquarters to Malta at the end of June; Admiral Sir Andrew B. Cunningham took up personal command at the Naval Headquarters on 4th July; three days later saw the arrival of the Supreme Commander himself, General Dwight D. 'Ike' Eisenhower, who was joined by Lord Louis Mountbatten, Chief of Combined Operations. On the 8th, the Deputy Supreme Commander, General Harold Alexander, opened a Tactical Headquarters for 15th Army Group. It was necessary for Air Marshal Arthur Coningham to move to Malta as well to supervise tactical air operations. Since Air Chief Marshal Sir Arthur Tedder, the Allied Air Commander, retained his Mediterranean Air Command Headquarters in Tunisia, he shuttled between North Africa and Malta and appointed Air Vice-Marshal H.E.P. Wigglesworth for better liaison with General Eisenhower.

Under the dynamic leadership of Air Vice-Marshal Sir Keith Park, the same airfields which only a few months earlier had resembled derelict scrapyards, now housed no fewer than 32 British squadrons with 527 aircraft, whilst 3 American squadrons operated 75 Spitfires from Gozo. (See Appendix **S**)

(US Army)
General Eisenhower, Lord Gort and Air Chief Marshal Sir Arthur Tedder outside War Headquarters at Lascaris.

(N. Russell)

LCTs (Landing Craft Tank) berthed at Ta' Xbiex.

(NWM)

Landing craft in No 4 Dock.

(The Times)

Aircraft-carriers in the Grand Harbour during Operation 'Husky'.

D-Day was fixed for 10th July, 1943, and as the weather unexpectedly deteriorated, the very fate of the operation was at stake. Although the velocity of the wind increased, the Supreme Commander ordered the launching of the assault, since most of the invasion fleet from east and west had sailed from their *rendezvous* near Malta: 3,000 ships and major landing craft, carrying 115,000 British and Commonwealth soldiers and 66,000 American troops. The assault vessels, including a large number of landing craft from Malta, were tossed by heavy seas and high winds as they headed for the landing beaches. The airborne troops left from six landing strips in Tunisia on board 104 Dakotas of the American Troop Carrier Command and eleven Albermarles of the Royal Air Force. These, together with Halifaxes and Stirlings, which were towing eight Waco and eleven Horsa gliders carrying men and anti-tank guns of the 1st Airlanding Anti-Tank Battery, flew in a tight V-formation towards Malta, where searchlight beams pointed skywards to enable the American pilots to set course towards Sicily.

General Eisenhower and the other commanders watched with concern from a vantage point on the Island as the large force of airborne men and material flew over in inclement weather. The strong wind was not the only obstacle this Force had to contend with. On nearing the Sicilian coastline, through some tactical error, Allied naval vessels off the landing beaches, opened fire; several of the Dakotas were shot down while others were damaged and had to return to North Africa. Some pilots, facing this unexpected hostile reception from their own side, altered course to avoid further punishment and dropped the troops away from the appointed sites, some as far away as on the Italian mainland. Despite this unfortunate experience and the raging freak storm, the Allies established a number of beachheads and advanced inland. The ships and troops received extensive aerial protection from the Maltese Islands and the Allied airfield on Pantelleria.

The Filter Room plotting table at Malta's War Headquarters was one mass of plots. The bombing of Sicily, intensified a week before the invasion, was sustained after the actual landing. British Liberators and Halifaxes, and American Flying Fortresses, Mitchells and Venturas, operating from Tripolitania and Tunisia, joined bombers from Malta in a fierce offensive; a continuous fighter umbrella was provided by groups of about 80 Spitfires from local airfields. Mrs Maria Warren, one of several Maltese plotters, remembers that for three days she and her colleagues worked without respite tracking the numerous British and American aircraft engaged in the operation.[154]

Among the first troops to land in Sicily were men of 231 Infantry Brigade, who were assigned the beachhead at Marzameni on the south-east corner of Sicily. These soldiers, with the Maltese Cross as their Brigade Sign, (See Appendix **T**) drew the admiration and respect of the commanders for their performance.

It was from Malta that three days later the Allied Supreme Commander set foot on Axis-dominated Europe to visit the Allied positions and to discuss tactics with the Field Commanders. On 1st August, following his return to Malta, General Eisenhower issued a message to the people of Malta. John Gunther, the noted American journalist and writer, recounts: "Once I was sitting with him (Eisenhower) in Malta when he suddenly had the idea of dictating a brief memorandum congratulating the people of Malta on their heroic resistance to the forces of the Axis; the time had come when the role Malta played in the Allied invasion of Sicily could be made publicly known. It was a Sunday and his aides were taking time off. So the General dictated the memorandum to me. He worked on it over and over again, changing a word here, a word there, as he paced up and down the room, nervously excited. "Let's make it epigrammatic; let's make it exquisite," he exclaimed. Then he paused with a chuckle. "I suppose you think 'exquisite' is a hell of a word for a soldier to be using."[155] The message, printed on the front pages of local newspapers on 5th August, 1943, reads: "The epic of Malta is symbolic of the experience of the United Nations in this war. Malta has passed successively through the stages of woeful unpreparedness, tenacious endurance, intensive preparation and the initiation of a fierce offensive. It is resolutely determined to maintain a rising crescendo of attack until the whole task is complete. For this inspiring example the United Nations will be forever indebted to Field-Marshal Lord Gort, the fighting services under his command and to every citizen of the heroic Island."

The Allied Fleet covered the landings and pounded the shore batteries. Force 'H', comprising capital ships, provided an outer protective ring but the Italian Fleet once again failed to make an appearance.

On 12th July, 1943, Force 'H' entered the Grand Harbour to refuel and revictual. The ships in port included *Rodney* and *Nelson*, the first battleships to enter Malta since Admiral Cunningham's two-day visit in HMS *Warspite* on 20th December, 1940.

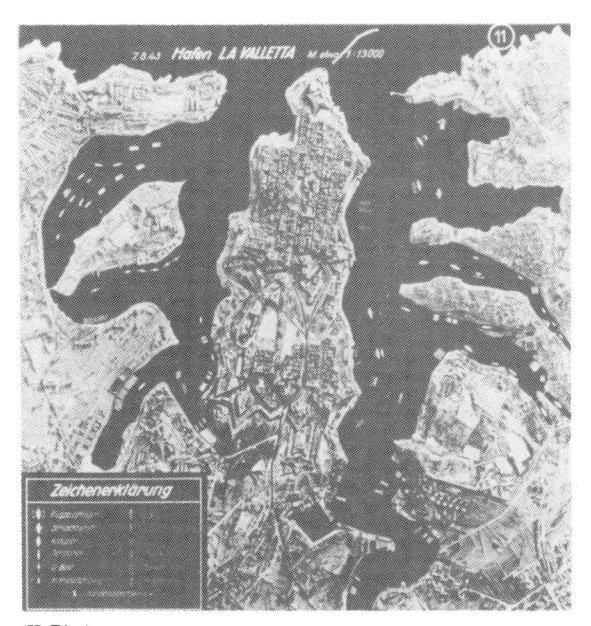

(K. Ries)
A German reconnaissance photograph, taken on 7th August, 1943, showing a vast array of naval units anchored in the harbours.

The Allied armies landed in three sectors in southern Sicily; the Americans on the west, the Canadians in the centre and the British on the east. Patton's Seventh Army advanced rapidly eastwards to join Montgomery's Eighth Army, which had encountered stiffer resistance from the Germans. The two Armies fought their way up north, capturing Messina on 16th August. Most of the German troops retreated by crossing over to Italy and, after thirty-eight days of fierce fighting, Sicily was occupied.

The Maltese Islands, now out of the front-line, were still in the Germans' minds. When the sirens sounded before dawn on Tuesday, 20th July, 1943, few took notice. Yet this turned out to be a fairly heavy raid reminiscent of those of a few months earlier. Bombs fell over various parts of the Island; six civilians were killed, two reported missing, fourteen seriously injured and thirteen received minor injuries. German bombers returned six days later, shortly after midnight on 26th July. As parachute flares illuminated the Island, a concentrated barrage was put up by ground batteries and naval units in the Grand Harbour; the gunners and night-fighters each shot down three bombers. Vincent Attard of Zabbar was killed during this raid; he was the last civilian to lose his life through aerial bombing.

As the population had grown complacent, exposing themselves to unnecessary risk, the Authorities issued a warning, advising people to take cover before the barrage started. Several civilians were still being injured by splinters from our own anti-aircraft shells.

(W.J. Jones)
The Maltese parading an effigy of Mussolini along Kingsway, Valletta, during celebrations marking his downfall.

As soon as Sicilian airfields fell into Allied hands, the locally-based fighters crossed over, their place being taken by a large number of light bombers, including three squadrons of Baltimores and Bostons of the United States Army Air Force, which pounded enemy positions further inland. Whilst the Sicilian campaign lasted, the Royal Air Force in Malta flew four million miles using two million gallons of aviation fuel.

It was at the height of the Sicilian Campaign that news of Mussolini's downfall on 25th July reached Malta to the delight and relief of all. His effigy was paraded in mockery along the main streets of Valletta and the suburbs to the jeers of the crowds. King Vittorio Emanuele III, assuming the role of Head of the Italian State, appointed *Maresciallo* Pietro Badoglio as Prime Minister.

Chapter Twenty-Two

Italy's surrender — Churchill and Roosevelt visit Malta — Allied Chiefs of Staff meet at Malta — Churchill and Roosevelt revisit Malta prior to Yalta Conference — Reconstruction — End of hostilities in Europe and Far East

The 8th of September, marking the end of the Great Siege of 1565, when the Turks left the Island after being routed by the Knights of St John and the Maltese, is also the feast day of the Nativity of Our Lady, titular feast of Senglea. It was indeed fitting for the people of Senglea to celebrate that day in a special way in 1943. The statue of Our Lady, known as *Il-Bambina*, was taken back to Senglea from Birkirkara, where it had been kept for safe-keeping immediately after the attack on HMS *Illustrious* in January 1941. Many Sengleans, including those who had sought refuge outside the City, welcomed Her back and congregated in fulfilment of vows for their deliverance from the onslaught that had threatened their life for three years. As the procession reached the devastated wharf, shortly after leaving St Philip's Church, destroyers in Dockyard Creek coned their searchlights onto the statue of *Il-Bambina*, whilst a loudspeaker from one of the naval ships blared out the joyous news of Italy's surrender. It became an occasion of double rejoicing, as evident from the tears of joy on the face of all present to see the statue that had been returned to the City she belonged to.

The terms of the Armistice with Italy provided for co-belligerency and the surrender at Malta of the Italian Fleet, which sailed from La Spezia and Taranto under the vigilance of *Warspite*, *Valiant* and the 8th Destroyer Flotilla. *En route* the flagship *Roma* was sunk by a German PC 1400 FX radio-controlled bomb, with the loss of many men, including the Commander-in-Chief *Ammiraglio d'Armata* Carlo Bergamini. The Fleet steamed on with *Ammiraglio* Romeo Oliva flying his flag from the cruiser *Eugenio di Savoia*. The first three ships arrived on 10th September, to be followed on the morrow by another twelve, including four battleships, six cruisers and six destroyers, which dropped anchor at St Paul's Bay, Marsaxlokk Bay and outside Grand Harbour. For the Maltese this was a moment of moral revenge.

On his arrival at Malta on 11th September, 1943, Admiral Sir Andrew Cunningham sent this signal to the Admiralty: "Be pleased to inform their Lordships that the Italian Battle fleet now lies at anchor under the guns of the fortress of Malta." By the end of the month, seventy-six Italian naval units had surrendered at Malta, some of which sailed to Alexandria a few days later. (See Appendix U).

The British Commander-in-Chief met *Ammiraglio* Alberto da Zara, in command of the 9th Division which had sailed from Taranto, to give him instructions for the dismantling and disposal of the Italian Fleet. The Italian Admiral, on coming ashore at the Customs House, was received by Commodore Royar Dick, representing Admiral Cunningham, and was accorded full military honours. Although Cunningham's office was no more than about sixty steps up a circular stairway, the British Admiral, feeling that da Zara should see some of the devastation caused, ordered that he be brought to his office in a roundabout way by car.[156]

Surrendered Italian naval units at anchor at St Paul's Bay.

Ammiraglio *Alberto da Zara*, followed by Commodore Royar Dick, receiving the salute from a naval guard of honour at the Customs House before meeting Admiral Cunningham.

Italian submarines anchored in Lazaretto Creek after surrendering at Malta.

Celebrations marking the National Day and the surrender of Italy and of the Italian Fleet went on for a few days, reaching a climax on Sunday, 12th September. The whole of Malta thronged into Valletta, which was beflagged and decorated in a manner reminiscent of pre-war festivities. Civilians and soldiers were joined by a large number of sailors from the many British warships that had accompanied the Italian Fleet to Malta. The Valletta band clubs, the "King's Own" and "La Valette", together inched their way down Kingsway in a triumphant Victory March. The Palace Square could contain only a fraction of the crowd that had assembled, and everyone jostled to catch a glimpse of the Palace balcony. When Lord Gort appeared, the applause drowned the music of the combined bands playing the National Anthem. As the roar subsided, the Governor delivered a speech which was repeatedly interrupted by the cheering crowd: "... The events which have happened during the past twelve months have surpassed our most optimistic dreams. Who would have foretold on 8th September last year that the bells of the Three Unconquered Cities would ring again this year, as of old, in commemoration of the great victory of 1565? Who would have prophesied that the Statue of Our Lady of Victories would again be carried through the ruined streets of Senglea Invicta, and that the bells, which would ring in 1943 in celebration of Malta's National Day, would continue their joyous peals to celebrate the downfall of Italy — the Italy who had so recently and so arrogantly boasted that Malta had been 'rubbed out'. Again, who would have dared to predict that the news would flash round the world on 11th September, 1943, announcing that the great Italian Fleet would be at anchor off the shores of our unconquered Island Fortress..." The people, who were now tasting victory, availing themselves of the extension by one hour of the emergency bus service, celebrated long after the Governor had left the Palace.

Maresciallo Pietro Badoglio left Brindisi on 28th September on an Italian cruiser to sign "The Longer Instrument" of Italy's surrender at Malta. The Italian Prime Minister and his party, which included *Ammiraglio* Raffaele De Courten, Minister of Marine and Chief of Staff of the Italian Navy, and *Generale* Vittorio Ambrosio, Chief of General Staff, were met on HMS *Nelson* in the Grand Harbour by Generals Eisenhower, Bedell Smith and Alexander, Admiral Cunningham, Air Chief Marshal Tedder, Lord Gort, Mr Harold Macmillan, British Minister attached to Allied Forces Headquarters Mediterranean Command, and Mr Robert Murphy of the American State Department. *Maresciallo* Badoglio was received by a guard of honour provided by the Royal Marines, after which the delegations proceeded to Vice-Admiral Algernon Willis' quarters to sign the document. The Italian Prime Minister tried to negotiate the clause relating to unconditional surrender, but the

(IWM)
Maresciallo Badoglio with General Eisenhower on board HMS Nelson *in the Grand Harbour on 29th September, 1943. In background, left to right, are Lord Gort, Sir Arthur Tedder, General Sir Frank Mason-MacFarlane and General Harold Alexander.*

Allied commanders refused discussion on any of the terms and the document was signed.

In view of the loss of *Roma*, it was felt that the Germans might attack the Italian Fleet as it lay dismantled in our harbours. To guard against that, British and Maltese units were moved to vulnerable areas and tactically deployed in defence of the Italian Fleet. Brigadier Alfred Samut-Tagliaferro CBE, then a Major commanding 10th Light Anti-Aircraft Battery, Royal Malta Artillery, one of the units involved in that unusual task, recalls: "The last operational role of the war which the Coast and Anti-Aircraft gunners of the Royal Malta Artillery had to carry out in partnership with British units, was affording protection to the Italian Battle Fleet against possible German bombing after Italy's unilateral surrender in September 1943. As the Fleet lay 'anchored under the Guns of Malta' at Marsaxlokk and St Paul's bays within striking distance of German bombers, one could not help pondering on the frailty of men and nations. For the nation which had dropped the first bomb on our soil was also the first to drop out of the conflict and its fleet then lay in our waters, under the protection of our guns! The wheel of fate had turned a full circle. Victory over Fascism was complete." [157]

Memories of the early days of the war were evoked on Friday, 3rd September, 1943, when Air Vice-Marshal Sir Keith Park presented to the People of Malta the sole survivor of the Gloster Sea Gladiators. The crowd watched in silence as *Faith*, surrounded by contingents from the Royal Air Force and the Malta Police Force, was parked in the centre of the Palace Square, later destined to find an honoured place in Malta's National War Museum. After nine Spitfires had dipped low over the Square in a final salute to the old warrior, Sir Keith Park addressed the crowd: "... The part played by *Faith*, *Hope* and *Charity* is symbolic of the courage and endurance displayed by the people of Malta during the long struggle against vastly superior Axis Air Forces..." Sir George Borg, in accepting the relic, spoke of the significance attached to the three legendary biplanes: "... And well did they perform their task, guided by hearts of oak who defied the immensely superior power of a ruthless enemy.

(S. Ward)
An American gun crew, manning a Bofors at St Paul's Bay, joined British and Maltese artillerymen in protecting units of the Italian Navy.

And well did they symbolise the unswerving faith which the people of Malta always had in the invincible nation that protects them, the never failing hope of ultimate victory, then apparently so remote, the smiling rays of charity that would mete out mercy to the vanquished but ask for none..."

On Friday, 22nd October, Major-General W.H. Oxley handed over, on Castille Square, the first Italian gun captured in Sicily by the 51st Highland Division in July 1943. The General Officer Commanding Troops Malta told the crowd: "I have the very pleasant duty today of handing over to the Citizens of Valletta, the gun which you see before you. This weapon was the first one captured by the 51st Highland Division when it landed on the beaches of Sicily. The General Officer Commanding this famous Division sent it to Malta with the request that it should be presented to the People of Valletta, to commemorate the stay of the Division on this Island preparatory to the invasion of Sicily. Although these troops were only here a few days, they received from everyone such a friendly and kindly welcome that the GOC wished to make this presentation as a mark of esteem in which the Units of his Division held the Maltese people." The gun, a 75mm Vickers Terni field-gun, received on behalf of the People of Valletta by Mr Salvino Galea, Regional Protection Officer, is now likewise preserved at the National War Museum.

Prime Minister Winston Churchill and President Franklin Roosevelt had long expressed their wish to visit Malta to see for themselves the ravages of war. The visits took place in November and December 1943 respectively. Churchill arrived in Malta on 17th November and remained here until the 19th; his visit was not given any publicity nor was a programme of public appearances prepared. This was due to the fact that he was suffering from a feverish cold, which confined him to bed for most of the time. He did manage, however, to attend a Staff conference and to visit the dockyard where the workers gave him an enthusiastic welcome. Afterwards, Churchill and Gort drove into Valletta where a sizeable crowd had gathered on the Palace Square. On entering the Palace, Churchill appeared on the balcony, waving his black naval cap and giving the 'V' sign; he made three appearances in response to the repeated cheers of the swelling crowd. During his visit, the British Prime Minister was accompanied by the Chiefs of Staff and by his two children, Major Randolph Churchill and Section Officer Sarah Oliver, WAAF.

(Crown)
Mr Churchill giving the 'V' sign to dockyard workers while being shown around the Yard by Rear-Admiral Kenneth Mackenzie, Vice-Admiral L.H.K. Hamilton and Field-Marshal Lord Gort.

A more formal welcome awaited President Roosevelt on his arrival on 8th December, 1943. His C 54 Douglas aircraft, escorted by twenty Lightnings and Spitfires, landed at Luqa at 9.30 am where he was met by the Island's leading Civil and Service dignitaries, as well as by a number of American personalities, including Generals Eisenhower, Spaatz, Bedell Smith and Wilson and Rear-Admirals Wilson Brown and Ross Macintire. On leaving the aircraft, the President and Lord Gort boarded the Willys jeep 'Husky',[158] presented in July by General Eisenhower to Sir Keith Park, and took the salute as the RMA band played the American National Anthem. After inspecting the guard of honour provided by the Three Services, President Roosevelt addressed the gathering:

"Lord Gort, Officers and Men, good People of Malta. Nearly a year ago the Prime Minister (Mr Churchill) and I were in Casablanca shortly after the landings by British and American troops in North Africa and, at that time, I told the Prime Minister some day we would control once more the whole of the Mediterranean and that then I would go to Malta. For many months I have wanted on behalf of the American people to pay some little tribute to this Island and to all the people, civil and military, who, during these years have contributed so much to democracy, not just here but all over the civilised world and so at last we have been able to come. At last I have been able to see something of the historic land and I wish I could stay but I have many things to do. May I tell you though that during these past three weeks the Prime Minsiter and I feel that we two have struck strong blows for the future of the human race and so in this simple way I am taking the opportunity to do what all American people would join me in doing. I have here a little token, a scroll, a citation from the President of the United States speaking on behalf of all the people and may I read it to you:

'In the name of the People of the United States of America I salute the Island of Malta, its people and defenders, who, in the cause of freedom and justice and decency throughout the world, have rendered valorous service far above and beyond the call of duty.

'Under repeated fire from the skies, Malta stood

IN THE NAME OF THE PEOPLE OF THE UNITED STATES OF AMERICA I SALUTE THE ISLAND OF MALTA, its people and defenders, who, in the cause of freedom and justice and decency throughout the world, have rendered valorous service far above and beyond the call of duty.

Under repeated fire from the skies, Malta stood alone but unafraid in the center of the sea, one tiny bright flame in the darkness -- a beacon of hope for the clearer days which have come.

Maltas bright story of human fortitude and courage will be read by posterity with wonder and with gratitude through all the ages. What was done in this Island maintains the highest traditions of gallant men and women who from the beginning of time have lived and died to preserve civilization for all mankind.

December 7th 1943
Date

Franklin D Roosevelt

(The Times) President Roosevelt inspecting a guard of honour at Luqa airfield.

alone but unafraid in the center of the sea, one tiny bright flame in the darkness — a beacon of hope for the clearer days which have come.

'Malta's bright story of human fortitude and courage will be read by posterity with wonder and with gratitude through all the ages.

'What was done in this Island maintains the highest traditions of gallant men and women who from the beginning of time have lived and died to preserve civilisation for all mankind.'

December 7th, 1943.   Franklin D. Roosevelt

"I have signed it at the bottom and I wrote on it not today, but yesterday, December 7, because that was the second anniversary of the entry into the war of the American people. We will proceed until that war is won but more than that we will stand shoulder to shoulder with the British Empire and our other Allies in making it a victory worth while."

The President then handed the case containing the illuminated scroll to his son-in-law, Major John Boettiger, who presented it to Lord Gort. Following the Governor's address of appreciation, Mr Roosevelt, while on his way back to his aircraft, expressed a desire to visit the harbour area. He was transferred to the Governor's car and toured Marsa, Pawla, Zabbar, St Peter's, Ricasoli, Kalkara, Vittoriosa, Senglea, Cospicua and the dockyard, after which he left Malta at 1.00 pm.

The list of other distinguished personalities who visited Malta at the height of the blitz and after the raising of the siege is a long one; they included General Wladyslaw Sikorski, Premier of the Polish Government -in-Exile and C-in-C of the Free Polish Forces; General Jan Christiaan Smuts, Prime Minister and C-in-C of South Africa; General Henri Giraud, Chief of the French Armed Forces; Mr. Anthony Eden, Secretary of State for Foreign Affairs; Viscount Cranborne, Secretary of State for the Colonies and Mr Henry Morgenthau, Jr, United States Secretary to the Treasury. Tributes speak for themselves:

General Sikorski — "The ruins of Valletta and of the Maltese churches, just as the ruins of Poland, bear testimony to the love for freedom felt equally by Maltese and Poles."

Air Chief Marshal Tedder — "Undying honour is due to the Maltese themselves, men, women and children, who never lost faith even in the darkest hours of blitz and starvation."

Viscount Cranborne — "No one who has visited the Island, who has seen what I have already seen, could fail to realise how cruel is the ordeal through which you have passed and are passing. Your cities and towns have been ravaged by bombing; your ancient and beautiful churches and monuments of long and honourable history have been wrecked and blasted; your homes have been reduced to heaps of broken stone ... After two years of siege and bombardment almost unrivalled in history, the defences of Malta remain unbroken and you still carry on your daily life, serene and undismayed."

General Sir Alan Brooke — "The destruction (at the docks and at Valletta) is inconceivable and reminds me of Ypres, Arras, Lens at their worse during the last war."

Mr Morgenthau — "I came here at the special request of General Eisenhower to see why the war costs so much. I am seeing it. What Malta has done during the past three years interests me more than what the Knights did. It's amazing what the Maltese people did. We all take off our hats to Malta."

The capture of Sicily, the first step in the Allied plan for the liberation of Europe from Nazi domination, was followed by the landings at Salerno in Italy on 9th September, 1943, and by those at Normandy in France on 6th June, 1944. The Allied armies, converging on Germany from the south, west and east, were involved in long and bitter fighting.

The situation in Malta improved with the retreat of the Germans from Italy. Between October 1943 and August 1944, there were only eight alerts, which did not result in any damage or casualty. The last alert was sounded at 8.43 pm on 28th August, 1944, and the final 'All Clear' at 9.00 pm. Since the start of hostilities on 11th June, 1940, Malta had experienced 3,340 alerts, totalling 2,357 hours 6 minutes. (See Appendix **V**).

Although the Allies had achieved complete mastery in the Mediterranean, certain commodities were still in short supply and rationed. A new rationing scheme for footwear and textiles was introduced at the end of 1943 and, as soon as supplies became available, knitting wool was distributed for children's garments. Between March 1944 and July 1946 babies' baths, layettes and teats for feeding

(D. Nithsdale)
On 4th June, 1944, the American Fifth Army, under General Mark Clark, entered Rome. Photograph shows a poster printed in Malta to mark the occasion.

bottles could be obtained on a ration basis. Families had been unable to buy ordinary household goods for a few years and it was only in February 1945 that a distribution of crockery and brooms could be made, priority being given to large families. In March 1945, when a consignment of 5,000 vacuum flasks was received, about 22,000 applications were submitted and lots had to be drawn. [159]

In 1944, Malta saw the arrival of a large United Nations naval force. The harbours accommodated no fewer than six British and two American aircraft-carriers, one American and one French battleship, four British, two American and one French cruiser, four British, twelve American, one Greek and one Yugoslav destroyer, one Chinese and two Italian sloops, in addition to several supply ships, troopships and submarines. Sailors from these ships roamed the streets of Valletta, together with Maltese, British, Basuto, Mauritian and Palestinian Jewish soldiers, WRNS, Poles, Free French, Yugoslav Royalists, and Partisans of both sexes.

(NWM)
The American cruiser Philadelphia, *which had collided with USS* Laub *off Anzio on 23rd May, 1944, entered No 4 Dock four days later. The shattered bow, seven feet out of line to starboard, was repaired at the Malta Dockyard, enabling the ship to return to active service. Photographs show the cruiser before and after repairs were carried out. Such work was commonplace during the Sicilian and Italian Campaigns, much to the credit of Maltese workmanship.*

On 7th April, 1944, after a three-year lapse, the Good Friday processions were again held in most towns and villages. At Rabat, twenty-four Yugoslav Partisans took part in the procession together with their Field Commander and twelve female partisans in their battledress with the Red Star on their forage caps.

The Island played a minor role in yet another invasion when, on 15th August, 1944, Allied naval units from Malta escorted the British forces that landed on the French Riviera.

The respect and gratitude that the Maltese felt for Lord Gort was marked by a ceremony that took place at Zebbug on Sunday, 12th March, 1944, when the Governor was presented with a Sword of Honour by the Band and Allied Clubs in Malta and Gozo. A huge crowd crammed St Philip Square, which was elaborately decorated; on arrival, Lord Gort was greeted with rounds of applause as the flags of sixty-four Band and Allied clubs of Malta waved in salute. Receiving the sword from Professor Philip Farrugia, representing all the Clubs, Lord Gort said: " ... I shall never cease to regard this Sword with affectionate pride all my life and I shall do so not only because men have always regarded the sword as the symbol of military honour but also on account of the many memories of wartime Malta and Gozo with which I shall always associate it. As the years pass by it will never fail to remind me of the many dangers and the many trials which we mutually suffered and mutually surmounted, many kindnesses and, in particular, the wonderful gesture of spontaneous generosity and goodwill which prompted the Maltese people to honour me as they have honoured me today..." The 38-inch sword, the work of 83-year old Tom Beasley, from the Wilkinson Sword Company, bore the following inscription: "Presented by the Band and Allied Clubs in Malta and Ghawdex, interpreters of the People's admiration, gratitude, devotion and love to H.E. Field-Marshal The Viscount Gort, V.C., their Leader and Governor during the Second Siege of Malta." The silver scabbard carried on it an embossed silver-gilt cross-guard. The show side featured a field marshal's badge and the

(The Times)
Lord Gort holding the Sword of Honour. On right is Mr David Campbell, the Lieutenant-Governor, and on left is Lt Col V.C. Micallef, the Governor's Aide de Camp.

Arms of Malta on the reverse. The ivory grip was held by four Tudor roses and a laurel wreath eyelet for the gold bullion sword knot. Besides the inscription, the blade carried a floral design and the George Cross on one side, and the Arms of Lord Gort and the Royal Cypher on the reverse.

The Maltese turned out again in great numbers to see Viscount Gort for the last time on Saturday, 5th August, 1944, when he was *fêted* down Kingsway prior to his departure to take up his appointment as High Commissioner and Commander-in-Chief Palestine. He was succeeded by Lieutenant-General Sir Edmond Acton Schreiber KCB.

Members of the Home Guard and of the Special Constabulary served their country well in the hour of need. Their services were now no longer necessary and the two Organisations stood down on 10th December, 1944, and 4th February, 1945, respectively. Parades marking the disbandment of the Home Guard were held in various districts, while the Special Constables held their last parade at Police War Headquarters, where they were inspected by General Schreiber.

As the Allied armies closed in onto the heart of Germany, the 'Big Three', Churchill, Roosevelt and Stalin, decided on a meeting at Yalta in the Crimea in February 1945. This was preceded by a series of meetings of the British and American Chiefs of Staff at Montgomery House (now Middle Sea House) in Floriana from 30th January to 1st February, 1945. The British delegation included Admiral Sir Andrew Cunningham, Admiral Sir James Somerville, Air Chief Marshal Sir Charles Portal, Field-Marshal Sir Henry Maitland Wilson, Field-Marshal Sir Alan Brooke, Field-Marshal Sir Harold Alexander, General Sir Hastings Ismay, Major-General Robert Laycock, Lord Leathers and Sir Ralph Metcalfe. The Americans were represented by General George Marshall, Fleet Admiral Joseph King, Major-General Lawrence S. Kuter, Brigadier-General A.G. McFarland, Lieutenant-General Breban B. Somerwell, Major-General W. Bedell Smith, Rear-Admiral Lynde Daniel McCormick and Vice-Admiral Charles N. "Savvy" Cooke. The smiles of the Combined Chiefs of Staff must have been mainly reserved to the Press photographers. It is recorded that the delegations had been engaged in the most turbulent disputes during the entire war, though this does not appear in the official minutes of these meetings. The discussion centred on the selection of a strategic plan for the final assault against Germany. The British plan differed from that proposed by General Eisenhower, who was represented during the meetings by General Bedell Smith. The heated arguments reached a point where General Marshall is stated to have

(The Times)
Allied Commanders outside St John's Co-Cathedral. Left to right: Mr. George Zarb (Information Officer), Admiral Somerville, Admiral King, Admiral Cunningham, Field-Marshal Brooke, Air Chief Marshal Portal, Major-General Kuter, Mr (later Sir) Hannibal Scicluna (Librarian), Field-Marshal Wilson and General Marshall.

said that were the British plan to be chosen, he would advise Eisenhower to relinquish command. Eventually the Combined Chiefs of Staff opted for Eisenhower's plan.[160] Also in Malta to discuss major political issues were Mr Anthony Eden, British Secretary of State for Foreign Affairs, and Mr Edward Stettinius, American Secretary of State.

Mr Churchill, his official party and the rest of his staff, travelled from Northolt on three aircraft. The Prime Minister's plane and one of the two other aircraft arrived at Luqa before dawn on 30th January, 1945. On landing, Mr Churchill was distressed to learn that the third aircraft had crashed near Pantelleria, with the loss of twelve.

Churchill, on coming to know that Roosevelt would be joining him in Malta, cabled the American President: "We shall be delighted if you will come to Malta. I shall be waiting on the quay. You will also see the inscription of your noble message to Malta of a year ago. Everything can be arranged to your convenience. No more let us falter! From Malta to Yalta! Let nobody alter!"

From the deck of HMS *Orion* berthed in the Grand Harbour, Mr Churchill watched as President Roosevelt and his party, including Mr Harry Hopkins, sailed into harbour on the USS *Quincy* on the morning of February 2nd. The two leaders conferred on the American cruiser, after which Mr Roosevelt visited Mdina, Ghajn Tuffieha and Valletta, whilst his car stopped at the Palace Square to enable the President to read his citation on the marble tablet on the Palace facade. Late in the afternoon, Mr Churchill received a delegation from the Chamber of Commerce, who presented him with a silver replica of an old Maltese cannon.

The presence in Malta of the Premier, their President and the Joint Chiefs of Staff was shrouded in secrecy. The night of 2nd/3rd February was one of busy activity at Luqa; transport planes took off at ten-minute intervals, carrying about seven hundred people, including Mr Churchill and Mr Roosevelt, to Saki airfield in the Crimea, a distance of fourteen hundred miles. During the eight plenary meetings of the Yalta Conference, which started on 5th February, the 'Big Three' took vital decisions. This conference not only planned the crushing of Nazism, but was to give Europe a new geographic physiognomy.

In Malta, the Government and the people were now facing the formidable task of reconstruction. New dwellings had to be built and thousands of others repaired by a population still suffering the after effects of prolonged under-nourishment and strain. In 1944, the Government commissioned two British architects, Mr Austen St B. Harrison and Mr P. Pearce S. Hubbard, to submit proposals for reconstruction work in Valletta and the Three Cities. Their report, published in January 1945, produced a plan aimed at providing better housing facilities, the

(US Army)
Roosevelt, Churchill and Hopkins aboard USS Quincy *at the Dockyard. On left are Anna Roosevelt Boettiger and Section Officer Sarah Oliver, daughters of Roosevelt and Churchill respectively.*

demolition of several slum areas as well as road improvements. To meet the cost necessary for reconstruction, the British Parliament in 1942 approved the allocation of the sum of £10,000,000, subsequently raised to £30,000,000.

The rehabilitation of ex-servicemen, especially of conscripts, was no easy task both for Government and the individuals themselves who had to take very important decisions concerning their future.

In Central Europe, events of great significance were taking place. On 25th April, 1945, Benito Mussolini, dressed in a German uniform, tried to escape into Switzerland. Recognised by a group of partisans, he and other leading Fascists were shot the following morning; their bodies, strung up by the feet on meat hooks, were exhibited in the market place in Milan. Four days later, the Germans in Italy surrendered unconditionally to Field-Marshal Alexander.

On the day of Mussolini's capture, American and Russian troops encircling Berlin joined hands as they poised to storm the German capital, where Hitler had sought refuge in the Chancellery bunker. As the Russians were only a few blocks away from Hitler's hide-out, the Führer appointed Grand Admiral Karl Doenitz as his successor and, on 30th April, shot himself.

(via V.E. Stafrace)
The lights of Victory illuminate the harbour area. On left is Fort St Angelo whilst on right are the Upper Barracca Gardens.

The war in Europe came to an end on 7th May, 1945, when *General* Alfred Jodl, on behalf of the German General Staff, signed the unconditional surrender to the representatives of Britain, America, Russia and France at Rheims in France; hostilities were to cease at midnight May 8th.

Malta, with the rest of the free world, celebrated Victory in Europe. In Valletta, Maltese civilians, British and other servicemen from Allied countries joined hands and marched down beflagged Kingsway with bands playing and church bells ringing.

With the cessation of hostilities in Europe, the Allied leaders met at Potsdam to plan the final victory with the subjugation of Japan. On 26th July the Japanese Imperial Command ignored an ultimatum offering unconditional surrender. On 6th August, Colonel Paul W. Tibbets, Jr, in a Superfortress of the United States Air Force, flying at 30,000 feet dropped the first atomic bomb, on Hiroshima, destroying the Japanese industrial city and killing a quarter of the 320,000 inhabitants. A second bomb was dropped three days later from a B-29 piloted by Major Charles W. Sweeny, on Nagasaki, with the same devastating effect. Just before midnight on 14th August, 1945, Japan conceded defeat, marking the end of the Second World War.

The long-awaited news reached Malta at 1.00 am on 15th August, 1945, the third anniversary of the arrival of *Ohio*. At six in the morning of that historic day, the Maltese woke to the terrific din created by the sounding of sirens, the pealing of bells and the hooting from ships in harbour.

On Sunday, 19th August, 1945, His Grace Mgr Michael Gonzi held a Victory Thanksgiving Service at St John's Co-Cathedral in Valletta. Addressing the congregation before the singing of the *Te Deum*, the Archbishop said: "*Exultemus:* Let us rejoice..."

SOURCES AND NOTES

1. General Sir Charles Bonham-Carter, Governor of Malta since 3rd March, 1936, left Malta for medical treatment in England on 24th May, 1940; health reasons prevented him from returning to the Island. Lieutenant-General Sir William Dobbie, who had arrived in Malta on 28th April, 1940, assumed the duties of Officer Administering the Government on the day of the Governor's departure.

2. *The Story of The Royal Army Service Corps 1939-1945*, published under the direction of The Institution of The Royal Army Service Corps; page 215.

3. Interview by the National War Museum Association on 27th January, 1976.

4. The Yellow Garage was originally located in a tunnel beneath the bastion on the left hand side of the bridge leading to City Gate. In 1971 the garage was moved to the old railway tunnel on the right hand side.

5. During the First World War, General Dobbie held the rank of Lieutenant Colonel and was on the staff of Field-Marshal Sir Douglas Haig at General Headquarters. At 0630 hours on 11th November, 1918, he received a message to be circulated to all British units. As GSO 1 on duty at the time, he signed this message; it brought hostilities to an end at 1100 hours that same day. (Source: Sybil Dobbie; *Faith and Fortitude*; page 114.)

6. Interview by NWMA on 11th May, 1982.

7. Interview by NWMA on 8th July, 1977.

8. Interview by NWMA on 13th November, 1979.

9. Debates of The Council of Government; Vol. VI, page 650.

10. Interview by NWMA on 1st March, 1980.

11. This Section later assumed responsibility for photographing destroyed and damaged buildings in connection with claims for compensation submitted under the War Damage Ordinance.

12. Black-out regulations were introduced with effect from Friday, 3rd May, 1940. These imposed that all lights in Malta and Gozo had to be turned off, or masked to render them invisible from the air and from the sea, between 7.00 pm and sunrise.

    Curfew came into force on Monday, 27th May, 1940. Everyone in the Maltese Islands, with the exception of authorised persons, had to remain indoors from 11.00 pm until 5.00 am.

13. The first streets to be named in English were those in Valletta, Vittoriosa, Cospicua and Senglea, as directed by Government Notice No 423 published in *The Malta Government Gazette* No 8745 dated 13th August, 1940.

14. NWMA Archives.

15. Letter from Ronald Lucking dated October 1981.

16. Interview by NWMA on 3rd March, 1975.

17. NWMA Archives.

18. Ibid

19. Letter from Ronald Lucking dated October 1981.

20. Account by Major Reginald Parker GM dated 1979.

21. Interview by NWMA on 5th September, 1978.

22. Picchi was eventually recognised by an interrogator and later shot as a spy.

23. Interview by NWMA on 19th July, 1975.

24. Major-General I.S.O. Playfair; *The Mediterranean and Middle East;* Vol. II, page 46.

25. *Leħen is-Sewwa;* 10th May, 1980.

26. The English translation reads 'There it is'. The motto is now given in the masculine form '*Ara fejn hu*' ('There he is'). It is not known when or why the change was effected.

27. Air Marshal Sir Hugh P. Lloyd; *Briefed to Attack*; page 13.

28. Ibid, page 45.

29. *Generale* Corrado Ricci; *Vita di Pilota*, page 188.

30. Interview by NWMA on 7th February, 1975.

31. The tablet, unveiled on 26th May, 1973, by the Hon Dr Joseph Cassar LL.D., Minister of Labour, Employment and Welfare, was blessed by Fr Gabriel Bartolo OFM Cap., son of Giuseppe who had lost his life on *Moor*.

    From research carried out by the National War Museum Association, it results that the name of Toni Bonnici on the tablet should read Alfred Bonnici.

32. When the Germans had invaded Norway on 9th April, 1940, four Heinkel 115 floatplanes of the Norwegian Naval Air Force (Marinens Flyvaaben) made their way to Britain. These were eventually sold by the Norwegian Government to the Air Ministry and two of them, bearing serial numbers BV 185 and BV 187, ended up in Malta.

33. J. Valerio Borghese; *Decima Flottiglia Mas*, page 121.

34. Ibid, page 124.

35. Such an eventuality had been foreseen by the Military Authorities and searchlights were positioned to cover this area, officially known as the Illuminated Area.

36. *The Malta Land Force Journal*, Issue No 7 dated July 1971, pages 63-65.

37. Interview by NWMA on 10th February, 1976.

38. J. Valerio Borghese; op. cit., page 142.

39. Tullio Marcon; *Operazione Malta Due*, page 23, and correspondence.

40. Interview by NWMA on 13th November, 1979.

41. Interview by NWMA on 22nd November, 1983.

42. Ministry of Information; *His Majesty's Submarines*, pages 32-33.

43. Major-General I.S.O. Playfair; op. cit., Vol. II, page 269.

44. Peter C. Smith and Edwin Walker; *The Battles of the Malta Striking Forces*, page 61.

45. Albert Kesselring; *The Memoirs of Feld-Marshal Kesselring*, page 109.

46. *Our Penelope*, page 31.

47. No bronze coins were delivered to Malta between 1939 and 1943. From the Annual Reports of the Royal Mint for the wartime period, it results that in 1940 there was an excessive quantity of pennies in circulation in Britain. Consequently, on 20th June, 1940, The Master of the Mint announced in the House of Commons that the minting of pennies was being suspended to conserve labour and copper. Such coins were again supplied to Malta in 1944. A consignment of nickel-brass threepences, with a face value of £9,380, reached Malta in 1943.

48. Interview by NWMA on 21st March, 1975.

49. Interview by NWMA on 1st July, 1977.

50. Interview by NWMA on 29th June, 1977.

51. G.W.G. Simpson; *Periscope View*, pages 205-206.

52. NWM Archives.

53. Harry Grossett; *Down to the Ships in the Sea*, page 227.

54. *Times of Malta* dated 13th October, 1942.

55. *Debates of the Council of Government*, Question No 734, Vol. 7, page 1216.

56. Daily allowances recommended in 1950 by the Nutrition Committee of the British Medical Association; reproduced in *Teach Yourself Nutrition* by Magnus Pyke, page 125.

57. H.J. Desson, T. Agius Ferrante, H.G.G. Bernstein and R.E. Tunbridge; *The Poliomyelitis Epidemic in Malta 1942-43; The Quarterly Journal of Medicine* No 53 dated January 1945.

58. Air Marshal Sir Hugh P. Lloyd; op. cit., pages 149-150.

59. Interview by NWMA on 12th April, 1975.

60. Letter from Mr. J. Max Surman RIBA dated March 1981 to Malta High Commissioner in London.

61. R.V. Jones; *Most Secret War*, pages 329-330.

62. Brigadier B.B. Kennett CBE and Colonel J.A. Tatman; *REME — Craftsmen of the Army*, page 109.

63. Brigadier A.H. Fernyhough; *History of the R.A.O.C. 1920-1945*, page 332.

64. *The Story of the Royal Army Service Corps 1939-1945;* published under the direction of The Institution of The Royal Army Service Corps, page 211.

65. *News from Israel* No 018 dated May 1977.

66. *A Short History of 7th Heavy A.A. Regiment (3rd September, 1939 — 5th March, 1944) in the Defence of Malta;* pages 24 and 25.

67. Letter dated 18th October, 1983, from Arnold Green, who served in Malta with No 1 Independent Troop RTR from 1940 to 1943.

68. Interview by NWMA on 12th July, 1980.

69. Interview by NWMA on 17th September, 1979.

70. Interview by NWMA on 8th March, 1975.

71. Ibid

72. Ibid

73. Ibid

74. Albert Kesselring; op. cit., page 121.

75. Interview by NWMA on 5th April, 1975.

76. Interview by NWMA on 15th September, 1982.

77. Interview by NWMA on 30th March, 1975.

78. Interview by NWMA on 19th March, 1975.

79. Rev Joseph Micallef; *Rahal Fi Gwerra*, pages 69 to 74.

80. Cajus Bekker; *The Luftwaffe War Diaries*, page 304.

81. Interview by NWMA on 13th May, 1982.

82. Ibid

83. Brigadier A.H. Fernyhough; op. cit., page 334.

84. Account sent on 12th April, 1983, by Lt Col Franklin F. Clark DSC and Bar.

85. Interview by NWMA on 20th December, 1975.

86. Interview by NWMA on 1st February, 1975.

87. *A Short History of 7th Heavy A.A. Regiment (3rd September, 1939 — 5th March, 1944) in the Defence of Malta;* pages 6 and 7.

88. Interview by NWMA on 31st July, 1980.

89. Alan Moorehead; *The March to Tunis,* page 310.

90. Interview by NWMA on 9th February, 1975.

91. R.T. Gilchrist; *Malta Strikes Back,* page 7.

92. Ibid

93. Cajus Bekker; op. cit., pages 305-306.

94. G.W.G. Simpson; op. cit., page 299.

95. Commander F.W. Lipscomb, *The British Submarine,* pages 109-110.

96. The George Cross was instituted by King George VI on 23rd September, 1940, to be bestowed on civilians and servicemen displaying 'acts of the greatest heroism or of the most conspicuous courage in circumstances of extreme danger.' It is of equivalent status as the Victoria Cross, which is awarded to servicemen performing 'some signal act of valour or devotion' in the presence of the enemy. The George Cross is in the form of a plain cross of silver with four equal limbs bearing the motto 'For Gallantry'. The name of the recipient and the date of the act of bravery are engraved on the reverse of the cross. The George Cross awarded to Malta is inscribed 'To The Island of Malta 15 April 1942'. The colour of the ribbon is garter blue and the medal is 1.375 inches in diameter. Malta is the only country awarded this prestigious medal. During the First World War, Dunkirk was awarded the Distinguished Service Cross, while Ypres and Verdun received the Military Cross. (Source: VC and GC, published by Imperial War Museum in 1970.)

97. Letter from Major Reginald Parker GM dated 1st May, 1980.

98. Citation dated 6th November, 1942; NWMA Archives.

99. Report No UBC 3872/42 dated 27th April, 1942; NWMA Archives.

100. NWMA Archives and letters from Lieut-Cdr Edward D. Woolley GM and Bar dated 16th April and 15th May, 1984.

101. On 10th July, 1942, Flt Lt (later Sqn Ldr) H.B.H. Dickinson was awarded the George Medal for outstanding courage, initiative and devotion to duty while performing dangerous work.

102. Sir Hugh P. Lloyd; op. cit., pages 143-144.

103. NWMA Archives.

104. Report dated 26th August, 1942, regarding unexploded bombs; NWMA Archives.

105. *Official History of the Second World War, Army Medical Services, Campaigns in General History;* pages 631-632.

106. Interview by NWMA with Louis F. Tortell on 27th February, 1981. During the war years, Mr. Tortell was employed as Clerk Assistant to the Council of Government.

107. Interview by NWMA on 13th October, 1975.

108. Reminiscences by Alex Randon of Sliema.

109. Account by John Galea dated 1st November, 1977.

110. Douglas S. Bader CBE DSO DFC; *Fight for the Sky,* page 133.

111. Nicola Malizia; *Inferno su Malta,* page 191.

112. W.J.A. Wood; *Royal Air Force Year Book 1979,* page 29.

113. Interview by NWMA on 15th September, 1981.

114. Ian Cameron; *Red Duster White Ensign,* pages 176-177.

115. NWMA Archives.

116. Reminiscences recorded by Philip A. Dixon RIBA Dip. Arch.

117. George R. Crockett; *The Airman is a Sailor;* unpublished manuscript reproduced by permission of Mrs Vera Crockett.

118. Interview by NWMA on 15th February, 1975.

119. Letter from Leo Nomis dated 11th March, 1983.

120. Talk given to members of the NWMA by Group Captain Edward W.T. Hardie CBE M Mar at the British Council, Valletta, on 7th May, 1975.

121. George R. Crockett; op, cit.

122. Ibid

123. Ibid

124. Ibid

125. Ibid

126. Ibid

127. Albert Kesselring; op. cit., page 125.

128. Ibid, page 123.

129. NWMA Archives.

130. Brigadier Kenneth P. Smith OBE; *Malta; The Part Played by the Infantry; Army Quarterly,* January 1944, pages 247 and 248.

131. Letter from J.S. Houghton dated 27th October, 1981.

132. Emiliani, Ghergo and Vigna; *Regia Aeronautica: Il Settore Mediterraneo,* pages 104-105.

133. *Evening Standard* dated 16th March, 1943.

134. Foreword to *Pedestal: The Malta Convoy of August 1942.*

135. Interview by NWMA with Albert Mallia on 13th July, 1976.

136. Shortly after her cargo was discharged, *Ohio* was moored at Rinella Bay, where she broke in half and rested in shallow water. As it was technically impossible to join the two halves, each was made watertight. The hulks, at first used for storage, later served as a base ship for small units of the Royal Navy and the Royal Yugoslav Navy; eventually, no further use could be made of the hulks. The fore part was taken out of the Grand Harbour on 19th September, 1946, and sunk ten miles to the north-east of Malta by gunfire from the destroyer HMS *Virago*. The stern part was towed out on 2nd October, 1946, by the salvage vessel *Salventure* and the tugs *Robust, Empire Ace* and *Expert*. At dawn the following day, Commander Newman, Salvage Officer Malta, and Chief Petty Officer Shepherd boarded the hulk for the last time to check the explosive charges; these were set off and the stern slid beneath the surface.

137. Letter from Earl Mountbatten of Burma dated 22nd June, 1978.

138. Interview by NWMA on 3rd July, 1976.

139. Letter from Frank Hewlett dated 22nd November, 1980.

140. Winston S. Churchill; *The Second World War,* Volume IV, page 411.

141. Interview by NWMA on 3rd July, 1976. Besides the Enquiry mentioned by Mr Treves, a debate took place in the House of Lords on 14th October, 1942, on the following Question about Shipping Secrecy tabled by The Earl of Cork and Orrery: "To ask His Majesty's Government whether they consider that every possible step is taken at the ports of the United Kingdom to keep secret the destination of ships that are loading therein." (Hansard, pages 647 to 656.)

142. L. Hurst; *Report on the Working of the Rationing Office for the Years 1941-1945*, dated 4th November, 1946; published in *The Malta Government Gazette*, Supplement No V of 17th January, 1947.

143. Interview by NWMA on 30th January, 1984.

144. Interview by NWMA on 31st December, 1983.

145. NWMA Archives.

146. Air Vice-Marshal Sandy Johnstone CB DFC; *Where No Angels Dwell*, page 122.

147. Christopher Shores, Hans Ring and William Hess; *Fighters Over Tunisia*, page 65.

148. NWMA Archives.

149. General Dwight D. Eisenhower; *Crusade in Europe*, pages 170 and 171.

150. Diary of King George VI; reproduced by the gracious permission of HM Queen Elizabeth II.

151. Alfred Wagg and David Brown; *No Spaghetti for Breakfast*, page 39.

152. Mr (later Sir) David C. Campbell succeeded Sir Edward St John Jackson as Lieutenant Governor on 12th February, 1943. The latter had held this appointment since 31st January, 1940.

153. John W. Wheeler-Bennett; *King George VI: His Life and Reign*, page 578.

154. Interview by NWMA on 8th February, 1981.

155. John Gunther; *Procession*, page 317.

156. Admiral of the Fleet Viscount Cunningham of Hyndhope KT GCB OM DSO; *A Sailor's Odyssey*, page 564.

157. Account by Brigadier Alfred Samut-Tagliaferro CBE dated 20th February, 1983.

158. This jeep, presented to the People of Malta by Air Vice-Marshal Sir Bryan V. Reynolds, AOC Malta, on 16th April, 1955, is exhibited at the National War Museum.

159. L. Hurst; op. cit.

160. Robert E. Sherwood; *Roosevelt and Harry Hopkins*, page 848.

Appendix A

BRITISH ARMY UNITS SERVING IN MALTA DURING THE SECOND WORLD WAR

Headquarters Malta Command

Royal Armoured Corps
Independent Troop Malta

Royal Regiment of Artillery
Headquarters Royal Artillery Malta
Headquarters Fixed Defences
Headquarters 10 HAA Brigade
Headquarters 7 LAA Brigade
12 Field Regiment
12 Gun Operations Room Regiment
4 Coast Regiment
4 HAA Regiment
7 HAA Regiment
10 HAA Regiment (later 68 HAA Regiment)
32 LAA Regiment
65 LAA Regiment
74 LAA Regiment
107 LAA Regiment
26 Defence Regiment
Coastal Observation Detachments
Searchlight Batteries

Royal Malta Artillery
1st Coast Regiment
  1 Coast Battery
  2 Coast Battery
  3 Coast Battery
  4 Coast Battery

2nd Heavy Anti-Aircraft Regiment
  5 HAA Battery (in Middle East from 7 May 1940 to February 1943)
  6 HAA Battery
  7 HAA Battery
  9 HAA Battery

3rd Light Anti-Aircraft Regiment
  10 LAA Battery
  15 LAA Battery
  22 LAA Battery
  30 LAA Battery (formerly Dockyard Defence Battery)

4th Searchlight Regiment RA/RMA
  8 Searchlight Battery

5th Coast Regiment
  11 Coast Battery
  12 Coast Battery
  13 Defence Battery

11th Heavy Anti-Aircraft Regiment (Territorial)
  20 HAA Battery
  21 HAA Battery
  23 HAA Battery

Corps of Royal Engineers
16 Fortress Company
24 Fortress Company
1 Tunnelling Company
171 Tunnelling Company
173 Tunnelling Company
1 (Works) Company
2 (Works) Company

Royal Corps of Signals
Malta Signal Company
No 4 Company Air Formation Signals
Pigeon Loft Unit

Infantry of the Line
Headquarters 231 Infantry Brigade
Headquarters 232 Infantry Brigade
Headquarters 233 Infantry Brigade
Headquarters 234 Infantry Brigade
4th Battalion The Buffs
8th Battalion The King's Own Royal Lancaster Regiment
2nd Battalion The Devonshire Regiment
11th Battalion The Lancashire Fusiliers
1st Battalion The Cheshire Regiment
1st Battalion The Hampshire Regiment
1st Battalion The Dorsetshire Regiment
2nd Battalion The Queen's Own Royal West Kent Regiment
8th Battalion The Manchester Regiment
1st Battalion The Durham Light Infantry
2nd Battalion The Royal Irish Fusiliers
1st Battalion The King's Own Malta Regiment
2nd Battalion The King's Own Malta Regiment
3rd Battalion The King's Own Malta Regiment
Static Group The King's Own Malta Regiment (later 10th Battalion)

Royal Army Chaplains Department

Royal Army Service Corps
Headquarters RASC Malta
32 (GT) Company
651 (GT) Company
178 (GT) Company (Palestinian)
468 (GT) Company (Palestinian)
Supply Depot

Royal Army Medical Corps
30 Company
33 General Hospital
39 General Hospital
45 General Hospital
90 General Hospital
15 Field Ambulance (East African)
161 Field Ambulance (East African)
11 Field Surgical Unit
57 Field Hygiene Section
Convalescent Depot

Royal Army Ordnance Corps
Ordinance Depot
Ammunition Depot

Royal Electrical and Mechanical Engineers
Command Workshops

Corps of Military Police

226 Provost Company

Royal Army Pay Corps

72 Detachment

Army Dental Corps

Field Dental Centre

Pioneer Corps

Malta Pioneer Corps
2600 Company
2601 Company
2602 Company
Headquarters 87 Group
1501 (Mauritian) Company
1502 (Mauritian) Company
1505 (Mauritian) Company
1507 (Mauritian) Company
1921 (Basuto) Company
1923 (Basuto) Company
1949 (Basuto) Company
1950 (Basuto) Company
612 (Palestine Arab) Company
Smoke Company

Intelligence Corps

69 Field Section
Special W/T Section

(Compiled by Alex Randon)

Appendix B

PRESENTATION SPITFIRES
MALTA W3210 and *GHAWDEX* W3212

The two Presentation Spitfires *Malta* and *Ghawdex* were delivered to No 8 Maintenance Unit at Little Rissington, Oxfordshire, on 14th and 16th May, 1941, respectively. Released to No 74 Squadron on 18th May, both aircraft took part in the several sweeps and patrols as recorded further on.

Most of the service career of W3210 erroneously appears under serial number W3120 in No 74 Squadron Form 541.

On 27th June, 1941, after a very positive action over North Eastern France, probably between Amiens and Abbeville, three Spitfires from No 74 Squadron were posted missing at about 2130 hours. One of the aircraft lost was *Malta* W3210 flown by Pilot Officer W.J. Sandman RNZAF, the sole survivor taken prisoner.

The accident that virtually put an end to *Ghawdex* W3212's career in the Royal Air Force was a chapter of misfortunes. On 6th February, 1942, the aircraft, together with other Mk VBs from No 92 Squadron, was flown from RAF Station Digby to RAF Station Colerne for delivery to No 417 Squadron Royal Canadian Air Force. Four days later, it was taken up for a formation flight over Bath, during the course of which it ran out of fuel as it was not refuelled after arrival at Colerne. Although the fuel gauge read 'full', this related only to the contents of the bottom one of two integral fuselage fuel tanks (a matter of only 37 gallons), whereas Form 700 was signed-up to show that the fuel content was 80 gallons. The pilot, Sergeant R.L. Hazel RCAF, force-landed in a field just short of RAF Station Charmy Down. W3212 was eventually taken to a Civilian Repair Unit before being re-issued on 26th May, 1942, to No 9 Maintenance Unit. In February 1943 the aircraft was modified to Seafire Mk IB configuration; its serial number was changed to NX 883. On 5th April, 1943, it was ferried to the Royal Naval Air Station at Lee-on-Solent for service with the Royal Navy.

Malta W3210 — Form 78

14.5.41	No 8 Maintenance Unit
18.5.41	No 74 Squadron
27.6.41	F.B. CAT E — Missing
4.7.41	Struck off charge

Ghawdex W3212 — Form 78

16.5.41	No 8 Maintenance Unit
18.5.41	No 74 Squadron
10.7.41	A.S.T.
9.9.41	No 6 Maintenance Unit
17.9.41	No 92 Squadron
6.2.42	No 417 Squadron
10.2.42	F.A. CAT AC
	C.R.U.
26.5.42	No 9 Maintenance Unit
17.2.43	A.S.T. Modification to Seafire Mk IB. Serial number changed to NX 883
5.4.43	RNAS Lee-on-Solent; service thereafter with the Royal Navy

Malta W3210 No 74 Squadron Operational Record

23 May 41	1145 — 1155	Sgt Dykes	Gravesend — West Malling
23	1400 — 1410	Sgt Dykes	West Malling — Gravesend
23	1755 — 1805	Sgt Wilson	Gravesend — West Malling
23	1850 — 1900	Sgt Wilson	West Malling — Gravesend
24	0945 — 0955	Plt Off Krol	Gravesend — West Malling
24	1155 — 1205	Plt Off Krol	West Malling — Gravesend
25	1525 — 1555	Fg Off Boulding	Gravesend — Ipswich

25	2010 — 2040	Fg Off Boulding	Ipswich — Gravesend
26	1140 — 1215	Plt Off Sandman	Air Firing
26	1725 — 1800	Plt Off Parkes	Air Firing
7 Jun	0500 — 0700	Plt Off Krol	Convoy Patrol
7	0735 — 0750	Plt Off Krol	Hawkinge — Gravesend
7	2145 — 2155	Plt Off Sandman	Gravesend — West Malling
8	1215 — 1225	Plt Off Sandman	West Malling — Gravesend
9	1400 — 1510	Plt Off Sandman	Patrol. One Me 109 Probable
11	0920 — 1045	Plt Off Sandman	Convoy Patrol
11	1430 — 1505	Plt Off Sandman	Air Firing
11	1555 — 1730	Plt Off Sandman	Bomber Escort
12	0545 — 0720	Plt Off Sandman	Patrol
12	0815 — 0845	Plt Off Sandman	Patrol
12	1405 — 1530	Plt Off Sandman	Blenheim Escort
13	0905 — 1035	Sgt Hilken	Patrol
13	1155 — 1235	Sgt Hilken	Patrol
13	1425 — 1610	Plt Off Sandman	Patrol
14	0650 — 0810	Plt Off Sandman	Patrol
14	0840 — 0855	Plt Off Sandman	Manston — Gravesend
14	1840 — 1955	Plt Off Parkes	Bomber Escort
15	1530 — 1630	Plt Off Sandman	Practice Flying
15	1825 — 2005	Plt Off Sandman	Sweep
17	1130 — 1245	Plt Off Sandman	Patrol
17	1600 — 1610	Plt Off Krol	Gravesend — Biggin Hill
17	1835 — 2005	Plt Off Krol	Sweep
18	0640 — 0740	Plt Off Sandman	Patrol
20	1805 — 1840	Plt Off Sandman	Formation Flying
21	0905 — 1035	Plt Off Sandman	Patrol
21	1205 — 1350	Plt Off Sandman	Sweep
21	1525 — 1535	Plt Off Sandman	Gravesend — Biggin Hill
21	1600 — 1730	Plt Off Sandman	Sweep
21	1805 — 1815	Plt Off Sandman	Biggin Hill — Gravesend
22	1405 — 1415	Plt Off Mould	Gravesend — Biggin Hill
22	1530 — 1645	Plt Off Mould	Sweep. One Me 109 Damaged
22	1715 — 1740	Plt Off Mould	Sweep
22	1830 — 1840	Plt Off Mould	Biggin Hill — Gravesend
23	1120 — 1130	Plt Off Poulton	Gravesend — Biggin Hill
23	1245 — 1305	Plt Off Poulton	Sweep
23	1500 — 1525	Plt Off Sandman	Air Test
23	1805 — 1815	Plt Off Sandman	Gravesend — Biggin Hill
23	1940 — 2110	Plt Off Sandman	Sweep
24	1705 — 1715	Plt Off Sandman	Gravesend — Biggin Hill
24	2025 — 2115	Plt Off Sandman	Sweep
25	1420 — 1430	Plt Off Sandman	Gravesend — Biggin Hill
25	1545 — 1705	Plt Off Sandman	Sweep
26	0915 — 0925	Flt Off Sandman	Gravesend — Biggin Hill
26	1045 — 1220	Plt Off Sandman	Sweep
27	1655 — 1705	Plt Off Sandman	Gravesend — Biggin Hill
27	2050 — +	Plt Off Sandman	Missing

Also Missing on the 27th June, 1941, from the same Sweep were Sqn Ldr Mungo-Park X4668 and Sgt Hilken W3252.

Ghawdex W3212 No 74 Squadron Operational Record

24 May 41	1200 — 1210	Sgt Doerr	Gravesend — West Malling
24	1420 — 1430	Sgt Doerr	West Malling — Gravesend
27	1140 — 1220	Fg Off Baker	Air Firing
3 Jun	1055 — 1125	Fg Off Baker	Air Firing
7	1150 — 1315	Fg Off Parkes	Sweep
7	2145 — 2155	Fg Off Boulding	Gravesend — West Malling
8	1215 — 1225	Fg Off Boulding	West Malling — Gravesend
11	1020 — 1130	Plt Off Skinner	Convoy Patrol

12	0630 — 0800	Plt Off Skinner	Patrol
12	1405 — 1530	Plt Off Skinner	Blenheim Escort
13	0905 — 1035	Plt Off Skinner	Patrol
13	1155 — 1210	Plt Off Skinner	Patrol
13	1425 — 1525	Plt Off Skinner	Patrol
14	0650 — 0810	Plt Off Skinner	Patrol
14	0840 — 0855	Plt Off Skinner	Manston — Gravesend
15	1520 — 1615	Sgt Carter	Practice Flying
16	1535 — 1655	Plt Off Sandman	Blenheim Escort. One Me 109F Probable
16	1800 — 1815	Plt Off Sandman	Hawkinge — Gravesend
17	1600 — 1610	Sgt Wilson	Gravesend — Biggin Hill
17	1835 — 2005	Sgt Wilson	Sweep
20	1805 — 1840	Sgt Evans	Formation Flying
21	1205 — 1350	Sgt Wilson	Sweep
21	1525 — 1535	Sgt Wilson	Gravesend — Biggin Hill
21	1600 — 1615	Sgt Wilson	Biggin Hill — Gravesend
21	1900 — 1910	Plt Off Skinner	Air Test
21	2025 — 2150	Plt Off Sandman	Convoy Patrol
23	0915 — 0925	Plt Off Skinner	Air Test
23	1120 — 1130	Plt Off Skinner	Gravesend — Biggin Hill
23	1245 — 1415	Plt Off Skinner	Sweep
23	1805 — 1815	Plt Off Skinner	Gravesend — Biggin Hill
23	1940 — 2110	Plt Off Skinner	Sweep
24	1705 — 1715	Plt Off Skinner	Gravesend — Biggin Hill
24	1950 — 2125	Plt Off Skinner	Sweep
25	1035 — 1105	Plt Off Skinner	Gravesend — Biggin Hill
25	1150 — 1315	Plt Off Skinner	Sweep
25	1420 — 1430	Sgt Mallett	Gravesend — Biggin Hill
25	1545 — 1710	Sgt Mallett	Sweep
27	1655 — 1705	Sgt Wilson	Gravesend — Biggin Hill
27	2050 — 2215	Sgt Wilson	Sweep
28	0625 — 0635	Sgt Wilson	Gravesend — Biggin Hill
28	0745 — 0925	Sgt Wilson	Sweep
29	0725 — 0850	Plt Off Skinner	Convoy Patrol
29	1120 — 1200	Plt Off Skinner	Sweep
29	1425 — 1545	Plt Off Skinner	Sweep
1 Jul	0915 — 1040	Plt Off Stokoe	Patrol
1	1545 — 1645	Plt Off Stokoe	Blenheim Escort
1	1900 — 2010	Plt Off Stokoe	Patrol
2	1035 — 1045	Sqn Ldr Mears	Gravesend — Biggin Hill
2	1155 — 1315	Plt Off Henderson	Sweep
3	1320 — 1330	Sgt Stuart	Gravesend — Biggin Hill
3	1445 — 1625	Sgt Stuart	Sweep
3	1630 — 1645	Sgt Stuart	Manston — Gravesend
4	1255 — 1305	Flt Lt Saunders	Gravesend — Biggin Hill
4	1525 — 1540	Sgt Mason	Biggin Hill — Gravesend
5	1105 — 1115	Sgt Lockhart	Gravesend — Biggin Hill
5	1215 — 1355	Sgt Lockhart	Sweep
5	1425 — 1440	Sgt Lockhart	Hawkinge — Gravesend
5	1610 — 1615	Sgt Lockhart	Gravesend — Biggin Hill
6	1335 — 1510	Sgt Lockhart	Sweep

Ghawdex W3212 No 92 Squadron Operational Record

25 Sep 41	1515 — 1525	Flt Lt Lund	Biggin Hill — Gravesend
2 Oct	1135 — 1150	Sgt Samouelle	Gravesend — Biggin Hill
2	1240 — 1255	Sgt Samouelle	Biggin Hill — Gravesend
3	1135 — 1150	Sgt Samouelle	Gravesend — Biggin Hill
3	1345 — 1400	Sgt Carpenter	Biggin Hill — Gravesend
12	1030 — 1045	Sgt Samouelle	Gravesend — Biggin Hill
12	1125 — 1250	Sgt Samouelle	Sweep
13	1320 — 1505	Sgt Samouelle	Sweep
13	1535 — 1555	Sgt Samouelle	Manston — Gravesend

15	0645 — 0810	Sgt Samouelle	Patrol Manston
15	0815 — 0835	Sgt Samouelle	Manston — Gravesend
20	1000 — 1100	Sgt Samouelle	Gravesend — Digby
24	1350 — 1515	Sgt Samouelle	Patrol for Ju 88
28	1340 — 1525	Sgt Samouelle	Convoy Patrol
1 Nov	0815 — 0835	Sgt Samouelle	Digby — Manby
1	0920 — 0940	Sgt Samouelle	Manby — Digby
1	1040 — 1130	Sgt Pavely	Aerobatics
3	1345 — 1445	Sgt Ryder	Patrol
4	0740 — 0845	Sgt Ryder	Convoy Patrol
6	0830 — 0855	Sgt Brown	Digby — Sutton Bridge
6	0940 — 1005	Sgt Brown	Air Firing
6	1145 — 1220	Sgt Brown	Sutton Bridge — Digby
6	1530 — 1545	Sgt Samouelle	Digby — Manby
6	1610 — 1735	Sgt Samouelle	Convoy Patrol
8	0850 — 0905	Sgt Samouelle	Digby — Manby
8	1100 — 1120	Sgt Samouelle	Manby — Digby
8	1155 — 1325	Sgt Clapson	Patrol for Ju 88
9	1520 — 1535	Sgt Samouelle	Digby — Manby
9	1635 — 1655	Sgt Samouelle	Manby — Digby
11	1150 — 1325	Sgt Brown	Sea Sweep
11	1415 — 1450	Sgt Samouelle	Practice Combat
11	1545 — 1620	Sgt Rose	Practice Combat
15	1030 — 1155	Sgt James	Battle Climb
17	1000 — 1035	Sgt James	Formation Flying
18	1020 — 1115	Sgt Seifert	Formation Flying
18	1150 — 1305	Sgt Rose	Formation Flying
18	1500 — 1550	Sgt Atkins	Formation Flying
18	1650 — 1820	Sgt Atkins	Dusk Patrol
23	1215 — 1315	Sgt Samouelle	Air Firing
24	1025 — 1055	Sgt Samouelle	Formation Flying
24	1415 — 1500	Sgt Samouelle	Formation Flying and Air Firing
25	1145 — 1400	Sgt Samouelle	Sea Sweep
25	1440 — 1525	Sgt Samouelle	Camera-gun Practice
25	1530 — 1605	Sgt Seifert	Camera-gun Practice
26	1030 — 1110	Plt Off Smith	Camera-gun Practice
26	1425 — 1530	Sgt Samouelle	Air Firing
26	1600 — 1615	Sgt Atkins	Air Firing
27	1030 — 1120	Plt Off James	Practice Combat
27	1145 — 1245	Sgt Samouelle	Air Firing
5 Dec	1140 — 1225	Plt Off James	Camera-gun Practice
5	1445 — 1530	Plt Off Smith	Camera-gun Practice
5	1605 — 1615	Plt Off Smith	Formation Flying
7	0955 — 1125	Plt Off James	Air Firing
8	1455 — 1625	Plt Off James	Camera-gun Practice
9	1130 — 1200	Sgt Rose	Instrument Flying
10	1155 — 1215	Sgt Samouelle	Formation Flying
10	1430 — 1540	Plt Off James	Formation Flying
11	1100 — 1215	Sgt Brown	Camera-gun Practice
11	1440 — 1605	Sgt Rose	Air Firing
11	1630 — 1705	Plt Off James	Dusk Landings
13	1020 — 1120	Plt Off Samouelle	Instrument Flying
13	1615 — 1720	Plt Off Samouelle	Dusk Landings
15	0955 — 1120	Plt Off Samouelle	Squadron Formation Flying
15	1210 — 1220	Plt Off Samouelle	Digby — Cranwell
16	0950 — 1035	Plt Off Samouelle	Air Firing
16	1105 — 1210	Plt Off Samouelle	Wing Formation Flying
17	0825 — 1005	Flt Lt Beake	Convoy Patrol
21	1145 — 1230	Plt Off Samouelle	Formation Flying
21	1550 — 1635	Plt Off Samouelle	Air Firing
23	1120 — 1215	Sgt Rose	Camera-gun Practice
24	0950 — 1045	Sgt Rose	Air Firing

24	1205 — 1310	Sgt Rose	Air Firing
26	1030 — 1205	Sgt Rose	Convoy Patrol
27	1525 — 1555	Sgt Rose	Manby — Digby
6 Jan 42	1120 — 1140	Plt Off Samouelle	Local Flying
6	1410 — 1510	Plt Off Samouelle	Formation Flying
7	1100 — 1115	Plt Off Samouelle	Weather Test
8	1030 — 1120	Plt Off Samouelle	Formation Flying
8	1455 — 1550	Plt Off Samouelle	Camera-gun Practice
9	1015 — 1115	Plt Off Samouelle	Local Flying
9	1400 — 1500	Plt Off Samouelle	Formation Flying
9	1550 — 1610	Plt Off Samouelle	Search for Sgt Payne missing in BL 298
11	1215 — 1300	Sgt Thomson	Practice Combat
15	1425 — 1530	Flt Lt Morgan	Camera-gun Practice
17	1110 — 1155	Sgt Thomson	Practice Scramble
17	1415 — 1455	Sgt Mitchell	Formation Flying
18	1510 — 1520	Sgt Thomson	Camera-gun Practice
19	1530 — 1625	Sgt Thomson	Formation Flying
31	1120 — 1220	Plt Off Samouelle	Formation Practice
6 Feb		W3212 (along with all the No 92 Squadron Mk VBs) was collected by a pilot from No 417 Squadron Royal Canadian Air Force and flown from Digby to Colerne, departing at 1518 hrs.	

Ghawdex W3212 No 417 Squadron RCAF Operational Record

10 Feb		Sgt Hazel	Ran out of fuel during formation flight over Bath and force-landed Charmy Down

(Compiled by Henry T.N. Ling. Acknowledgement is made to the Public Record Office at Kew for permission to reproduce the extracts from Crown copyright material; the relative references are AIR 27 641 for the list of sorties for both aircraft with No 74 Squadron; AIR 27 744 in the case of W3212 with No 92 Squadron; AIR 50 32 in respect of the extracts from the collective Combat Reports.)

Appendix C

CONVOYS TO MALTA: 1940-1942

Operation 'Hats', August-September 1940, from Alexandria.
Cargo Ships: *Cornwall* (11,288 grt), *Volo* (1,587 grt) and RFA *Plumleaf* (12,300 dwt).
Escort Force: 2 carriers, 1 battleship, 1 battle cruiser, 3 cruisers and 16 destroyers.
Losses: Damaged — *Cornwall* on 31 August.
Supplies delivered: 40,000 tons.

Operation 'Collar', November 1940, from Gibraltar.
Cargo Ships: *Clan Forbes* (7,529 grt), *Clan Fraser* (7,529 grt). (*New Zealand Star*, 12,436 grt, bound for Alexandria).
Escort Force: 1 carrier, 1 battle cruiser, 4 cruisers, 10 destroyers and 4 corvettes.
Losses: Nil
Supplies delivered: 20,000 tons.

Operation 'Excess', January 1941, from Gribraltar.
Cargo Ships: *Essex* (13,500 grt).
(3 other ships bound for Alexandria).
Escort Force: 1 carrier, 1 battleship, 1 battle cruiser, 2 cruisers and 11 destroyers.

Operation 'MW 5½', January 1941, from Alexandria.
Cargo Ships: *Breconshire* (10,000 grt) and *Clan Macaulay* (10,500 grt).
Escort Force: 1 carrier, 2 battleships, 6 cruisers and 12 destroyers.
Losses in Operations 'Excess' and 'MW 5½':
Sunk: 1 cruiser (*Southampton* on 11 January).
Damaged: 1 carrier (*Illustrious* on 10 January), 1 cruiser (*Gloucester* on 11 January) and 1 destroyer (*Gallant* on 10 January).
Supplies delivered in both Operations: 10,000 tons.

Operation 'MW 6', March 1941, from Alexandria.
Cargo Ships: *City of Lincoln* (8,000 grt), *Perthshire* (grt not known), *Clan Ferguson* (7,500 grt) and *City of Manchester* (8,000 grt).
Escort Force: Not known.
Losses: Damaged: 1 cruiser (*Bonaventure* on 23 March), 1 destroyer (*Griffin* on 23 March), *City of Lincoln*, *Clan Ferguson* and *Perthshire* on 23 March.
Supplies delivered: Not known.

Operation 'Substance', July 1941, from Gibraltar.
Cargo Ships: *Melbourne Star* (11,000 grt), *Sydney Star* (12,500 grt), *City of Pretoria* (8,000 grt), *Port Chalmers* (8,500 grt), *Durham* (13,000 grt) and *Deucalion* (7,500 grt).
Escort Force: 1 carrier, 1 battleship, 1 battle cruiser, 4 cruisers, 1 minelayer and 17 destroyers.
Losses: Sunk: 1 destroyer (*Fearless* on 23 July).
Damaged: 1 cruiser (*Manchester* on 23 July), 1 destroyer (*Firedrake* on 23 July) and *Sydney Star* on 24 July.
Supplies delivered: 65,000 tons.

Operation 'Halberd', September 1941, from Gibraltar.
Cargo Ships: *Clan Macdonald* (9,500 grt), *Clan Ferguson* (7,500 grt), *Ajax* (7,500 grt), *Imperial Star* (12,500 grt), *City of Lincoln* (8,000 grt), *Rowallan Castle* (8,000 grt), *Dunedin Star* (14,000 grt), *City of Calcutta* (8,000 grt) and *Breconshire* (10,000 grt).
Escort Force: 1 carrier, 3 battleships, 5 cruisers and 18 destroyers.
Losses: Sunk: *Imperial Star* on 27 September.
Damaged: 1 battleship (*Nelson* on 27 September).
Supplies delivered: 85,000 tons.

Operation 'MF 2', January 1942, from Alexandria.
Cargo Ship: *Glengyle* (10,000 grt).
Escort Force: Not known.
Losses: Not known.
Supplies delivered: Not known.

Operation 'MF 3', January 1942, from Alexandria.
Cargo Ships: *Ajax* (7,500 grt), *Thermopylae* (6,500 grt), *Clan Ferguson* (7,500 grt) and *City of Calcutta* (8,000 grt).
Escort Force: Not known.
Losses: Sunk: *Thermopylae* on 19 January.
Supplies delivered: Not known.

Operation 'MF 4', January 1942, from Alexandria.
Cargo Ship: *Breconshire* (10,000 grt).
Escort Force: Not known (probably none).
Losses: Not known (probably none).
Supplies delivered: Not known.

Operation 'MF 5', February 1942, from Alexandria.
Cargo Ships: *Rowallan Castle* (8,000 grt), *Clan Chattan* (7,200 grt) and *Clan Campbell* (7,200 grt).
Escort Force: 3 cruisers and 16 destroyers.
Losses: Sunk: *Rowallan Castle* and *Clan Chattan* on 14 February.
Damaged: *Clan Campbell* on 13 February (returned to Alexandria).
Losses sustained by escorts not known.
Supplies delivered: Nil.

Operation 'MW 10', March 1942, from Alexandria.
Cargo Ships: *Breconshire* (10,000 grt), *Clan Campbell* (7,200 grt), *Pampas* (5,500 grt) and *Talabot* (7,000 grt).
Escort Force: 5 cruisers and 17 destroyers.
Losses: Sunk: 1 destroyer (*Southwold* on 24 March), *Clan Campbell* on 23 March. *Pampas* and *Talabot* were sunk in the Grand Harbour on 26 March, and *Breconshire* in Marsaxlokk Bay on 27 March.
Damaged: 1 cruiser (*Cleopatra* on 22 March), 3 destroyers (*Havock* and *Kingston* on 22 March, and *Legion* on 23 March. The last-named destroyer was sunk in the Grand Harbour on 26 March).
Supplies delivered: 5,000 tons.

Operation 'Harpoon', June 1942, from Gibraltar.
Cargo Ships: *Troilus* (7,500 grt), *Burdwan* (6,000 grt), *Chant* (5,500 grt), *Orari* (10,000 grt), *Tanimbar* (8,000 grt) and *Kentucky* (5,500 grt).
Escort Force: 2 carriers, 1 battleship, 4 cruisers, 1 minelayer, 17 destroyers and 4 minesweepers.
Losses: Sunk: 2 destroyers (*Bedouin* and *Kujawiak* on 15 June), *Tanimbar* on 14 June, *Burdwan*, *Chant* and *Kentucky* on 15 June.
Damaged: 2 cruisers (*Liverpool* on 14 June and *Cairo* on 15 June), 3 destroyers (*Partridge*, *Badsworth* and *Matchless* on 15 June), *Orari* on 16 June.
Supplies delivered: 25,000 tons.

Operation 'Vigorous', June 1942, from Alexandria.
Cargo Ships: *City of Calcutta*, *Ajax*, *Potaro*, *Elizabeth Vakke*, *Aagtekirk*, *City of Edinburgh*, *Bhutan*, *City of Pretoria*, *Rembrandt*, *City of Lincoln* and *Bulkoil*.
Escort Force: 1 dummy battleship, 8 cruisers, 26 destroyers, 4 corvettes, 2 minesweepers and 2 rescue ships.
Losses: Sunk: 1 cruiser (*Hermione* on 16 June), 3 destroyers (*Hasty*, *Airedale* and *Nestor* on 15 June), *Aagtekirk* on 12 June and *Buthan* on 14 June.
Damaged: 1 dummy battleship (*Centurion* on 15 June), 3 cruisers (*Newcastle*, *Birmingham* and *Arethusa* on 15 June), 1 corvette, *City of Calcutta* on 12 June and *Potaro* on 13 June.
Supplies delivered: Nil. Surviving merchant ships returned to Alexandria.

Operation 'Pedestal', August 1942, from Gibraltar.
Cargo Ships: *Port Chalmers* (8,500 grt), *Clan Ferguson* (7,500 grt), *Melbourne Star* (11,000 grt), *Brisbane Star* (13,000 grt), *Almeria Lykes* (8,000 grt), *Santa Elisa* (8,500) grt), *Rochester Castle* (8,000 grt), *Empire Hope* (12,500 grt), *Glenorchy* (9,000 grt), *Dorset* (13,000 grt), *Deucalion* (7,500 grt), *Wairangi* (12,500 grt), *Waimarama* (13,000 grt) and *Ohio* (10,000 dwt).
Escort Force: 4 carriers, 2 battleships, 7 cruisers, 24 destroyers.
Support Group: 2 oilers, 4 corvettes and 2 tugs.
Losses: Sunk: 1 carrier (*Eagle* on 11 August), 2 cruisers (*Cairo* on 12 August and *Manchester* on 13 August), 1 destroyer (*Foresight* on 12 August), *Deucalion*, *Empire Hope* and *Clan Ferguson* on 12 August, *Waimarama*, *Almeria Lykes*, *Wairangi*, *Glenorchy*, *Santa Elisa* and *Dorset* on 13 August).
Damaged: 1 carrier (*Indomitable* on 12 August), 2 cruisers (*Kenya* and *Nigeria* on 12 August), *Brisbane Star* on 12 August, *Rochester Castle* on 13 August, and *Ohio* on 12 and 13 August.
Supplies delivered: 55,000 tons.

Operation 'Stoneage', November 1942, from Alexandria
Cargo Ships: *Denbighshire* (9,000 grt), *Bantam* (9,300 grt), *Robin Locksley* (7,100 grt) and *Morcamoon* (8,000 grt).
Escort Force: 5 cruisers and 17 destroyers.
Losses: Damaged: 1 cruiser (*Arethusa* on 18 November)
Supplies delivered: 35,000 tons.

Operation 'Portcullis', December 1942, from Alexandria.
Cargo Ships: *Suffolk* (11,145 grt), *Glenartney* (9,796 grt), *Alcoa Prospector* (6,797 grt) and *Yorba Linda* (6,900 grt).
Escort Force: 1 cruiser, 18 destroyers and 1 minelayer.
Losses: Nil.
Supplies delivered: 55,000 tons.

(Based on information supplied by the Naval Historical Branch of the Ministry of Defence, London, the Fleet Air Arm Museum, Yeovilton, and from the Association's Archives.)

Appendix D

HONOURS AND AWARDS

Knight Bachelor
HH Chief Justice Dr George Borg

Commander of the Order of the British Empire
(Civil Division)
Mr E.L. Petrococchino
Prof A.V. Bernard
Dr A.V. Laferla
Mr O. Sammut

Officer of the Order of the British Empire
(Military Division)
Lt Col E.J. Salomone RMA
Lt Col J. Terreni RMA
Lt Col A.J. Bartolo
Sqn Ldr E.H. Mallia
Lt Col G.T. Curmi KOMR
Lt Col A.J. Dunkerley RMA

Officer of the Order of the British Empire
(Civil Division)
Hon Dr P. Boffa MD
Mr J.E. Axisa
Mr E. Camilleri
Mr J.C. Degiorgio
Mr L.V. Farrugia
Marquis Barbaro of St George
Prof V. Vassallo
Hon Dr H. Sacco MD
Prof P.P. Debono MD
Hon Mabel Strickland
Mr C. Scicluna

Member of the Order of the British Empire
(Military Division)
Lt J. Buttigieg KOMR
T/Maj H.R. Micallef RMA
Capt. A. Sammut-Tagliaferro RMA
2/Lt J. Bartolo Parnis KOMR
BSM E. Buttigieg RMA
Capt. E.E. Demarco
T/Maj F.E. Amato-Gauci RMA

Member of the Order of the British Empire
(Civil Division)
Capt W. Parnis
Mr L. Agius A&CE
Mr L. Demajo Albanese
Mr A. Attard
Mr J. Attard
Mr A.S. Mortimer A&CE
Mr R.E. Said
Mr C. Zammit Marmara
Capt P. Muscat Azzopardi
Mr S. Dandria
Rev Can E. Brincat

Mr P.J. Mercieca BE&A
Mr O. Paris
Capt S. Xuereb
Mr J. Vella Gera
Dr R. Cauchi Inglott MD
Mr C. Jones

Military Cross

103649 Lt J.E. Agius RMA
 58681 T/Maj E.R.P. Amato RMA
115560 2/Lt G. Amato-Gauci RMA

Military Medal

 8129 Sgt L. Apap RMA(T)
 8135 Bdr G. Balzan RMA(T)
 6829 Cpl A. Kitney KOMR
 4236 L/Bdr C. Cuschieri RMA
 3665 W/Sgt J. Abela RMA
10840 L/Bdr J. Vella RMA
20219 A/Sgt J. Camilleri RMA
 4371 A/Sgt F. Zarb RMA
 8126 W/Sgt H. Andrews RMA
 4314 Sgt C. Camilleri RMA
20262 A/Sgt C. Polidano RMA
 4201 Bdr C. Schembri RMA
20386 Gnr J. Camilleri RMA
 6413 Sgt C. Tabone KOMR
50801 A/Cpl C. Caruana KOMR
50698 A/Cpl J. Glanville KOMR

George Medal

Mr F. Mallia
PC 347 C. Camilleri
Mr L. Thake
BSM C. Caruana RMA

British Empire Medal
(Military Division)

  576 Spr S. Zammit RE
20148 A/Sgt A. Stevens RMA(T)
 6408 L/Cpl J. Mallia KOMR
 4487 Gnr E. Abela RMA
 8238 A/Sgt H. Agius RMA
 4775 Gnr J. Barbara RMA
51314 Gnr J. Cassar RMA
776656 F/Sgt E. Aquilina RAF
      Gnr P. Galea RMA

British Empire Medal
(Civil Division)

Mr J. Storace
Mr J. Gauci
A/Supt V.B. de Gray
Mr F. Calleja
Mr C. Galea
PC 509 M. Fenech
PC 44 C. Cassar
Mr J. Panzavecchia
Mr D. Archer
PC 661 J. Bayliss
Mr A. Sciberras
Police Sgt Major D. Florian

Mr L. Ebejer
Mr J. Saliba
Mr T. Formosa
Mr E. Pisani
Mr E. Abela
Mr C. Guliano
Mr S. Mahoney
Mr M. Mifsud
Mr C.J.L. Demaria
Mr J.M. Farrugia
Mr J. Cassar
Mr V. Grech
Miss C.E. Galea
Mr F. Pace
Mr F. Agius
Mr P. Costa
Miss M. Gatt
Mr J. Penza
Mr E. Psaila
Mr L. Vassallo
Mr J. Ellul
Mr W. St John
Mr G. Fenech
Mr C. Attard
Mr A. Buhagiar
Mr N. Busuttil
Mr L. Farrugia
Mr A. Grech
Mrs M. Denaro Testaferrata
Mr A. Gatt
Police Sgt Major H. Catania
Mr A.G.A. Micallef
Mr J. Spiteri

An official list of Maltese servicemen and civilians awarded honours and decorations for service rendered in Malta during the Second World War could not be traced. The lists published here have been compiled from records held by the National War Museum Association and from reports appearing in the *Times of Malta*. They cover the period from June 1940 to June 1945 and, as far as possible, are in chronological order.

No information is available regarding awards made to Maltese serving overseas with the Armed Forces and Merchant Navy, and to Maltese civilians residing abroad.

The Association regrets any omissions.

Appendix E

SUCCESSES BY MALTA-BASED SUBMARINES

The 10th Submarine Flotilla, also known as Malta Force Submarines, comprised Royal Navy and Allied submarines. Operating from HMS *Talbot* at Manoel Island, they inflicted severe losses on Axis shipping. Between 1st January 1941 and 1st May 1942, the following successes were registered:

UPHOLDER:	2 destroyers 3 submarines 3 transports	10 supply-ships 2 tankers 1 trawler	128,353 tons
URGE:	2 cruisers 1 destroyer 1 transport	5 supply-ships 2 tankers	74,669 tons
UTMOST:	1 transport	6 supply-ships	43,993 tons
UNBEATEN:	2 submarines 2 supply-ships 1 tanker	1 collier 2 schooners	30,616 tons
UPRIGHT:	1 cruiser 1 destroyer	4 supply-ships 1 floating dock	23,408 tons
UNIQUE:	1 armed merchant cruiser 1 transport	2 supply-ships	20,382 tons
UNA:	1 supply-ship 1 tanker	1 schooner	15,355 tons
URSULA:	2 supply-ships		14,640 tons
P 31:	1 cruiser	1 supply-ship	12,100 tons
SOKOL:	1 destroyer 2 supply-ships	1 schooner	7,642 tons
P 33:	1 supply-ship		6,600 tons
P 35:	1 supply-ship	1 salvage-tug	4,471 tons
P 38:	1 supply-ship		4,170 tons
UNION:	1 supply-ship		2,800 tons
P 34:	1 submarine		1,461 tons
		Grand total...	390,660 tons

(Reproduced from Periscope Patrol *by J F Turner, published by George G Harrap & Co Ltd, London, 1957)*

Appendix F

TRANSFER OF GOVERNMENT DEPARTMENTS

Government Departments transferred, in whole or in part, from Valletta:

Department	*Where housed*
Lieutenant-Governor's Office	Police Headquarters, St Venera
Attorney-General	Police Headquarters, St Venera
Councils	Police Headquarters, St Venera
Transport	Police Headquarters, St Venera
Treasury (in part)	Police Headquarters, St Venera
Printing Office (in part)	St Joseph's Press, Hamrun
F.C.C.O. & Customs (in part)	'Colorado', Fleur-de-Lys, Birkirkara
Food Distribution Office	'Reinatrop', Fleur-de-Lys, Birkirkara
Bread Distribution Office	'Walmar', Fleur-de-Lys, Birkirkara
Public Works	Old Railway Station, Birkirkara
Water & Electricity	Hamrun School
Medical & Health (in part)	St Aloysius College, Birkirkara
Post Office (in part)	Junior Lyceum, Hamrun
Audit	Villa Concetta, Balzan
Education	285, Fleur-de-Lys, Birkirkara
Agriculture	Junior Lyceum, Hamrun
Land Valuation Office	47, Bakery Street, Lija
Imposts and Lotto	85, High Street, Lija
Superior Courts	Lija Girls' School (High Street, Balzan)
Inferior Courts	St Cajetan Band Club, Hamrun
Public Registry and Notary to Government	Duke of Connaught Band Club, Birkirkara
Labour and Emigration	Junior Lyceum, Hamrun
Information Office	St Joseph Institute, Hamrun
Controller of Engineering and Building Material	Fra Diego Institute, Hamrun
State Law Revision Commission	56, Valley Road, Balzan

(Extracted from a Paper laid on the Table of the Council of Goverment by the Lieutenant-Governor on 16th June, 1942.)

Appendix G

CIVILIAN RATION ENTITLEMENT — 1942

Ration per half month for a family of five (man, wife and three children, 8 years, 3 years and 10 months):

		Jan/Jun	Jul/Dec
Bread	ozs	52½ (daily)	55 (daily)
Paste	,,	—	38
Flour	,,	—	—
Rice	,,	13	7
Preserved Meat	,,	24	24
Preserved Fish	,,	8	22
Frozen Meat	,,	—	—
Cheese	,,	—	8½
Powdered Egg	,,	—	—
Fats	,,	28	21
Oil	,,	37	33
Sugar	,,	108	55½
Tea	,,	—	3½
Coffee	,,	13	10½
Powdered Milk	,,	—	39½
Tinned Milk		—	—
Semolina	,,	—	3½
Dried Fruit	,,	—	—
Chocolate	,,	—	—
Jam	,,	—	—
Sweets	,,	—	—
Soap	,,	42	21
Matches	boxes	3	2
Kerosene	gallons	1½	$1^{1}/_{8}$

(Reproduced from Report on the Working of the Rationing Office for the years 1941-45, *published in the Malta Government Gazette Supplement No. V of 17th January, 1947.)*

Appendix H

DAILY ARMY RATIONS — SPRING/AUTUMN 1942

Bread	11 ozs
Biscuits	1 "
Flour	1 "
Tinned meat	4 "
M. & V.	1 "
Steak & Kidney (tinned)	1 "
Bacon (tinned)	-
Cheese (tinned)	-
Chocolate	
Milk (tinned)	1 "
Sugar	1½ "
Tea	½ "
Salt	¼ "
Sardines	
Salmon	-
Herrings	-
Pilchards	-
Potatoes (tinned)	1 "
Onions	-
Vegetables (tinned)	2 "
Vegetables (fresh)	2 "
Tomatoes	-
Peas (processed)	1 "
Peas (dried)	-
Marmite	
Cooking fat	-
Jam	½ "
Fruit (tinned)	-
Fruit (fresh)	1 "
Meat and fish paste	-
Margarine	1 "
Cigarettes	40 per week
Tobacco	2 ozs per week
Matches	1 box per week

(Reproduced from the Official History of the Second World War, Army Medical Services, Campaigns in General History, *pages 623-4.)*

Appendix I

ORDER OF DEPORTATION

"WHEREAS the Emergency Powers (Removal of Detained Persons) Ordinance, 1942, enables the Governor to make an order directing that any person as therein specified and subject to the conditions therein set forth shall be removed from Malta in persuance of arrangements made as there is recited;

AND Whereas the persons hereunder mentioned have been lawfully ordered to be detained in Malta;

AND Whereas it appears to me that, with a view of securing the public safety or defence of Malta, the continued detention in Malta of the persons hereunder mentioned is inexpedient;

AND Whereas arrangements have been made with the Governor of Uganda, which is a country to which the Emergency Powers (Defence) Act, 1939, of the United Kingdom has been extended by Order in Council made under Section 4 of that Act, for the removal of the persons hereunder mentioned to that country;

NOW, therefore, I, Sir William George Sheddon Dobbie, Governor and Commander-in-Chief of Malta and its Dependencies, enabled as aforesaid DO hereby ORDER that the following persons, namely:

Guido Abela
Vincent Bonello
Charles Chetcuti
Emanuel Cossai
Charles Farrugia
Charles Formosa
Herbert Ganado
Albert Gauci
Ladislau Klein
Carmelo Lateo
Orazio Laudi
Eric Maitland Woolf
Umberto Perrone
Vic. Savona
Alexander Stilon de Piro

Albert Bajona
Vincent Caruana
Joseph Cini
Frank Curmi
Wm Farrugia
Ifar Gabel
Henry Gatt
Daniel German
Edgar Laferla
Edgar Lateo
Salv. Laudi
Enrico Mizzi
Charles Saffrette
Jos. Scicluna
Sir Arturo Mercieca
Miss Mercieca

Alfred Bencini
John Casabene
Giulio Cortis
Anthony Farrugia
Paul Felice
Emmanuel Galleri
Salvatore Gatt
Joseph Grech Marguerat
Carmelo Lateo
Jos. Laudi
Georges Leprè
Joe W. Naudi
John Sammut
Edgar George Soler
Lady Mercieca
Mgr. A.V. Pantalleresco

shall be removed in custody from Malta to Uganda.

Given at the Palace, Valletta, in the Island of Malta, this 12th day of February 1942".

(By courtesy of Rev Fortunato Mizzi)

Appendix J

MONTH BY MONTH SUMMARY OF ENEMY AIRCRAFT DESTROYED OR DAMAGED OVER MALTA BY ANTI-AIRCRAFT ARTILLERY

	A — Confirmed			B — Unconfirmed			C — Damaged		
	BY DAY			BY NIGHT			TOTALS		
	A	B	C	A	B	C	A	B	C
1940									
June	½	3	—	—	—	—	½	3	—
July	3	2½	—	—	—	—	3	2½	—
September	—	3	—	—	—	—	—	3	—
November	2	3	—	—	—	—	2	3	—
1941									
January	18	1	—	—	—	—	18	1	—
February	6	5	—	—	—	—	6	5	—
March	15	2	—	—	—	—	15	2	—
April	1	—	1	3	1	1	4	1	2
May	—	1	2	3	—	1	3	1	3
June	—	1	—	—	—	—	—	1	—
July	—	—	4	—	—	—	—	—	4
August	—	—	2	—	—	—	—	—	2
September	—	1	—	—	—	—	—	1	—
October	—	—	—	—	—	6	—	—	6
November	—	—	—	1	2	3	1	2	3
December	—	3	—	3	—	10	3	3	10
1942									
January	5	—	5	—	1	—	5	1	5
February	9	2	9	—	—	—	9	2	9
March	27	3	31	1	—	—	28	3	31
April	101	12	67	1	—	—	102	12	67
May	11½	—	16	1	—	—	12½	—	16
June	—	—	—	6	—	2	6	—	2
July	4½	—	—	4	—	1	8½	—	1
August	—	—	—	1	1	—	1	1	—
October	7½	1	4	1	—	—	8½	1	4
1943									
May	1	—	—	—	—	—	1	—	—
June	1	—	—	—	—	—	1	—	—
July	—	—	—	3	—	—	3	—	—
TOTALS	213	43½	141	28	5	24	241	48½	165

(Reproduced from Appendix 'C' to R.A. Notes No 24; reference para. 1380)

Appendix K

ANTI-AIRCRAFT SUCCESSES AND AMMUNITION EXPENDITURE
Analysis for the period 15 December 1941 to 20 April 1942

(a) Heavy Anti-Aircraft

    (i)   Destroyed: 63 enemy aircraft
            Probably destroyed: 13 ″ ″
            Damaged: 56 ″ ″

    (ii)   Ammunition expenditure

	Total	Rounds per gun
4.5 inch	23,379	1,948
3.7 inch	140,675	1,675
3 inch	18,911	1,182

    (iii)   Rounds expended per enemy aircraft destroyed: 2,904

(b) Light Anti-Aircraft

    (i)   Destroyed: 85 enemy aircraft
            Probably destroyed: 7 ″ ″
            Damaged: 71 ″ ″

    (ii)   Ammunition expenditure

Total	Rounds per gun
154,492	1,111

    (iii)   Rounds expended per enemy aircraft destroyed: 1,817

(c) In April 1942:

    102 enemy aircraft were destroyed by AA
     12 ″ ″ probably destroyed
     67 ″ ″ damaged

Appendix L

HM SHIPS, MERCHANT VESSELS ETC SUNK AT OR NEAR MALTA

Date	Name	Type	Cause	Location
HM Ships				
7.9.40	*Hellespont*	Tug	Aircraft	Dockyard Creek
8.4.41	*Moor*	Mooring Vessel	Mine	Inside Breakwater
30.4.41	*Coral*	A/S Trawler	Aircraft	No 3 Dock
2.5.41	*Jersey*	Destroyer	Mine	Entrance to Grand Harbour
3/4.5.41	*Fermoy*	Minesweeper	Aircraft	No 5 Dock
12.2.42	*Maori*	Destroyer	Aircraft	French Creek
24.3.42	*Southwold*	Destroyer	Mine	Zonqor Point
26.3.42	*P 39*	Submarine	Aircraft	Marsa
26.3.42	*Legion*	Destroyer	Aircraft	French Creek
1.4.42	*Pandora*	Submarine	Aircraft	French Creek
1.4.42	*P 36*	Submarine	Aircraft	Lazaretto Creek
1.4.42	*Sunset*	M/S Drifter	Aircraft	French Creek
4.4.42	*Abingdon*	Minesweeper	Aircraft	Kalkara Creek
9.4.42	*Lance*	Destroyer	Aircraft	No 2 Dock
11.4.42	*Kingston*	Destroyer	Aircraft	No 4 Dock
21.4.42	*Jade*	A/S Trawler	Aircraft	Dockyard Creek
18.4.42	*Andromeda*	M/S Tug	Aircraft	Grand Harbour
8.5.42	*Olympus*	Submarine	Mine	5 miles off Malta
26.5.42	*Eddy*	M/S Drifter	Mine	7 cables off St Elmo Breakwater
Royal Fleet Auxiliary				
26.3.42	*Plumleaf*	Oiler	Aircraft	French Creek
Allied Warships				
4.4.42	*Glaucos*	Greek Submarine	Aircraft	French Creek
16.6.42	*Kujawiak*	Polish Destroyer	Mine	096° St Elmo Breakwater Light 3.8 miles
Floating Dock				
20.6.40	*AFD 8*	40,000 GRT	Aircraft	Off Magazine Wharf
Merchant Ships (Allied)				
26.3.42	*Pampas*	5,415 GRT	Aircraft	Ras Hanzir
26.3.42	*Talabot*	6,798 GRT	Aircraft	No 6 Buoy
27.3.42	*Breconshire*	9,776 GRT	Aircraft	Marsaxlokk Bay
Merchant Ships (Italian)				
23.3.41	*Adige*	1,006 GRT	Aircraft	Kalkara Creek
30.4.41	*Polinice*	1,373 GRT	Aircraft	Kalkara Creek

(By courtesy of the Naval Historical Branch, Ministry of Defence, London. Revised by the Author.)

Appendix M

HISTORICAL BUILDINGS — DESTROYED OR DAMAGED

ATTARD
Church of the Annunciation badly damaged by a near miss.
Church of St Saviour completely destroyed by a direct hit.

COSPICUA
Church of St Paul seriously damaged.
Church of St John badly damaged.
Almonry of St John extensively damaged.

FLORIANA
Polverista Curtain badly hit.
Hornworks damaged by direct hits.
Magazine Bastion damaged by direct hits.
Pietà *Lunette* damaged by direct hits.
Porte-des-Bombes slightly damaged by splinters.
Parish Church of St Publius badly damaged.
Monastery of the Minor Observants almost completely wrecked.
Chapel of St Roch completely destroyed.
Central Civil Hospital badly damaged.
Ospizio badly damaged.
Wignacourt Water Tower slightly damaged by blast and splinters.

GUDJA
Church of St Mary *Ta' Bir Miftuh* badly damaged.

GZIRA
Fort Manoel very badly damaged; Chapel of St Anthony of Padua reduced to a shattered shell; Courtyard extensively damaged.
Lazaretto very badly damaged.

HAMRUN
None, except for the oldest church, an anonymous sixteenth-century structure badly damaged by bombing

KALKARA
Parish Church completely destroyed.
Villa Bighi completely destroyed.
Fort Ricasoli; Gatehouse received at least one direct hit causing severe damage; Governor's House completely destroyed; *Porte-Cochere* blasted and shattered.

LUQA
Church of St Andrew extensively damaged.

MARSA
Church of the Annunciation damaged.

MARSAXLOKK
It-Torri tal-Pont damaged by bombing.

MDINA
Chapel of Our Lady of Victory, on Mdina-Valletta road near Ta' Qali, badly damaged by bombs.

MOSTA
The Rotunda damaged by bombs.
Church of St Sylvester badly damaged by a bomb.

Church of St Mary, *Ta' Wejda*, damaged by a bomb.
Church of the Immaculate Conception demolished; its material used to make aircraft pens at Ta' Qali.

MQABBA
Parish Church of St Mary badly damaged.

PAWLA
Villa of Grandmaster Caraffa demolished.

QRENDI
Church of St Matthew extensively damaged.

ST PAUL'S BAY
Church of St Paul wrecked by a direct hit.

SANTA VENNERA
Wignacourt Aqueduct hit by a bomb.

SENGLEA
Parish Church of Our Lady of Victory demolished by bombs.

VALLETTA
St John's Co-Cathedral; the Chapel of the Langue of Germany damaged by a bomb, wrecking the north *loggia* and sucking out the end wall of the chapel; the great vault shaken; the timber spires shaken and pulled down.
Grand Prior's House damaged.
St Ursula's Monastery wrecked.
Church of St Mary of Damascus completely destroyed.
Carmelites Church damaged.
Augustinian Church extensively damaged by a direct hit on one of the belfries.
Dominican Church slightly damaged.
Royal University of Malta partly destroyed.
Franciscan Church cloister destroyed.
Church of *Notre Dame de Liesse* severely damaged.
St Nicholas Church extensively damaged.
St Saviour Church extensively damaged.
Nibbia Chapel destroyed.
Chapel of Bones completely destroyed.
St Paul's Anglican Cathedral, pinnacle knocked off the steeple.
St Elmo Castle hit but not seriously damaged.
Palace of the Grandmasters; Marble Staircase and Dining Hall destroyed; much of the walling of the Armoury sucked out by a heavy bomb which fell on the Market.
Auberge de Castille; a heavy-calibre bomb destroyed the signal tower and wrecked the grand staircase; part of the two-storied cloister destroyed.
Auberge d'Italie twice hit and badly damaged.
Auberge d'Auvergne hit several times and badly damaged.
Auberge de France completely destroyed by a heavy-calibre bomb.
Auberge de Baviere hit and damaged.
Hospital of the Order of St John; the Great Ward received a direct hit at its eastern end, destroying part of the fine timber ceiling and roof; gateway from Merchants Street wrecked.
Prison of the Slaves badly bombed.
Treasury of the Order of St John (*Casino Maltese*) extensively damaged by a direct hit.
Royal Malta Library shaken by nearby explosions but not seriously damaged.
Conventual Chaplains' Houses (opposite St John's Cathedral) extensively damaged.
Upper Barracca Arcades hit and partly destroyed.
Fishmarket extensively damaged.
Palazzo Parisio hit by a bomb bringing down most of the main facade.
Casa Dorell badly damaged.
Palazzo Hompesch destroyed.
Palazzo St Poix destroyed.
Cottoner Foundation badly damaged by several direct hits.

VITTORIOSA
Parish Church of St Lawrence, chapels adjoining the south side wrecked.
Church of St Mary of Damascus completely destroyed.
Oratory of the Crucifix badly damaged.
St Joseph Oratory damaged.
Church of the Annunciation destroyed except for the bell-tower.
Church of St Anthony destroyed.
Church of the Holy Trinity destroyed.
Church of St Philip damaged.
Church of St Mary (in Fort St Angelo), above-ground building destroyed by a direct hit.
Captain's House (in Fort St Angelo) badly shaken by a near miss.
Palace of the Inquisitors considerably shaken by bombing.
Auberge de France slightly damaged.
Victory Tower sliced in half by bombing; the remaining portion laboriously pulled down stone by stone.
Galley Houses badly damaged.
Slave Prisons badly damaged.
Galley-Captain's House badly damaged.
House of the General of the Galleys badly damaged.

ZEBBUG
Church of Our Lady of Light hit and damaged.

(Extracted from 'Works of Art in Malta: Losses and Survivals in the War,' *compiled by Hugh Braun, FSA, FRIBA, and published by HMSO London in 1946. Reproduced by permission of the Controller of Her Majesty's Stationery Office. Revised by the Author.)*

Appendix N

OTHER BUILDINGS — DESTROYED OR DAMAGED

	A	B	C	D	Total
Private dwellings	5,524	5,077	4,848	14,225	29,674
Churches, convents, etc.	11	32	21	47	111
Hospitals, institutes, colleges, etc.	4	23	10	13	50
Theatres, clubs, hotels, etc.	10	11	8	7	36
Auberges, palaces and villas	4	10	9	23	46
Government offices, banks, garages, cemeteries, printing presses, etc.	4	14	5	8	31
Factories, bakeries and flour mills	14	23	18	24	79
Grand total					30,027

A = Totally destroyed

B = Extensively damaged, needing reconstruction

C = Damaged but repairable

D = Damaged by blast

(Extracted from O.D.C. Report as appearing in 'X'Garrbet Malta' by Salv. Mifsud, published by A.C. Aquilina & Co., 1949.)

Appendix O

AIRCRAFT FLOWN TO MALTA FROM AIRCRAFT CARRIERS 1940-1942

Date	Name of Operation	Carriers	Aircraft Ferried	Aircraft Reaching Malta
Aug 2, 1940	Hurry	*Argus*	12 Hurricanes	12 Hurricanes
Nov 17, 1940	White	*Argus*	12 Hurricanes	4 Hurricanes
Apr 3, 1941	Winch	*Ark Royal*	12 Hurricanes	12 Hurricanes
Apr 27, 1941	Dunlop	*Ark Royal*	24 Hurricanes	23 Hurricanes
May 21, 1941	Splice	*Ark Royal* *Furious*	48 Hurricanes	46 Hurricanes
Jun 6, 1941	Rocket	*Ark Royal* *Furious*	44 Hurricanes	43 Hurricanes
Jun 14, 1941	Tracer	*Ark Royal* *Victorious*	48 Hurricanes	45 Hurricanes
Jun 27, 1941	Railway I	*Ark Royal*	22 Hurricanes	21 Hurricanes
Jun 30, 1941	Railway II	*Ark Royal* *Furious*	42 Hurricanes	34 Hurricanes
Jul 24, 1941	Substance	*Ark Royal*	7 Swordfish	7 Swordfish
Sep 9, 1941	Status I	*Ark Royal*	14 Hurricanes	14 Hurricanes
Sep 13, 1941	Status II	*Ark Royal* *Furious*	46 Hurricanes	45 Hurricanes
Oct 18, 1941	Callboy	*Ark Royal*	11 Albacores	11 Albacores
Nov 12, 1941	Perpetual	*Argus* *Ark Royal*	37 Hurricanes	34 Hurricanes
Mar 7, 1942	Spotter	*Eagle* *Argus*	15 Spitfires	15 Spitfires
Mar 21, 1942	Picket I	*Eagle*	9 Spitfires	9 Spitfires
Mar 29, 1942	Picket II	*Eagle*	7 Spitfires	7 Spitfires
Apr 20, 1942	Calendar	*Wasp*	47 Spitfires	46 Spitfires
May 9, 1942	Bowery	*Wasp* *Eagle*	64 Spitfires	60 Spitfires
May 19, 1942	L.B.	*Argus* *Eagle*	17 Spitfires	17 Spitfires
Jun 3, 1942	Style	*Eagle*	31 Spitfires	27 Spitfires
Jun 9, 1942	Salient	*Eagle*	32 Spitfires	32 Spitfires
Jul 15, 1942	Pinpoint	*Eagle*	32 Spitfires	31 Spitfires
Jul 21, 1942	Insect	*Eagle*	30 Spitfires	28 Spitfires
Aug 11, 1942	Bellows●	*Furious*	38 Spitfires	37 Spitfires
Aug 17, 1942	Baritone	*Furious*	32 Spitfires	29 Spitfires
Oct 29, 1942	Train	*Furious*	31 Spitfires	29 Spitfires
Totals	25 Operations		764 aircraft ferried	718 aircraft delivered to Malta●● 34 aircraft lost (plus some escorting carrier aircraft) 12 aircraft returned with carriers

● Part of Operation 'Pedestal'.
●● In addition, several Swordfish and Fulmars from HMS *Illustrious* operated from Malta after that carrier was severely damaged in January 1941.

Appendix P

TOP-SCORING 'MALTA' FIGHTER PILOTS

All claims made whilst serving at Malta. Figures indicate 'confirmed victories', 'probables', 'damaged' and 'total credited victories for whole of war' respectively. Ranks are those achieved whilst at Malta and decorations are those held at the time or awarded for Malta operations:-

Pilot	Confirmed	Probable	Damaged	Total	Nationality	Sqn/s
P/O G.F. Beurling DSO DFC DFM+	26⅓	1	8	31⅓	Canadian	249
F/S P.A. Schade DFM	14	2	3	14	b. Malaya	126
F/L H.W. McLeod DFC+ (RCAF)	13	2	9¼	21	Canadian	603/1435
F/L J.A. Plagis DFC+	12	4¾	4	16	Rhodesian	249/185
P/O J.W. Yarra DFM (RAAF)	12	2	6	12	Australian	185
P/O J.F. McElroy DFC (RCAF)	12	1	8½	16½	Canadian	249
P/O R.B. Hesselyn DFM+ (RNZAF)	12	1	6	21½	New Zealander	249
P/O C. Weaver DFM (RCAF)	11½	2	0	13½	American	185
P/O A.P. Goldsmith DFC DFM (RAAF)	10¾	0	7	14¾	Australian	126
Sgt F.N. Robertson DFM	10	3	7	12	British	261
P/O V.P. Brennan DFC+ (RAAF)	10	1	6	10	Australian	249

(By courtesy of Christopher Shores and Brian Cull with Nicola Malizia, co-authors of 'Malta: The Hurricane Years 1940-41'.)

Appendix Q

MEN AND EQUIPMENT TO BE LANDED DURING OPERATION C 3

Troops and equipment	Day X	Night after day X + 1	Night after day X + N	Day X + N	Totals
Men	300	35,805	9,000	16,700	61,895*
Motor cycles	—	768	26	207	1,001
Motor vehicles	—	62	62	358	482
Half tracks	—	56	12	85	153
20 mm guns	—	56	8	8	72
47 mm guns	—	92	24	43	159
47 mm self propelled guns	—	19	—	—	19
65 mm guns	—	8	—	—	8
75 mm guns	—	56	24	32	112
75 mm self propelled guns	—	8	—	—	8
90 mm guns	—	—	—	6	6
100 mm guns	—	—	—	12	12
105 mm guns	—	—	—	24	24
149 mm guns	—	—	—	12	12
81 mm mortars	—	180	45	45	270

* The number of men does not include the parachutists and the airborne *La Spezia* Division, which would have brought the strength of the invading Force to just under 100,000 men.

(Reproduced from 'Operazione C3: Malta', *published by the* 'Ufficio Storico Della Marina Militare, Roma,' *1965).*

Appendix R

OPERATION 'PEDESTAL' — ESCORTING FORCES

Name	Type	Commanding Officer
FORCE 'Z'		
Nelson	Battleship	Capt H.B. Jacomb
		(flag of Acting Vice-Admiral E.N. Syfret CB)
Rodney	Battleship	Capt J.W. Rivett-Carnac DSC
Victorious	Aircraft carrier	Capt H.C. Bovell CBE
		(flag of Rear-Admiral A.L. St. G. Lyster CB CVO DSO)
Indomitable	Aircraft carrier	Capt T.H. Troubridge
Eagle	Aircraft carrier	Capt L.D. Mackintosh DSC
Sirius	Cruiser	Capt P.W.B. Brooking
Phoebe	Cruiser	Capt C.P. Frend
Charybdis	Cruiser	Capt G.A.W. Voelcker
Laforey	Destroyer	Capt R.M.J. Hutton
Lightning	Destroyer	Cdr H.G. Walters DSC
Lookout	Destroyer	Cdr C.P.F. Brown DSC
Quentin	Destroyer	Lieut-Cdr A.H.P. Noble DSC
Tartar	Destroyer	Cdr St. J.R.J. Trywhitt DSC
Eskimo	Destroyer	Cdr E.G. le Geyt
Somali	Destroyer	Cdr E.N.V. Currey DSC
Wishart	Destroyer	Cdr H.G. Scott
Zetland	Destroyer	Lieut J.V. Wilkinson
Ithuriel	Destroyer	Lieut-Cdr D.H. Maitland-Makgill-Crichton DSC
Antelope	Destroyer	Lieut-Cdr E.N. Sinclair
Vansittart	Destroyer	Lieut-Cdr T. Johnston DSC
Keppel	Destroyer	Cdr J.E. Broome
Westcott	Destroyer	Cdr I.H. Bockett-Pugh DSO
Venomous	Destroyer	Cdr H.W. Falcon-Steward
Malcolm	Destroyer	A Cdr A.B. Russell
Wolverine	Destroyer	Lieut-Cdr P.W. Gretton OBE DSC
Amazon	Destroyer	Lieut-Cdr Lord Teynham
Wrestler	Destroyer	Lieut R.W.B. Lacon DSC
Vidette	Destroyer	Lieut-Cdr E.N. Walmsley DSC
FORCE 'R'		
Jonquil	Corvette	Lieut-Cdr R.E.H. Partington RD RNR
Spirea	Corvette	Lieut-Cdr R.S. Miller DSC RD RNR
Geranium	Corvette	Lieut-Cdr A. Foxhall RNR
Coltsfoot	Corvette	Lieut the Hon. W.K. Rouse RNVR
Salvonia	Tug	
Brown Ranger	Fleet oiler	
Dingledale	Fleet oiler	
FORCE 'X'		
Nigeria	Cruiser	Capt S.H. Paton
		(flag of Rear-Admiral H.M. Burrough CB DSO)
Kenya	Cruiser	Capt A.S. Russell
Manchester	Cruiser	Capt H. Drew DSC
Cairo	Anti-aircraft ship	A Capt C.C. Hardy DSO
Ashanti	Destroyer	A Capt R.G. Onslow DSO
Intrepid	Destroyer	Cdr C.A. de W. Kitcat
Icarus	Destroyer	Lieut-Cdr C.D. Maud DSC

Foresight	Destroyer	Lieut-Cdr R.A. Fell
Fury	Destroyer	Lieut-Cdr C.H. Campbell DSC
Derwent	Destroyer	Cdr R.H. Wright DSC
Bramham	Destroyer	Lieut E.F. Baines
Bicester	Destroyer	Lieut-Cdr S.W.F. Bennetts
Ledbury	Destroyer	Lieut-Cdr R.P. Hill
Pathfinder	Destroyer	Cdr E.A. Gibbs DSO
Penn	Destroyer	Lieut-Cdr J.H. Swain
Wilton	Destroyer	Lieut A.P. Northey DSC
Jaunty	Tug	Lieut-Cdr H. Osburn OBE RNR

MALTA ESCORT FORCE
(A/Cdr H.J.A.S. Jerome, Senior Officer, in *Speedy*)

Speedy	Minesweeper	Lieut-Cdr A.E. Doran
Hebe	Minesweeper	Lieut-Cdr G. Mowatt RD RNR
Hythe	Minesweeper	Lieut-Cdr L.B. Miller
Rye	Minesweeper	Lieut J.A. Pearson DSC RNR
No 121	Motor launch	
No 126	Motor launch	
No 134	Motor launch	
No 135	Motor launch	Lieut-Cdr E.J. Strowlger RNVR
No 168	Motor launch	in No 121, Senior Officer
No 459	Motor launch	
No 462	Motor launch	

OPERATION 'BELLOWS'

Furious	Aircraft carrier	Capt T.O. Bulteel

SUBMARINES

North of Sicily
P.211	Submarine	Cdr B. Bryant DSC
P.42	Submarine	Lieut A.C.G. Mars

Between Malta and Tunisia
P.44	Submarine	Lieut T.E. Barlow
P.222	Submarine	Lieut-Cdr A.J. Mackenzie
P.31	Submarine	Lieut J.B. Kershaw DSO
P.34	Submarine	Lieut P.R. Harrison DSC
P.46	Submarine	Lieut J. Stevens
Utmost	Submarine	Lieut A.W. Langridge

(By courtesy of the Naval Historical Branch, Ministry of Defence, London)

Appendix S

OPERATION 'HUSKY'
Order of Battle
Royal Air Force Malta
D − 5 to D + 1

HAL FAR

324 Wing HQ

72 Spitfire	16
93 Spitfire	16
43 Spitfire	16
243 Spitfire	16

ASR/COMM

Walrus	6
Wellington	2
Hudson	
Harvard	1
5 Squadrons	75

SAFI

111 Spitfire	16
126 Spitfire	16
1435 Spitfire	16
3 Squadrons	48

GOZO

31st Group USAAF HQ

307 Spitfire	25
308 Spitfire	25
309 Spitfire	25
3 Squadrons	75

LUQA

244 Wing HQ

1 SAAF Spitfire	16
92 Spitfire	16
145 Spitfire	16
601 Spitfire	16
417 Spitfire	16
683 PRU Spitfire	15
40 Spitfire (Tac. R)	16
23 Intr. Mosquito	16
108 (½) NF Beaufighter	10
600 NF Beaufighter	20
221 (½) NR TB	8
69 (½) Baltimore GR	6
PRU Mosquito	1
Hurricane	1
10½ Squadrons	173

KALAFRANA & ST PAUL'S BAY

230 (½) Sunderland	3
(½) Catalina	3
1 Squadron	6

TOTALS

Spitfire	20 Squadrons
PRU Spitfire	1 Squadron
Spitfire (Tac. R)	1 Squadron
Albacore	1½ Squadron
Intruder Mosquito	1 Squadron
NF Beaufighter	1½ Squadron
Baltimore GR	½ Squadron
NR TB	½ Squadron
ASR/Comm.	1 Squadron
Sunderland	½ Squadron
Catalina	½ Squadron
	29 Squadrons

USAAF

Spitfire	3 Squadrons
Kittyhawk	3 Squadrons
	6 Squadrons

Grand Total: 35 Squadrons

TA' QALI

322 Wing HQ

81 Spitfire	16
154 Spitfire	16
232 Spitfire	16
242 Spitfire	16
152 Spitfire	16
Fulmar	3
Hurricane	3
826 Albacore	12
815 (½) Alb. (F)	4
6½ Squadrons	102

QRENDI

229 Spitfire	16
249 Spitfire	16
185 Spitfire	16
3 Squadrons	48

PANTELLERIA

33rd Group USAAF HQ

58 Kittyhawk	25
59 Kittyhawk	25
60 Kittyhawk	25
3 Squadrons	75

(Operation Order No 52, dated 27th May, 1943)

Appendix T

MILITARY FORMATION SIGNS IN MALTA

During the last War (1939-1945) "Formation signs" were worn on the upper arm of battledress, by almost all ranks in the Army. During the "Great War" these were also worn but were largely semi-official. These signs (usually of printed or woven cloth) as worn by the Royal Artillery, Royal Malta Artillery and The King's Own Malta Regiment during the last war are described below:

Artillery

    a. Headquarters and the two mobile units, namely:

        HQ Royal Artillery
        12th Field Regiment RA
        26th Defence Regiment RA

On a black background the Maltese cross Red/Blue (each arm of the cross divided equally) edged Silver.

    b. Fixed Defences:

        HQ Fixed Defences   1st Coast Regiment RMA
        4th Coast Regiment RA   5th Coast Regiment RMA'

On a black background the Maltese cross White and Red (each arm divided equally).

    c. Heavy Anti-Aircraft:

        HQ 10th HAA Brigade
        4th HAA Regiment RA   2nd HAA Regiment RMA
        7th HAA Regiment RA   11th HAA Regiment RMA (T)
        10th HAA Regiment RA

On a black background the Maltese cross Yellow/Blue (each arm divided equally) edged in Red.

    d. Light Anti-Aircraft:

        HQ 7th LAA Brigade
        32nd LAA Regiment RA   3rd LAA Regiment RMA
        65th LAA Regiment RA   4th S/L Regiment RA/RMA
        74th LAA Regiment RA

On a black background the Maltese cross Yellow/Blue (each arm divided equally) edged in White.

At first, signs woven in silk were used. An initial issue of 1000 of each type were provided by a private contractor; the subsequent issues manufactured by Ordnance, were printed. Officers wore the woven badges and soldiers the printed ones.

It is interesting to note that 1st and 5th Coast Regts RMA bore the Maltese cross in White and Red while 2nd, 3rd and 11th Regts RMA bore the cross in Blue and Yellow edged in White or red (White for Light AA and Red for Heavy AA). The White and Red are the colours of our National Flag while the Yellow and Blue, possibly because of the units' role, may have symbolized the sky and the sun!

The Mobile units and HQRA, composed entirely of Royal Artillerymen bore the cross in Red and Blue edged White, maybe to represent, as near as possible, the Union Flag (sometimes incorrectly called the Union Jack) with its red, white and blue colours.

Infantry
    a. 231st Infantry Brigade — On a red shield a white Maltese cross.
    b. The King's Own Malta Regiment.

The 1st, 2nd and 3rd Battalions wore a triangle (point upright), a diamond and a square respectively. The left half of these geometrical figures was White and the right half Red.

The 10th Battalion or Static Group wore a triangle also but point downwards, the top half was White and the bottom half Red.

The Infantry formation signs were thus comparatively uninteresting — the colours of the different Battalions being always white and red, appearing and reappearing in different shapes and designs. These signs were also painted on the right hand side of the steel helmets of all ranks.

(The above article by Captain C.A. Strickland KOMR appeared in 'The Malta Land Force Journal', Issue No 6, April 1971, and is reproduced by courtesy of the Publisher/Editor, Brigadier Alfred Samut-Tagliaferro CBE).

Appendix U

UNITS OF THE ITALIAN NAVY SURRENDERED AT MALTA IN TERMS OF THE ARMISTICE OF SEPTEMBER 1943:

Battleships (Corazzate)   Day of arrival

Vittorio Veneto   11th
Italia   11th
Duilio   10th
Doria   10th
Cesare   13th

Cruisers (Incrociatori)

Eugenio di Savoia   11th
Duca D'Aosta   11th
Montecuccoli   11th
Duca degli Abruzzi   11th
Garibaldi   11th
Pompeo Magno   10th

Destroyers (Cacciatorpediniere)

Velite   11th
Gregale   11th
Artigliere   11th
Legionario   11th
Oriani   11th
Riboty   13th

Escorts (Torpediniere)

Aliseo   20th
Animoso   20th
Ardimentoso   20th
Fortunale   20th
Idromito   20th
Orione   12th
Ariete   20th
Calliope   20th
Libra   12th
Carini   21st
Fabrizi   21st
Mosto   20th

Corvettes (Corvette)

Ape   20th
Cormorano   20th
Danaide   20th
Gabbiano   20th
Minerva   20th
Pellicano   19th

Submarines (Sommergibili)

Alagi   16th
Axum   20th

247

Brin	16th
Corridoni	20th
Galatea	16th
Giada	16th
H 1	20th
H 2	20th
H 4	20th
Nichelio	20th
Platino	16th
Turchese	28th
Marea	16th
Atropo	13th
Bandiera	13th
Bragadino	17th
Jalea	13th
Menotti	12th
Onice	17th
Settembrini	17th
Squalo	17th
Vortice	17th
Zoea	17th

Anti-Submarine Launches (VAS)

201	20th
204	20th
224	20th
233	20th
237	20th
240	20th
241	20th
246	20th
248	20th

Motor Torpedo Boats (Motosiluranti)

35	20th
54	23rd
55	20th
56	23rd
61	23rd
64	20th

Auxiliary Vessels (Navigli Ausiliari)

Regina Elena	20th
Liscanera	13th
Miraglia	13th

(By courtesy of Ufficio Storico, Stato Maggiore della Marina, Roma.)

Appendix V

SUMMARY OF AIR RAID ALERTS OVER MALTA

No. of alerts during	1940	1941	1942	1943	1944
January		57	263	25	2
February		107	236	5	—
March		105	275	7	1
April		92	282	7	1
May		98	246	30	—
June	53	68	169	30	—
July	51	73	184	10	1
August	22	30	101	9	3
September	25	31	57	4	
October	10	57	153	—	
November	32	76	30	—	
December	18	169	35	—	
Total	211	963	2,031	127	8

The 3,340 alerts totalled 2,357 hours and 6 minutes.

The first air raid took place on 11th June, 1940, at 6.55 am, whilst the sirens sounded the last alert on 28th August, 1944, at 8.43 pm; the final 'all clear' was given at 9 pm.

Appendix W

GOVERNORS AND SERVICE COMMANDERS 1939-45

GOVERNORS AND COMMANDERS-IN-CHIEF

Date of Appointment

General Sir Charles Bonham-Carter GCB CMG DSO ADC — 3rd March 1936 (Oath of Office 6th April 1936)

Lieutenant-General Sir William Dobbie GCMG KCB DSO — 19th May 1941 (Act. Governor from 24th May 1940)

Field-Marshal Viscount Gort VC GCB CBE DSO MVO MC ADC — 4th May 1942 (Oath of Office 7th May 1942)

Lieutenant-General Sir Edmond Schreiber KCB DSO — 19th September 1944 (Oath of Office 26th September 1944)

FLAG OFFICERS

Vice-Admiral Sir Wilbraham Ford KBE CB	26th December 1936
Vice-Admiral Sir Ralph Leatham KCB	1st January 1942
Vice-Admiral Sir Stuart Bonham-Carter KCB CVO DSO	1st December 1942
Vice-Admiral A.J. Power CB CVO	7th May 1943
Vice-Admiral L.H.K. Hamilton CB DSO and Bar	29th September 1943
Vice-Admiral Sir Frederick Dalrymple-Hamilton KCB	April 1945

GENERAL OFFICERS COMMANDING TROOPS

Major-General Sir John P. Scobell KBE CB CMG DSO	27th October 1939
Major-General D.M.W. Beak VC DSO MC	6th January 1942
Major-General R. MacK. Scobie CB CBE MC	6th August 1942
Major-Geneal W.H. Oxley CBE MC ADC	30th March 1943
Major-General W. Robb CBE DSO MC	7th October 1944

AIR OFFICERS COMMANDING

Air Cmdre R. Leckie DSO DSC AFC	2nd December 1938
Air Vice-Marshal Forster H.M. Maynard AFC	20th January 1940
Air-Vice Marshal Hugh Pughe Lloyd CB CBE MC DFC	1st June 1941
Air Vice-Marshal Sir Keith R. Park KBE CB MC DFC	15th July 1942
Air Cmdre J.R. Scarlett-Streatfeild	6th January 1944
Air Vice-Marshal A.H. Wann	6th February 1944
Air Vice-Marshal R.M. Foster DFC	26th March 1944
Air Vice-Marshal K.B. Lloyd CBE AFC	19th October 1944

General Sir Charles Bonham-Carter.

Lieutenant-General Sir William Dobbie.

Field-Marshal Viscount Gort.

Lieutenant-General Sir Edmond Schreiber.

Appendix X

RAF, SAAF, RAAF, RCAF, RN-FAA AND USAAF SQUADRONS AND DETACHMENTS BASED AT MALTA BETWEEN JUNE 1940 AND DECEMBER 1943:

Squadron	Base	Dates
No 18	Luqa	Oct 41 — Mar 42
No 18	Luqa	Jul 43
No 21	Luqa	Apr 41 — May 41
No 21	Luqa	Dec 41 — Mar 42
No 23	Luqa	Dec 42 — Sep 43
No 37	Luqa	Oct 40 — Nov 40
No 37	Luqa	Feb 42 — Mar 42
No 38	Luqa	Aug 41 — Oct 41
No 38	Luqa	Jun 42 — Jul 42
No 39	Luqa	Jun 42 — Jun 43
No 40	Luqa	Oct 41 — Mar 42
No 40	Luqa	Nov 42 — Jan 43
No 43	Hal Far	Jun 43 — Jul 43
No 46	Hal Far	Jun 41 — Jun 41
No 55	Luqa	Jul 43 — Aug 43
No 69	Luqa	Jan 41 — Feb 44
No 72	Hal Far	Jan 43 — Jul 43
No 73	Luqa	Jun 43 — Jul 43
No 81	Ta' Qali	Jun 43 — Jul 43
No 82	Luqa	May 41 — Mar 42
No 89	Ta' Qali	Jun 42 — Feb 43
No 92	Luqa	Jun 43 — Jul 43
No 93	Hal Far	Jun 43 — Jul 43
No 104	Luqa	Oct 41 — Jan 42
No 104	Luqa	May 42 — Jun 42
No 104	Luqa	Nov 42 — Jan 43
No 105	Luqa	Jul 41 — Oct 41
No 107	Luqa	Sep 41 — Jan 42
No 108	Luqa	Apr 43 — Jul 44
No 110	Luqa	Jul 41 — Jul 41
No 111	Safi	Jun 43 — Jul 43
No 112	Safi	Jul 43 — Jul 43
No 113	Luqa	Sep 41 — Sep 41
No 114	Luqa	Jul 43 — Aug 43
No 126	Ta' Qali	Jun 41 — May 42
No 126	Luqa	May 42 — Jun 43
No 126	Safi	Jun 43 — Sep 43
No 139	Luqa	May 41 — Jun 41
No 145	Luqa	Jun 43 — Jul 43
No 148	Luqa	Dec 40 — Mar 41
No 148	Luqa	Apr 41 — Apr 41
No 148	Luqa	Dec 42 — Dec 42
No 152	Ta' Qali	June 43 — Jul 43
No 154	Ta' Qali	Jun 43 — Jul 43
No 185	Hal Far & Ta' Qali	May 41 — Jun 43
No 185	Qrendi	Jun 43 — Oct 43
No 185	Hal Far	Oct 43 — Jul 44
No 217	Luqa	Jun 42 — Aug 42
No 219		Jun 42 —
No 221 (Special Duties Flight)	Luqa	Oct 41 —
No 221	Luqa	Jan 42 — Aug 42
No 221	Luqa	Jan 43 — Mar 44
No 223	Luqa	Jul 43 — Aug 43

Unit	Location	Dates
No 227	Luqa	Aug 42 — Nov 42
No 227	Ta' Qali	Nov 42 — Mar 43
No 228	Kalafrana	Jun 40 — Mar 41
No 229	Hal Far	Mar 42 — Apr 42
No 229	Ta' Qali	Aug 42 — Dec 42
No 229	Qrendi	Dec 42 — Sep 43
No 229	Hal Far	Sep 43 — Jan 44
No 230	Kalafrana	Jul 40 —
No 232	Ta' Qali	Jun 43 — Jul 43
No 235	Luqa	Jun 42 — Aug 42
No 242	Hal Far & Luqa	Nov 41 —
No 242	Ta' Qali	Jun 43 — Jul 43
No 243	Hal Far	Jun 43 — Jul 43
No 248	Ta' Qali	Aug 42 — Aug 42
No 249	Ta' Qali	May 41 — Nov 42
No 249	Qrendi	Nov 42 — Sep 43
No 249	Hal Far	Sep 43 — Oct 43
No 250	Hal Far	Jul 43 — Jul 43
No 250	Luqa	Jul 43 — Jul 43
No 252	Luqa	May 41 — May 41
No 252	Luqa	Jul 41 — Aug 41
No 252	Luqa	Dec 41 — Dec 41
No 256	Luqa	Jul 43 — Oct 43
No 256	Luqa	Oct 43 — Apr 44
No 260	Luqa	Jun 43 — Jul 43
No 261	Luqa	Aug 40 — Oct 40
No 261	Ta' Qali	Oct 40 — May 41
No 272	Luqa	Aug 41 — Sep 41
No 272	Ta' Qali	Nov 42 — Jun 43
No 272	Luqa	Jun 43 — Jul 43
No 417 RCAF	Luqa	Jun 43 — Jul 43
No 600	Luqa	Jun 43 — Jul 43
No 601	Luqa	Apr 42 — Jun 42
No 601	Luqa	Jun 43 — Jul 43
No 603	Ta' Qali	Apr 42 — Aug 42
No 605	Hal Far & Luqa	Nov 41 — Feb 42
No 605	Ta' Qali	Feb 42 — Mar 42
No 683	Luqa	Feb 43 — Nov 43
No 1435	Luqa	Aug 42 — Oct 43
No 418 Flight	Luqa	Aug 40 — Aug 40
No 431 Flight	Luqa	Sept 40 — Dec 40
No 1435 Flight		Dec 41 —
Fighter Flight	Hal Far	Apr 40 — Aug 40
Malta Night Fighter Unit	Ta' Qali	Jul 41 — Dec 41
No 3 RAAF	Ta' Qali	Jul 43 — Jul 43
No 450 RAAF	Luqa	Jul 43 — Jul 43
No 458 RAAF	Luqa	Jan 43 — May 43
No 1 SAAF	Luqa	Jun 43 — Jul 43
No 4 SAAF		
No 12 SAAF	Hal Far	Jul 43 — Aug 43
No 21 SAAF		Jul 43 — Aug 43
No 24 SAAF	Hal Far	Jul 43 — Aug 43
No 40 SAAF (Tac.R)	Luqa	Jun 43 — Jul 43
307th USAAF	Xewkija, Gozo	Jun 43 — Jul 43
308th USAAF	Xewkija, Gozo	Jun 43 — Jul 43
309th USAAF	Xewkija, Gozo	Jul 43 — Jul 43
47th Light Bombardment Group	Ta' Qali	Jul 43 — Aug 43
800X RN-FAA	Hal Far	May 41 — Nov 41
806 RN-FAA	Hal Far	Jan 41 — Mar 41
815 RN-FAA	Hal Far	Jan 41 — Jan 41
819 RN-FAA	Hal Far	Jan 41 — Jan 41
820 RN-FAA	Hal Far	Aug 43 — Aug 43
821 RN-FAA	Hal Far	Nov 42 — Jul 43

826 RN-FAA	Hal Far	Dec 42 — Feb 43
828 RN-FAA	Hal Far	Oct 41 — Jul 43
830 RN-FAA	Hal Far	Jun 40 — Mar 43

(Compiled by Frederick R. Galea)

Appendix Y

ROYAL NAVY SHIPS, FLEET AIR ARM SQUADRONS AND MOTOR LAUNCHES GRANTED THE "MALTA CONVOYS" BATTLE HONOUR:

Ajax	1941	*Fleur de Lys*	1941
Amazon	1942	*Foresight*	1941-42
Antelope	1942	*Forester*	1941
Arethusa	1941-42	*Fortune*	1941-42
Argus	1942	*Foxhound*	1941
Ark Royal	1941	*Furious*	1942
Arrow	1942	*Fury*	1941-42
Ashanti	1942		
Aurora	1941	*Gallant*	1941
Avon Vale	1941-42	*Geranium*	1942
		Gloucester	1941
Badsworth	1942	*Gloxinia*	1941
Beaufort	1942	*Greyhound*	1941
Bedouin	1942	*Griffin*	1941-42
Beverley	1941	*Gurkha*	1941-42
Bicester	1942		
Blankney	1942	*Hasty*	1941-42
Bonaventure	1941	*Havock*	1941-42
Boston	1942	*Hebe*	1942
Bramham	1942	*Hereward*	1941
Breconshire	1941-42	*Hermione*	1941-42
		Hero	1941-42
Cachalot	1941	*Heythrop*	1941-42
Cairo	1942	*Hurworth*	1942
Calcutta	1941	*Hyacinth*	1941
Carlisle	1941-42	*Hythe*	1942
Charybdis	1942		
Cleopatra	1942	*Icarus*	1942
Clyde	1942	*Ilex*	1941
Coltsfoot	1942	*Illustrious*	1941
Cossack	1941	*Indomitable*	1942
		Inglefield	1942
Dainty	1941	*Intrepid*	1942
Decoy	1941-42	*Ithuriel*	1942
Defender	1941		
Derwent	1942	*Jaguar*	1941-42
Diamond	1941	*Janus*	1941
Dido	1942	*Jervis*	1941-42
Dulverton	1942	*Jonquil*	1942
Duncan	1941	*Juno*	1941
Eagle	1942	*Kandahar*	1941
Echo	1942	*Kelvin*	1942
Edinburgh	1941	*Kenya*	1941-42
Encounter	1941	*Keppel*	1942
Eridge	1941-42	*Kimberley*	1941
Escapade	1942	*Kingston*	1941-42
Eskimo	1942	*Kipling*	1941-42
Euryalus	1941-42		
		Laforey	1941-42
		Lance	1941-42
Farndale	1941	*Ledbury*	1942
Faulknor	1941	*Legion*	1941-42
Fearless	1941	*Lightning*	1941-42
Firedrake	1941	*Lively*	1941-42

Liverpool	1942		*Sikh*	1941-42
Lookout	1942		*Sirius*	1942
			Somali	1942
Malaya	1941-42		*Southampton*	1941
Malcolm	1942		*Southwold*	1942
Manchester	1941-42		*Speedy*	1942
Manxman	1941-42		*Spirea*	1942
Maori	1941-42			
Marne	1942		*Talisman*	1941
Matchless	1942		*Tartar*	1942
Middleton	1942		*Thunderbolt*	1941-42
Mohawk	1941		*Triumph*	1941
			Trusty	1941
Naiad	1941-42			
Nelson	1941-42		*Unbeaten*	1941-42
Neptune	1941		*Unique*	1941
Nestor	1941-42		*Upholder*	1941-42
Nigeria	1942		*Upright*	1941
Nizam	1941		*Urge*	1941
Nubian	1941		*Ursula*	1941
			Utmost	1941-42
Onslow	1942			
Oribi	1941		*Valiant*	1941
Orion	1941		*Vansittart*	1942
Olympus	1941-42		*Venomous*	1942
Osiris	1941		*Victorious*	1942
Otus	1941		*Vidette*	1942
P.31	1942		*Warspite*	1941
P.32	1941		*Welshman*	1942
P.34	1942		*Westcott*	1942
P.36	1941		*Wilton*	1942
P.42	1942		*Wishart*	1942
P.43	1942		*Wolverine*	1942
P.44	1942		*Wrestler*	1942
P.46	1942			
P.211	1942		*York*	1941
P.222	1942			
Pandora	1941-42		*Zetland*	1942
Parthian	1942		*Zulu*	1941-42
Partridge	1942			
Pathfinder	1942			
Penelope	1941-42		**F.A.A. Squadrons:**	
Penn	1942		*800*	1941-42
Peony	1941		*801*	1942
Perth	1941		*806*	1942
Phoebe	1942		*807*	1941-42
Porpoise	1942		*808*	1941
Prince of Wales	1941		*809*	1942
Proteus	1942		*812*	1941
			813	1942
Quentin	1942		*816*	1941
			820	1941
Renown	1941-42	**Motor Launches:**	*824*	1942
Rodney	1941-42	*121*	*825*	1941
Rorqual	1941-42	*134*	*827*	1942
Rye	1942	*135*	*831*	1942
		168	*832*	1942
Salvia	1941	*459*	*884*	1942
Sheffield	1941	*462*	*885*	1942

(*By courtesy of the Naval Historical Branch, Ministry of Defence, London.*)

Appendix Z

CODE NAMES

Code names of Operations destined to, or originating from, Malta:

APOLOGY and HATS	Fast convoy, United Kingdom to Malta and Egypt (8-9/40)
APPLEDORE	Move of 1st Malta Infantry Brigade from Malta to Middle East for training for HUSKY
ASCENDANT	Passage of *Troilus* and *Orari* from Malta to Gibraltar (8/42)
ASTROLOGER and BANDOLIER	Eastbound convoy for Malta (11/41)
BANJO	Gozo (after HUSKY)
BARITONE	Despatch of aircraft to Malta (8/42);
BELLOWS	Aircraft to Malta (8/42)
BENEDICT	Hurricanes to Malta;
BLOODSTOCK	Capture of Kerkenna Island, Tunisia— German human torpedo base (4/43)
BOWERY	Reinforcement of aircraft to Malta (5/42)
BREASTPLATE	; also use of force from Malta against Sicily (4/43)
CALENDAR	Aircraft for Malta from USS *Wasp* (4/42)
CALLBOY	Reinforcements of aircraft to Malta
CHILDHOOD	Attack by MTBs from Malta on moles at Tripoli to stop demolition and blocking of the harbour (1/43)
COAT	Passage of reinforcements for fleet and troops to Malta (11/40)
COLLAR	; also fast convoy of merchant ships for Malta and Alexandria (11/40)
COLOSSUS	Airborne combined operations attack on the aqueduct at Tragino, carrying water for Taranto, Brindisi and Bari (2/41)
CORKSCREW	Capture of Pantelleria, Linosa and Lampedusa Islands, Mediterranean (6/43)
CRICKET	Malta Conference, 1945
CRUPPER	; also movement of supply ships, Gibraltar to Malta
CUCUMBER	Bombing of Tripoli from Malta (7/41);
DUNLOP	Reinforcements of fighters to Malta and Middle East (4/41)
EXCESS	Convoy of fast merchant ships for Greece, troops for Malta and aircraft to Alexandria (1/41)

FINANCE	Malta (after HUSKY)
FULLSIZE	8th Army operation to divert enemy air forces during passage of convoy to Malta (3/42)
GANYMEDE	Convoy, Gibraltar to Malta (1942)
GIBBON	Control and surrender of Italian warships and merchant ships at the time of Italian armistice (9/43)
GILMAN	Despatch of aircraft reinforcements to Malta
GLOVER	Reinforcement of fighters to Malta, 1941
GRINNELL	Reinforcement of Spitfires to Malta from HMS *Furious*
HALBERD	Movement of storeships, Gibraltar to Malta (8-9/41);
HARLEY	Reinforcement of fighters to Malta, 1941
HARPOON	Convoy from UK to Malta (6/42)
HATS	See APOLOGY
HURRY	Reinforcement of aircraft to Malta from HMS *Argus* (7-8/40)
HUSKY	Invasion of Sicily (7/43)
INSECT	Movement of aircraft for Malta (7/42)
JAGUAR	; also air reinforcement of Malta, 1941
JULIUS	Two convoys to Malta (Western see HARPOON, Eastern see VIGOROUS)
KNAPSACK	Despatch of aircraft to Malta
LANDAU	Fast ship, Gibraltar to Malta
LANDSMAN	Despatch of aircraft reinforcements to Malta (7/42)
LANDSDALE	Shipment of stores to Malta
L.B.	Aircraft for Malta (5/42)
LOADER	Visit of King, Secretary of State and VIPs to North Africa and Middle East, including Malta (1943)
LOTUS	Bomber force from UK to Malta for operations against Italy (1941)
MANDATE	Protection by Beaufighters of Alexandria-Malta convoy (6/42)
MANOTICK	Stores for Malta via Middle East
M.B. 6	Malta convoy (10/40)
M.F. 3, 5	Convoys to Malta (1/42)
M.G. 1	Convoys to Malta (3/42)
MOLECULE	Stores for Malta via Middle East

NEWMAN	Direct reinforcement of aircraft to Malta by carrier
NORDIC	Further reinforcement of fighters to Malta
OPPIDAN	Despatch of Spitfires from USS *Wasp* to Malta;
PANTALOON	Reinforcement of Hurricanes to Malta (10/41);
PEDESTAL	Convoy to Malta from UK; the last to be seriously attacked (8/42)
PERPETUAL	Reinforcement of Spitfires to Malta by HMS *Argus* (3/42);
PICKET	Reinforcement of Spitfires to Malta by HMS *Eagle* (3/42);
PINNACE	Passage of HMS *Centurion* to Malta
PINPOINT	Reinforcement of Spitfires to Malta (7/42)
POPLAR	Despatch of aircraft reinforcements to Malta
PORTCULLIS	Egypt to Malta convoy (12/42)
PRINCIPAL	Transport by air of stores and personnel to Malta;
PROPELLER	Eastbound convoy for Malta (9/41)
QUADRANGLE	Series of slow convoys, Egypt to Malta (12/42)
QUARTER	Aircraft reinforcements to Malta, 1942
QUICK	Reinforcements of two squadrons already in Malta, 1941
RAILWAY	Reinforcements of aircraft to Malta and Gibraltar (7/41)
RANDOM	RAF portion of special reinforcement to Malta (1941)
ROCKET and TRACER	Movement of aircraft to Malta (6/41)
RUPERT	Eastern convoy to Malta (6/42);
SALIENT	; also reinforcements of Spitfires to Malta (6/42)
SCANTLING	Despatch of aircraft reinforcements to Malta
SCARLET	Reinforcement of fighter aircraft in Malta (1941)
SCRIMMAGE	RAF portion of HALBERD (8-9/41)
SKIRMISH	Despatch of Beaufighters to Malta, 1941
SPLICE	Reinforcement of Hurricanes to Malta (5/41)
SPOTTER	Reinforcement of fighters in Malta (3/42);
STATUS	Reinforcement of aircraft to Malta (9/41)
STONEAGE	Convoy from Alexandria to Malta (11/42)
STYLE	Passage of warships with personnel to Malta (8/41); second phase of TILDEN
SUBSTANCE	Convoy from Gibraltar to Malta (7/41)

SWEEP	Convoy, Gibraltar to Malta (1942)
TANKER	Slow follow-up convoy, Gibraltar to Malta
TECHNICAL	Fast follow-up convoy, Gibraltar to Malta
TEMPLE	Special stores for Malta
TIGER	British naval operation: fast convoy of tanks and Hurricane fighters from UK via Gibraltar to Egypt, slow and fast convoys from Alexandria to Malta, and bombardment of Benghazi (5/41);
TILDEN	Reinforcement of Spitfires to Malta
TRAIN	Twenty-nine Spitfires to Malta (10/42)
TRACER	See ROCKET
TUREEN	Movement of drafts to Malta (6/42)
VIGOROUS	Alexandria to Malta convoy (6/42)
WHITE	Air reinforcement of Malta by *Argus* (12/40)
WINCH	Reinforcement of fighters in Malta (1940-41)

Extracted by John A. Agius from The Second World War: A Guide to Documents in the Public Records Office, *published by HMSO London in 1972. Reproduced by permission of the Controller, Her Majesty's Stationery Office.*

Notes:
* Entries containing a semi-colon indicate that the operation includes some other activity not related to Malta.
* Figures shown in brackets refer to the month and year.

THE WAR MEMORIAL

A War Memorial, commemorating the Maltese who lost their life during the First World War, was unveiled on 11th November, 1938, — Armistice Day — by the Governor of Malta, General Sir Charles Bonham-Carter.

The fifty-foot high memorial, designed by Louis Naudi, takes the form of five superimposed crosses made of hard Gozo stone. On one side of the plinth, the message sent by King George V recording Malta's part in the Great War was originally reproduced, while the other three sides showed the names, in bronze letters, of the 592 Maltese who paid the supreme sacrifice.

Less than a year after the unveiling ceremony, Britain and Germany were at war again. The Memorial escaped with a few splinter scars during the aerial bombardment of Malta, following Italy's entry into the war as Germany's ally.

With the return of peace, Government decided that the Memorial should commemorate the dead of the two Great Wars. The original panels at the base of the Memorial were replaced by tablets reproducing Malta's armorial bearings and the text of the tributes paid to Malta by King George V, King George VI and President Franklin D. Roosevelt.

When unveiling the tablets on 8th December, 1949, HRH Princess Elizabeth (now Queen Elizabeth II) said "... It is most fitting that those tributes should be recorded on your Cenotaph, which commemorates those whose supreme sacrifice deserves all honour and glory...." The Prime Minister of Malta, Dr (later Sir) Paul Boffa, replied: "... Recalling with pride the role Malta has played in the cause of Freedom, it is highly befitting that on this day we pay tribute to the Service and civilian men and women of Malta who, fighting side by side with fellow-members of the British Commonwealth, have paid with their lives that we may live and continue to enjoy our heritage; we solemnly pledge ourselves never to forget their sacrifice...."

Consequent to the reconstruction of Floriana and the redevelopment of the approaches to Valletta, in 1954 the War Memorial was moved to come in alignment with the centre of St Anne's Street.

THE COMMONWEALTH AIR FORCES MEMORIAL

The Commonwealth Air Forces Memorial, built on a prominent site at Floriana provided by the Government of Malta, takes the shape of a fifty-foot high column of travertine marble, surmounted by a 7-foot 9-inch high gilded bronze eagle. The column stands on a circular base bearing bronze panels with the names of 2,301 airmen, made up as follows:

Royal Air Force	1,542	Royal New Zealand Air Force	85
Of Newfoundland	3	South African Air Force	171
Royal Canadian Air Force	286	British Overseas Airways Corporation	3
Royal Australian Air Force	211		

The central panel bears the following dedicatory inscription:

OVER THESE AND NEIGHBOURING
LANDS AND SEAS THE AIRMEN
WHOSE NAMES ARE RECORDED HERE
FELL IN RAID OR SORTIE AND
HAVE NO KNOWN GRAVE.

MALTA   GIBRALTAR
MEDITERRANEAN
ADRIATIC   TUNISIA
SICILY   ITALY
YUGOSLAVIA   AUSTRIA

PROPOSITI INSULA TENAX
TENACES   VIROS
COMMEMORAT

The Latin epigram translates: An Island resolute of purpose remembers resolute men.

The Memorial was unveiled by HM Queen Elizabeth II on 3rd May, 1954, in the presence of several distinguished personalities, about 500 relatives of the deceased airmen and thousands of Maltese. In a brief address, Her Majesty said: "Many of you here today have, I know, come from far to Malta to join with my husband and myself in paying tribute to the fallen whose names are inscribed here. Most of you will inevitably be turning your minds back, recalling past memories and wondering, perhaps, whether their sacrifice has been in vain. To you I give this message of hope — if we show in all our dealings the same integrity of purpose, and the same resolution in fulfilling it as was shown by them in the war, then surely we shall be able to extract from the dark and desperate difficulties which beset us a victory no less glorious than that which we commemorate here today ...".

The Malta Branch of the Commonwealth War Graves Commission looks after the maintenance of the Memorial as well as of the graves of British Commonwealth servicemen buried in the four military cemeteries.

ROLL OF HONOUR

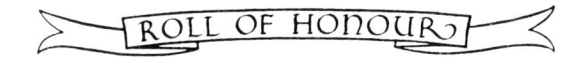

CIVILIANS

Surname	Name	Age	Residence at time of death	Date of death
ABDILLA,	Anthony	28	Gzira	24 Dec 41
ABDILLA,	Grezzja	45	Zabbar	2 Mar 42
ABDILLA,	Jessie	9	Luqa	9 Apr 42
ABDILLA,	John	16	Zurrieq	16 May 41
ABDILLA,	Joseph	14	Zebbug	3 Nov 42
ABDILLA,	Josephine	32	Gzira	2 Jan 42
ABDILLA,	Mary	15	Zabbar	2 Mar 42
ABELA,	Amante	30	Qormi	7 Jul 40
ABELA,	Carmel	3 months	Ghaxaq	27 Dec 41
ABELA,	Carmela	52	Rabat	21 Mar 42
ABELA,	Carmela	14	Zejtun	2 May 42
ABELA,	Dolores	60	Floriana	24 Apr 42
ABELA,	Francis	22	Tarxien	15 Jun 41
ABELA,	Gaetana	20	Birkirkara	3 Aug 42
ABELA,	Harry			26 Jun 40
ABELA,	John	33	Ghaxaq	27 Dec 41
ABELA,	Joseph		Msida	5 Apr 42
ABELA,	Joseph	13	Ghaxaq	27 Jul 42
ABELA,	Melita	26	Sliema	15 Feb 42
ABELA,	Michael	26	Ghaxaq	17 May 42
ABELA,	Pauline	55	Valletta	7 Apr 42
ABELA,	Sr Rosaria	82	Mdina	2 May 42
ABELA,	Santo	14	Mgarr	29 Sep 42
ABELA,	Teresa	1	Ghaxaq	27 Dec 41
ABELA,	Vincenza	26	Ghaxaq	27 Dec 41
ADAMI,	Albert	2	Rabat	21 Mar 42
ADAMI,	Louise	29	Rabat	21 Mar 42
ADAMI,	Mary	6	Rabat	21 Mar 42
AGIUS,	Angelo	29	Zejtun	5 Apr 42
AGIUS,	Anthony	29	Birkirkara	31 Jul 42
AGIUS,	Catherine	50	Valletta	1 Nov 41
AGIUS,	Dolores	6	Qormi	9 Mar 42
AGIUS,	Emanuel	16	Qormi	9 Apr 42
AGIUS,	Emanuel	7	Msida	13 Apr 42
AGIUS,	Francis	30	Floriana	8 May 42
AGIUS,	Joseph	60	Zebbug	3 Apr 42
AGIUS,	Louis	20	Rabat	20 Apr 42
AGIUS,	Marianna	66	Hamrun	3 Jul 42
AGIUS,	Mary	31	Pawla	12 Feb 42
AGIUS,	Sr Paola	73	Balzan	21 Mar 42
AGIUS,	Saviour	68	Qormi	6 Apr 42
AGIUS,	Victor	29	Pawla	12 Feb 42
ALVAREZ,	Mary	88	Sliema	25 Mar 42
AMAIRA,	Onorato	45	Floriana	25 Apr 42
AMODIO	Joseph	24	Sliema	15 Feb 42
ANCILLERI,	Joseph		Cospicua	11 Jun 40
ANDREWS,	W			29 Mar 42
APAP,	Eleanora	66	Hamrun	3 Jul 42
AQUILINA,	Carmel	77	Qormi	17 Mar 42
AQUILINA,	Joseph	38	Qrendi	30 Jan 42
AQUILINA,	Josephine	64	Valletta	14 Feb 41
AQUILINA,	Liza	50	Qormi	10 Feb 42
AQUILINA,	Mary Rose	24	Qrendi	30 Jan 42
AQUILINA,	Michael	60	Cospicua	8 Apr 41
AQUILINA,	Toussaints	17	Pawla	24 Mar 42

ROLL OF HONOUR

ASHMORE,	Agnes	9	Senglea	30 Apr 41
ASHMORE,	Iris	11	Senglea	30 Apr 41
ASHMORE,	Tommy	4	Senglea	30 Apr 41
ATTARD,	Andrew	12	Luqa	9 Apr 42
ATTARD,	Anna	75	Hamrun	19 Apr 42
ATTARD,	Anthony	8	Luqa	9 Apr 42
ATTARD,	Antonia	50	Floriana	5 Apr 42
ATTARD,	Paskalina	3	Luqa	9 Apr 42
ATTARD,	Br Bonaventura	21	Zebbug	29 Apr 41
ATTARD,	Carmel	50	Valletta	1 Mar 41
ATTARD,	Carmel	15	Zejtun	16 May 41
ATTARD,	Carmel	16	Zejtun	23 Dec 41
ATTARD,	Carmel	72	Xaghra, Gozo	10 Feb 42
ATTARD,	Carmel	50	Zebbug	1 Apr 42
ATTARD,	Carmela	22	Pawla	7 Jul 41
ATTARD,	Concetta	47	Tarxien	11 Oct 42
ATTARD,	Frances	16	Zebbug	1 Apr 42
ATTARD,	Gaetano	28	Marsa	8 Jun 42
ATTARD,	Giovanna	56	Valletta	15 Mar 42
ATTARD,	Innocenza	42	Luqa	9 Apr 42
ATTARD,	John	20	Pawla	15 Feb 42
ATTARD,	John	25	Sliema	26 Jun 42
ATTARD,	John	17	Qrendi	19 Dec 42
ATTARD,	Joseph	33	Zabbar	20 Jan 41
ATTARD,	Lawrence	23	Kercem, Gozo	14 Jun 43
ATTARD,	Leonard	57	Siggiewi	29 Jan 42
ATTARD,	Mary	17	Valletta	24 Apr 42
ATTARD,	Marianna	70	Xaghra, Gozo	10 Feb 42
ATTARD,	Marianna	70	Hamrun	19 Apr 42
ATTARD,	Michael	10	Luqa	9 Apr 42
ATTARD,	Nazzarena	28	San Lawrenz, Gozo	7 Aug 42
ATTARD,	Nicola	6	Luqa	9 Apr 42
ATTARD,	Robert	60	Floriana	1 Mar 42
ATTARD,	Salvina	17	Luqa	9 Apr 42
ATTARD,	Vincent	86	Zabbar	26 Jul 43
AXIAQ,	Carmel	40	Zurrieq	20 May 42
AXISA,	Vincent	68	Zejtun	23 May 42
AZZOPARDI,	Alfred	56	Naxxar	3 May 42
AZZOPARDI,	Carmel	24	Hamrun	4 Jul 41
AZZOPARDI,	Carmel	17	Xaghra, Gozo	12 Apr 42
AZZOPARDI,	Carmela	52	Luqa	9 Apr 42
AZZOPARDI,	Coronato	9	Nadur, Gozo	14 Sep 43
AZZOPARDI,	Edwin	21	Sliema	6 May 42
AZZOPARDI,	Filomena	70	Hamrun	19 Apr 42
AZZOPARDI,	Francis	16	Floriana	21 Mar 42
AZZOPARDI,	Francis	58	Xaghra, Gozo	23 Apr 42
AZZOPARDI,	John	15	Sliema	1 Apr 42
AZZOPARDI,	Joseph	7	Nadur, Gozo	14 Sep 43
AZZOPARDI,	Josephine	30	Gzira	2 Jan 42
AZZOPARDI,	Katherine	80	Rabat	21 Mar 42
AZZOPARDI,	Lawrence	1	Zejtun	8 May 42
AZZOPARDI,	Michael	6 months	Sannat, Gozo	10 Oct 42
AZZOPARDI,	Paul	52	Ghajnsielem, Gozo	29 Dec 41
AZZOPARDI,	Paul	39	Lija	19 Mar 42
AZZOPARDI,	Paul	17	Mtarfa	11 Oct 42
AZZOPARDI,	Rosaria	67	Hamrun	19 Apr 42
AZZOPARDI,	Rosaria	25	Zejtun	8 May 42
AZZOPARDI,	Teodoro	23	Naxxar	7 Oct 42
AZZOPARDI,	Walter	16	Hamrun	5 Jul 41

ROLL OF HONOUR

BALDACCHINO,	Carmel	44	Siggiewi	17 Mar 42
BALDACCHINO,	Joseph	36	Tarxien	11 Oct 42
BALDACCHINO,	Saviour	55	Zejtun	2 May 42
BALDACCHINO,	Wistin	58	Siggiewi	9 Feb 42
BALZAN,	Augustine	16	Hamrun	5 Apr 42
BALZAN,	Carmel	71	Sliema	6 Mar 42
BARBARA,	Alfred	27	Zebbug	5 Apr 42
BARBARA,	Andrew	5	Luqa	9 Apr 42
BARBARA,	Anthony	55	Tarxien	11 Oct 42
BARBARA,	Annetta	41	Floriana	28 Apr 42
BARBARA,	Carmela	5 months	Luqa	9 Apr 42
BARBARA,	Frances	25	Luqa	9 Apr 42
BARBARA,	Francis	56	Qormi	8 Apr 42
BARBARA,	John	9	Luqa	9 Apr 42
BARBARA,	Josephine	16	Zurrieq	9 Apr 42
BARBARA,	Louis	60	Mosta	19 Jan 42
BARBERI,	Mary	74	Mosta	12 Jun 41
BARTOLI,	Emanuel LL.D.	55	Rabat	10 Sep 41
BARTOLO,	Eddie	38	St Julian's	17 Mar 42
BARLOLO,	Joseph	52	Tarxien	8 Apr 41
BARTOLO,	Joseph	38	Sliema	17 Mar 42
BARTOLO,	Joseph	40	Mosta	22 Mar 42
BARTOLO,	Joseph	18	Valletta	24 Mar 42
BARTOLO,	Leone	20	Pawla	24 Apr 42
BARTOLO,	Paul	24	Cospicua	4 Apr 42
BARTOLO,	Spiro	73	Kirkop	21 May 42
BATES,	Carmen	6	Sliema	1 Apr 42
BATES,	George	9 months	Sliema	1 Apr 42
BATES,	Imelda	5	Sliema	1 Apr 42
BELLIZZI,	Alfred	72	Gzira	25 Mar 42
BELLIZZI,	Anthony	65	Hamrun	10 Apr 42
BELLIZZI,	Joseph	66	Valletta	15 Mar 42
BELLOTTI,	Saviour	52		2 May 42
BEN ALI,	Abdul	61	Valletta	4 Apr 42
BEZZINA,	Albino	11	Mosta	29 May 42
BEZZINA,	Carmel	73	Mosta	16 Sep 42
BEZZINA,	Francis	12	Mosta	29 May 42
BEZZINA,	Giovanna Maria	20	Rabat	20 Apr 42
BEZZINA,	Louis		Hamrun	8 Apr 41
BIANCO,	Francesca	70	Msida	19 Apr 42
BIGENI,	Felic	32	Ghajnsielem, Gozo	29 Dec 41
BLOCK,	John	20	Sliema	13 Oct 42
BONANNO,	Antonia	16	Zebbug	3 Nov 42
BONANNO,	Matthew	4	Mosta	23 Jun 42
BONANNO,	Paul	45	Mosta	23 Jun 42
BONANNO,	Salvina	7	Zebbug	3 Nov 42
BONAVIA,	Joseph	9	Zejtun	18 Apr 42
BONDIN,	Consolat	6	Pawla	18 May 42
BONDIN,	Josephine	35	Pawla	24 Apr 42
BONDIN,	Josephine	10 months	Zurrieq	23 Jul 42
BONDIN,	Mary	6 months	Pawla	24 Apr 42
BONDIN,	Teresa	2	Pawla	24 Apr 42
BONE,	Violet	16	Valletta	19 Apr 42
BONELLO,	Alfred	45	Sliema	8 May 42
BONELLO,	Frances	75	Hamrun	19 Apr 42
BONELLO,	Mary	11	Tarxien	6 Apr 42
BONELLO,	Michael	21	Rabat	29 Apr 42
BONELLO,	Robert M.D.	52	Valleta	15 Feb 42
BONETT,	Peter	52	Marsa	1 Nov 41
BONGAILAS,	Emanuel	28	Zabbar	15 Mar 42

ROLL OF HONOUR

BONNICI,	Alfred		Pawla	8 Apr 41
BONNICI,	Alexander	38	Luqa	24 Mar 42
BONNICI,	Carmel	50	Zejtun	2 Jan 42
BONNICI,	Carmel	45	Qormi	9 Feb 42
BONNICI,	Carmel	12	Zebbug	11 Jul 42
BONNICI,	Carmela	44	St Paul's Bay	18 Oct 41
BONNICI,	Emanuel	4	St Paul's Bay	18 Oct 41
BONNICI,	Frances	6	St Paul's Bay	18 Oct 41
BONNICI,	Francis	50	St Paul's Bay	18 Oct 41
BONNICI,	John	17	Zabbar	20 May 41
BONNICI,	Joseph	16	St Paul's Bay	18 Oct 41
BONNICI,	Joseph	56	Tarxien	5 Sep 42
BONNICI,	Philip	38	Qormi	20 Jul 43
BONNICI,	Rosa	60	Luqa	27 May 42
BONNICI,	Salvina	15	Zejtun	12 Feb 42
BONNICI,	Tarcisio	12	Zejtun	2 May 42
BONO,	Silvia	71	Hamrun	19 Apr 42
BORDA,	Sr Alexandra	31	Attard	9 May 42
BORDA,	Joseph	82	Hamrun	6 Apr 42
BORDA,	Marianna	77	Hamrun	6 Apr 42
BORG,	Annunziata	60	Sliema	21 Aug 41
BORG,	Anthony	26	Hamrun	15 Jun 40
BORG,	Anthony	48	Gudja	19 Apr 42
BORG,	Anthony	59	Qormi	26 Jun 42
BORG,	Anthony	60	Gzira	25 Feb 42
BORG,	Antonia	58	Tarxien	6 Apr 42
BORG,	Carmel	61	Rabat	10 Sep 41
BORG,	Carmel	39	Rabat	24 Dec 41
BORG,	Carmel	25	Attard	18 Apr 42
BORG,	Carmel	3	Senglea	28 Apr 42
BORG,	Carmel	3	Hamrun	26 May 42
BORG,	Carmel	35	Hamrun	26 May 42
BORG,	Carmel	27	Birkirkara	31 Jul 42
BORG,	Carmel	27	Qormi	20 Jul 43
BORG,	Carmela	23	Victoria, Gozo	24 Dec 41
BORG,	Carmela	91	Hamrun	19 Apr 42
BORG,	Carmela	27	Senglea	28 Apr 42
BORG,	Carmela	10	Rabat	24 Jul 42
BORG,	Cettina	3	Kalkara	7 Jul 40
BORG,	Cettina	25	Tarxien	6 Apr 42
BORG,	Charles	55	Pawla	7 Jul 41
BORG,	Concetta	66	Hamrun	20 Jul 42
BORG,	Dolores	60	Sliema	1 Mar 42
BORG,	Domenica	19	Rabat	7 Mar 42
BORG,	Doris	6	Mosta	21 Mar 42
BORG,	Edward	16	Valletta	1 Nov 41
BORG,	Eliza	28	Pawla	7 Jul 41
BORG,	Emanuel	46	Xewkija, Gozo	15 Mar 41
BORG,	Emanuel	60	St Paul's Bay	16 Feb 42
BORG,	Emanuel	16	Sliema	19 Apr 42
BORG,	Emanuel	11	Siggiewi	10 Feb 43
BORG,	Frances	30	Hamrun	4 Apr 42
BORG,	Francis	5	Siggiewi	11 Feb 43
BORG,	George	5	Kalkara	7 Jul 40
BORG,	George	63	Tarxien	8 Apr 42
BORG,	George	35	Qormi	26 Jun 42
BORG,	Giorgia	22	Sliema	11 Mar 42
BORG,	Giorgia	43	Qormi	10 Feb 42
BORG,	Giorgina	52	Balzan	11 Jul 42
BORG,	Giovanna	72	Hamrun	19 Apr 42

ROLL OF HONOUR

BORG,	Giovanna	76	Harmun	2 May 42
BORG,	Grace	30	Attard	3 Jul 42
BORG,	Br Hilarion	22	Zebbug	29 Apr 41
BORG,	Irene	8 months	Kalkara	7 Jul 40
BORG,	John	25	Qormi	26 Jun 40
BORG,	John	24	Sliema	11 Mar 41
BORG,	John	51	Cospicua	24 Feb 42
BORG,	John	53	Qormi	20 Jul 43
BORG,	Joseph	13	Sliema	11 Mar 41
BORG,	Joseph	8	Floriana	1 Mar 42
BORG,	Joseph	70	Floriana	5 Apr 42
BORG,	Joseph	14	Valletta	19 Apr 42
BORG,	Joseph	15	Gzira	19 Apr 42
BORG,	Josephine	4	Kalkara	7 Jul 40
BORG,	Josephine	44	Mgarr	11 Apr 41
BORG,	Josephine	24	Rabat	11 Oct 42
BORG,	Lucrezia	55	Hamrun	19 Apr 42
BORG,	Maggie	10	Kalkara	7 Jul 40
BORG,	Mary	18	Tarxien	6 Apr 42
BORG,	Marion	14	Birkirkara	13 Apr 42
BORG,	Mary	46	Birkirkara	13 Apr 42
BORG,	Mary	33	Mosta	13 Apr 42
BORG,	Marie Assunta	48	Sliema	12 Jun 40
BORG,	Melania	42	Kalkara	7 Jul 40
BORG,	Michael	64	Sliema	19 Mar 42
BORG,	Nikolina	62	Siggiewi	7 Jul 42
BORG,	Paul	17	Birkirkara	24 Mar 42
BORG,	Pauline	31	Mqabba	11 Apr 42
BORG,	Rosario	21	Birkirkara	10 Jul 42
BORG,	Saviour	20	Birkirkara	15 Mar 42
BORG,	Speranza	80	Valletta	14 Feb 41
BORG,	Stella	35	Hamrun	26 May 42
BORG,	Spiro	25	Zebbug	11 Oct 42
BORG,	Vincent	2	Kalkara	7 Jul 40
BORG,	Vincent	55	Mosta	9 Feb 42
BORG BELLIZZI,	Domenica	39	Valletta	15 Mar 42
BOXALL,	John	42	Vittoriosa	13 Feb 43
BRICCIO,	Elicio	70	Senglea	16 Jan 41
BRIFFA,	Carmel	13	Marsa	22 Dec 41
BRIFFA,	Carmela	60	Qormi	17 Feb 42
BRIFFA,	Carmela	6	Birzebbuga	7 Apr 42
BRIFFA,	Catherine	4	Birzebbuga	7 Apr 42
BRIFFA,	Concetta	53	Qormi	9 Mar 42
BRIFFA,	John	33	Qormi	10 Feb 42
BRIFFA,	John Mary	54	Mqabba	21 Jan 42
BRIFFA,	Manwela	8	Birzebbuga	7 Apr 42
BRIGNOLI,	Albert	51	Zejtun	16 Jan 41
BRIMMER,	Carmela	62	Hamrun	26 May 42
BRIMMER,	William	38	Hamrun	26 May 42
BRINCAT,	Carmelo	54	Hamrun	20 Jan 42
BRINCAT,	John	32	Sliema	24 Feb 42
BRINCAT,	Joseph	33	Marsa	8 Apr 41
BRINCAT,	Melita	50	Balzan	8 Mar 42
BRINCAT,	Saviour		Zabbar	17 Oct 40
BRINCAT,	Spiro	60	Gudja	6 May 41
BROCKLEBANK,	Muriel	47	Valletta	17 Mar 42
BROOKS,	Arthur	18	Gzira	12 Jun 40
BUGEJA,	Carmel	5	Mosta	19 Jan 42
BUGEJA,	Carmel	58	Mosta	19 Jan 42
BUGEJA,	Carmel	76	Pawla	12 Feb 42

ROLL OF HONOUR

BUGEJA,	Carmel	47	Rabat	11 Jul 42
BUGEJA,	Catherine	13	Zurrieq	23 Jul 42
BUGEJA,	Ines	4	Mosta	19 Jan 42
BUGEJA,	Jane	11	Zurrieq	23 Jul 42
BUGEJA,	Joseph	19	Marsa	4 Apr 42
BUGEJA,	Joseph	7	Mosta	19 Jan 42
BUGEJA,	Josephine	68	Valletta	7 Apr 42
BUGEJA,	Josephine	68	Ghaxaq	9 Apr 42
BUGEJA,	Liberata	75	Sliema	5 Feb 42
BUGEJA,	Mary	9	Mosta	21 Jan 42
BUGEJA,	Marianna	43	Mosta	19 Jan 42
BUGEJA,	Rosario	65	Zejtun	2 May 42
BUGEJA,	Saviour	8	Mgarr	16 Sep 42
BUHAGIAR,	Bartholomew	80	Naxxar	4 Feb 42
BUHAGIAR,	Carmel	10	Zurrieq	28 Jul 42
BUHAGIAR,	Emanuel	29	Zebbug	3 Nov 42
BUHAGIAR,	Joseph	50	Mosta	4 Feb 42
BUHAGIAR,	Joseph		Zurrieq	28 Jul 42
BUHAGIAR,	Nicola	70	Senglea	16 Jan 41
BURLO,	Anthony	23	Hamrun	4 Jul 41
BURLO,	Carmel	57	Hamrun	4 Jul 41
BURLO,	Lorenza	58	Hamrun	4 Jul 41
BUSUTTIL,	Anthony	16	Kalkara	24 Mar 42
BUSUTTIL,	Anthony	16	Tarxien	6 Apr 42
BUSUTTIL,	Antonia	4	Pawla	12 Feb 42
BUSUTTIL,	David	7	Ghaxaq	9 Apr 42
BUSUTTIL,	Doris	2	Zejtun	6 Apr 42
BUSUTTIL,	Emanuel	26	Pawla	12 Feb 42
BUSUTTIL,	Francis	44	Tarxien	6 Apr 42
BUSUTTIL,	Jane	41	Mqabba	9 Apr 42
BUSUTTIL,	John	13	Tarxien	6 Apr 42
BUSUTTIL,	John	16	Birkirkara	31 Jul 42
BUSUTTIL,	Joseph	7	Tarxien	6 Apr 42
BUSUTTIL,	Joseph	58	Zejtun	11 Nov 42
BUSUTTIL,	Mary	38	Tarxien	6 Apr 42
BUSUTTIL,	Mary	15	Mqabba	9 Apr 42
BUSUTTIL,	Michelina	47	Ghaxaq	27 Dec 41
BUSUTTIL,	Michelina	60	Valletta	15 Mar 42
BUSUTTIL,	Rose	18	Tarxien	6 Apr 42
BUSUTTIL,	Rosina	32	Sliema	14 May 42
BUSUTTIL,	Salvina	14	Mqabba	9 Apr 42
BUSUTTIL,	Vincent	30	Valletta	15 Mar 42
BUTLER,	Christopher	1	St Julian's	15 Mar 42
BUTTIGIEG,	Anthony	30	Sliema	11 Mar 41
BUTTIGIEG,	Emanuel	40	Sliema	11 Mar 41
BUTTIGIEG,	Joseph	60	Qala, Gozo	7 Apr 42
BUTTIGIEG,	Joseph	64	Floriana	29 Apr 42
BUTTIGIEG,	Josephine	14	Zejtun	12 Feb 42
BUTTIGIEG,	Margherita	44	Valletta	20 Mar 42
BUTTIGIEG,	Pauline	5	Birkirkara	31 Jul 42
BYERS,	Charles J		Cospicua	9 Apr 42
CACHIA,	Anthony	8	Birkirkara	5 Jan 42
CACHIA,	Carmel	33	Birkirkara	26 Jun 40
CACHIA,	Carmel	53	Siggiewi	24 Apr 42
CACHIA,	Carmela	52	Pawla	12 Feb 42
CACHIA,	Carmela	8	Safi	29 June 42
CACHIA,	Concetta	34	Safi	28 June 42
CACHIA,	Helen	38	Birkirkara	5 Jan 42
CACHIA,	John	48	Valletta	22 Mar 42

ROLL OF HONOUR

CACHIA,	Joseph	49	Valletta	8 Apr 42
CACHIA,	Lawrence	24	Marsascala	30 Dec 41
CACHIA,	Michael	11	Mqabba	27 Aug 42
CACHIA,	Nazzareno	38	Zebbug	29 Apr 41
CACHIA,	Nazzareno	7	Safi	28 Jun 42
CACHIA,	Rita	13	Siggiewi	8 Jul 42
CACHIA,	Vincent	40	Valletta	16 Jan 41
CACHIA,	Vincent	65	Qormi	24 Dec 41
CACHIA ZAMMIT SLYTHE,	Helen	58	Valletta	7 Apr 42
CACHIA ZAMMIT SLYTHE,	Luigia	60	Valletta	7 Apr 42
CACHIA ZAMMIT SLYTHE,	Rev Robert	55	Valletta	7 Apr 42
CACHIA ZAMMIT SLYTHE,	Rosina	50	Valletta	7 Apr 42
CALAFATO,	Lawrence	35	Cospicua	26 Jun 40
CALAPAI,	Alfred	54	Sliema	17 Mar 42
CALASCIONE,	Mary	40	Hamrun	19 Apr 42
CALASCIONE,	Rosa	70	Hamrun	19 Apr 42
CALLEJA,	Alfred	35	Birkirkara	17 Mar 42
CALLEJA,	Arthur	6	Mellieha	15 Oct 42
CALLEJA,	Carmel	54	Marsa	12 Feb 42
CALLEJA,	Carmel	54	Gudja	9 Apr 42
CALLEJA,	Carmel	58	Qormi	28 Apr 42
CALLEJA,	Carmela	33	Gudja	9 Apr 42
CALLEJA,	Carmela	37	Hamrun	22 Oct 42
CALLEJA,	Doris	17	Sliema	11 Mar 41
CALLEJA,	Grace	30	Gudja	9 Apr 42
CALLEJA,	John	32	Tarxien	17 Jan 41
CALLEJA,	Joseph		Floriana	8 Apr 41
CALLEJA,	Joseph	40	Birkirkara	6 May 41
CALLEJA,	Joseph	51	Gudja	9 Apr 42
CALLEJA,	Joseph	75	Birkirkara	31 Jul 42
CALLEJA,	Luigi	75	Mosta	24 Apr 42
CALLEJA,	Mary	11	Hamrun	22 Oct 42
CALLEJA,	Peter			8 Apr 41
CALLEJA,	Peter	30	Gudja	9 Apr 42
CALLEJA,	Rev Robert	58	Rabat	21 Mar 42
CALLEJA,	Teresa	65	Gudja	9 Apr 42
CALLUS,	Annunziato	65	Balzan	28 Apr 42
CALLUS,	Carmel	43	Zurrieq	19 Apr 42
CALLUS,	John	49	Birzebbuga	24 Mar 42
CAMENZULI,	Mary	78	Luqa	8 Jan 42
CAMENZULI,	Michael	39	Gzira	11 Jun 40
CAMERON,	Una Patricia	18	Floriana	1 Mar 42
CAMILLERI,	Alexander	50	Attard	20 Mar 42
CAMILLERI,	Alphonse	52	Tarxien	12 Feb 42
CAMILLERI,	Anthony	42	Rabat	5 Apr 42
CAMILLERI,	Anthony	32	Zejtun	3 May 42
CAMILLERI,	Anthony	40	Birkirkara	17 Oct 42
CAMILLERI,	Anthony	56	Lija	3 Nov 42
CAMILLERI,	Antonia	24	Zurrieq	5 Oct 41
CAMILLERI,	Antonia	76	Tarxien	11 Oct 42
CAMILLERI,	Carmel	9	Cospicua	12 Jun 40
CAMILLERI,	Carmel	30	Pawla	12 Feb 42
CAMILLERI,	Carmel	11	Hamrun	20 Mar 42
CAMILLERI,	Carmel	18	Zejtun	1 Apr 42
CAMILLERI,	Francis	21	Cospicua	10 Mar 41
CAMILLERI,	Francis	11	Zurrieq	26 Dec 41

ROLL OF HONOUR

CAMILLERI,	Ganna	65	Gharghur	25 Apr 42
CAMILLERI,	Gerald	33	Valletta	12 May 41
CAMILLERI,	Gerald	33	Mosta	24 Jun 42
CAMILLERI,	John Mary	67	Ghaxaq	24 Apr 42
CAMILLERI,	Joseph	30	Birkirkara	24 Mar 42
CAMILLERI,	Joseph	16	Floriana	15 May 42
CAMILLERI,	Josephine	25	Pawla	12 Jun 40
CAMILLERI,	Louis	43	Pieta	20 Mar 42
CAMILLERI,	Maria	65	Hamrun	19 Apr 42
CAMILLERI,	Mary	79	Hamrun	19 Apr 42
CAMILLERI,	Mary	60	Gharghur	24 Apr 42
CAMILLERI,	Mary	68	Zejtun	2 May 42
CAMILLERI,	Paul	14	Valletta	1 Nov 41
CAMILLERI,	Paul		Gzira	11 Feb 43
CAMILLERI,	Philip	63	Valletta	14 Feb 41
CAMILLERI,	Philip	64	Floriana	6 Apr 42
CAMILLERI,	Philip	28	Siggiewi	19 Dec 42
CAMILLERI,	Vincent	29	Senglea	8 Apr 41
CAMPBELL,	Concetta	59	Pawla	26 Apr 42
CANNATACI,	Pauline	26	Sliema	15 Mar 42
CANAVAUGH,	Carmela	24	Valletta	20 Jul 43
CANAVAUGH,	Mary	46	Valletta	20 Jul 43
CAPPELLO,	Anthony		Pawla	7 Jul 41
CAPPELLO,	Joseph		Pawla	7 Jul 41
CAPPELLO,	Salvatore		Pawla	7 Jul 41
CARABOTT,	Emanuel	53	Zejtun	29 Nov 42
CARABOTT,	Pio	34	Birkirkara	15 Feb 42
CARBONE,	Teresa	36	Floriana	8 May 42
CARDONA,	Calcedonia	79	Floriana	28 Apr 42
CARDONA,	Catherine	50	Zabbar	24 Mar 42
CARDONA,	Joseph	76	Qormi	11 Oct 42
CARDONA,	Mary		Vittoriosa	16 Jan 41
CARUANA,	Alfred			1 Jun 42
CARUANA,	Angelo	84	Gudja	26 Feb 41
CARUANA,	Anthony	13	Gzira	26 Jun 42
CARUANA,	Anthony	10	Rabat	11 Oct 42
CARUANA,	Antonia	35	Valletta	27 Apr 41
CARUANA,	Carmela	71	Valletta	30 Apr 41
CARUANA,	Christopher	77	Zejtun	1 Apr 42
CARUANA,	Emanuel	50	Senglea	16 Jan 41
CARUANA,	Francis	54	Pawla	26 Jun 40
CARUANA,	Giovanna	43	Floriana	1 Mar 42
CARUANA,	John	7	Mosta	19 Jan 42
CARUANA,	Joseph	43	Pawla	4 Apr 42
CARUANA,	Joseph	33	Gzira	7 Apr 42
CARUANA,	Joseph	12	Zejtun	16 Apr 42
CARUANA,	Joseph	77	Hamrun	19 Apr 42
CARUANA,	Lawrence	35	Zejtun	26 Jun 40
CARUANA,	Lawrence	52		26 Jun 40
CARUANA,	Leonard	56	Zejtun	20 Mar 42
CARUANA,	Lewis	2	Rabat	21 Mar 42
CARUANA,	Br Raphael	69	Birkirkara	3 Jan 42
CARUANA,	Saviour	21	Hamrun	24 Apr 42
CARUANA GALIZIA,	Anton LL.D.	46	Valletta	15 Feb 42
CARUANA MAMO,	Vincenza	74	Msida	19 Apr 42
CASABENE,	Teresa	58	Hamrun	19 Apr 42
CASHA,	Annie	17	Hamrun	31 Mar 42
CASHA,	Elizabeth	18	Hamrun	31 Mar 42
CASSAR,	Carmel	8	Hamrun	21 Dec 41
CASSAR,	Carmela	29	Mosta	15 Apr 41

ROLL OF HONOUR

CASSAR,	Emanuel	53	Zebbug	26 Jun 40
CASSAR,	Francis	14	Zabbar	22 Mar 41
CASSAR,	George	27	Sliema	1 Apr 42
CASSAR,	Henry	2	Gzira	26 Jun 42
CASSAR,	Jane	20	Senglea	16 Jan 41
CASSAR,	Joseph	17	Valletta	15 Feb 42
CASSAR,	Joseph	30	Hamrun	15 Feb 42
CASSAR,	Lawrence	19	Luqa	7 Apr 42
CASSAR,	Leonard	76	Kirkop	1 May 42
CASSAR,	Lucrezio	26	Qormi	26 Jun 40
CASSAR,	Mary	19	Hamrun	15 Feb 42
CASSAR,	Marianna	65	Hamrun	19 Apr 42
CASSAR,	Modesta	37	Qormi	10 Jul 40
CASSAR,	Nicolo	40	Msida	19 Apr 41
CASSAR,	Paul	43	Hamrun	7 Apr 42
CASSAR,	Rita	18	Senglea	16 Jan 41
CASSAR,	Salvino	7	Qormi	10 Feb 42
CASSAR,	Tessie	8	Senglea	16 Jan 41
CASSAR,	Vincenza	20	Sliema	1 Apr 42
CASTAGNA,	Laura	22	Sliema	6 Mar 42
CASTLES,	David	62	Birkirkara	26 Jun 40
CATANIA,	John	60	Vittoriosa	7 Apr 42
CAUCHI,	Anthony	29	Nadur, Gozo	27 Feb 41
CAUCHI,	Carmel	38	Qormi	20 Jul 43
CAUCHI,	Catherine	66	Hamrun	19 Apr 42
CAUCHI,	Censa	80	Sliema	1 Apr 42
CAUCHI,	Fr Clement	67	Floriana	5 Apr 42
CAUCHI,	John Mary	56	Mosta	9 Apr 42
CAUCHI,	Lawrence	26	Floriana	2 Jul 42
CAUCHI,	Raphael			8 Apr 41
CAUCHI,	Samuel	55	Hamrun	24 Dec 41
CECI,	Dominic	84	Rabat	21 Mar 42
CEFAI,	Spiro	45	Valletta	9 Feb 42
CHEESEMAN,	Doris	45	St Julian's	1 Mar 42
CHETCUTI,	Francis	29	Mosta	4 Feb 42
CHETCUTI,	John Mary	12	Mosta	11 Feb 42
CHIRCOP,	Philip	68	Zebbug	18 Jan 42
CHURCHILL,	Dorothy	4	Sliema	11 Mar 41
CHURCHILL,	George	6 weeks	Sliema	11 Mar 41
CHURCHILL,	James	50	Sliema	11 Mar 41
CHURCHILL,	James Henry	9	Sliema	11 Mar 41
CIANTAR,	Gerald	19	Floriana	15 Feb 42
CIANTAR,	Grace	40	Zejtun	8 May 42
CIANTAR,	Joseph	49	Qormi	4 Apr 42
CIANTAR,	Nazzareno	40	Zejtun	8 May 42
CIAPPARA,	Anthony	12	Qormi	10 Feb 42
CIARLO,	Francis	14	Valletta	5 Jul 42
CILIA,	Michael		Tarxien	6 Apr 42
CILIA,	Michael	18	Marsa	24 Apr 42
CINI,	Joseph	50	Sannat, Gozo	10 Oct 42
CINI,	Publio	52	Pawla	7 Jul 41
CINI,	Raphael	55	Pawla	26 Jun 40
CIOFFI,	Carmel	55	Zejtun	4 Apr 42
CLARKE,	Hilda	34	Sliema	1 Apr 42
CLARKE,	Ivy	5	Sliema	1 Apr 42
CLARKE,	Joseph	2	Sliema	1 Apr 42
COLEIRO,	Andrew	53	Luqa	4 Jul 42
COLEIRO,	Anthony	30	Pawla	7 Jul 41
COLEIRO,	Anthony	22	Hamrun	26 Apr 42
COLEIRO,	Teodora	68	Zebbug	4 Apr 42

ROLL OF HONOUR

COLOMBO,	Ophelia	25	Gzira	1 Apr 42
COOK,	Maggie	56	Tarxien	11 Oct 42
COPPOLA,	Carmel	50	Sliema	26 Mar 42
COPPOLA,	Doris	17	Sliema	26 Mar 42
CORDINA,	Joseph	22	Hamrun	26 Jun 40
CORDINA,	Martha	45	Zabbar	10 Apr 42
CORDINA,	Peter	57	Sliema	2 Jul 42
COSTA,	Carmel	35	Ghajnsielem, Gozo	15 Mar 41
COSTER,	Filomena	54	Kalkara	24 Mar 42
COSTER,	Gustu	30	Kalkara	24 Mar 42
COSTER,	Joseph	26	Kalkara	24 Mar 42
COSTER,	Mary	48	Kalkara	24 Mar 42
CREMONA,	Anthony	54	Valletta	15 May 41
CREMONA,	Francis	15	Valletta	15 Feb 42
CREMONA,	Joseph	27	Valletta	15 Feb 42
CREWS,	Raymond Robert	21		23 Apr 42
CRIMINALE,	Carmelo	21	Hamrun	4 Jul 41
CRIMINALE,	Frances	47	Hamrun	4 Jul 41
CRIMINALE,	Mary	12	Hamrun	4 Jul 41
CRIMINALE,	Paul	17	Hamrun	4 Jul 41
CURMI,	Joseph	38	Pawla	6 Apr 42
CURMI,	Saviour	80	Sannat, Gozo	10 Oct 42
CUSCHIERI,	John Mary	57	Mosta	21 Mar 42
CUSCHIERI,	Rev Joseph	63	Zurrieq	23 Jul 42
CUSCHIERI,	Josephine	3	Hamrun	21 Mar 42
CUSCHIERI,	Josephine	75	Hamrun	19 Apr 42
CUSCHIERI,	Teresa	70	Mosta	21 Mar 42
CUTAJAR,	Carmel	31	Birzebbuga	18 Apr 42
CUTAJAR,	Carmel	9	Siggiewi	10 Feb 43
CUTAJAR,	Ernest	33	Hamrun	26 Jun 40
CUTAJAR,	Francis	48	Nadur, Gozo	15 Jan 42
CUTAJAR,	John Baptist	14	Tarxien	13 Feb 42
CUTAJAR,	Joseph	19	Zejtun	19 Aug 41
CUTAJAR,	Lawrence	62	Siggiewi	3 Jul 42
CUTAJAR,	Nicholas	75	Zebbug	2 Jun 42
CUTAJAR,	Saviour	55	Cospicua	21 Dec 41
CUTAJAR,	Saviour	50	Qormi	6 May 42
CUTAJAR,	Saviour	48	Lija	3 Nov 42
CUTTER,	Frances Patricia	19	Pieta	15 Feb 42
D'AGOSTINO,	Erminia	12	Vittoriosa	16 Jan 41
D'AGOSTINO,	Joseph	11	Vittoriosa	16 Jan 41
D'AGOSTINO,	Josephine	41	Vittoriosa	16 Jan 41
D'AGOSTINO,	Lawrence		Vittoriosa	16 Jan 41
D'ALFONSO,	Michael	18	Tarxien	24 Apr 42
DALLI,	Bonvicino	14	Zejtun	3 May 42
DALLI,	Grezzju	52	Qrendi	12 Sep 42
DALLI,	Joseph	62	Valletta	28 Apr 42
D'AMATO,	Paul	77	Marsa	6 Apr 42
D'AMATO,	Salvina	18	Zurrieq	28 Jul 42
DARMANIN,	Catherine	13	Zurrieq	24 Jun 42
DARMANIN,	Concetta	70	Hamrun	19 Apr 42
DARMANIN,	Dominic		St Julian's	11 Feb 43
DARMANIN,	Emanuel			8 Apr 41
DARMANIN,	Emanuel	11	Rabat	12 Jul 42
DARMANIN,	Joseph	60	Floriana	1 Mar 42
DARMANIN,	Joseph	68	Hamrun	26 May 42
DARMANIN,	Sosa	50	Vittoriosa	16 Jan 41
DEBATTISTA,	Antonia	26	Marsa	12 Jul 41
DEBATTISTA,	John	61	Marsa	12 Jul 41

ROLL OF HONOUR

DEBATTISTA,	Michael	30	Floriana	13 Feb 42
DEBATTISTA,	Stella	19	Floriana	1 Mar 42
DEBONO,	Anthony	54	Hamrun	22 Oct 42
DEBONO,	Carmela	80	Hamrun	19 Apr 42
DEBONO,	Carmela	42	Hamrun	22 Oct 42
DEBONO,	George	32	Gzira	2 Jan 42
DEBONO,	George	43	Hamrun	17 Mar 42
DEBONO,	George	7	Sliema	11 Apr 44
DEBONO,	Helen	70	Birkirkara	13 Apr 42
DEBONO,	Joseph	55	Gzira	1 Jan 42
DEBONO,	Joseph	45	St Julian's	20 Mar 42
DEBONO,	Joseph	40	Mellieha	30 Apr 42
DEBONO,	Joseph	25	Tarxien	11 Oct 42
DEBONO,	Lonza	25	Tarxien	11 Oct 42
DEBONO,	Ludgarda	60	Zabbar	7 Apr 42
DEBONO,	Saviour	24	Gzira	2 Jan 42
DECELIS,	Concetta	64	Hamrun	26 May 42
DEFELICE,	Emilia	65	Qormi	11 Feb 42
DEFELICE,	Nazzareno	44	Zabbar	10 Apr 42
DEGABRIELE,	Alphonse	67	Vittoriosa	16 Jan 41
DEGABRIELE,	Angela	75	Zabbar	19 Apr 42
DEGABRIELE,	Dolores	5 days	Zejtun	11 May 41
DEGABRIELE,	Francis			8 Apr 41
DEGABRIELE,	Joseph	21	Vittoriosa	16 Jan 41
DEGABRIELE,	Joseph	2	Zejtun	11 May 41
DEGABRIELE,	Joseph	9	Tarxien	11 Oct 42
DEGABRIELE,	Lawrence	56	Vittoriosa	16 Jan 41
DEGIORGIO,	Anthony	79	Mosta	21 Mar 42
DEGIORGIO,	Carmela	34	Senglea	29 Apr 41
DEGIORGIO,	Carmela	77	Mosta	21 Mar 42
DEGIORGIO,	George	22	Hamrun	4 Apr 42
DEGIORGIO,	Mary	34	Mosta	21 Mar 42
DEGIOVANNI,	Andrew	43	Sliema	11 Mar 41
DEGUARA,	Joseph	20	Naxxar	14 May 42
DEGUARA,	Joseph	45	Mosta	30 Jul 42
DEGUARA,	Pauline	9	Rabat	11 Jul 42
DELIA,	Joseph	4	Pawla	17 Mar 42
DELIA,	Joseph	60	Pawla	17 Mar 42
DELIA,	Joseph	20	Birkirkara	24 Apr 42
DEMAJO,	Charles	13	Hamrun	24 Apr 42
DEMANUELE,	Annunziata	13	Floriana	1 Mar 42
D'EMMANUELE,	Spiro	48	Pieta	8 Apr 41
DE MAURO,	Louis	59	Birkirkara	3 Jan 42
DEMICOLI,	Saviour	15	Luqa	29 Dec 41
DESIRA,	Annunziato	21	Zejtun	1 Apr 42
DESIRA,	John	70	Pawla	12 Feb 42
DESIRA,	Saviour	50	Zejtun	13 Jul 42
DESPOTT,	Paul	16	Zejtun	19 Apr 42
DIMECH,	Antonia		Zejtun	8 May 42
DIMECH,	Carmela	22	Ghaxaq	9 Apr 41
DIMECH,	Carmeline	12	Msida	26 Jun 42
DIMECH,	Giorgina	28	Birkirkara	31 Jul 42
DIMECH,	Joseph	11	Marsa	28 Apr 41
DIMECH,	Josephine	7	Msida	26 Jun 42
DIMECH,	Lawrence		Zejtun	8 May 42
DIMECH,	Lilian	17	Msida	26 Jun 42
DIMECH,	Mary	6	Msida	26 Jun 42
DIMECH,	Rita	2	Msida	26 Jun 42
DIMECH,	Saviour	70	Mosta	20 Mar 42
DINGLI,	Joseph	14	Attard	4 Mar 42

ROLL OF HONOUR

DINGLI,	Tessie	4	Attard	4 Mar 42
DINGLI,	Valentine	1	Attard	4 Mar 42
DINGSTAD,	Petra Christine	30	Valletta	24 Apr 42
DOUBLET,	Lilian	7	Gzira	11 Jun 40
DOUBLET,	Mary	46	Gzira	11 Jun 40
DOUGALL,	Giorgina	42	Mosta	21 Mar 42
EBEJER,	Carmel	24	Zabbar	26 Feb 43
ELLUL,	Angiolina	73	Rabat	21 Mar 42
ELLUL,	Carmel	70	Zurrieq	23 Jul 42
ELLUL,	Carmel	18	Qormi	20 Jul 43
ELLUL,	Carmela	30	Birzebbuga	31 Aug 42
ELLUL,	George	17	Qormi	9 Mar 42
ELLUL,	John M	51	Luqa	9 Apr 42
ELLUL,	Joseph	36	Mqabba	11 Jun 40
ELLUL,	Mary	13	Gudja	24 Feb 43
ELLUL,	Pauline	64	Zurrieq	12 Mar 42
ELLUL,	Rose	65	Qrendi	9 Apr 42
ELLUL,	Vincent	67	Zejtun	12 Apr 42
ENRIQUEZ,	Francis	60	Ghaxaq	9 Apr 42
ENRIQUEZ,	Joseph	65	Floriana	28 Apr 42
FABRI,	Adelaide	32	Hamrun	26 May 42
FABRI,	John	9	Mosta	21 Mar 42
FACCIOL,	Joseph	23	Cospicua	12 Jun 40
FALZON,	Angelo	73	Sliema	14 May 42
FALZON,	Angiolina	14	Rabat	11 Oct 42
FALZON,	Antonia	60	Hamrun	26 May 42
FALZON,	Concetta	9	Tarxien	6 Apr 42
FALZON,	Francis	16	Vittoriosa	16 Jan 41
FALZON,	Iro	37	Sliema	27 Jun 42
FALZON,	Joseph	17	Valletta	15 Feb 42
FALZON,	Mary	11	Tarxien	6 Apr 42
FALZON,	Michael	70	Naxxar	6 Jul 40
FALZON,	Pauline	38	Tarxien	6 Apr 42
FALZON,	Rita	19	Gzira	28 Oct 42
FALZON,	Sarah	67	Sliema	14 May 42
FALZON,	Vincent	56	Tarxien	6 May 41
FARRELL,	Antonia	27	Senglea	16 Jan 41
FARRELL,	William	38	Senglea	16 Jan 41
FARRUGIA,	Andrew	16 months	Luqa	9 Apr 42
FARRUGIA,	Andrew	10	Luqa	9 Apr 42
FARRUGIA,	Andrew	8	Luqa	23 May 42
FARRUGIA,	Angelo	50	Birzebbuga	14 Jun 40
FARRUGIA,	Annie	67	Sliema	11 Mar 41
FARRUGIA,	Anthony	5	Pieta	11 Jun 40
FARRUGIA,	Anthony	19	Valletta	28 Feb 41
FARRUGIA,	Anthony	18	Hamrun	8 Sep 41
FARRUGIA,	Anthony	49	Zurrieq	5 Dec 41
FARRUGIA,	Anthony	6	Zejtun	31 Jan 42
FARRUGIA,	Anthony	14	Pawla	15 Feb 42
FARRUGIA,	Anthony	43	Valletta	9 Apr 42
FARRUGIA,	Antonia	25	Pieta	11 Jun 40
FARRUGIA,	Arthur	40	Birkirkara	26 Jun 40
FARRUGIA,	Calcedonio	15	Tarxien	11 Oct 42
FARRUGIA,	Carmel	4 months	Luqa	9 Apr 42
FARRUGIA,	Carmela	35	San Lawrenz, Gozo	5 Aug 42
FARRUGIA,	Consiglia	48	Zejtun	19 Aug 41
FARRUGIA,	Felicissima	42	Luqa	9 Apr 42
FARRUGIA,	Francis	50	Valletta	26 Jun 40

ROLL OF HONOUR

FARRUGIA,	Frank	13	Valletta	15 Feb 42
FARRUGIA,	Francis	13	Hamrun	20 Mar 42
FARRUGIA,	George	51	Floriana	8 May 42
FARRUGIA,	Jane	50	Hamrun	6 Apr 42
FARRUGIA,	John	5	Safi	28 Jun 42
FARRUGIA,	Joseph	4	Pieta	11 Jun 40
FARRUGIA,	Joseph	31	Gzira	26 Jun 40
FARRUGIA,	Joseph	36	Qormi	12 Feb 42
FARRUGIA,	Joseph	5	Luqa	9 Apr 42
FARRUGIA,	Joseph	10	Gudja	1 May 43
FARRUGIA,	Josephine	48	Hamrun	6 Apr 42
FARRUGIA,	Josephine	66	San Lawrenz, Gozo	5 Aug 42
FARRUGIA,	Louis	42	Marsa	16 Jun 41
FARRUGIA,	Louis	22	Zurrieq	15 Jan 42
FARRUGIA,	Louis	41	Hamrun	2 Jun 42
FARRUGIA,	Mary	8	Senglea	16 Jan 41
FARRUGIA,	Mary	35	San Lawrenz, Gozo	6 Aug 42
FARRUGIA,	Mary	44	Birzebbuga	20 Nov 42
FARRUGIA,	Michael	31	Kirkop	16 Feb 42
FARRUGIA,	Nicholas	43	Siggiewi	15 Jun 42
FARRUGIA,	Pauline	70	Sannat, Gozo	10 Oct 42
FARRUGIA,	Peter	62	Luqa	8 Mar 42
FARRUGIA,	Rosario	7	Luqa	9 Apr 42
FARRUGIA,	Saviour	8	Luqa	9 Apr 42
FARRUGIA,	Vincent	24	Siggiewi	13 Jan 42
FARRUGIA,	Walter	34	Balzan	2 Apr 42
FAVA,	Albert	1	Sliema	1 Apr 42
FAVA,	Antonio	20	Sliema	17 Mar 42
FAVA,	Mary	8	Zabbar	16 May 42
FEARNLEY,	J			3 May 41
FELICE,	Carmel	17	Hamrun	4 Apr 42
FELICE,	Carmela	66	Hamrun	26 May 42
FELICE,	Francis	56	Qormi	9 Feb 42
FELICE,	Gracie	14	Zejtun	2 May 42
FELICE,	Josephine	2	Qormi	15 Apr 42
FELICE,	Mary Rose	5	Zejtun	2 May 42
FENECH,	Alfred	73	Hamrun	22 Oct 42
FENECH,	Antonia	28	Cospicua	12 Jun 40
FENECH,	Carmelo	11	Mosta	21 Mar 42
FENECH,	Carmela	6	Ghaxaq	9 Apr 42
FENECH,	Esther	10 months	Ghaxaq	9 Apr 42
FENECH,	Francis	33	Cospicua	12 Jun 40
FENECH,	Francis	18	Birkirkara	14 Oct 42
FENECH,	Grezzju	28	Marsaxlokk	8 Jun 41
FENECH,	Jane	50	Attard	18 Jul 41
FENECH,	John	27	Lija	19 Jan 42
FENECH,	John	11	Mosta	28 Jul 42
FENECH,	Joseph	35	Pawla	12 Feb 42
FENECH,	Joseph	11	Mosta	21 Mar 42
FENECH,	Josephine	11	Zejtun	2 May 42
FENECH,	Louis	47	Lija	20 Jan 42
FENECH,	Louis	64	Birkirkara	30 Mar 42
FENECH,	Mary	6	Cospicua	12 Jun 40
FENECH,	Mary	31	Ghaxaq	9 Apr 42
FENECH,	Michael	47	Birkirkara	31 Jul 42
FENECH,	Nazzareno	8	Ghaxaq	9 Apr 42
FENECH,	Peter	82	Lija	4 Nov 42
FENECH,	Saviour	8	Cospicua	12 Jun 40
FENECH,	Spira	46	Zejtun	2 May 42
FENECH,	Victoria	10	Zejtun	2 May 42

ROLL OF HONOUR

FERRO,	Pauline	80	Hamrun	19 Apr 42
FILLETTI,	John	34	Gzira	2 Jan 42
FILLETTI,	Mary	22	Gzira	2 Jan 42
FITENI,	Carmel	40	Hamrun	27 Jun 40
FLERI,	Lilian	1 month	Pawla	12 Feb 42
FLERI,	Mary	29	Pawla	12 Feb 42
FLORES,	Dominic		Cospicua	8 Apr 41
FLORES,	Renzo	65	Hamrun	15 Feb 42
FLORIDIA,	Ramiro	66	Sliema	20 Jul 43
FORMOSA,	Anthony	37	Valletta	15 Mar 42
FORMOSA,	Aristide		Sliema	14 Feb 43
FORMOSA,	Carmela	31	Tarxien	6 Apr 42
FORMOSA,	Georgia	56	Tarxien	6 Apr 42
FORMOSA,	Joseph	78	Marsa	18 Apr 42
FORMOSA,	Paul	50	Sliema	17 Mar 42
FRENDO,	Antonia	19	Valletta	24 Dec 41
FRENDO,	Carmela	29	Marsa	26 Jun 40
FRENDO,	Concetta	16	Siggiewi	4 Jul 42
FRENDO,	Eric	15	Sliema	11 Apr 44
FRENDO,	Francis	15	Pawla	4 Apr 42
FRENDO,	Francis	30	Zejtun	2 May 42
FRENDO,	Giovanna	75	Mosta	20 Mar 42
FSADNI,	Girolamo	77	Valletta	15 Mar 42
FSADNI,	Joseph	28	Rabat	11 Oct 42
GALEA,	Anna	9	Vittoriosa	16 Jan 41
GALEA,	Anthony	51	Ghaxaq	24 Apr 42
GALEA,	Carmel	40	Birkirkara	11 Jun 40
GALEA,	Carmela	56	Victoria, Gozo	2 Nov 42
GALEA,	Clara	40	Sannat, Gozo	10 Oct 42
GALEA,	Dominic	28	Valletta	26 Jun 40
GALEA,	Doris	5 months	Cospicua	11 Jun 40
GALEA,	Doris	30	Birkirkara	10 Jul 42
GALEA,	Frank	31	Rabat	12 Jun 42
GALEA,	Francis	3 months	Birkirkara	10 Jul 42
GALEA,	Grazio	42	Mosta	4 Feb 42
GALEA,	John	66	Mosta	21 Mar 42
GALEA,	John	18	Birkirkara	11 Jul 42
GALEA,	Joseph	20	Zabbar	21 Dec 41
GALEA,	Joseph	77	Senglea	4 Apr 42
GALEA,	Joseph	13	Birkirkara	1 Aug 42
GALEA,	Joseph	4	Sannat, Gozo	10 Oct 42
GALEA,	Joseph	55	Lija	3 Nov 42
GALEA,	Joseph	62	Sliema	20 Jul 43
GALEA,	Josephine	70	Hamrun	19 Apr 42
GALEA,	Josephine	30	Sannat, Gozo	10 Oct 42
GALEA,	Lawrence	39	Birkirkara	10 Jul 42
GALEA,	Maddalena	28	Rabat	11 Oct 42
GALEA,	Margaret	6	Sannat, Gozo	10 Oct 42
GALEA,	Michael	8	Sannat, Gozo	10 Oct 42
GALEA,	Paul	37	Msida	11 Jun 40
GALEA,	Rita	15	Nadur, Gozo	15 Jan 42
GALEA,	Saviour	82	Mosta	7 May 41
GALEA,	Saviour	42	Pawla	7 Jul 41
GALEA,	Saviour	41	Mosta	21 Mar 42
GALEA,	Saviour	17	Zejtun	2 May 42
GALEA,	Spiro	63	Rabat	21 Mar 42
GALEA,	Susanna	41	Balzan	8 Oct 41
GALEA,	Teresa	42	Rabat	21 Mar 42
GALEA,	Victor	39	Mosta	21 Mar 42

ROLL OF HONOUR

GALDES,	Fr Diego	52	Sliema	1 Apr 42
GATT,	Adelaide	60	Senglea	28 Apr 42
GATT,	Alfred	50	Sliema	1 Apr 42
GATT,	Anthony	12	Birkirkara	20 Mar 42
GATT,	Anthony	71	Zejtun	6 May 42
GATT,	Carmel	51	Luqa	7 May 41
GATT,	Carmel	2	Nadur, Gozo	3 Jan 42
GATT,	Carmela		Vittoriosa	16 Jan 41
GATT,	Carmela	45	Birkirkara	17 Oct 42
GATT,	Cettina		Vittoriosa	16 Jan 41
GATT,	Doris	24	Vittoriosa	16 Jan 41
GATT,	Edwin	11	Mosta	29 May 42
GATT,	Emanuela	60	Birkirkara	22 Apr 42
GATT,	Felice	80	Marsa	25 Mar 42
GATT,	Francis	13	Mosta	21 Mar 42
GATT,	George	7	Marsa	27 Jun 40
GATT,	Giulia	46	Sliema	1 Apr 42
GATT,	Jane	55	Pawla	12 Feb 42
GATT,	Jane	64	Senglea	16 Jan 41
GATT,	John	24	Gzira	12 Jun 40
GATT,	Joseph	2	Marsa	27 Jun 40
GATT,	Joseph	9	Mosta	21 Mar 42
GATT,	Joseph	31	Vittoriosa	4 Apr 42
GATT,	Josephine	34	Zabbar	19 Apr 42
GATT,	Kalang	42	Mosta	21 Mar 42
GATT,	Lawrence		Vittoriosa	16 Jan 41
GATT,	Lawrence	62	Senglea	28 Apr 42
GATT,	Mary	23	Vittoriosa	16 Jan 41
GATT,	Rose Marie	4	Sliema	1 Apr 42
GATT,	Saviour	47	Qormi	10 Feb 42
GATT,	Saviour	49	Attard	20 Mar 42
GARCIA,	Joseph	14	Tarxien	7 Jul 40
GARIBALDI,	Sr Maria	53	Hamrun	19 Apr 42
GAUCI,	Anthony	60	Zurrieq	23 Jul 42
GAUCI,	Emanuel	50	Cospicua	14 Jun 40
GAUCI,	Emanuel	9	Kalkara	24 Mar 42
GAUCI,	Felice	30	Rabat	15 Jul 42
GAUCI,	George	80	Pawla	17 Mar 42
GAUCI,	Jimmy	3	Mosta	20 Feb 42
GAUCI,	Joseph	16	Valletta	20 May 41
GAUCI,	Joseph	60	Rabat	12 Jul 42
GAUCI,	Mary	8	Mosta	21 Mar 42
GAUCI,	Mary	53	Attard	3 Jul 42
GAUCI,	Michael	40	Birkirkara	4 Mar 42
GAUCI,	Paul	25	Hamrun	16 Jan 41
GAUCI,	Rokku	2	Kalkara	24 Mar 42
GAUCI,	Saviour		Sliema	26 Apr 42
GAUCI,	Stella	12	Kalkara	24 Mar 42
GAUCI,	Vincent	5	Mosta	21 Mar 42
GELLEL,	Carrie	20	Senglea	28 Apr 42
GENOVESE,	Joseph	21	Birkirkara	30 Jun 40
GERA,	Anna	75	Pawla	12 Feb 42
GERMAN,	Lorenza	11	Vittoriosa	16 Jan 41
GERMAN,	Victor	17	Sliema	12 Jun 40
GHIGO,	Angela	55	Mqabba	26 Jun 40
GHIGO,	Anthony	24	Mqabba	21 Feb 42
GHIGO,	Emanuel	18	Mqabba	26 Jun 40
GHIGO,	Giulio	25	Mqabba	26 Jun 40
GIBBONS,	L			7 Jul 40
GINGELL,	Josephine	40	Gzira	19 Apr 42

ROLL OF HONOUR

Surname	Given name	Age	Place	Date
GIORDIMAINA,	Emanuel	11	Qormi	10 Feb 42
GIORDIMAINA,	Joseph	8	Qormi	10 Feb 42
GIORDIMAINA,	Mary	5	Qormi	10 Feb 42
GIORDIMAINA,	Peter	65	Rabat	21 Mar 42
GIORGIO,	Albert	11	Sliema	11 Apr 44
GIORGIO,	John	9	Sliema	11 Apr 44
GLEAVES,	Emily	28	Tarxien	11 Oct 42
GOURA,	Manoel	49	Msida	8 May 42
GRECH,	Alex	15	Sliema	11 Mar 41
GRECH,	Angela	7	Ghajnsielem, Gozo	29 Jan 42
GRECH,	Annie	11	Sliema	11 Mar 41
GRECH,	Anthony	51	Rabat	29 Mar 41
GRECH,	Aurelia	19	Pawla	12 Feb 42
GRECH,	Carmel	15	Naxxar	14 Jul 42
GRECH,	Carmel	30	Rabat	11 Oct 42
GRECH,	Carmel	47	Zejtun	11 Oct 42
GRECH,	Carmela	49	Ghajnsielem, Gozo	29 Jan 42
GRECH,	Carmela	53	Pawla	12 Feb 42
GRECH,	Carmelina	9	Birkirkara	23 Oct 42
GRECH,	Connie	45	Zebbug	29 Apr 41
GRECH,	Emanuel	52	Naxxar	29 Oct 42
GRECH,	Emilia	17	Ghajnsielem, Gozo	29 Jan 42
GRECH,	George	34	Qormi	10 Feb 42
GRECH,	Ines	16	Ghajnsielem, Gozo	29 Jan 42
GRECH,	John	14	Ghajnsielem, Gozo	29 Jan 42
GRECH,	John	28	St Paul's Bay	7 Apr 42
GRECH,	Joseph	17	Sliema	2 Apr 42
GRECH,	Joseph	76	Msida	19 Apr 42
GRECH,	Joseph	52	St Paul's Bay	25 Apr 42
GRECH,	Joseph	62	Valletta	28 Apr 42
GRECH,	Joseph	64	Zejtun	3 May 42
GRECH,	Joseph	8	Hamrun	14 Jul 42
GRECH,	Louis	31	Zejtun	1 Apr 42
GRECH,	Mary	18	Sliema	11 Mar 41
GRECH,	Mary	21	Pawla	12 Feb 42
GRECH,	Mary	54	Mosta	21 Mar 42
GRECH,	Michelina	72	Tarxien	12 Feb 42
GRECH,	Orazia	4	Birkirkara	31 Jul 42
GRECH,	Pauline	46	Zurrieq	15 Aug 42
GRECH,	Philip	23	Zebbug	29 Apr 41
GRECH,	Robert	21	Floriana	16 Jan 41
GRECH,	Rosemary	3	Mosta	6 Jul 42
GRECH,	Saviour	50	Ghajnsielem, Gozo	15 Mar 41
GRECH,	Saviour	35	Zabbar	10 Apr 42
GRECH,	Teresa	3	Sliema	11 Mar 41
GRECH,	Zaru	30	Naxxar	20 Mar 42
GREEN,	Carrie	20	Senglea	28 Apr 42
GRIMA,	Carmel	44	Hamrun	12 Jul 41
GRIMA,	Carmel	37	Floriana	20 Jan 42
GRIMA,	Emanuel	15	Hamrun	5 Apr 42
GRIMA,	Jane	19	Pawla	12 Feb 42
GRIMA,	Joseph	64	Floriana	28 Apr 42
GRIMA,	Lawrence		Pawla	8 Apr 41
GRIMA,	Mary	3	Pawla	7 Jul 41
GRIMA,	Saviour	57	Marsa	7 Apr 42
GRIMA,	Vincenza	50	Senglea	16 Jan 41
GRISCTI,	Lina	8	Gzira	22 Dec 41
GRIXTI,	Antonia	46	Rabat	11 Oct 42
GRIXTI,	Joseph	51	Hamrun	24 Mar 42

ROLL OF HONOUR

HAIG,	Jessie	40	Mosta	20 Feb 42
HAMILTON,	Florence May		Imtarfa	13 Jul 42
HARMSWORTH,	Thomas	54	Hamrun	4 Apr 42
HARRIS,	Joseph	11	Zejtun	2 May 42
HATCHINGS,	Emanuel		Cospicua	8 Apr 41
HEALEY,	Mary	66	Valletta	16 Jan 41
HERRERA,	Alphonse	80	Valletta	20 May 41
HILI,	Anthony		Vittoriosa	16 Jan 41
HILI,	Anton	16	Sannat, Gozo	15 May 42
HILI,	Concetta	20	Kalkara	24 Mar 42
HILI,	Grezzja	44	Kalkara	24 Mar 42
HILI,	John	4	Kalkara	24 Mar 42
HILI,	Pauline	12	Kalkara	24 Mar 42
HISCOCK,	Alice		St George	15 Feb 42
HOCKEY,	Doris	4	Pawla	11 Oct 42
HOCKEY,	Joseph	30	Pawla	11 Oct 42
HOCKEY,	Rosy	25	Pawla	11 Oct 42
HYZLER,	Antonia	75	Hamrun	19 Apr 42
HYZLER,	Emanuel M.D.	56	Zejtun	2 May 42
ILES,	William	25	Senglea	28 Apr 42
INCORVAJA,	Adelaide	6	Sliema	5 Feb 42
INGUANEZ,	Anthony	13	Zurrieq	19 Apr 42
KAMM,	Angolina	50	Senglea	16 Jan 41
KELLY,	Aida	26	Hamrun	24 Apr 42
KELLY,	Mary	90	Hamrun	19 Apr 42
LAFERLA,	Albert A. & C.E.	45	Rabat	21 Mar 42
LAFERLA,	Emanuela	70	Hamrun	19 Apr 42
LANZON,	Charles	36	Lija	17 Mar 42
LETARD,	Josephine	65	Sliema	15 Oct 42
LEWIS,	Charles	17	Valletta	20 May 41
LEWIS,	Thomas	54	Sliema	1 Apr 42
LIA,	Joseph	12	Zabbar	15 Mar 42
LIA,	Mary	38	Zabbar	19 Apr 42
LIJA,	Anthony	76	Zabbar	20 Dec 41
LIVORI,	Carmel		Pawla	4 Apr 42
LONG,	Frederick			28 Jan 42
LYNCH,	Tony			1 Mar 42
MACGILL,	Vincenza	33	Valletta	30 Apr 41
MAGGI,	Benjamin	15	Floriana	1 Mar 42
MAGRI,	Paul	16	Luqa	22 Sep 40
MAGRI,	Saviour	58	St Julian's	27 May 42
MAGRO,	Catherine	54	Qrendi	19 Dec 42
MAGRO,	Francis	60	Qrendi	19 Dec 42
MAGRO,	Grezzju	16	Floriana	1 Mar 42
MAGRO,	Pauline	18	Birkirkara	13 Apr 42
MALLIA,	(child)		Vittoriosa	16 Jan 41
MALLIA,	Angelo	43	Gzira	3 Jan 42
MALLIA,	Carmel	75	Luqa	23 Jul 42
MALLIA,	Emanuel		Vittoriosa	16 Jan 41
MALLIA,	Francis		Vittoriosa	16 Jan 41
MALLIA,	Francis		Rabat	17 Mar 42
MALLIA,	Francis	66	Qrendi	19 Dec 42
MALLIA,	John	72	Naxxar	6 May 42
MALLIA,	Joseph	30	Zabbar	19 Apr 42
MALLIA,	Lawrence	55	Vittoriosa	16 Jan 41
MALLIA,	Louis	9	Pawla	12 Feb 42

ROLL OF HONOUR

MALLIA,	Lora		Vittoriosa	16 Jan 41
MALLIA,	Michael	65	Senglea	16 Jan 41
MALLIA,	Raphael	54	Valletta	15 Feb 42
MALLIA,	Rosina	56	Pawla	12 Feb 42
MALLIA,	Saviour	45	Lija	20 Mar 42
MALLIA,	Saviour	33	Zabbar	19 Apr 42
MALLIA PULVIRENTI,	Ena	12	Rabat	17 Mar 42
MAMO,	Attilio	45	Sliema	20 Jan 42
MAMO,	Carmela	44	Valletta	16 Jan 41
MAMO,	Frances	17	Valletta	15 Feb 42
MAMO,	Joseph	68	Zejtun	2 May 42
MAMO,	Mary	4	Birkirkara	10 Jul 42
MAMO,	Stella	32	Birkirkara	10 Jul 42
MAMO,	Teresa	80	Valletta	16 Jan 41
MANGANI,	Doris	20	Rabat	21 Mar 42
MANGION,	Emanuel	16	Zurrieq	22 Apr 42
MANGION,	James	67	Mosta	23 Jun 42
MANGION,	Josephine	4	Pieta	11 Jun 40
MANGION,	Mary	74	Floriana	28 Apr 42
MANGION,	Lawrence	61	Mqabba	11 Apr 42
MANICOLO,	Carmel	55	St Julian's	31 Jan 42
MANICOLO,	Joseph	44	Tarxien	11 Oct 42
MANSUETO,	Gaetan	40	Birkirkara	19 Aug 42
MAYMAN,	Marianna	35	Valletta	15 Mar 42
MAZZELLI,	Joseph	47	Mdina	8 Apr 41
MAZZELLO,	John	75	Pawla	12 Feb 42
MEDATI,	Mary Melita	50	Birkirkara	31 Jul 42
MEILAK,	John	28	Nadur, Gozo	3 Jan 42
MEILAK,	Lawrence	55	Kalkara	2 Mar 42
MEILAK,	Teresa	90	Hamrun	19 Apr 42
MERCIECA,	Carmel	64	Zejtun	29 Dec 41
MERCIECA,	Joseph	45	Zejtun	17 Mar 42
MERCIECA,	Publio	16	Floriana	25 Mar 42
MERCIECA,	Susanna	85	Valletta	14 Feb 41
MICALLEF,	Alfred	16	Sliema	14 May 42
MICALLEF,	Amadeo	44	Tarxien	6 Apr 42
MICALLEF,	Anthony	9	Kalkara	24 Mar 42
MICALLEF,	Carmel	8	Gharghur	12 Feb 42
MICALLEF,	Carmela	42	Gzira	28 Oct 42
MICALLEF,	Catherine	57	Mosta	23 Jun 42
MICALLEF,	Domenica	18	Mosta	20 Mar 42
MICALLEF,	Elvira	23	Gzira	14 Jun 40
MICALLEF,	Emanuela	3	Hamrun	31 Mar 42
MICALLEF,	Ines	13	Hamrun	4 Jul 41
MICALLEF,	Jane	17	Siggiewi	15 Jan 42
MICALLEF,	Joseph	11	Sliema	17 Mar 42
MICALLEF,	Josephine	54	Sliema	17 Mar 42
MICALLEF,	Julian	65	Gzira	11 Jun 40
MICALLEF,	Lonza	50	Sliema	1 Apr 42
MICALLEF,	Louis	55	Hamrun	20 Jan 42
MICALLEF,	Mary	31	Kalkara	24 Mar 42
MICALLEF,	Mary	39	Senglea	28 Apr 42
MICALLEF,	M'Anna	45	Hamrun	31 Mar 42
MICALLEF,	Peter	45	Mosta	20 Mar 42
MICALLEF,	Rita	24	Mosta	20 Mar 42
MICALLEF,	Samuel	10	Kalkara	24 Mar 42
MICALLEF,	Stella	13	Gzira	2 Jan 42
MICALLEF,	Teresa	60	Hamrun	19 Apr 42
MICALLEF,	Vincent	48	Senglea	16 Jan 42

ROLL OF HONOUR

MICALLEF,	Violet	13	Gzira	2 Jan 42
MICALLEF,	Virginia	60	Hamrun	19 Apr 42
MICELI,	John	21	Sliema	9 Jun 42
MIDLANE,	Rose	41	Pawla	2 Apr 42
MIFSUD,	Albert	10	Gzira	2 Jan 42
MIFSUD,	Albert	14	Sliema	17 Mar 42
MIFSUD,	Albert	19	Rabat	21 Mar 42
MIFSUD,	Alfred	2	Gzira	2 Jan 42
MIFSUD,	Bernarda	33	Zejtun	11 May 41
MIFSUD,	Blanche	14	Gzira	2 Jan 42
MIFSUD,	Carmel	55	Mosta	2 Jan 42
MIFSUD,	Carmel	35	Qormi	14 May 43
MIFSUD,	Concetta	80	Mosta	20 Apr 42
MIFSUD,	Edward	12	Attard	22 Jul 42
MIFSUD,	Emanuel	20	Birkirkara	13 Oct 42
MIFSUD,	Felicia	26	Rabat	21 Mar 42
MIFSUD,	Francis	38	Naxxar	25 May 41
MIFSUD,	Gaetan	54	Zejtun	9 May 42
MIFSUD,	Gerald	27	Valletta	31 May 43
MIFSUD,	Gisualda	10 months	Rabat	21 Mar 42
MIFSUD,	Herman	42	Sliema	26 Mar 42
MIFSUD,	Jane	60	Qrendi	9 Apr 42
MIFSUD,	Joseph	13	Gzira	2 Jan 42
MIFSUD,	Joseph	66	Sliema	17 Mar 42
MIFSUD,	Joseph	47	Valletta	24 Mar 42
MIFSUD,	Rev Joseph	50	Mosta	20 Apr 42
MIFSUD,	Joseph	36	Gzira	9 May 42
MIFSUD,	Giulio	19	Floriana	15 Feb 42
MIFSUD,	Mary	36	Gzira	2 Jan 42
MIFSUD,	Mary	57	Valletta	15 Mar 42
MIFSUD,	Rosaria	8	Gharghur	11 Apr 41
MIFSUD,	Saviour	56	Zejtun	16 Jun 40
MIFSUD,	Saviour	34	Qormi	12 Jul 42
MIFSUD,	Tancred	15	Gzira	2 Jan 42
MIFSUD,	Victor	7	Xaghra, Gozo	23 Apr 43
MIFSUD,	Walter	14	Attard	22 Jul 42
MIFSUD,	Winnie	4	Gzira	2 Jan 42
MIFSUD ELLUL,	Annetto A. & C.E.	53	Mosta	9 Feb 42
MIFSUD ELLUL,	Concetta	43	Gzira	1 Apr 42
MIFSUD SPERANZA,	Frances	17	Pawla	8 Jul 42
MIGGIANI,	Vincent	38	Pieta	4 Apr 42
MILES,	Harold R	38	Valletta	15 Mar 42
MILLER,	William	55	Zabbar	20 Feb 42
MILLER,	Mary Anne	10	Gzira	1 Apr 42
MINTOFF,	Augustine	16	Kalkara	24 Mar 42
MINTOFF,	Carmela	80	Kalkara	24 Mar 42
MINTOFF,	Josephine	48	Kalkara	24 Mar 42
MIZZI,	Albert		Vittoriosa	16 Jan 41
MIZZI,	Anthony		Vittoriosa	16 Jan 41
MIZZI,	Francis	32	Vittoriosa	16 Jan 41
MIZZI,	John	59	Zabbar	8 Apr 41
MIZZI,	Kalang	60	Gharb, Gozo	4 Aug 42
MIZZI,	Vincent	13	Rabat	21 Mar 42
MOAKES,	Henry	42	Floriana	20 Apr 42
MONTAGUE,	Carmela	33	Cospicua	5 Apr 42
MONTAGUE,	Daniel	13	Cospicua	5 Apr 42
MONTAGUE,	Joseph	11	Cospicua	5 Apr 42
MONTAGUE,	Mary	8	Cospicua	5 Apr 42
MONTANARO,	Alfred	63	Mosta	21 Mar 42
MONTANARO,	Annetto LL.D.	79	Hamrun	20 Apr 42

ROLL OF HONOUR

MONTANARO,	John	18	Mosta	21 Mar 42
MONTANARO,	Mary	60	Mosta	21 Mar 42
MONTGOMERY,	Albert J	41	St Julian's	25 Apr 42
MONTIFORT,	Alfred	75	Sliema	25 Apr 42
MONTIFORT,	Perina	68	Sliema	25 Apr 42
MORANA,	Saviour	66	Floriana	28 Apr 42
MORRIS,	Carmela	68	Pawla	12 Feb 42
MULIETT,	Jane	3	Valletta	24 Apr 42
MUSCAT,	Alfred	4	Hamrun	22 Oct 42
MUSCAT,	Anna	15	Qormi	10 Feb 42
MUSCAT,	Anthony	18	Zebbug	3 Nov 42
MUSCAT,	Antonia	33	Xaghra, Zabbar	31 Mar 42
MUSCAT,	Carmel	17	Sliema	27 Dec 41
MUSCAT,	Carmel	58	Mosta	2 Jan 42
MUSCAT,	Carmela	72	St Paul's Bay	18 Mar 42
MUSCAT,	Carmela	23	Attard	9 May 42
MUSCAT,	Carmela	5	Zebbug	3 Nov 42
MUSCAT,	Charles R		Hamrun	1 Jun 42
MUSCAT,	Emanuel	22	Siggiewi	3 Jul 42
MUSCAT,	Francis	14	St Paul's Bay	18 Mar 42
MUSCAT,	Joseph	35	Sannat, Gozo	30 Dec 41
MUSCAT,	Joseph	9	Nadur, Gozo	15 Jan 42
MUSCAT,	Joseph	35	Sliema	1 Mar 42
MUSCAT,	Joseph,	32	Balzan	21 Mar 42
MUSCAT,	Josephine	51	Siggiewi	3 Jul 42
MUSCAT,	Grazzia	50	Sannat, Gozo	10 Oct 42
MUSCAT,	Lewis	3	Tarxien	6 Apr 42
MUSCAT,	Mary	30	Sannat, Gozo	10 Oct 42
MUSCAT,	Mary Annunziata	26	Tarxien	6 Apr 42
MUSCAT,	Mary Concetta	16	Siggiewi	3 Jul 42
MUSCAT,	Philip	57	Zebbug	3 Nov 42
MUSCAT,	Rosanna	20	Siggiewi	3 Jul 42
MUSCAT,	Rose	9 months	Tarxien	6 Apr 42
MUSCAT,	Saviour	17	Siggiewi	3 Jul 42
NAUDI,	James	45	Sliema	24 Apr 42
O'NEIL,	Harriet	56	Rabat	21 Mar 42
O'NEILL,	William	22	Rabat	4 Apr 42
ORLAND,	Angiolina	30	Tarxien	27 Jun 40
PACE,	Anthony	75	Dingli	7 Jan 42
PACE,	Anthony	24	Attard	21 Mar 42
PACE,	Antonia	77	Sliema	21 May 42
PACE,	Carmel	30	Birzebbuga	19 May 42
PACE,	Carmela	5	Hamrun	26 May 42
PACE,	Clara	70	Hamrun	19 Apr 42
PACE,	Emanuel	20	Floriana	1 Mar 42
PACE,	Filomena	60	Marsa	26 Jun 40
PACE,	Frances	45	Sannat, Gozo	10 Oct 42
PACE,	Francis	22	Hamrun	13 Feb 42
PACE,	Fr Gerald	50	Valletta	15 Feb 42
PACE,	Grace	80	Hamrun	19 Apr 42
PACE,	Jane	15	Floriana	1 Mar 42
PACE,	Michael	15	Hamrun	24 Apr 42
PACE,	Paul	48	Birkirkara	10 Feb 42
PACE,	Regina	64	Pawla	12 Feb 42
PACE,	Romeo	35	Cospicua	11 Jun 40
PACE BONELLO,	Edward	51	Sliema	6 Feb 42
PALMIER,	Calcedonio	40	Zejtun	2 May 42

ROLL OF HONOUR

PANTALLERESCO,	Emanuel	70	Valletta	20 May 41
PARIS,	Emanuel		Pawla	31 Aug 42
PARLAR,	Paul	62	Birkirkara	18 Oct 42
PARNIS,	Calcedonio	50	St Julian's	10 Mar 42
PARNIS,	Joseph	26	Birkirkara	9 Nov 41
PARNIS,	John	17	Birkirkara	10 Nov 41
PARNIS,	Capt William	48	Valletta	28 Feb 42
PEEL,	Albert	20	Tarxien	26 Jun 40
PENZA,	Joseph	71	Luqa	8 Jan 42
PERINI,	Irene	8 months	Birkirkara	13 Apr 42
PERINI,	Marianna	26	Birkirkara	13 Apr 42
PETRONI,	Joseph	29	Zebbug	17 Mar 42
PIKE,	Anthony	4	Gzira	8 May 42
PISANI,	Anthony	38	Sliema	17 Mar 42
PISANI,	Carmel	5	Kalkara	7 Sep 40
PISANI,	Carmel	29	Hamrun	16 Aug 41
PISANI,	Carmel	10	Birkirkara	10 Jul 42
PISANI,	Carmela	34	Pawla	12 Feb 42
PISANI,	Gaetan	31	Pawla	24 Apr 42
PISANI,	Jane	50	Pawla	12 Feb 42
PISANI,	John	49	Nadur, Gozo	24 Oct 41
PISANI,	Joseph	1	Kalkara	7 Sep 40
PISANI,	Joseph	64	Pawla	12 Feb 42
PISANI,	Lorenza	3	Kalkara	7 Sep 40
PISANI,	Lorenza	32	Vittoriosa	16 Jan 41
PISANI,	Br Marcellino	22	Zebbug	29 Apr 41
PISANI,	Mary	27	Kalkara	7 Sep 40
PISANI,	Mary	8	Birkirkara	10 Jul 42
PISANI,	Paul	3	Birkirkara	10 Jul 42
PISANI,	Victoria	45	Birkirkara	10 Jul 42
PISANI,	Vincent		Vittoriosa	16 Jan 41
PISCOPO,	Joseph	75	Zejtun	2 May 42
PISCOPO,	Lawrence	24	Tarxien	11 Oct 42
PIZZUTO,	Anthony	38	Marsa	7 Apr 42
PIZZUTO,	Marietta	50	Mosta	9 Feb 42
POLIDANO,	Mary	17	Floriana	9 May 42
PORTELLI,	Anthony	14	Zabbar	10 Apr 42
PORTELLI,	Carmelina	4	Floriana	1 Mar 42
PORTELLI,	Carrie	23	Msida	1 Mar 42
PORTELLI,	Consiglio	53	Rabat	2 Jul 42
PORTELLI,	Gaetana	60	Zejtun	2 May 42
PORTELLI,	Gisualda	71	Rabat	21 Mar 42
PORTELLI,	John	34	Qormi	10 Feb 42
PORTELLI,	John	55	Attard	20 Mar 42
PORTELLI,	Joseph	44	Valletta	5 May 42
PORTELLI,	Rev Paul	52	Floriana	28 Apr 42
PORTELLI,	Sarah	39	Floriana	1 Mar 42
PORTELLI,	Saviour	37	Rabat	17 Mar 42
PORTER,	Charles	71	Tarxien	11 Oct 42
POTENZA,	Giovanna	70	Hamrun	19 Apr 42
PSAILA,	Anna	82	Zabbar	15 May 41
PSAILA,	Anthony	16	Zabbar	21 Dec 41
PSAILA,	Emanuel		Zejtun	8 Apr 41
PSAILA,	John	12	Birkirkara	7 Apr 42
PSAILA,	Josephine	25	Luqa	8 Jan 42
PSAILA,	Josephine	70	Qrendi	9 Apr 42
PSAILA,	Lewis	45	Qormi	20 Jul 43
PSAILA,	Micheline	16	Hamrun	4 Apr 42
PULIS,	Angelo	45	Zabbar	10 Jul 40
PULIS,	Louis	41	Tarxien	14 Jun 42

ROLL OF HONOUR

PULIS,	Vincent	37	Zabbar	28 Apr 42
PULLICINO,	Clementa	48	Zabbar	5 Dec 41
PULLICINO,	Joseph	27	Qormi	20 Jul 43
PULO,	Antonia	27	Floriana	1 Mar 42
PULO,	Francis	62	Floriana	14 Mar 42
PXINGA,	Francis	56	Valletta	20 Feb 43
RAPA,	Saviour	74	Nadur, Gozo	15 Mar 41
RAPINETT,	Assunta	43	Valletta	16 Jan 41
RAPINETT,	Charles	60	Valletta	28 Apr 42
RAPINETT,	Mary	6	Valletta	16 Jan 41
REDMAN,	Edward	64	Tarxien	11 Oct 42
REGINIANO,	Manasser	18	Valletta	15 Feb 42
REMIGIO,	Rosina	35	Senglea	16 Jan 41
RICE,	Vincenza	41	Gzira	28 Oct 42
RIOLO,	Assunta	30	Mosta	19 Jan 42
RIOLO,	Frances	71	Mosta	19 Jan 42
RIVIERA,	Michael	49	Sliema	1 Apr 42
RIZZO,	Doris	18	Hamrun	26 May 42
RIZZO,	Emanuel	4	Zejtun	9 Apr 42
RIZZO,	Paul	70	Hamrun	26 May 42
RODO,	Anthony	26	Zebbug	6 Jun 42
ROGERS,	Carmela	71	Sliema	20 Apr 42
SACCO,	Alfred	3	Hamrun	22 Jul 42
SACCO,	Anthony	18	Zurrieq	11 Feb 43
SACCO,	Joseph	23	Birkirkara	13 Apr 42
SACCO,	Louis	60	Birkirkara	24 Mar 42
SEGONA,	Josephine	50	Senglea	28 Apr 42
ST JOHN,	Alfred	2	Mosta	26 Mar 42
ST JOHN,	Olga	26	Mosta	21 Mar 42
ST JOHN,	Nazzareno	3 months	Mosta	21 Mar 42
SALIBA,	Anthony	38	Victoria, Gozo	6 May 42
SALIBA,	Angelo	16	Sliema	11 Mar 41
SALIBA,	Carmel	55	Qormi	10 Feb 42
SALIBA,	Carmela	30	Mqabba	26 Jun 40
SALIBA,	Carmela	20	Marsa	4 Apr 42
SALIBA,	Calcedonio	25	Qormi	26 Jun 40
SALIBA,	Catherine	72	Mqabba	21 Jun 42
SALIBA,	Catherine	35	Sannat, Gozo	10 Oct 42
SALIBA,	Josephine	3	Mqabba	26 Jun 40
SALIBA,	Luke	27	Siggiewi	5 Jan 42
SALIBA,	Paul	7	Vittoriosa	26 Jun 40
SALIBA,	Pauline	6	Mqabba	26 Jun 40
SALIBA,	Spiro	40	Qormi	27 Aug 42
SALIBA,	Saviour	9	Siggiewi	10 Feb 43
SALIBA,	Saviour	50	Zejtun	13 Feb 43
SALNITRO,	Caroline	14	Valletta	24 Apr 42
SALSERO,	Charles	3	Tarxien	11 Oct 42
SALSERO,	Mary	17	Pawla	12 Feb 42
SALSERO,	Saviour	66	Pawla	28 Apr 42
SAMMUT,	Amabile	21	Birkirkara	30 Jul 42
SAMMUT,	Anthony	33	Msida	26 Apr 41
SAMMUT,	Carmel	42	Qormi	17 Jan 41
SAMMUT,	Carmela	23	Birkirkara	30 Jul 42
SAMMUT,	Emanuel	16	Hamrun	12 Jul 41
SAMMUT,	Emanuel	7	Qormi	10 Feb 42
SAMMUT,	Francis	70	Floriana	8 May 42
SAMMUT,	Francis	16	Rabat	1 Sep 42
SAMMUT,	Mary	6	Qormi	10 Feb 42

ROLL OF HONOUR

SAMMUT,	Marianna	24	Naxxar	8 Apr 42
SAMMUT,	Michael	46	Siggiewi	11 Apr 41
SAMMUT,	Michael	40	Msida	19 Apr 41
SAMMUT,	Rita	18	Rabat	11 Jul 42
SAMMUT,	Saviour	62	Zurrieq	12 Mar 42
SAMMUT,	Saviour	64	Zurrieq	12 Mar 42
SAMMUT,	Teresa	68	Luqa	8 Jan 42
SAMMUT,	Teresa	20	Qormi	9 May 42
SAMMUT,	Valent	33	Balzan	26 Mar 42
SAMMUT BARDON,	Louis	48	Sliema	5 May 42
SAMPSON,	Claude Philip	34		25 Apr 42
SANDHAM,	William		Zabbar	23 Jan 43
SANT,	Francis	56	Hamrun	4 Jul 41
SANT MANDUCA,	Stella	76	Mdina	16 May 42
SAPIANO,	Anthony	53	Mdina	7 May 42
SAPIANO,	Jane	58	Mdina	7 May 42
SAPIANO,	Mary	17	Birkirkara	13 Apr 42
SAYDON,	Joseph	48	Zurrieq	23 Jul 42
SAYDON,	Peter Paul	42	Luqa	8 Mar 42
SCERRI,	Calcedonio	63	Floriana	28 Apr 42
SCERRI,	Herman	14	Valletta	19 Apr 42
SCERRI,	Jane	19	Qormi	20 Jul 43
SCERRI,	Jennie	17	Hamrun	22 Oct 42
SCERRI,	Joseph	70	Rabat	11 Jul 42
SCERRI,	Lawrence	55	Pawla	12 Feb 42
SCERRI,	Marguerite	75	Valletta	20 Jul 43
SCERRI,	Mary	9	Birkirkara	31 Jul 42
SCERRI,	Salvina	28	Mosta	9 Feb 42
SCERRI,	Vincent	64	Pawla	23 Apr 42
SCERRI,	Vincent	60	Tarxien	11 Oct 42
SCHEMBRI,	Anna	75	Zurrieq	6 Apr 42
SCHEMBRI,	Carmel	14	Naxxar	4 May 42
SCHEMBRI,	Carmel	16	Zurrieq	23 Jul 42
SCHEMBRI,	Frances	30	Zejtun	2 May 42
SCHEMBRI,	Francis	13	Luqa	9 Apr 42
SCHEMBRI,	Giorgia	56	Gzira	2 Jan 42
SCHEMBRI,	Grezzju	9	Mosta	22 Mar 42
SCHEMBRI,	Grezzju	53	Luqa	9 Apr 42
SCHEMBRI,	Joseph	13	Ghaxaq	9 Apr 42
SCHEMBRI,	Joseph	11	Mosta	12 May 42
SCHEMBRI,	Josephine	50	Siggiewi	3 Jul 42
SCHEMBRI,	Louis	3	Siggiewi	13 Jan 42
SCHEMBRI,	Nicholas	50	Siggiewi	29 Dec 41
SCHEMBRI,	Horatio	19	Mosta	19 Jan 42
SCHEMBRI,	Paul	15	Birkirkara	13 Apr 42
SCHEMBRI,	Ursula	58	Zurrieq	18 Mar 42
SCHEMBRI,	Vincent	60	Valletta	22 Apr 41
SCIBERRAS,	Catherine	86	Qrendi	9 Apr 42
SCIBERRAS,	Carmel	30	St Julian's	4 Apr 42
SCIBERRAS,	Carmela	56	St Julian's	22 Oct 42
SCIBERRAS,	Joseph	18	Naxxar	20 Mar 42
SCIBERRAS,	Sr Marie	85	Hamrun	19 Apr 42
SCIBERRAS,	Vincent	44	Birkirkara	20 Nov 42
SCIBERRAS,	Vincent	78	Qrendi	19 Dec 42
SCICLUNA,	Adeodata	60	Hamrun	13 May 41
SCICLUNA,	Fred	45	Gudja	8 Apr 42
SCICLUNA,	Alfred	33	Hamrun	2 Jun 42
SCICLUNA,	Andrew	40	Rabat	27 Apr 42

ROLL OF HONOUR

SCICLUNA,	Beatrix	14	Sliema	14 May 42
SCICLUNA,	Benedict	17	Sliema	11 Mar 41
SCICLUNA,	Concetta	24	Cospicua	12 Jun 40
SCICLUNA,	Gaetan	18	Hamrun	29 Dec 41
SCICLUNA,	John	44	Sliema	11 Mar 41
SCICLUNA,	Joseph	52	Qormi	12 Apr 42
SCICLUNA,	Joseph	18	Zejtun	23 Apr 42
SCICLUNA,	Joseph	48	Gzira	15 Oct 42
SCICLUNA,	Josephine	24	Cospicua	13 Jun 40
SCICLUNA,	Kenneth	6 months	Sliema	6 Mar 42
SCICLUNA,	Veneranda	45	Attard	28 Jun 42
SCICLUNA,	Zarenu	50	Sliema	11 Mar 41
SERRA,	Aldo	10	Hamrun	5 Jul 41
SERRA,	Carmelina	5	Hamrun	5 Jul 41
SERRA,	Ines	14	Hamrun	5 Jul 41
SERRA,	Nello	13	Hamrun	5 Jul 41
SGHENDO,	Carmela	15	Sliema	17 Mar 42
SIZELAND,	Antonia	46	Senglea	28 Apr 42
SIZELAND,	Charles	8	Senglea	28 Apr 42
SMITH,	Agnes	47	Ta' Xbiex	26 Jun 42
SMITH,	Reginald de N	53	Valletta	26 Feb 42
SMITH,	Winnie	56	Sliema	14 May 42
SPAGNOL,	Rosario	14	Valletta	14 Feb 41
SPITERI,	Alfred	7 months	Gzira	2 Jan 42
SPITERI,	Andrew	17	Rabat	17 Mar 42
SPITERI,	Anna	21	Zejtun	21 Apr 41
SPITERI,	Anthony	54	Zejtun	6 Apr 42
SPITERI,	Antonia	24	Zejtun	8 Jul 41
SPITERI,	Benedetta	15	Gzira	2 Jan 42
SPITERI,	Carmela	10	Gzira	2 Jan 42
SPITERI,	Carmela	70	Qrendi	1 Jul 42
SPITERI,	Dominic	10	Gzira	2 Jan 42
SPITERI,	Dominic	50	Gzira	2 Jan 42
SPITERI,	Doris	8	Birkirkara	18 Oct 42
SPITERI,	Emanuel	65	Cospicua	16 Jun 40
SPITERI,	Emanuel	48	Valletta	16 Jan 41
SPITERI,	Emanuel	2	Gzira	2 Jan 42
SPITERI,	Eugene	48	Senglea	8 Apr 41
SPITERI,	Francis	14	Sliema	17 Mar 42
SPITERI,	John	23	Mosta	19 Jan 42
SPITERI,	Joseph	15	Marsa	12 Jul 41
SPITERI,	Joseph	12	Hamrun	24 Apr 42
SPITERI,	Joseph	36	Siggiewi	12 Jun 42
SPITERI,	Joseph	55	Zejtun	23 Jun 42
SPITERI,	Joseph	3 months	Zurrieq	23 Jul 42
SPITERI,	Josephine	5	Gzira	2 Jan 42
SPITERI,	Lawrence	62	Zejtun	23 Jun 42
SPITERI,	Mary	12	Gzira	2 Jan 42
SPITERI,	Maria Carmela	6	Birkirkara	18 Oct 42
SPITERI,	Saviour	30	Zejtun	20 Mar 42
SPITERI,	Vincenza	3	Gzira	2 Jan 42
STILON,	Albert LL.D.	64	Rabat	21 Mar 42
STIVALA,	Mariano	62	Kalkara	24 Mar 42
SULTANA,	Concetta	6	Hamrun	4 Apr 42
SULTANA,	Emanuel	40	Hamrun	12 Jul 41
SULTANA,	Emanuel	5	Xaghra, Gozo	23 Apr 43
SULTANA,	Francis	7	Xaghra, Gozo	23 Apr 43
SULTANA,	Joseph	2	Hamrun	4 Apr 42
SULTANA,	Michael	73	Birkirkara	27 Oct 42
SULTANA,	Publius	31	Hamrun	4 Apr 42
SULTANA,	Teresa	26	Hamrun	4 Apr 42

ROLL OF HONOUR

TABONE,	Antonia	7	Sliema	1 Apr 42
TABONE,	Assunta	48	Floriana	28 Apr 42
TABONE,	Josephine	22	Mosta	21 Mar 42
TABONE,	Josephine	22	Sliema	1 Apr 42
TABONE,	Lawrence	35	Mosta	8 Apr 41
TABONE,	Mary	14	Sannat, Gozo	10 Oct 42
TABONE,	Mary	12	Tarxien	11 Oct 42
TANTI,	Carmel	14	Rabat	1 Sep 42
TANTI,	Concetta	13	Gzira	26 Jun 42
TANTI,	Mary	17	Gzira	26 Jun 42
TANTI,	Saviour	70	Pawla	7 Jul 41
TANTI,	Victor	2	Pawla	7 Jul 41
TEDESCO,	Grace	23	Zabbar	19 Apr 42
TESTAFERRATA de NOTO,	Alfio	12	Zejtun	15 Jun 43
TEUMA,	Bice	5	Senglea	16 Jan 41
TEUMA,	Carmela	30	Senglea	16 Jan 41
TEUMA,	Emily	21	Senglea	16 Jan 41
TEUMA,	Rev Can John	28	Senglea	16 Jan 41
TEUMA,	Marcel	51	Ghajnsielem, Gozo	29 Dec 41
THEOBALD,	Charles	77	Pawla	13 Feb 42
THEUMA,	Carmela	64	Sannat, Gozo	10 Oct 42
TIKAMADAS,	Rochani	48	Valletta	29 Apr 41
TONNA,	Elia	51	Mosta	4 Feb 42
TONNA,	Joseph	31	Mosta	4 Feb 42
TONNA,	Mary	60	Birkirkara	26 Nov 42
TONNA,	Santu	32	Mosta	21 Mar 42
TONNA BARTHET,	Emilie	74	Birkirkara	13 Apr 42
TONNA BARTHET,	Valentin	76	Birkirkara	13 Apr 42
TRAPANI,	John	50	Gzira	11 Jun 40
ULLO,	Josephine	75	Valletta	20 May 41
VASSALLO,	Anthony	22	Pawla	1 Apr 42
VASSALLO,	Dominic	15	Marsa	16 Jan 41
VASSALLO,	Emanuel	47	Attard	20 Mar 42
VASSALLO,	Hector LL.D.	41	Sliema	14 May 42
VASSALLO,	John	75	Pawla	12 Feb 42
VASSALLO,	Joseph	39	Marsa	1 May 41
VASSALLO,	Lawrence	9	Siggiewi	9 May 43
VASSALLO,	Lucarda	70	Msida	20 Apr 41
VASSALLO,	Margherita	28	Rabat	21 Mar 42
VASSALLO,	Paul	50	Gzira	19 Mar 42
VASSALLO,	Rosina	33	Gzira	11 Jun 40
VASSALLO,	Samuel	25	Rabat	17 Mar 42
VELLA,	Alfred	45	Sliema	17 Mar 42
VELLA,	Andrew	7	Naxxar	28 Aug 41
VELLA,	Angelo	46	Tarxien	8 Apr 41
VELLA,	Anthony	74	Valletta	5 Jul 42
VELLA,	Bartholomew	41	Mosta	21 Mar 42
VELLA,	Carmel	4	Naxxar	28 Aug 41
VELLA,	Carmel	12	Mosta	21 Mar 42
VELLA,	Carmel	17	Valletta	24 Mar 42
VELLA,	Carmel	28	Qormi	20 Jul 43
VELLA,	Carmela	14	Zabbar	7 Feb 41
VELLA,	Carmela	11	Naxxar	28 Aug 41
VELLA,	Catherine	17	Zebbug	29 Jun 43
VELLA,	Censa	70	Luqa	9 Apr 42
VELLA,	Evangelista	34	Mosta	19 Jan 42
VELLA,	Evelyn	17	Senglea	16 Jan 41

ROLL OF HONOUR

VELLA,	Francis	29	Victoria, Gozo	27 Feb 41
VELLA,	Gerald	37	Birkirkara	8 Apr 41
VELLA,	John	14	Mellieha	8 Jun 41
VELLA,	John	41	Zabbar	8 May 42
VELLA,	Joseph	9	Mosta	21 Mar 42
VELLA,	Joseph	43	Pawla	23 Apr 42
VELLA,	Joseph	14	Mosta	6 Jul 42
VELLA,	Joseph	53	Sliema	20 Jul 43
VELLA,	Lino	11	Sliema	20 Jul 43
VELLA,	Louis	22	Zebbug, Gozo	4 Mar 42
VELLA,	Melita	45	Valletta	15 Mar 42
VELLA,	Mary	36	Mgarr	11 Apr 41
VELLA,	Mary	14	Naxxar	28 Aug 41
VELLA,	Mary	69	Hamrun	19 Apr 42
VELLA,	Marianna	42	Naxxar	28 Aug 41
VELLA,	Michael	74	Valletta	15 Mar 42
VELLA,	Br Norbert	20	Rabat	13 Jun 42
VELLA,	Paul		Tarxien	8 Apr 41
VELLA,	Paul	75	Valletta	15 May 41
VELLA,	Paul	11	Naxxar	15 Jun 42
VELLA,	Peter	70	Luqa	8 Jan 42
VELLA,	Peter	52	Rabat	11 Oct 42
VELLA,	Rita	6	St Paul's Bay	28 Mar 42
VELLA,	Rosina	47	Luqa	11 Jan 42
VELLA,	Saviour	60	Mgarr	11 Apr 41
VELLA,	Saviour	45	Msida	21 Mar 42
VELLA,	Spira	70	Kalkara	24 Mar 42
VELLA,	Spiro	20	Qormi	10 Feb 42
VELLA,	Teresa	3	Naxxar	28 Aug 41
VELLA,	Ubaldesca	32	Ghaxaq	24 Feb 42
VELLA,	Vincent	50	Hamrun	28 Apr 42
VENTURA,	Angelica	66	Kalkara	24 Mar 42
VENTURA,	Michael	75	Kalkara	24 Mar 42
VERZIN,	Pauline	70	Hamrun	12 Jul 41
VINCENTI,	Edwidge	37	Mosta	19 Jan 42
VINCENTI,	John	45	Mosta	19 Jan 42
WALTON,	John Peter	40	Imtarfa	18 Apr 42
WARD,	Joseph	19	Hamrun	2 Jun 42
WARNE,	Stanley	13	Pawla	12 Feb 42
WHIDDATT,	Filippa	12	Hamrun	22 Oct 42
WHIDDATT,	Joan	10	Hamrun	22 Oct 42
WHIDDATT,	William	8	Hamrun	22 Oct 42
WICKMAN,	Michael	19	Pawla	15 Feb 42
WOODHOUSE,	Joseph	18	Hamrun	4 Jul 41
WOODWARD,	Albert	37	Marsa	12 Jul 41
XERRI,	John Mary			8 Apr 41
XERRI,	Vincent			8 Apr 41
XUEREB,	Carmel	23	Gzira	10 Nov 41
YABSLEY,	Caroline Ethel	72	Sliema	5 Feb 42
ZAHRA,	Anthony	11	Msida	14 Oct 42
ZAHRA,	Antonia	10	Zejtun	31 Jan 42
ZAHRA,	Carmel	15	Zejtun	27 Mar 42
ZAHRA,	Doris	60	Sliema	11 Mar 41
ZAHRA,	Edgar	43	Birkirkara	2 Apr 42
ZAHRA,	George	44	Luqa	8 Apr 41
ZAHRA,	Joseph	27	Dingli	23 Mar 41

ROLL OF HONOUR

ZAHRA,	Mary	54	Zurrieq	12 Mar 42
ZAHRA,	Mary	44	Rabat	11 Oct 42
ZAHRA,	Peter Paul	54	Qormi	20 Jul 43
ZAHRA,	Rosa	70	Hamrun	19 Apr 42
ZAMMIT,	Alfred	4	Sliema	1 Apr 42
ZAMMIT,	Alfred	24	Zebbug	8 May 42
ZAMMIT,	Albert	22	Hamrun	15 Feb 42
ZAMMIT,	Andrew	76	Pawla	12 Feb 42
ZAMMIT,	Anthony	19	Valletta	28 Feb 41
ZAMMIT,	Anthony	70	Cospicua	2 Mar 42
ZAMMIT,	Anthony	10	Lija	3 Nov 42
ZAMMIT,	Antoinette	18	Balzan	6 Jun 42
ZAMMIT,	Carmel	32		8 Apr 41
ZAMMIT,	Carmel	53	Birkirkara	8 Apr 41
ZAMMIT,	Carmel	33	Pawla	12 Feb 42
ZAMMIT,	Carmel	15	Sliema	1 Apr 42
ZAMMIT,	Carmela	24	Lija	3 Nov 42
ZAMMIT,	Doris	24	Floriana	1 Mar 42
ZAMMIT,	Emanuel	24	Zejtun	2 May 42
ZAMMIT,	Emanuel	7	Mqabba	27 Aug 42
ZAMMIT,	George	32	Hamrun	26 Jun 40
ZAMMIT,	George	65	Rabat	13 Jul 42
ZAMMIT,	George	8	Birkirkara	17 Oct 42
ZAMMIT,	Jane	60	Msida	19 Apr 41
ZAMMIT,	John	50	Msida	19 Apr 42
ZAMMIT,	John Mary	11	Zejtun	31 Jan 42
ZAMMIT,	Joseph	65	Msida	19 Apr 41
ZAMMIT,	Joseph	1	Zejtun	31 Jan 42
ZAMMIT,	Joseph	72	Benghaisa	8 Jun 42
ZAMMIT,	Joseph	6	Mqabba	27 Aug 42
ZAMMIT,	Louis	46	Zejtun	27 Jun 42
ZAMMIT,	Lydia	2	Sannat, Gozo	10 Oct 42
ZAMMIT,	Mary	30	Zejtun	31 Jan 42
ZAMMIT,	Marianna	45	Sliema	1 Apr 42
ZAMMIT,	Paul	7	Ghaxaq	9 Apr 42
ZAMMIT,	Paul	13	Rabat	22 Jul 42
ZAMMIT,	Peter	62	Gudja	9 Apr 42
ZAMMIT,	Randa	30	Birzebbuga	8 May 42
ZAMMIT,	Rose	16	Comino	24 Apr 42
ZAMMIT,	Samuel	63	Birkirkara	4 Aug 42
ZAMMIT,	Saviour	54	Zurrieq	23 Jul 42
ZAMMIT,	Stephen	62	Pawla	12 Feb 42
ZAMMIT,	Vincent	39	Mosta	21 Mar 42
ZAMMIT PSAILA,	Rev Joseph	68	Zurrieq	23 Jul 42
ZARB,	Charlie	13	Senglea	30 Apr 41
ZARB,	Edward	12	Senglea	30 Apr 41
ZARB,	Jane	48	Mosta	21 Mar 42
ZARB,	Lawrence	44	Vittoriosa	16 Jan 41
ZARB,	Mary	10	Senglea	30 Apr 41
ZARB,	Marianna	50	Pawla	12 Feb 42
ZARB COUSIN,	Edwidge	5	Valletta	30 Apr 41
ZERAFA,	Joseph	33	Pawla	7 Jul 41
ZERAFA,	Mary	15	Pawla	7 Jul 41
ZERAFA,	Kalang	47	Zurrieq	14 Mar 42
ZERAFA,	Paul	22	Pawla	7 Jul 41

ROLL OF HONOUR

ROYAL NAVY

(This list contains the names of members of the Malta Port Division only.)

AGIUS,	Emanuel	Std	E/LX	23547	*Glorious*	9 Jun 40
AGIUS,	John	Std	E/LX	23361	*Fiona*	18 Apr 41
AGIUS,	Joseph	P O Std	E/LX	20734	*Juno*	21 May 41
ANASTASI,	Emanuel	L/Std	E/LX	23185	*St Angelo*	29 Jun 40
AQUILINA,	Anthony	O C 2	E/LX	20866	*Hunter*	10 Apr 40
AQUILINA,	Joseph	L/Std	E/LX	22505	*Cossack*	13 Nov 40
ATTARD,	Anthony	Asst Std	E/LX	25382	*Kent*	17 Sep 40
ATTARD,	Francis	P O Ck (O)	E/LX	20770	*Royal Oak*	14 Oct 39
ATTARD,	Joseph	L/Std	E/LX	22396	*Kent*	17 Sep 40
ATTARD,	Joseph	P O Std	E/LX	21784	*St Angelo*	30 Jun 42
ATTARD,	Lawrence	Std	E/LX	21773	*Royal Oak*	14 Oct 39
AZZILLA,	Demitri	L/Ck (O)	E/LX	22182	*Barham*	25 Nov 41
AZZOPARDI,	Anthony	Std	E/LX	22321	*Royal Oak*	14 Oct 39
AZZOPARDI,	Joseph	L/Ck (O)	E/LX	22087	*Kandahar*	20 Dec 41
AZZOPARDI,	Vincent	Ck (O)	E/LX	23401	*Ouse*	20 Feb 41
BAJADA,	Anthony	A B	E/JX	163727	*Sunset*	31 Jan 42
BALZAN,	Calcedonio	P O Ck			*Barham*	25 Nov 41
BALZAN,	Vincent	L/Std	E/LX	21715	*Barham*	25 Nov 41
BARTOLO,	Emanuel	Std	E/LX	21301	*Glorious*	9 Jun 40
BARTOLO,	John	Std	E/LX	22582	*Royal Oak*	14 Oct 39
BERTUELLO,	Joseph	P O Std	E/LX	22088	*Kandahar*	20 Dec 41
BIANCO,	Joseph	P O Std	E/LX	20700	*Mohawk*	16 Apr 41
BONELLO,	Joseph	L/Std	E/L	13188	*Glorious*	9 Jun 40
BONELLO,	Salvatore	L/Std	E/L	11922	*Royal Oak*	14 Oct 39
BONELLO,	Walter	Std	LX	22829	*Glorious*	9 Jun 40
BONNICI,	Carmel	P O Std	E/L	12291	*Cornwall*	5 Apr 42
BONNICI,	Joseph	P O	E/JX	132594	*Ploughboy*	10 Mar 41
BORDA,	Alfred	L/Std	E/LX	20695	*Glorious*	9 Jun 40
BORG,	Joseph	P O Std	E/LX	21269	*Gloucester*	22 May 41
BORG,	Paul	L/Std	E/LX	22156	*Barham*	25 Nov 41
BORG,	Salvatore	A/P O	E/JX	138980	*Eddy*	26 May 42
BRIFFA,	Anthony	Asst Std	E/LX	22989	*Barham*	25 Nov 41
BRIFFA,	Joseph	P O Std	E/L	14986	*Barham*	25 Nov 41
BRIFFA,	Joseph	P O Std	E/L	12364	*Fiona*	18 Apr 41
BRINCAT,	G	Asst Std			*Glorious*	9 Jun 40
BURLO,	John	Std	E/LX	21950	*Kimberley*	12 Jan 42
BUSUTTIL,	Carmel	A B	E/JX	164549	*Eddy*	26 May 42
BUTTERS,	Cyril	Std	E/LX	20620	*Glorious*	9 Jun 40
BUTTIGIEG,	Carmel, DSM	Sto	E/KX	117749	*St Angelo*	23 Aug 43
CACHIA,	Carmel	Ck (O)	E/LX	23949	*Gloucester*	22 May 41
CACHIA,	Joseph	L/Std	E/LX	20812	*Royal Oak*	14 Oct 39
CACHIA,	Joseph	Std	E/LX	22506	*Glorious*	9 Jun 40
CALLEJA,	Dominic	O C 2	E/LX	21330	*Curlew*	26 May 40
CALLEJA,	Paul	L/Std	E/LX	22307	*Diamond*	27 Apr 41
CALLUS,	Joseph	Std	E/LX	25499	*Hereward*	29 May 41
CAMENZULI,	Anthony	L/Std	E/LX	21144	*Decoy*	14 Nov 40
CAMENZULI,	Dominic	L/Std	E/LX	22083	*Kelly*	25 May 41
CAMILLERI,	Alfred	P O Std	E/LX	15003	*Diamond*	27 Apr 41
CAMILLERI,	Rocco	P O Std	E/LX	20469	*Barham*	25 Nov 41
CARUANA,	Gregory	O S	E/LX	22029	*Glorious*	9 Jun 40
CARUANA,	Joseph	L/Sea	E/JX	138967	*St Angelo*	11 Jun 40
CARUANA,	Vincent	A/P O	E/JX	138978	*Justified*	16 Jun 42
CASHA,	Gaetan	Std	E/LX	22630	*Cromer*	9 Nov 42

292

ROLL OF HONOUR

CASSAR,	Joseph	Std	E/LX	23053	*Fiona*	18 Apr 41
CATANIA,	Carmel	Std	E/LX	24312	*Cromer*	9 Nov 42
CAUCHI,	Dominic	L/Std	E/LX	21861	*Fiona*	18 Apr 41
CHETCUTI,	Carmel	A B	E/JX	165102	*Ouse*	20 Feb 41
CHETCUTI,	John	L/Std	E/LX	22787	*Barham*	25 Nov 41
CHURCH,	Ovidio	Asst Std	E/LX	23166	*Royal Oak*	14 Oct 39
CINI,	Dominic	O C 1	E/LX	20934	*Gloucester*	22 May 41
CIOFFI,	Anthony	O C 2	E/LX	20536	*Cornwall*	5 Apr 42
CONSIGLIO,	William	Std	E/LX	22308	*Glorious*	9 Jun 40
CONTI,	Vincent	L/Ck (O)	E/LX	358073	*St Angelo*	22 Jul 40
COPPOLA,	John	Ck (O)	E/LX	22050	*Huntley*	3 Feb 41
CORDINA,	Carmel	L/Std	E/LX	21893	*Fiona*	18 Apr 41
CORESCHI,	Emanuel	Ck (O)			*Royal Oak*	14 Oct 39
COSAITIS,	Joseph	O C Ck	E/L	12533	*Glorious*	9 Jun 40
CREMONA,	Emanuel	A B	E/JX	165092	*Eddy*	25 May 42
CUSCHIERI,	Dominic	O C 3	E/L	9476	*Dainty*	24 Feb 41
D'AGOSTINO,	Dominic	L/Std	E/L	15078	*Grafton*	29 May 40
D'ANDREA,	Carmel	Ck (O)	E/LX	23204	*Gloucester*	22 May 41
DEBATTISTA,	Joseph	L/Sea	E/JX	146442	*St. Angelo*	30 May 42
DEGABRIELE,	Peter	Sto	E/KX	87275	*Medusa*	26 Jun 40
DIACONO,	Vincent	L/Std	E/LX	20044	*Glorious*	9 Jun 40
ELLUL,	Joseph	Std	E/LX	22653	*Cornwall*	5 Apr 42
FAIELLA,	Joseph	A B	E/JX	164541	*St Angelo*	24 Nov 40
FALZON,	Angelo	Std	E/LX	25509	*Neptune*	19 Dec 41
FALZON,	Francis	Sto	E/KX	98144	*Nile*	8 Nov 42
FALZON,	Gaetan	Ck (O) 2	E/LX	21856	*Barham*	25 Nov 41
FARRELL,	Joseph	Std	E/LX	22996	*Glorious*	9 Jun 40
FARRUGIA,	Anthony	L/Std	E/LX	30632	*Fiona*	18 Apr 41
FARRUGIA,	Carmel	A B	E/JX	165086	*Ploughboy*	1 Mar 41
FARRUGIA,	John	P O Std	E/LX	12430	*Barham*	25 Nov 41
FARRUGIA,	Joseph	Sto 1st Cl	E/KX	87274	*St Angelo*	11 Jun 40
FARRUGIA,	Joseph	O C 2	E/LX	20246	*Wryneck*	27 Apr 41
FARRUGIA,	Vincent	A B	E/JX	251984	*St Angelo*	30 May 42
FENECH,	Carmel	Sto 1st Cl	E/KX	98133	*St Angelo*	30 Mar 41
FENECH,	Gio	Cook (O)	E/LX	22030	*Glorious*	9 Jun 40
FENECH,	Joseph	S P O	E/KX	80262	*Lazzaretto*	12 Feb 42
FRANCICA,	Joseph	L/Cook (S)	E/LX	21089	*Glorious*	9 Jun 40
GALEA,	Carmel	L/Std	E/L	12182	*Glorious*	9 Jun 40
GALEA,	Carmel	L/Std	E/LX	20149	*St Angelo*	7 May 44
GALEA,	Joseph	A B	E/JX	148313	*St Angelo*	19 Apr 42
GALEA,	Michael	Std	E/LX	23459	*Decoy*	13 Nov 40
GATT,	Henry	A B	E/JX	283058	*Justified*	16 Apr 42
GATT,	John	O C 2	E/LX	20868	*Hythe*	1 Oct 43
GATT,	Philip	L/Std	E/L	13162	*Gloucester*	22 May 41
GAUCI,	John	L/Std	E/L	11706	*Mohawk*	16 Apr 41
GAUCI,	Nunzio	A B	E/JX	165085	*Nile*	8 Nov 42
GIGLIO,	Benjamin	O C 1	E/LX	20840	*Glorious*	9 Jun 40
GITTOS,	Hector	Sto	E/KX	95622	*St Angelo*	11 Jun 40
GIUSTI,	Ignazio	L/Std	E/X	15022	*Royal Oak*	14 Oct 39
GOODLIP,	William	L/Std			*Pangbourne*	29 May 40
GRECH,	Carmel	Std	E/LX	22795	*Gipsy*	20 Nov 39
GRECH,	Joseph	Std	E/LX	22806	*Royal Oak*	14 Oct 39
GRIMA,	Paul	Sto	E/KX	117530	*St Angelo*	30 May 42
GRISCTI,	Joseph	L/Ck (O)	E/LX	20333	*Glorious*	9 Jun 40

293

ROLL OF HONOUR

HALES,	Joseph	O C 2	E/L	12226	Royal Oak	14 Oct 39
HOWARD,	George	P O Std	E/LX	21672	St Angelo	26 Jun 40
JAMES,	John	L/Std	E/LX	6313	Dunoon	30 Apr 40
JONES,	Alfred	L/Std	E/L	14950	Glorious	9 Jun 40
LANDOLINA,	Salvatore	Std	E/LX	227788	Glorious	9 Jun 40
LAUTIER,	Salvatore	Sto	E/KX	98150	St Angelo	11 Jun 40
LEWIS,	Joseph	P O Std	E/LX	20857	Calcutta	1 Jun 41
LONGHURST,	Henry				Nile	8 Nov 42
MALLIA,	Lawrence	Std	E/LX	22995	Talbot	19 Jul 44
MAMO,	Francis	O C 2	E/L	6426	Royal Oak	14 Oct 39
MANGION,	Joseph	P O Std	E/LX	20458	Royal Oak	14 Oct 39
MARMARA,	Anthony	P O Std	E/LX	11937	Barham	25 Nov 41
MEDINA,	Joseph	Sto	E/KX	98141	Justified	16 Jun 42
MERCIECA,	Anthony	Cook (O)	E/LX	21860	Hunter	10 Apr 40
MICALLEF,	Emanuel	O C 1	E/LX	21166	Barham	25 Nov 41
MICALLEF,	Espedito	L/Std	E/LX	12523	Barham	25 Nov 41
MICALLEF,	George	A B	E/JX	283054	Lazzaretto	25 Oct 42
MICALLEF,	John	Ck (O)	E/LX	23399	Barham	25 Nov 41
MICALLEF,	Joseph	L/Std	E/LX	21220	Gloucester	22 May 41
MIFSUD,	Publius	L/Ck (O)	E/LX	20063	Barham	25 Nov 41
MIZZI,	Francis	A B	E/JX	583827	St Angelo	2 Oct 44
MONTANARO,	Emanuel	Std	E/LX	25454	Neptune	19 Dec 41
MULLIGAN,	Henry	Std	E/LX	22037	Barham	25 Nov 41
MUSCAT,	Joseph	Std	E/LX	22991	Medway	4 Aug 41
PACE,	Joseph	O C 2	E/LX	21000	Glorious	9 Jun 40
PARNIS,	Carmel	Ck (O)	E/LX	23599	Neptune	13 Jan 42
PESCI,	Emanuel	Ck (O)	E/LX	22099	Royal Oak	14 Oct 39
PIZZUTO,	Gerald	P O Sto	E/KX	87270	Eddy	25 May 42
POLIDANO,	Charles	Std	E/LX	25652	Lively	11 May 42
POLIDANO,	Francis	Std	E/LX	28325	Glorious	9 Jun 40
PORTELLI,	Anthony	P O Std	E/LX	21880	Glowworm	8 Apr 40
PORTANIER,	Paul	Std	E/LX	22369	Cornwall	5 Apr 42
PSAILA,	John	Std	E/LX	21959	St Angelo	2 May 42
RAPA,	Joseph	L/Std	E/LX	22782	Barham	25 Nov 41
SAID,	Joseph	Sto	E/KX	87265	St Angelo	30 May 42
SAID,	Peter	A B	E/JX	251702	Talbot	23 Aug 43
ST JOHN,	Walter	L/Std	E/LX	22789	Juno	21 May 41
SALIBA,	Lawrence	Std	E/LX	207769	Royal Oak	14 Oct 39
SAMMUT,	Francis	P O Std	E/LX	20536	Stoke	7 May 41
SAMMUT,	Joseph	L/Std	E/LX	14973	Cornwall	5 Apr 42
SARSERO,	Lawrence	A B	E/JX	164539	Justified	26 May 42
SAVONA,	Francis	Sto 1st Cl	E/KX	117981	Nile	8 Nov 42
SCHEMBRI,	Andrew	L/Std	E/LX	22681	Kandahar	20 Dec 41
SCHEMBRI,	Francis	Std	E/LX	23056	Glorious	9 Jun 40
SCHEMBRI,	Joseph	A B	E/JX	91714	St Angelo	29 May 45
SCHIAVONE,	Emanuel	CK (O)	E/LX	22979	Royal Oak	14 Oct 39
SCIBERRAS,	Edward	Ck (O)	E/LX	23472	Barham	11 Nov 40
SCICLUNA,	Anthony	Ck (O)	E/LX	22446	Glorious	9 Jun 40
SCICLUNA,	Michael	L/Std	E/LX	20710	Grafton	9 May 40
SHORT,	William	O C 1	E/L	5468	Royal Oak	14 Oct 39
SIMLER,	Joseph	Std	E/LX	25396	Gloucester	22 May 41
SPITERI,	Alfred	Std	E/LX	22825	Nile	20 Jun 42
SPITERI,	Egidio	Sto 1st Cl	E/KX	98322	Nile	8 Nov 42
SPITERI,	Francis	Ck (O)	E/LX	21958	Glorious	9 Jun 40

ROLL OF HONOUR

SPITERI,	Joseph	Std	E/LX	22791	*Barham*	25 Nov 41
SPITERI,	Joseph	A B	E/JX	146466	*Eddy*	20 May 42
SPITERI	Paul	P O Std	E/LX	20727	*Eagle*	10 Mar 41
SPITERI,	Salvo	C P O Std	E/LX	20717	*Glorious*	9 Jun 40
STAFRACE,	Vincent	L/Std	E/LX	21726	*Barham*	25 Nov 41
SULTANA,	Alfred	P O Std	E/LX	21828	*Hereward*	29 May 41
SULTANA,	Charles	L/Std	E/LX	23184	*Decoy*	13 Nov 41
SULTANA,	Vincent	Std	E/LX	22654	*Glorious*	9 Jun 40
TABONE,	Alfred	Sto	E/KX	117700	*Eddy*	26 May 42
TABONE,	Joseph	P O Std	E/LX	20744	*Zulu*	31 Oct 40
TAYLOR,	Joseph	Ck (O)	E/LX	23194	*Medway*	1 Jul 40
TESTA,	Anthony	O C 2	E/LX	23186	*Glowworm*	8 Apr 40
TIRCHETT,	Joseph	Std	E/LX	25643	*Lively*	11 May 42
TONNA,	Carmel	Ck (O)	E/LX	23469	*Diamond*	28 Apr 41
TONNA,	Nicholas	P O	E/JX	136892	*Nile*	8 Nov 42
TROISI,	Anthony	Std	E/LX	24325	*Kent*	17 Sep 40
VALLETTA,	Louis	Ck (O)	E/LX	22981	*Cornwall*	5 Apr 42
VASSALLO,	Carmel	P O Std	E/LX	21705	*Glorious*	9 Jun 40
VASSALLO,	Joseph	L/Std	E/LX	20820	*Gipsy*	20 Nov 39
VELLA,	Anthony	Std	E/LX	22885	*Glowworm*	8 Apr 40
VELLA,	Emanuel	Std	E/LX	583768	*Erebus*	25 Jul 43
VELLA,	Joseph	L/Std	E/LX	21139	*Juno*	21 May 41
VIDAL,	Henry	Ck (O)	E/LX	22317	*Decoy*	14 Nov 40
WADGE,	William	O C 3	E/LX	21093	*Glorious*	9 Jun 40
XERRI,	Emanuel	P O Std	E/LX	11125	*Gloucester*	22 May 41
XUEREB,	John	Ck (O)	E/LX	22100	*Royal Oak*	14 Oct 39
ZAHRA,	Carmel	Ck (O)	E/LX	22135	*Glorious*	9 Jun 40
ZAHRA,	John	Std	E/LX	20554	*Royal Oak*	14 Oct 39
ZAHRA,	Joseph	Std	E/LX	22982	*Glorious*	9 Jun 40
ZAMMIT,	Alfred	P O Std	E/LX	21720	*Decoy*	13 Nov 40
ZAMMIT,	Alfred	Std	E/LX	25380	*Medway*	19 Apr 42
ZAMMIT,	Emanuel	C P O Std	E/LX	13163	*Decoy*	13 Nov 40
ZAMMIT,	John	L/Std	E/LX	21887	*St Issey*	28 Dec 42
ZAMMIT,	Joseph	Ck (O)	E/LX	23471	*Glorious*	9 Jun 40
ZAMMIT,	Louis	Std	E/LX	25645	*Hyacinth*	19 Aug 42
ZARB,	Salvatore	P O Std	E/LX	20832	*Glorious*	9 Jun 40
ZARB,	Spiridione	A B	E/J	54002	*St Angelo*	5 Sep 41

ADDENDA

AZZOPARDI,	Carmel	L/Std	E/LX	20238	*Devonshire*	11 Feb 40
CUSCHIERI,	Carmel	L/Ck(S)	E/LX	20060	*Juno*	21 May 41
CUSCHIERI,	Joseph	L/Std	E/	362115	*St Angelo*	6 Feb 43
DEMICOLI,	Vincent	Asst Std	E/LX	25433	*Gloucester*	22 May 41
MALLIA,	John	L/Std	E/L	14927	*Malaya*	2 May 41
MIFSUD,	Joseph	A B	E/JX	146456	*St Angelo*	5 Sep 39
POULTER,	William	L/Sea	E/JX	145944	*Eddy*	26 May 42
SPITERI,	Emanuel	PO Ck (S)	E/LX	20334	*St Angelo*	15 Apr 45
TEUMA,	Carmel	Asst Ck (O)	E/LX	23469	*Diamond*	28 Apr 41

ROLL OF HONOUR

ROYAL MALTA ARTILLERY

AGIUS,	Francis	Gnr	41440	3rd Regt	20 Jul 42
ALLISON,	Alfred	Gnr	10951	1st Regt	30 Apr 41
ATTARD,	Joseph	Gnr	10690	2nd Regt	9 Apr 42
ATTARD,	Paul	Bdr	4290	2nd Regt	8 May 42
BALDACCHINO,	Francis	Gnr	10774	3rd Regt	20 Jul 42
BARTOLO,	Edgar	2/Lt	132208	1st Regt	30 Apr 41
BORG,	Lawrence	Gnr	40450	11th Regt (T)	11 Oct 42
BORG,	Saviour	Gnr	10721	2nd Regt	11 Mar 41
BUSUTTIL,	Philip	Boy	10129	1st Regt	11 Jun 40
CACHIA,	Loreto	Gnr	8269	3rd Regt	15 Jun 42
CALLEJA,	Joseph	Gnr	40067	RTD	30 Apr 41
CAMILLERI,	Joseph	Gnr	41573	2nd Regt	25 Mar 42
CAUCHI,	Seraphim	Gnr	8109	3rd Regt	9 May 42
CHRISTINA,	Gaetan	Sgt	3908	1st Regt	18 Apr 42
CORDINA,	Carmel	Gnr	10069	1st Regt	11 Jun 40
CUTAJAR,	Emanuel	Gnr	40274	11th Regt (T)	7 Apr 42
DALLI,	Theodore	Gnr	8411	3rd Regt	11 Apr 42
DARMANIN,	Carmel	Gnr	40772	1st Regt	17 Mar 42
DEBONO,	Paul	Gnr	10127	1st Regt	11 Jun 40
DINGLI,	Carmel	Gnr	40687	RTD	5 Jul 41
DINGLI,	Carmel	Gnr	40729	1st Regt	24 Apr 42
ELLUL,	Consiglio	Gnr	20299	3rd Regt	26 Apr 42
ELLUL,	Joseph	Gnr	10809	3rd Regt	20 Jul 42
FAELLA,	Joseph	Gnr	8217	3rd Regt	11 Apr 42
FALZON,	George	Gnr	10649	1st Regt	8 Apr 42
FALZON,	Joseph	Gnr	40458	11th Regt (T)	9 May 42
FARRUGIA,	Emanuel	WOII	3901	3rd Regt	12 Feb 42
FILLETTI,	Joseph	Gnr	20169	11th Regt (T)	2 Jan 42
FRENDO,	John Baptist	Gnr	41577	2nd Regt	8 Mar 42
GALEA,	Joseph	Bdr	3570	1st Regt	11 Jun 40
GALEA,	Joseph	Gnr	40531	11th Regt (T)	18 Apr 42
GRAVINA,	Thomas	Gnr	41551	1st Regt	15 Jan 42
GRECH,	Anthony	Gnr	40127	11th Regt (T)	7 Apr 42
GRECH,	John Mary	L/Bdr	4182	1st Regt	8 Apr 42
MALLIA,	Joseph	Gnr	40925	11th Regt (T)	8 Apr 42
MANGION,	Saviour	L/Bdr	4088	1st Regt	11 May 41
MICALLEF,	Roger	Gnr	4345	1st Regt	11 Jun 40
MIFSUD,	Anthony	Gnr	20243	11th Regt (T)	1 Apr 42
MIFSUD,	Saviour	Gnr	20275	3rd Regt	19 Apr 42
MIZZI,	Emanuel	Gnr	10168	1st Regt	8 Apr 42
MIZZI,	Joseph	L/Bdr	4185	1st Regt	30 Apr 41
MIZZI,	Michael	Gnr	4706	2nd Regt	18 Apr 42
MIZZI,	Spiridione	L/Bdr	3309	11th Regt (T)	7 Apr 42
PORTELLI,	Peter	Gnr	20099	11th Regt (T)	9 May 42
PULIS,	Carmel	L/Bdr	3997	1st Regt	30 Apr 41
REDMAN,	Charles	Gnr	10743	3rd Regt	8 May 42
SALIBA,	Michael Angelo	Gnr	3084	1st Regt	11 Jun 40

ROLL OF HONOUR

SAMMUT,	Joseph	L/Sgt	3943	1st Regt	24 Apr 42
SAMMUT,	Michael	Gnr	40469	11th Regt (T)	10 May 42
SCHEMBRI,	Carmel	Gnr	8096	3rd Regt	13 Jul 42
SILLATO,	Saviour	Gnr	10677	3rd Regt	20 Jul 42
SPITERI,	Lawrence	Gnr	8290	3rd Regt	11 Apr 42
STORACE,	Anthony	Gnr	40762	1st Regt	15 Jan 42
TABONE,	Carmel	Gnr	40139	11th Regt (T)	7 Apr 42
TANTI,	Carmel	Gnr	40282	11th Regt (T)	7 Apr 42
TEDESCO,	Pius	Gnr	41560	2nd Regt	25 Mar 42
UNGARO,	Vincent	Gnr	41587	2nd Regt	6 Mar 42
VELLA,	Francis	L/Bdr	4714	3rd Regt	7 Jul 42
VELLA,	Joseph	Gnr	10674	RTD	30 Apr 41
VELLA,	Paul	Gnr	4331	2nd Regt	25 Mar 42
ZAHRA,	Carmel	WOII	3860	2nd Regt	23 May 42
ZAMMIT,	Albert	Gnr	10789	3rd Regt	20 Jul 42
ZAMMIT,	Paul	Gnr	4026	1st Regt	24 Apr 42
ZAMMIT,	Saviour	Gnr	20252	3rd Regt	16 May 41
ZARB,	Fidele, MM	L/Sgt	4371	3rd Regt	20 Jul 42
ZARB,	Gaetan	L/Bdr	40029	3rd Regt	13 Feb 42
ZARB,	Joseph	Gnr	4215	1st Regt	29 Apr 41

ROLL OF HONOUR

KING'S OWN MALTA REGIMENT

ABELA,	Joseph	Pte	6787	Static Grp	21 Mar 42
ATTARD,	John	Pte	6519	Static Grp	26 Dec 41
ATTARD,	Paul	Pte	6430	Static Grp	16 Apr 42
BALDACCHINO,	Anthony	Pte	51621	1st Bn	25 Apr 42
BONELLO,	Anthony	Pte	51111	Static Grp	18 Apr 42
BONELLO,	George	L/Cpl	35163	2nd Bn	15 Jul 42
CAMENZULI,	Carmel	Pte	51459	RTD	2 Apr 42
DEBONO,	Saviour	Pte	7793	2nd Bn	1 Mar 42
GRECH,	Nazzareno	Pte	51573	RTD	25 Apr 42
GRIMA,	Joseph	Pte	50849	1st Bn	7 Apr 42
McGILL,	Robert	Pte	7858	3rd Bn	13 Feb 41
MICALLEF,	Anthony	Pte	6793	Static Grp	24 Mar 42
MIFSUD,	Dominic	Pte	6675	Static Grp	15 Mar 42
REFALO,	Joseph	Cpl	6452	3rd Bn	5 Mar 42
SALIBA,	Anthony	Pte	6902	Static Grp	19 Apr 42
SAMMUT,	John	Pte	51611	RTD	25 Apr 42
SPITERI,	Gregory	L/Cpl	1275	1st Bn	24 Jan 42
SPITERI,	John	Pte	51163	3rd Bn	19 Jan 42
TANTI,	Emanuel	Pte	6783	Static Grp	6 Jul 41
TORPIANO,	Victor	L/Cpl	35180	3rd Bn	1 May 42
VELLA,	Dominic	Pte	1570	1st Bn	31 May 42
VELLA,	Vincent	Pte	50305	2nd Bn	15 Feb 42
XUEREB,	Publius	Cpl	1372	1st Bn	28 Apr 42

MALTA PIONEER GROUP

CASHA,	Vincent	Pte	6863		20 Oct 42
CUTAJAR,	Emanuel	Pte	6419		14 Aug 43
PORTELLI,	Carmel	Pte	7508		23 Aug 43
SANT,	Paul	Pte	80271		23 Aug 43

MALTA AUXILIARY CORPS

BORG,	Francis	Cook	3872		24 Jun 41
BROWNRIGG,	Joseph	Artificer	5957		10 May 42
DUCA,	Emanuel	Driver	5812		10 Mar 42
GRECH,	Francis				8 Feb 41
MICALLEF,	Vincent	Driver	4345		24 Mar 42

ROLL OF HONOUR

ROYAL REGIMENT OF ARTILLERY
12th FIELD REGIMENT

FOSTER,	Jack	Sgt	822839	26 Apr 41
HARRIS,	Ronald	L/Bdr	940950	6 Oct 42
HEMMINGFIELD,	Edward	Gnr	981780	11 Feb 43
HORNSEY,	Frederick	Gnr	805117	15 Aug 42
PATEMAN,	William	Gnr	816497	10 Apr 41
TUCKER,	Clarence	WOII	1058628	5 Jan 41

4th COAST REGIMENT

ALLEN,	Bertie	Gnr	859409	7 Apr 42
BEAUMONT,	Leonard	WOII	1418685	25 Feb 42
FITENI,	Antonis	WOII	850730	17 Jun 41
FULLER,	Herbert	Gnr	1603080	7 Apr 42
GATES,	Frederick	WOI	1056171	15 Nov 41
McCARTHY,	John	Sgt	845004	25 May 42
MORRIS,	Frederick	L/Sgt	1420719	26 Jul 41
NUNN,	Stanley	L/Bdr	4201368	6 Apr 42
THOMPSON,	Richard	Gnr	1784240	7 Apr 42
TRETHOWAN,	Tom	Sgt	1023014	12 Sep 43

4th HAA REGIMENT

ASHARD,	Edward	Gnr	1517550	7 Mar 42
ATKINS,	Sidney	Gnr	1560108	23 Feb 42
BARRETT,	Henry	Gnr	1676181	2 May 42
BROADHURST,	Alfred	L/Bdr	1778056	25 May 42
BURFIELD,	Thomas	Gnr	926754	1 Apr 42
CLARK,	Ernest	Gnr	869120	7 Mar 42
CLEE,	Richard	Bdr	1549773	22 Jun 42
DERBYSHIRE,	Frank	Gnr	1676219	10 Jul 43
FITZSIMONS,	John	Gnr	3598158	25 May 42
FRENCH,	Cecil	Gnr	1653736	22 Apr 42
GENTLE,	Harry	L/Bdr	1653655	22 Apr 42
GILBERT,	William	Gnr	1653691	22 Apr 42
GREEN,	George	Gnr	1535481	1 Aug 43
HALE,	Howard	Gnr	876394	15 Mar 40
HART,	Jack	Gnr	1626517	12 Feb 42
HOVELL,	John	L/Bdr	818856	12 Apr 42
INGRAM,	John	L/Sgt	784432	7 Mar 42
JAMES,	R F	Gnr	1777227	7 Mar 42
JONES,	William	Gnr	1611747	12 Feb 42
KELLY,	William	Gnr	3850045	25 May 42
LONGVILLE,	Walter	Bdr	806252	25 May 42
MADDEN,	Michael	Gnr	1512951	14 Mar 42
MORLAND,	Joseph	Gnr	4449802	12 Apr 40
MORRIS,	Evan	Gnr	1701591	18 Aug 41
NIXON,	Gilbert	Gnr	1523772	22 Apr 42
NORRIS,	Albert	Bdr	1560204	22 Apr 42
O'BRIEN,	George	Gnr	1777080	25 May 42
O'BRYAN,	Thomas	Gnr	822371	7 Mar 42
RICHARDSON,	Thomas	Gnr	1576257	1 May 42
SCARBOROUGH-TAYLOR,	John	L/Bdr	922034	1 Apr 42
SEAMARKS,	Walter	Gnr	5884025	25 Apr 42
SMITH,	Ernest	Gnr	1535523	1 Apr 42

ROLL OF HONOUR

SMITH,	Walter	Gnr	1783939	6 Mar 42
WALKER,	George	Sgt	4338070	25 Apr 42
WARD,	Harold	Gnr	791311	25 May 42
WHITTER,	Walter	Gnr	1676088	7 Mar 42
WOOD,	Jack	L/Sgt	815133	7 Mar 42

7th HAA REGIMENT

ANDREWS,	Robert	Bdr	1073436	25 Apr 42
BESANT,	Albert	Bdr	1071117	6 Jul 42
BLUNT,	Eric	Bdr	1528789	14 Apr 42
BROWN,	Edward	L/Bdr	868921	7 Jan 42
BROWN,	Philip	Gnr	1566822	1 Nov 41
CARDEN,	John	Bdr	2034362	28 Aug 43
CLARKE,	John	S/Sgt	1422511	10 Apr 42
CONNELL,	James	Gnr	4268906	1 Nov 41
CRANKSHAW,	Stanley	Gnr	1536243	24 Mar 41
CROSSLAND,	Beryl	Gnr	1778086	1 Nov 41
CUNNINGHAM,	Anthony	Gnr	1532087	19 Apr 42
DEAN,	Edward	Gnr	876392	29 Nov 40
DUTTON,	Randolph	L/Sgt	868889	3 Jul 42
FORD,	George	Gnr	5437991	18 Apr 42
GOATLEY,	Norman	Gnr	863564	18 Jan 41
HAMPTON,	Francis	Gnr	850568	1 Nov 41
HOPKINSON,	Frederick	L/Bdr	1503028	27 Jun 41
JONES,	Edward	Gnr	4690234	23 Jan 41
LEWIS,	Tom	Gnr	1536019	26 Mar 42
McFARLANE,	P	Gnr	4613592	29 May 43
MENGHAM,	Albert	Bdr	821121	10 May 42
RAFFERTY,	Frank	Gnr	868656	30 Mar 41
ROWLEY,	John	L/Bdr	856569	19 Jan 41
SHARPLES,	George	Bdr	3763471	1 Nov 41
SMITH,	Stanley	Gnr	880744	8 Apr 42
TAYLOR,	Peter	Gnr	1536395	7 Apr 42
TAYLOR,	Thomas	Gnr	872938	11 Jun 40
VAUGHAN,	John	Gnr	1535952	24 Dec 41

10th (later 68th) HAA REGIMENT

ALLEN,	Gerard	BQMS	1451651	30 Dec 42
ALLEN,	William	Gnr	1587348	25 Apr 42
ALLEN,	Wilfred	Gnr	1597300	2 Apr 42
ALLSOP,	Stephen	Gnr	1432931	26 Apr 42
ANDERSON,	Joseph	Capt	121499	5 Feb 42
BAINES,	Wilfred	Gnr	1446189	7 Apr 42
BARNES,	George	Gnr	1597309	7 Apr 42
BARRATT,	John	Gnr	1597308	7 Apr 42
BROAD,	Eric	L/Bdr	1512135	7 Apr 42
BROMLEY,	William	Gnr	1502830	7 Apr 42
BUDDEN,	James	Gnr	1602626	25 Apr 42
BUNN,	Cyril	Gnr	967202	19 Apr 42
CARRUTHERS,	William	Gnr	909018	7 Apr 42
CARTER,	Sydney	Gnr	1532683	19 Apr 42
CASTLE,	Charles	L/Bdr	967206	19 Apr 42
COLLINS,	William	Bdr	967209	2 Oct 43
COOPER,	Horace	Gnr	1592037	29 Apr 42
CULLEN,	Andrew	Bdr	1536802	19 Apr 42
DAVIES,	Gerald	L/Bdr	1062660	6 Apr 41

ROLL OF HONOUR

DITHERIDGE,	James	Gnr	846109	19 Apr 42
FAWCETT,	John	Gnr	1559901	19 Apr 42
GWINNUTT,	Charles	L/Sgt	820912	27 Apr 42
HILL,	John	Gnr	1597238	7 Apr 42
HILL,	William	Gnr	864583	25 Apr 42
HYDE,	Herbert	L/Bdr	1620227	27 Dec 44
JARY,	William	Gnr	1838517	2 Feb 45
JOHNSON,	Albert	L/Bdr	1431032	19 Apr 42
LLOYD,	Harold	Gnr	1536812	25 Apr 42
MANSELL,	John	Gnr	1777003	19 Apr 42
MILLS,	Leslie	Gnr	1562319	2 Feb 42
MOSS,	Michael	Bdr	869467	19 Aug 43
OSBORNE,	Jeffrey	Bdr	1471693	2 Apr 42
PUGHE,	Cyril	Bdr	879202	19 Apr 42
QUINE,	P			
SAFE,	P			
SANDELL,	John	Lt (QM)	183499	5 Feb 42
SIMM,	John	Gnr	911163	7 Apr 42
SMITH,	Thomas	Gnr	870213	19 Apr 42
STEWART,	James	Gnr	1559916	19 Apr 42
SUTTON,	Leslie	Bdr	1455859	2 Apr 42
TOMASINA,	Arthur	Sgt	1465215	1 Feb 45
TURNER,	Harry	Gnr	1428049	25 Apr 42
THREADGALL,	Thomas	Gnr	1575196	10 Apr 42
VERNON,	John	Gnr	865826	7 Apr 42
VICKERS,	Samuel	Gnr	1442589	19 Apr 42
WALKER,	Ernest	Gnr	2045989	25 Apr 42
WILES,	Cyril	Gnr	1602811	25 Apr 42
WORRALL,	Geoffrey	Bdr	1451583	8 Apr 42
YATES,	Bernard	L/Sgt	898582	25 Jan 45
YEOMANS,	Cyril	L/Bdr	864910	25 Apr 42

32nd LAA REGIMENT

BERRY,	Tom	Gnr	1734717	22 Apr 42
BOOTH,	James	Gnr	1734570	22 Apr 42
BOYINGTON,	Rowland	Gnr	1770930	30 Dec 41
BRODIE,	Thomas	Gnr	1599508	1 May 42
CAMPBELL,	Hugh	Sgt	934900	30 Dec 41
CASEY,	Thomas	Gnr	1590941	25 Apr 42
CASS,	Robert	Sgt	967387	15 Feb 42
DEMPSTER,	William	L/Bdr	1485178	1 Feb 42
DRYDEN,	Edward	Gnr	1736469	22 Apr 42
GASKIN,	Herbert	Gnr	1770161	30 Dec 41
HUNTER,	Thomas	Gnr	1738045	24 May 42
JOHNSON,	Leonard	L/Sgt	1734761	14 Feb 42
KELLY,	Michael	Gnr	915414	22 Apr 42
LAWRENCE,	Bernard	Sgt	1714867	13 Feb 42
MARSHALL,	Henry	Gnr	1484189	18 Apr 42
MOLONEY,	Joseph	Gnr	1597100	19 Mar 42
NAYLOR,	Harold	Bdr	1734764	23 Apr 42
SMITH,	John	Gnr	1545729	2 Apr 43
WHITCHER,	Edwin	Gnr	1768767	13 Feb 42

65th LAA REGIMENT

KEEGAN,	John	Gnr	1643620	28 Apr 42
WOODLEY,	William	BQMS	1432710	16 Feb 42

ROLL OF HONOUR

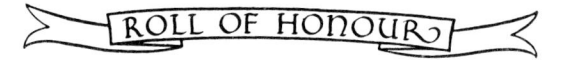

74th LAA REGIMENT

ANCIENT,	James	Gnr	1634664	4 May 42
BALAAM,	Alec	Gnr	1483563	26 Aug 42
BEARD,	Albert	L/Bdr	1601607	4 Feb 42
BURROWS,	Norman	Gnr	1616151	23 Feb 42
CHANDLER,	William	Gnr	1634689	31 May 42
DOWLING,	John	Gnr	1428571	23 Jan 42
FALVEY,	Cornelius	Gnr	1543021	22 Jun 42
FENSON,	Fred	Gnr	1523773	27 May 42
GLOVER,	Harold	L/Bdr	1616093	23 Feb 42
GOLDSMITH,	Alfred	Gnr	1657786	8 Jan 42
HANCOCKS,	Francis	L/Sgt	1634712	22 Jun 42
LEE,	David	L/Bdr	1429200	29 Jun 42
MORGAN,	Richard	2/Lt	185209	19 Mar 42
MUNDY,	Arthur	Gnr	1634757	29 Aug 42
THORNTON,	Jack	Gnr	1634782	29 Jun 42
WRIGHT,	Guy MC	Maj	45947	29 Dec 41

26th DEFENCE REGIMENT

ABBOTT,	James	Gnr	1725511	26 Oct 41
CANN,	William	Gnr	1714661	15 Mar 42
DAVIES,	Joseph	Sgt	780830	25 Mar 42
FURBER,	Leslie	Gnr	6344691	26 Apr 42
HINES,	Thomas	Gnr	1106177	7 Dec 41
KEATING,	James	Gnr	1106367	26 Apr 42
LAMBERT,	Fred	Sgt	884874	6 Jun 42
LODGE,	Thomas	Gnr	884176	14 Jan 42
MORRIS,	Percy	Gnr	1715565	25 Mar 42
MURPHY,	John	Gnr	1106718	11 Jul 42
NICHOLSON,	Harry	Gnr	1103085	26 Apr 42
SCOTT,	William	Sgt	1061642	18 Sep 43

4th SEARCHLIGHT REGIMENT RA/RMA

ANTHONY,	Frank	Gnr	2050606	21 Dec 41
BOWEN,	William	Bdr	2059893	1 Nov 41
BOWEN,	William	Gnr	2065899	6 Apr 42
COUPE,	Frank	Gnr	1628635	21 Dec 41
EVANS,	Lewis	Gnr	3953853	20 Apr 42
GOLDING,	James	L/Sgt	1052832	20 Apr 42
JAMES,	William	Gnr	1628644	21 Dec 41
MEYLER,	Harold	Gnr	2092526	7 Apr 42
MILLINGTON,	Walter	Gnr	1612313	22 Mar 42
NORTH,	Thomas	Gnr	1577517	27 Dec 41
NURSE,	Sidney	Gnr	3953122	20 Apr 42
PHILLIPS,	Alfred	Gnr	3947076	20 Apr 42
PORTER,	Alfred	Gnr	1576978	1 Nov 41
SEGON,	Alfred	Gnr	1601776	22 Mar 42
SELF,	Sidney	Gnr	1577185	6 Apr 42
SHAPLEY,	Frederick	L/Sgt	2021142	1 Nov 41
WATSON,	James	Gnr	1577333	2 Nov 41

ROLL OF HONOUR

ROYAL ARTILLERY — Miscellaneous

BOWYER,	Frank	Bdr	1698909	11 HAA Regt	6 Mar 42
BUTTERFIELD,	George	Gnr	840550	17 Defence Regt	9 Apr 41
COOTE,	Bert	Gnr	880829	13 Mobile Coast Defence Regt	3 Feb 41
DUFF,	Peter	L/Bdr	1776266	11 HAA Regt	6 Mar 42
GRIFFITHS,	William	Gnr	1612349	5 S/L Regt	23 Mar 42
HALL,	Alfred	Gnr	826513	5 HAA Regt	7 Mar 42
HOLTON,	Ernest	Gnr	1611735		24 Apr 41
LEE,	Edwin	Gnr	1810988	107 LAA Regt	24 Mar 44
MERINGO,	Frederick	Gnr	3856115	40 Bty 13 Mobile Coast Def Regt	5 Feb 41
POOLE,	Norman	Capt	143804		9 Jun 41
SKINNER,	James	Bdr	877987		25 Jun 41
STAPLES,	Henry	S/Sgt	1466413	11 HAA Regt	8 Apr 42
THORNTON,	Stephen	Gnr	6458318	12 LAA Regt	2 Jul 42

ARMY DENTAL CORPS

KELLY,	John	L/Cpl	7538008	28 Feb 41

ARMY — Miscellaneous

APSLEY, Allen Algernon Bathurst, Lord DSO, MC, TD — 1st Royal Gloucestershire Hussars, RAC	Major	17 Dec 42
MILLAR, Arthur David Curtis — Indian Army	Major	17 Dec 42

ROLL OF HONOUR

4th Bn THE BUFFS (ROYAL EAST KENT REGIMENT)

BOLAND,	Malachy	Sgt	6283806	22 Mar 41
BOORMAN,	James	Pte	6096441	15 Apr 41
CARD,	Royston	L/Cpl	6289876	13 Jul 43
DUNCAN,	John	Pte	5954539	24 Apr 41
FLETCHER,	Cyril	Pte	4396335	1 Oct 41
HARDY,	Aubrey	Pte	5954560	10 Jun 42
MATTHEWS,	Sydney	Pte	5954588	24 Apr 41
MILES,	John	Cpl	6394710	24 Apr 41
SIGRIST,	Arthur	Pte	6288342	3 Jan 42
SIVIOUR,	Raymond	Pte	6288229	21 Mar 42
STRINGER,	Albert	Pte	6286014	6 May 42
TAYLOR,	Victor	Pte	6288274	3 Jan 43
WOODWARD,	Harry	Pte	6286778	24 Apr 41

8th Bn THE KING'S OWN ROYAL REGIMENT (LANCASTER)

ATKINSON,	Frederick	Cpl	3714730	21 Mar 43
BATTEN,	Harold	Pte	1440953	12 Jan 43
CRAWFORD,	Robert	L/Cpl	2087421	22 Feb 42
LAIDLAW,	Robert	Pte	3178692	22 Jul 44
ROGERS,	George	Pte	4200733	15 Jun 43
SALKELD,	Joseph	Pte	3717811	21 Apr 40
SHARP,	Laurie	Lt.	153845	15 Jul 43
WADE,	Walter	Pte	3778302	20 Aug 42
WILSON,	Alexander	Pte	2070182	17 Feb 42

2nd Bn THE DEVONSHIRE REGIMENT

CHANNON,	Leonard	Pte	5616618	24 Mar 42
COLES,	Ronald	Pte	5625205	11 Dec 41
CONNOR,	William	Cpl	820624	8 May 42
EDWARDS,	Sydney	Pte	5619318	24 Mar 42
FOOTE,	John	Pte	5619974	29 Jul 40
FROST,	Ronald	Pte	5619814	8 Oct 40
GALTON,	Leonard	L/Cpl	5626532	18 Apr 42
HEARL,	William	Cpl	5615313	20 Jul 42
HILLMAN,	Walter	Pte	5615574	23 Jun 42
HOARE,	James	Pte	5613343	1 Jul 42
KELLOND,	Frederick	Sgt	5613668	9 Jul 40
KEYS,	William	Pte	878860	1 Feb 43
KITE,	Henry	Pte	5615850	13 Jun 40
LAKE,	Francis	Pte	5625172	27 May 42
LOCK,	Reginald	Pte	5615801	8 Dec 41
MARTIN,	Sidney	Pte	5620132	3 Apr 42
PAYNE,	Tom	Pte	5617558	3 Apr 42
PHILLIPS,	Arthur	Pte	5493555	14 Nov 40
PIPER,	Kenneth	Pte	5619245	7 Sep 41
ROOKE,	Ronald	Pte	5624769	4 Sep 42
ROWE,	Charles	Pte	2042213	1 Apr 42
SCOTT,	James	Pte	5623724	13 Feb 41
SHEPHERD,	Edmund	L/Cpl	5616622	8 May 42
SLADE,	John	Pte	7342748	13 Jun 40
SPRINGETT,	Thornton	Sgt	729888	1 Jul 42
STOCKHALL,	William	Pte	5614136	24 Mar 42
WALKE,	Felix	L/Cpl	5618892	28 Mar 42
WATSON,	Frank	Pte	5623376	6 Jul 41
WINGETT,	Frederick	Pte	5622174	21 Jan 42

ROLL OF HONOUR

11th Bn THE LANCASHIRE FUSILIERS

CROSLAND,	Ernest	Fus	3458424	7 Apr 42
HOPWOOD,	Herbert	Fus	3457389	8 Feb 42
MILNE,	Charles	Fus	3458263	8 Apr 42
NICKLIN,	George	Cpl	3452887	9 Apr 42
OWEN,	Norman	2/Lt	187022	20 Nov 41
PATT,	John	L/Cpl	3445968	20 Mar 42
PENNINGTON,	James	Fus	3460962	10 Aug 44
ROBINSON,	Harold	Fus	3457488	25 Apr 42
RUSSELL,	Harold	Fus	3457519	20 Mar 42
TAYLOR,	Cyril	Cpl	3457520	31 Aug 41
THARBY,	William	Fus	3457439	11 Aug 43
WALLWORK,	Thomas	Fus	3445096	15 Feb 42
WOOTTON,	William	Fus	3441960	26 Jun 42
WORSTER,	Henry	Fus	3070658	8 Apr 42

1st Bn THE CHESHIRE REGIMENT

BROWN,	Joseph	Pte	R/4131429	2 Jul 42
BYERS,	Francis	Pte	4126001	15 Feb 42
CONLON,	Samuel	Sgt	4189697	15 Jul 42
DAVIES,	Harry	Lt	216548	20 Jun 42
EDWARDS,	Thomas	Pte	4130237	8 May 42
HANNON,	John	Sgt	4122959	9 Apr 42
HARVEY,	Leonard	Pte	4121603	9 May 42
HAWKESLEY,	Alex	Pte	4127788	18 Feb 42
JOHNSON,	Albert	Cpl	4122825	25 Apr 42
JONES,	William	Pte	4130773	9 Mar 42
LEVER,	Lindon	Pte	4130692	9 May 42
LIVINGSTONE,	Henry	Pte	4123584	19 Apr 42
LODWICK,	Henry	Pte	4130814	8 May 42
MALONEY,	Thomas	Cpl	4122349	9 May 42
RIMMER,	Frederick	Pte	4122992	6 Dec 42
SCHOLEY,	Stephen	Pte	4130693	10 May 42
SMALL,	Raymond	Pte	4126274	9 May 42
TARR,	Gerald	L/Cpl	4131396	31 Oct 42
TAYLOR,	Arthur	Pte	4122844	28 Apr 42
WILSON,	Frank	Pte	4123514	15 Feb 42
YATES,	Ronald	Pte	4129635	23 Dec 41

1st Bn THE HAMPSHIRE REGIMENT

BARNES,	Kenneth	Pte	5504893	13 Jul 42
BEABEY,	Lorenzo	Pte	5505041	29 Aug 41
BRANDRETH,	John	Pte	3653408	13 Jan 42
CHANT,	Henry	Pte	5503654	13 Jan 42
CHINNOCK,	Robert	Sgt	844797	12 Apr 42
CLARKE,	Frederick	L/Cpl	5499177	26 Dec 41
DAWKINS,	Leonard	L/Cpl	5502887	25 Feb 42
DICKS,	Lenard	Pte	5495944	13 Jul 42
DUDMAN,	William	Pte	5498264	15 Feb 42
FLATMAN,	Robert	CQMS	5494437	14 May 41
FRAMPTON,	Thomas	Pte	4595776	23 Feb 42
GILES,	Victor	Pte	5497889	5 Mar 42
GREEN,	Edward	Pte	5494149	29 Jun 42
KELLY,	William	Pte	5498253	19 Aug 42
LAWRENCE,	James	Pte	5498441	9/10 Nov 41

ROLL OF HONOUR

LIPSCOMBE,	Leonard	Pte	5498286	14 Aug 43
MORGAN,	William	Pte	5499766	29 Jun 42
MURPHY,	Dennis	Pte	5498451	2 Jan 42
SMITH,	James	Pte	5498447	8 May 42
TOLCHER,	George	Sgt	5495946	29 Nov 41

1st Bn THE DORSETSHIRE REGIMENT

BARTLETT,	William	Pte	5726497	16 Jan 43
BELL,	John	L/Cpl	6539389	12 Jul 42
CARTER,	Arthur	L/Sgt	5724554	2 Jun 41
CARTER,	Reginald	L/Cpl	5725249	20 Jan 42
DALE,	Peter	2/Lt	117691	12 Jul 41
DAVIES,	George	Pte	5725764	2 Jun 41
EVANS,	Berkley	WOII	2815185	1 Dec 42
EVANS,	Edgar	Cpl	5497037	10 Apr 42
FOLLETT,	Guy	2/Lt	109027	30 Jan 41
FOOTE,	William	Cpl	804988	1 Apr 42
FRENCH,	Ernest	Pte	5733043	1 Apr 42
HOUSE,	Arthur	Pte	825185	7 Jul 40
JAMES,	Alfred	L/Cpl	5724574	19 Apr 42
JAMES,	Frederick	Pte	5723015	13 Dec 41
LE PROVOST,	George	Pte	5725620	12 Jul 40
MACPHERSON,	Donald	Pte	5495224	19 Apr 42
MALCOLM,	Maurice	L/Cpl	5724730	12 Jul 40
MEADER,	William	Pte	5728807	26 May 42
PEACE,	Cecil	Pte	5724298	8 Apr 42
PEARCE,	Charles	L/Cpl	5725738	1 Apr 42
PORTER,	George	L/Cpl	5728008	27 May 42
SEVILLE,	Thomas	Pte	5724290	3 Nov 42
SMITH,	Francis	Pte	5723854	23 Jan 42
TALBOT,	Francis	Pte	5728944	21 Nov 41
TREADWELL,	George	Lt	178951	20 Apr 42
WELLMAN,	John	Pte	5725052	15 Feb 41

2nd Bn THE QUEEN'S OWN ROYAL WEST KENT REGIMENT

BYRNE,	James	L/Cpl	6344674	24 Jun 42
EDWARDS,	Frederick	Pte	6343382	25 Apr 42
GREEN,	Herbert	Cpl	6343257	27 Apr 42
HIGGINS,	Arthur	Pte	6343638	3 Mar 41
HOLFORD,	Charles	Pte	6343628	3 Jan 42
HUMPHRIES,	Charles	Pte	6342696	23 Jan 43
HURLEY,	Raymond	Pte	6344521	31 Oct 42
JONES,	William	Pte	6343762	12 Nov 39
KENT,	Rodney	Pte	6287135	24 Jul 42
LEAGAS,	Thomas	Pte	6410606	17 Aug 43
MARTIN,	John	Pte	2045666	26 Nov 39
MOXON,	Charles	Cpl	6342058	19 Dec 40
O'SULLIVAN,	Patrick	Pte	6343265	25 Apr 42
PANTON,	Reginald	Pte	6342887	12 Feb 42
RYAN,	Thomas	Pte	6093595	27 Mar 42
SUTER,	Arthur	Pte	6342886	28 Apr 42
TURNER,	Percy	Pte	6344901	24 Jun 40
URQUHART,	Leslie	Pte	6344394	25 Apr 42
WALKER,	Edward	Pte	6343616	25 Apr 42

ROLL OF HONOUR

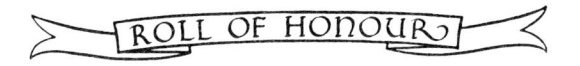

8th Bn THE MANCHESTER REGIMENT

ADAMS,	William	Pte	3511933	29 Jan 41
DUCKWORTH,	Lawrence	Pte	3530444	5 Feb 41
EATON,	Thomas	L/Cpl	3529357	29 Mar 42
GREENHALGH,	Herbert	Pte	3858177	13 Jul 43
LOCO,	Arthur	Pte	3525140	25 Apr 42
MAY,	Cyril	WOII	3524654	23 May 42
FARRINGTON,	John	Pte	3529187	29 Mar 42
MITCHELL,	Donald	Pte	3531808	9 Feb 42
PATTEN,	Charles	Pte	3524791	29 Mar 42
RATHBONE,	John	Pte	3526551	9 Apr 42
SPINKS,	William	Pte	3858001	9 Feb 42
THOMAS,	Philip	Pte	4196338	27 Jan 41
TINGEY,	William	L/Cpl	3531466	18 Dec 42
WALKER,	Edward	Pte	3858407	4 Jul 42

1st Bn THE DURHAM LIGHT INFANTRY

BARROWMAN,	James	Pte	2987569	22 Apr 42
CHAPMAN,	John	Pte	4470492	17 Aug 43
CLARKE,	Henry	Pte	4450608	21 Jun 42
DEWHURST,	John	Pte	4269895	22 Mar 42
DOUGLASS,	Roy	Pte	4463148	22 Apr 42
GARDINER,	Stephen	Pte	4462437	21 Mar 42
GARDNER,	Harry	L/Cpl	4450130	5 Jul 42
GARNICK,	James	Pte	4451285	21 Mar 42
HALL,	Gerald	Pte	4451559	4 Jul 42
HARROLD,	Ivan	Pte	6026833	8 Apr 42
LEVEY,	Charles	Pte	6025634	21 Mar 42
MURRAY,	James	Pte	4460644	21 Mar 42
ROGERSON,	William	Cpl	4269087	24 Apr 42
SADLER,	Robert	Pte	4459647	21 Mar 42
WAKE,	John	Pte	4460787	21 Mar 42
WARNER,	Tom	L/Cpl	4037190	20 Jun 42
WATERHOUSE,	Jack	Pte	2080445	27 Sep 43

2nd Bn THE ROYAL IRISH FUSILIERS

BALDWIN,	Douglas	Cpl	6978499	21 Mar 42
BROWN,	William	L/Cpl	3770585	21 Mar 42
BURKE,	Joseph	Fus	7043204	24 Jun 41
BYRNE,	Francis	Capt	45019	30 May 40
GALLAGHER,	Terence	L/Cpl	6207239	21 Mar 42
GOUGH,	Henry	Capt	71211	15 Feb 42
HAUNCE,	Albert	Fus	6978473	15 Feb 42
HAWKINS,	Harry	Fus	6978783	28 Apr 41
LOW,	Peter	Capt	95532	15 Feb 42
MILLAR,	John	Fus	3311596	24 Jul 41
NEEDHAM,	Fred	Fus	3860492	19 Aug 43
POLLOCK,	James	Fus	6978757	15 Sep 41
POYNTER,	Cyril	Cpl	5826568	25 Apr 42
PURVIS,	Samuel	Fus	6979112	26 Apr 42
REES,	Charles	Fus	4460365	13 Dec 41
THOMPSON,	Edward	Fus	6978732	20 Mar 42
TURNBULL,	John	Fus	6978944	5 Jul 42
VERNON,	Harold	Fus	6978496	21 Mar 42
WATTON,	Alexander	L/Cpl	6977994	29 Apr 41
WHELAN,	Michael	L/Cpl	7043205	1 Apr 41

ROLL OF HONOUR

ROYAL ENGINEERS

BODIAM,	William	L/Sgt	1866775	4 May 41
BRIFFA,	Paul	Spr	30216	5 Jun 42
BUGEJA,	Joseph	Spr	5052	24 Dec 43
CADOGAN,	William	Sgt	1485818	23 Aug 43
CALLEJA,	John	Cpl	30392	17 Apr 43
CHAPPELL,	Fred	Cpl	2069708	1 Apr 42
CHIRCOP,	Joseph	Spr	30272	27 May 41
CUMMING,	Francis	Spr	2030838	10 Jun 42
EVANS,	Evan	Spr	4194968	1 Apr 42
FALZON,	Pacifico	L/Cpl	30430	21 Mar 42
FELTHAM,	Ronald	Spr	1877322	1 Apr 42
FRASER,	Alexander	Spr	4391979	23 Aug 43
GALEA,	Carmel	L/Sgt	30101	17 Apr 43
GARNHAM,	Arthur	L/Cpl	1872250	3/4 May 41
GRECH,	Francis	Spr	579	10 May 42
HALL,	James	Spr	4537587	10 Jun 42
HARRINGTON,	John	Sgt	1863912	3/4 May 41
HART,	Bernard	Spr	4746694	3/4 May 41
HAYES,	Henry	Spr	3452214	1 Apr 42
HEWITSON,	Robert	L/Cpl	1858388	16 Dec 41
JOHNSTON,	John	Lt	158213	25 Apr 43
JONES,	Jackie	Dvr	1906201	23 Aug 43
LEIGHTON,	William	Spr	2763355	1 Apr 42
MAMO,	Gerald	L/Cpl	30380	10 Jul 42
MIZEN,	Daniel	Spr	920622	1 Apr 42
O'GRADY,	William	Cpl	1872375	3/4 May 41
PSAILA,	Paul	Spr	5075	1 Apr 42
REID,	Robert	Spr	902921	22 Jul 44
SANDILANDS,	John	Spr	1902055	1 Apr 42
SOPER,	Leonard	Spr	5671562	20 Apr 42
TAYLOR,	Charles	Spr	1872862	3 May 41
TROISI,	Anthony	Spr	91005	17 Apr 43
VELLA,	Emanuel	Spr	30208	26 Apr 42
WADSWORTH,	John	Spr	1874195	3/4 May 41
WALLER,	William	Spr	2194398	7 Apr 42
WATSON,	William, MC	Capt	137569	25 Apr 43
WEAVER,	Clarence	Spr	1872500	1 Apr 42
WEBBER,	Peter	L/Cpl	1872562	3/4 May 41
WILLIAMS,	Glanville	Spr	911385	18 Nov 42

ROYAL CORPS OF SIGNALS

CHILDS,	Walter	Dvr	2333127	20 Jan 44
MIFSUD,	Richard	Sigmn	70523	25 Apr 42
PAGE,	Edward	L/Cpl	2314544	5 Apr 41
SAUNDERS,	John Ernest	Sigmn	2325411	27 Jun 40
WARD,	Albert	Sigmn	2341138	24 Dec 41

ROYAL ARMY SERVICE CORPS

BASCOMBE,	Derek	Cpl	S/181155	13 Jan 43
DEACON,	Harry	2/Lt	143228	19 Apr 41
GUNNS,	Herbert	Pte	T/206351	25 Mar 41
HOLTOM,	Francis	L/Cpl	S/5622617	14 Apr 43
ROBERTS,	Robert	Dvr	T/125872	30 Jun 43
TERRILL,	John	Dvr	T/258498	6 Apr 42
THOMPSON,	Peter att RAMC	L/Cpl	T/876491	21 Mar 42
URE,	James att RAMC	Sgt	T/45744	21 Mar 42

ROLL OF HONOUR

ROYAL ARMY MEDICAL CORPS

ARMSTRONG,	Douglas	Maj	115202	24 Sep 42
BLANKSBY,	D.	Pte	7379046	25 Apr 42
CLINGO,	Walter	L/Cpl	7385258	25 Apr 42
COUSENS,	Walter	S/Sgt	7256929	5 Jul 42
GINIES,	Samuel	Pte	60166	24 Dec 41
HOURIGAN,	Cornelius	S/Sgt	7012189	6 Feb 42
KANTER,	Philip	Pte	7393158	24 Oct 42
LOGUE,	William	Pte	7382585	25 Apr 42
MAIR,	Stewart	Capt	175675	18 Apr 42
POWELL,	O J	Cpl	7265613	25 Apr 42
SAGE,	Stephen	Pte	7389302	25 Apr 42
SALMON,	Norman	Pte	7391660	15 Sep 42
SEARLE,	John	Pte	7389312	25 Apr 42
TIMMINS,	Dennis	Pte	7259501	25 Apr 42
WAIT,	Jack	Cpl	7390794	25 Apr 42

ROYAL ARMY ORDNANCE CORPS

CLAPHAM,	Frederick	Pte	7612754	9 Sep 41
HALL,	Thomas	Pte	7619988	20 Jan 42
MOORE,	Vernon	Sgt	7584502	25 Apr 42
Attached 2nd Bn The QORWK Regt				
NEWMAN,	Alfred	WOI	757715	20 Jan 42
WHITTAKER,	Jarvis	S/Sgt	7600582	1 Mar 42

ROYAL ELECTRICAL AND MECHANICAL ENGINEERS

CHAPMAN,	George	Cfn	7627750	10 Aug 43
CLARKE,	Ronald	Sgt	7590452	11 Jun 43
SPRAGG,	Percival	Cfn	7631695	19 Oct 43
WEST,	George	Cfn	7630986	11 Aug 43

CORPS OF MILITARY POLICE

GILMORE,	Francis	L/Cpl	6978163	28 Feb 41
HUMPHREYS,	James	L/Cpl	3645833	22 Nov 42
WALKER,	John	L/Cpl	4123183	25 Apr 42
WHITE,	Frederick	WOI	7683598	17 Jun 42

ROYAL ARMY PAY CORPS

BAILEY,	John	Pte	7665642	13 May 43
BECKETT,	Leslie	Cpl	5826157	3 Apr 42
DAVIES,	Charles	Pte	7678505	2 Apr 42
DILLEY,	Alfred	Pte	7673850	25 Apr 42
GOLDING,	James	Capt	157003	20 Sep 42
GOLLEDGE,	Albert	Pte	7675913	2 Apr 42
HARROD,	Frank	Lt	183518	2 Apr 42
HEYWOOD,	Arthur	Pte	7674864	25 Apr 42
MAGUIRE,	Cyril	Pte	7680168	25 Apr 42
PULLAN,	Arthur	Pte	7674870	2 Apr 42
RUST,	Philip	Pte	7666418	25 Apr 42
TAPPIN,	Cecil	Pte	7666431	25 Apr 42

ROLL OF HONOUR

ROYAL AIR FORCE

(This list contains the names of RAF personnel buried in Malta. Those who were lost and have no known grave are not included; their names are shown on the Commonwealth Air Forces Memorial at Floriana.)

Surname	Name	Rank	Role	Number	Squadron	Date
ABELA,	Anthony	AC1		795188		2 Oct 43
ALLEN,	David	Plt Off	Pilot	42783	148 Sqn	3 Nov 40
ALPE,	Henry	Sgt	Nav/Radar	1603261	108 Sqn	2 May 44
ASHTON,	Dennis	Sgt	Pilot	741212	261 Sqn	26 Nov 40
ASKIN,	Ralph	Sgt		40957	RNZAF	12 Jul 41
ASPELL,	Everard	Sgt	WOAG	1064105	108 Sqn	3 Dec 42
ASQUITH,	James	LAC		1001817		8 Mar 42
ATKINSON,	Leslie	Cpl		613918		29 Jul 42
BACKES,	Trevor	AC1		906019	148 Sqn	18 Jan 41
BAINES,	George	AC1		1017872		24 Mar 42
BAKER,	Cecil	Flt Lt	Pilot	89400	126 Sqn	21 Mar 42
BALINSON,	Alexander	F/Sgt		R/64389	148 Sqn	24 Apr 42
BARLOW,	Edward	AC1		954524		18 Jan 41
BARTON,	Arthur	Flg Off	Pilot	145326	108 Sqn	17 Apr 44
BEATTIE,	Evan	Sgt	Pilot	964587		16 Jun 41
BEER,	Archibald	Flt Lt		43314		18 Apr 42
BEVERIDGE,	Robert	Flt Lt	Pilot	86337	38 Sqn	14 Apr 42
BIGGS,	Stanley	WO	Pilot	1263193	229 Sqn	7 Jan 44
BLYTH,	Arthur	Cpl		530020		30 Dec 41
BOLTON,	John	Sgt	Pilot	903615		16 Jun 41
BOND,	George	LAC		1302238	72 Sqn	20 Mar 42
BOND,	James	AC1		776764		16 Sep 41
BOORMAN,	George	LAC		913535		2 Mar 42
BOOTH,	John	Flg Off	Pilot	60093	249 Sqn	21 Mar 42
BORG,	Joseph	AC1		776857		11 Mar 41
BOYD,	John, DFM	Plt Off		404548	185 Sqn	14 May 42
BOYD,	Victor	WO	WOAG	R/71778	69 Sqn	4 May 43
BOYS-STONES,	John	Flg Off	Pilot	33434	69 Sqn	7 Mar 41
BRENTON,	Edward	Sgt		402272		16 Oct 41
BROADBENT,	Trevor	WO	Pilot	547116	108 Sqn	2 May 44
BROADWAY,	John	Sgt	Obs	989687	110 Sqn	15 Jul 41
BROOKS,	Lucien	F/Sgt	Pilot	R/74800	229 Sqn	25 Apr 42
BROWN,	Eric	Sgt	Pilot	1289528	458 Sqn	13 Feb 43
BROWN,	Peter	WO	WOAG	R/92308	458 Sqn	13 Feb 43
BROWNE,	Cyril	LAC		1069726	138 Sqn	17 Dec 42
BRUNTON,	Frederick	LAC		909910		2 Jan 43
BUNN,	John	Sgt	Nav	1612957	108 Sqn	18 Jun 44
BUNNETT,	George	Sgt		1325479	148 Sqn	7 Dec 42
BUTLER,	Leslie	Sgt	WOAG	1051918		16 Jun 41
CACHIA,	George	AC1		776870	229 Sqn	3 Jul 43
CALTON,	Douglas	LAC		1054303		23 Feb 42
CAMERON,	Donald	Plt Off	Air Obs	J/3267		16 Jun 41
CAMERON,	Douglas	Sgt		517813		28 Jan 41
CAMPBELL,	Alexander	AC2		1370099	185 Sqn	24 Mar 42
CANNON,	John	AC1		1233431		21 Jun 43
CARSWELL,	Robert	Cpl		293124		8 Sep 43
CASSAR,	Carmel	AC2		795604	283 Sqn	11 Sep 44
CHAPMAN,	Robert	Flg Of	Pilot	402567	21 Sqn	9 Aug 43
CHARRON,	Arthur	F/Sgt		R/54061		24 Apr 42
CHILDE,	Frederick	F/Sgt	WOAG	279462V	21 Sqn	23 Jul 43
CHRISTIAN,	Douglas	F/Sgt	Nav	1108283	21 Sqn	9 Aug 43

ROLL OF HONOUR

CIARLO,	John	LAC		776833		5 Jul 42
CLARK,	Campbell	F/Sgt	WOAG	550958	69 Sqn	11 Aug 41
CLARK,	Norman	LAC		801812		2 Jul 42
CLARKE,	Cecil	AC1		1200534		2 Jul 42
CLARKE,	Douglas	LAC		907554		8 May 42
CLARKE,	John	AC1		1075909		9 May 42
CLARKE,	Peter	Cpl		572133		21 Apr 42
CLARKE,	Thomas	Sgt		341491		18 Dec 41
CLAY,	Lionel	Sgt	Obs	914496		12 Jul 41
CLEGG,	Richard	LAC		1233498	138 Sqn	17 Dec 42
CLIFF,	John	Cpl		334172		15 Jun 44
COLLINS,	Walter	LAC		917643		18 Apr 42
COOK,	Stanley	Cpl		1280167		8 May 42
COOKE,	Ivan	Flg Off	Nav	132845	69 Sqn	2 Sep 43
CORFE,	Douglas	WO	Pilot	810075	229 Sqn	25 Apr 42
CORRY,	Daniel	Flg Off		154268	267 Sqn	10 Sep 44
COSTER,	George	Flg Off	Obs	145040	108 Sqn	8 Mar 44
CRAIG,	Lincoln	F/Sgt	Pilot	411376	104 Sqn	7 Nov 42
CRIPPS,	Walter	Plt Off	Pilot	J/5806	601 Sqn	26 Apr 42
CRUICKSHANK,	Gilbert	Cpl		535425		2 Jul 42
CRUICKSHANK,	William	Plt Off	Pilot	157415	185 Sqn	19 Oct 43
CULBERT,	Wilfred	Sgt	WOAG	1260278		26 Jun 42
CUNNINGHAM,	James	F/Sgt		970824	39 Sqn	6 Sep 42
CURRIE,	Ian	Plt Off	Pilot	95944	261 Sqn	30 Jan 41
CURTIS,	James	LAC		912458	126 Sqn	2 Sep 41
DANIELL,	Charles	F/Sgt		414207		14 Dec 43
DAVID,	Ronald	Cpl		974066		1 Apr 42
DAVIES,	Ernest	Sgt	WO	915315	104 Sqn	22 Oct 41
DAVIES,	George	F/Sgt	Air Obs	R/78498	104 Sqn	29 May 42
DAVIS,	Jack	F/Sgt		365231		8 May 42
DAWES,	Vincent	LAC		542749		23 Nov 40
DEWHURST,	James, MM	Sgt		1100752		21 May 42
DIVE,	Peter	Sgt		401273		23 Dec 41
DONALD,	Keith	Sgt	Air Gnr	411070	104 Sqn	7 Nov 42
DONCASTER,	John	Plt Off	Pilot	J/6401	235 Sqn	13 Jun 42
DOWDS,	Robert	LAC		978632	221 Sqn	15 Aug 43
DOWLAND,	John, GC	Wg Cdr	Pilot	33239	69 Sqn	13 Jan 42
DOWNER,	James	LAC		1358217		27 Jan 43
DRAINER,	John	LAC		1100537		13 Jul 42
DYER,	Ralph	F/Sgt	Pilot	1137726	185 Sqn	6 Oct 43
EARLE,	Peter	Flt Lt	Obs	44315	138 Sqn	17 Dec 42
EARNEY,	Herbert	F/Sgt	Obs	405371	104 Sqn	7 Nov 42
EATON,	William	Sgt	WOAG	1199104	114 Sqn	15 Nov 41
EDWARDS,	Henry, DFC	Sqn Ldr	Pilot	36227	108 Sqn	5 May 43
ELLIS,	Michael	LAC		944388		1 Apr 42
ENRIGHT,	Peter	LAC		29729		25 Jul 43
FARRUGIA-GAY,	John	AC2		777215		8 May 42
FINLAY,	Colin	Sgt	Pilot	1288189	185 Sqn	14 May 42
FIRTH,	Kenneth	Sgt	Pilot	570681	108 Sqn	18 Jun 44
FISHER,	Walter	AC1		1141853		24 Mar 42
FLEMING,	William	Cpl		411135		21 Jul 43
FLETCHER,	John	Plt Off	Pilot	J/15319	185 Sqn	28 Apr 42
FLETCHER,	Ronald	Sgt	Obs	1053905	21 Sqn	6 Feb 42
FLOWER,	William	LAC		1010438		26 Apr 42
FOLEY,	Thomas	Plt Off	Pilot	J/6292	229 Sqn	28 Apr 42
FORD,	Ernest	LAC		1072270	148 Sqn	8 Dec 42
FORRESTER,	Philip	Sgt		740529		4 Nov 40

311

ROLL OF HONOUR

FORSYTH,	Michael	Sgt	Nav	955168	108 Sqn	17 Apr 44
FORTH,	Alfred	F/Sgt	Pilot	1007456	185 Sqn	29 Dec 41
FOX,	Harry	Sgt		405353		13 Aug 42
FRENCH,	Timothy	Cpl		553198	126 Sqn	16 May 42
FULLALOVE,	John	Sgt	Pilot	1058227	229 Sqn	21 Apr 42
FULLBROOK,	William	AC1		903164		7 Jan 42
GALLICHAN,	Henry	LAC		1178015	185 Sqn	24 Mar 42
GARRETT,	Alfred	Sgt		400950		30 Mar 42
GIBBS,	Harold	F/Sgt		560149		30 Apr 42
GODWIN,	Lewis	Sgt		590507		28 Feb 41
GOODFELLOW,	Emrys	Sgt	Obs	1176272	37 Sqn	9 Mar 43
GOODMAN,	Reginald	LAC		1172764		21 Jun 43
GOULDING,	Terence	Lt	Obs	103794V	12 Sqn	23 Jul 43
GRANARD,	John	Cpl		1053026		3 Jan 42
GRANDFIELD,	Clifford	Sgt	WOAG	1253914	148 Sqn	8 Dec 42
GRAYSMARK,	Charles	Sgt	Pilot	1267255	601 Sqn	12 May 42
GREENACRE,	Harold	LAC		910484	249 Sqn	19 Jan 42
GRIFFITH,	Thomas	LAC		959417		4 Feb 42
GROSVENOR,	Francis	Sgt	Obs	1266029		20 Jun 42
GUERIN,	James	Flg Off		403136		21 Mar 42
GUTHRIE,	James	Plt Off	Pilot	120153	185 Sqn	2 Aug 42
HALEY,	George	F/Sgt	Nav/Bomber	974370	23 Sqn	5 Jun 43
HALL,	Geoffrey	Sgt	Pilot	740543	148 Sqn	14 Jan 41
HALL,	Ronald	Sgt	WOAG	1381186	21 Sqn	6 Feb 42
HALLETT,	William	Plt Off	Pilot	66559	126 Sqn	21 Mar 42
HAMILTON,	Claud	Plt Off	Pilot	90964	185 Sqn	14 May 41
HANCOCK,	George	Sgt	WOAG	1381377		6 Feb 42
HANDLEY,	S J	Lt	Obs	205752V		18 Aug 43
HANKINS,	Percy	Sgt	WOAG	910438	59 Sqn	18 Jan 42
HARDY,	Keith	Sgt	WOAG	R/72509		9 Apr 42
HARVEY,	Ray	F/Sgt	Pilot	R/67086	242 Sqn	1 Mar 42
HASLAM,	Reginald	Cpl		570282	185 Sqn	24 Mar 42
HAWKINS,	John	Sgt	Obs	926333		5 Apr 42
HAWKSLEY,	Reginald	Sgt	Nav	1212996	272 Sqn	6 Jun 43
HAYNES,	James	LAC		974206	185 Sqn	24 Mar 42
HAYTER,	Kenneth	Cpl		571417		18 Apr 42
HERMON,	Herbert	LAC		614311		29 Apr 41
HERRING,	Duncan	Flg Off		145764	157 Sqn	27 Jan 44
HEYWOOD,	Frank	Sgt	WOAG	553746	203 Sqn	23 Mar 43
HOARE,	John	AC1		1211791	69 Sqn	15 Jan 42
HOGARTH,	George	F/Sgt	Pilot	R/95351	249 Sqn	4 Oct 42
HOLE,	Reginald	AC2		1234992		27 Dec 43
HOLMES,	Oliver	Sgt	Air Gnr	778622	104 Sqn	7 Nov 42
HOLT,	George	LAC		1017442		10 Aug 42
HORN,	George	AC1		1169517		7 Jan 42
HOSKIN,	Stanley	LAC		1171811		1 Apr 42
HOUNSLOW,	Douglas	Cpl		1165159	138 Sqn	17 Dec 42
HOWARD,	David	Sgt	Pilot	1082376	69 Sqn	18 Dec 42
HOWARD,	Frank	Sgt	Pilot	777674	601 Sqn	20 May 42
HOWIESON,	George	Sgt		803556	185 Sqn	16 Jun 43
HOWROYD,	Stanley	F/Sgt	Pilot	935037	22 Sqn	14 Apr 42
HUBBARD,	Donald	Sgt	Pilot	1197623		28 Jul 42
HUDSON,	William	Sgt	WOAG	1113431	69 Sqn	2 Sep 43
HUNTLEY,	Arthur	F/Sgt		410488		19 Apr 44
ILSLEY,	Kenneth	F/Sgt	Pilot	1169997		9 Mar 43
JEMMETT,	Frank	Plt Off	Pilot	116904	601 Sqn	22 Apr 42

ROLL OF HONOUR

JENNINGS,	Henry	Sgt	Pilot	754910	261 Sqn	7 May 41
JOHNSON,	John	LAC		1120713		2 Jul 42
JOHNSON,	Kirke	Flg Off	Obs	126967	69 Sqn	4 May 43
JONES,	Allen	Sgt		530722	228 Sqn	7 Mar 41
JONES,	James	Cpl		628449		26 Jun 42
JONES,	John	F/Sgt	Pilot	1231189	108 Sqn	8 Mar 44
KEAM,	Montague, DSM	F/Sgt	WOAG	363999		8 Nov 41
KEEBLE,	Peter	Flt Lt	Pilot	37186		16 Jul 40
KELLY,	Stanley	AC1		1493201	138 Sqn	17 Dec 42
KEMP,	Robert	AC1		1116632		15 Feb 42
KEMPTON,	Maurice	Flg Off		J/9516	458 Sqn	13 Feb 43
KENNETT,	Peter	Plt Off	Pilot	82685	261 Sqn	11 Apr 41
KENT,	David	Flg Off	Pilot	101026	229 Sqn	23 Jul 42
KIN,	Harry	Cpl		971724		24 Mar 42
KING,	Gerald	AC2		1256284		4 Feb 42
KING,	William	AC1		624199		21 May 42
KIRKHAM,	William	LAC		944053	126 Sqn	22 May 43
KITCHEN,	John	F/Sgt		560634	148 Sqn	7 Dec 42
KITCHER,	Charles	AC2		705526		12 Sep 43
KNIGHT,	Norman	Sgt		402077		9 Mar 42
KOZLOWSKI,	Stanley	WO	Pilot	R/54174	37 Sqn	8 Mar 42
LAKIN,	Conrad	LAC		1193016	5051 Sqn	29 Aug 43
LAMBLE,	Ronald	AC2		1213882	69 Sqn	15 Jan 42
LAPISH,	Harry	AC1		1078237	126 Sqn	2 Jul 42
LEA,	Roland	Sgt		570361	89 Sqn	4 Jan 43
LEAVESLEY,	Stanley	LAC		1065959		15 Mar 42
LEE,	Edward	AC1		1314070	185 Sqn	24 Mar 42
LEE,	Joseph	WO	Obs	581342	22 Sqn	14 Apr 42
LEGGO,	Douglas	Plt Off	Pilot	80356	249 Sqn	20 Mar 42
LEVERINGTON,	Gerald	LAC		1269209		24 Mar 42
LEVY,	Jack	Sgt	WOp	548053	69 Sqn	7 Mar 41
LEWIS,	William	F/Sgt	Pilot	919631	683 Sqn	2 Sep 43
LINDSAY,	Alec	Flt Lt	Pilot	83982	185 Sqn	23 Oct 42
LIVINGSTON,	Alexander	Sgt	Pilot	742426	249 Sqn	18 Jun 41
LOCKWOOD,	Frank	Cpl		546564		8 May 42
LONG,	David	AC2		1281983		21 Oct 41
LUNDY,	Martin	F/Sgt	Pilot	1114229	229 Sqn	21 Nov 42
MACDONALD,	Roderick	AC2		1023150		11 Dec 41
MACDOUGAL,	Charles	Sgt	Pilot	811002	261 Sqn	5 Mar 41
MACKIE,	Alexander	Plt Off	Pilot	109893		29 Jan 42
MacMILLAN,	Duncan	LAC		904533		4 Oct 41
MACNAMARA,	Thady	Plt Off	Pilot	65586	242 Sqn	24 Feb 42
MacPHERSON,	Robert	Sgt	Pilot	900860	260 Sqn	14 Jun 41
MACQUEEN,	Norman, DFC	Flt Lt	Pilot	86689	249 Sqn	4 May 42
MAGRO,	Walter	AC1		777171		19 Sep 43
MALTBY,	George	AC2		947113		7 Jan 42
MANCHIP,	Arnold	AC1		1315240	185 Sqn	24 Mar 42
MARCH,	George	Sgt	Air Gnr	955584	262 Sqn	24 Mar 43
MARSDEN,	Donald	Sgt	WOAG	1021118	69 Sqn	23 Mar 43
MARTIN,	Eric	Sgt	Pilot	1375103	104 Sqn	6 Jun 42
MARTIN,	Jack	Sgt	Nav	1082119	256 Sqn	25 Jul 43
MATTHEWS,	Robert	Flg Off	Pilot	61248	249 Sqn	22 Dec 41
MATTHEWS,	Stephen	Sgt	Obs	1064002		26 Jun 42
MAY,	Arthur	Sgt		365514		28 Jan 41
MAYALL,	John	Plt Off		400150		10 Mar 42
McALLISTER,	Samuel	Flg Off	Pilot	67671	107 Sqn	16 Oct 41
McCANN,	Thomas, BEM	AC1		619213	40 Sqn	24 Nov 41

ROLL OF HONOUR

McCARTY,	John	LAC		1008310		8 May 42
McCLURE,	Charles	Flg Off	Pilot	108802	69 Sqn	4 May 43
McCOLL,	Andrew	Sgt	WOAG	1061860	104 Sqn	29 May 42
McCRACKEN,	John	F/Sgt	Pilot	748004	249 Sqn	20 Jul 41
McCRIRICK,	Robert	Cpl		1035584		30 Dec 42
McEWEN,	Murray	LAC		932286		26 Apr 42
McFARLANE,	John	Plt Off	Pilot	J/7428		28 Apr 42
McKEE,	Hugh	Plt Off		J/5103		5 Apr 42
McMAHON,	Thomas	Sgt	Air Gnr	1179931	69 Sqn	4 May 43
McMILLAN,	Herbert	Flg Off		409574		19 Apr 44
McNAUGHTON,	Andrew	Plt Off	Pilot	J/7465	185 Sqn	1 Jun 42
McNICOL,	William	LAC		573027		31 Dec 41
MERRITT,	Arnold	Sgt	Pilot	1290036	104 Sqn	24 May 42
METCALFE,	Henry	F/Sgt	WOAG	653570	69 Sqn	23 Dec 41
MEYRICK,	George	AC1		1135504	126 Sqn	2 Jul 42
MILBURN,	Harold	Plt Off	Pilot	112542	249 Sqn	9 May 42
MOORE,	Arthur	Sgt	WOAG	746926		12 Feb 42
MORGAN,	Albert	Sgt	Pilot	1239536	69 Sqn	2 Sep 43
MORIARTY,	Alec	AC2		577254		23 Apr 42
MORRIS,	Victor	Sgt		647926		26 Jan 42
MORRISON,	Samuel	Flg Off	Pilot	115396	104 Sqn	7 Nov 42
MOSS,	Eric	Sgt	WO Obs	1047847	23 Sqn	9 Jan 43
MURCUTT,	Alfred	Sgt	Obs	919872	82 Sqn	5 Jul 41
MURPHY,	Joseph	Sgt	WOAG	1237993	221 Sqn	23 Oct 43
MURRAY,	Kenric	Plt Off		400152		10 Mar 42
MUTIMER,	Richard, DFM	Sgt	Obs	581062	69 Sqn	10 Aug 41
NASH,	Peter, DFC	Plt Off	Pilot	113759	249 Sqn	17 May 42
NEALE,	Donald	Sgt	Pilot	1375372	242 Sqn	22 Jan 42
NEWMAN,	H G	Flt Lt		62087		14 Jan 43
NICHOLS,	Bertie	Cpl		1055807		2 Jul 42
NICOLLS,	Victor	Flt Lt		44747		11 Feb 42
NIELSEN,	Theodore	Cpl		640037		4 Feb 42
NORMAN,	Denis	Sgt	WOAG	1169618	217 Sqn	10 Jun 42
NUTTALL,	Ernest	LAC		1305857		30 Jun 43
OATEN,	Jack	Sgt	WOAG	939727	82 Sqn	5 Jul 41
OLLEY,	Peter	Sgt	Pilot	1236217	23 Sqn	9 Jan 43
ORMROD,	Oliver, DFC	Plt Off	Pilot	110128	185 Sqn	22 Apr 42
OSBORNE,	Albert, GC	LAC		1058637		1 Apr 42
OTIS,	Joseph	F/Sgt	Pilot	R/82872	249 Sqn	19 Jul 42
PALMER,	Ivan	Flg Off		403783		6 Jan 43
PARK,	Robert	Flg Off		404981		19 Nov 42
PARKS,	Walter	F/Sgt		403476		29 Oct 42
PARMENTER,	Sidney	Cpl		958639		8 May 42
PARRIS,	Sidney	AC1		1318457		21 May 43
PASSMORE,	John	Sgt	Pilot	1202043		30 Jun 42
PATERSON,	Alastair	F/Sgt		406461		7 Nov 42
PAUL,	Isaac	Plt Off	Obs	102610	107 Sqn	24 Dec 41
PAWSON,	Kenneth	Plt Off	Pilot	112442	601 Sqn	25 Apr 42
PENFOLD,	George	AC2		1237400		9 Feb 43
PHIMISTER,	James	LAC		1059343		13 May 43
PIROTTA,	Joseph	AC1		776890		30 Dec 41
PITT,	John	LAC		1178272	185 Sqn	10 Oct 42
PITT,	Joseph	Cpl		991595		1 Apr 42
POLLOCK,	Thomas	Sgt		402393		30 Mar 42
POOLE,	Frederick	LAC		620341		16 Feb 42
PORTELLI,	Joseph	LAC		776772		2 Jul 42
POVEY,	Frederick	Flt Lt		80867		1 Apr 42

ROLL OF HONOUR

PRESTON,	Martin	AC1		900259		2 Sep 41
PROUT,	Donald	LAC		1410738		2 Sep 43
PUTNAM,	Hiram	Plt Off	Pilot	J/15079	126 Sqn	21 Apr 42
QUINN,	Leslie	LAC		1059690	40 Sqn	24 Mar 42
RAMSAY,	William	Sgt	WOAG	1002037		12 Jul 41
RATTEE,	William	F/Sgt	Pilot	R/75092	203 Sqn	23 Mar 43
RAWLINGS,	David	Sgt	Pilot	526314		4 Nov 40
REARDON,	James	Sgt	Obs	749561	148 Sqn	13 Jan 41
REAY,	Thomas	Sgt	Air Gnr	751646		28 Jan 41
REED,	Charles	Sgt		402774		30 Mar 42
RELTON,	Frederick	WO		547166		13 Jun 42
RIORDAN,	Kenneth	Sgt		402775		30 Mar 42
RIPPER,	Donald	F/Sgt		409276		26 Oct 43
ROBBINS,	Arthur	AC1		1212776		9 Oct 42
ROBERTS,	Elwyn	Sgt	WOAG	915495	104 Sqn	29 May 42
ROBERTS,	V P	F/Sgt	WOAG	206453V	21 Sqn	18 Aug 43
ROBINSON,	Alexander	LAC		817180	249 Sqn	5 Feb 42
ROSS,	Kenneth	F/Sgt	Air Gnr	545687	104 Sqn	29 May 42
RYAN,	Jeremiah	AC1		1008738		7 Jan 42
SALIBA,	Anthony	LAC		776833		5 Jul 42
SALTER,	Arthur	LAC		1357188	2934 Sqn	31 Oct 43
SANDERS,	Cyril	Sgt	WO	1251297		16 Jun 41
SARGENT,	William	F/Sgt	Pilot	745120	110 Sqn	22 Jul 41
SAUNDERS,	Raymond	Sgt	Pilot	1332534	185 Sqn	24 Oct 42
SCADENG,	Hubert	Plt Off		80908		28 Feb 41
SCICLUNA,	Eugenio	LAC		776753		24 Mar 42
SEMLEY,	Ronald	Sgt	Air Gnr	1087497	40 Sqn	3 Dec 42
SHEARSBY,	Walter	Sgt		347503		23 Nov 41
SHEPPERSON,	K O	F/Sgt	WOAG	279641V	21 Sqn	18 Aug 43
SIM,	James	LAC		1014574		19 Jan 42
SIMPSON,	R A E W	Lt	Pilot	103273V	21 Sqn	18 Aug 43
SINGER,	Gordon	Cpl		523138		15 Feb 42
SLY,	Raymond	Flt Lt		402260		9 May 42
SMALL,	John	Cpl		648295	249 Sqn	19 Jan 42
SMITH,	Arthur	Sgt	WOAG	968337		4 Nov 40
SMITH,	Edmund	Plt Off	WOAG	403591		5 Apr 42
SMITH,	Jack	Sgt		636422		18 Apr 42
SOUTHWELL,	John	Flg Off	Pilot	41959	261 Sqn	22 Mar 41
SPIBEY,	Dennis	Sgt		535526	138 Sqn	17 Dec 42
STANLEY,	Harold	Sgt	WOAG	R/91441	458 Sqn	13 Feb 43
STEELE,	Archibald	Plt Off	Pilot	993840	185 Sqn	31 Mar 42
STEVENSON,	James	Flg Off	Pilot	J/15340	126 Sqn	18 Oct 42
STORY,	Alan	Sgt	Pilot	1253997	59 Sqn	18 Jan 42
STREET,	Deryck	Sgt	Nav	930976	108 Sqn	5 May 43
STREETS,	Edward	Plt Off		67587		21 Mar 42
STRINGFELLOW,	Paul	Sgt	Obs	1052523	117 Sqn	6 Apr 43
STUART,	James	Plt Off	Pilot	64928	249 Sqn	9 Feb 42
STYLES,	Adrian	LAC		971966		27 Mar 42
SUNLEY,	Frank	Sgt	Pilot	1260361	40 Sqn	18 Dec 41
SUSSEMS,	Donald	Cpl		570324	126 Sqn	16 May 42
SUTTON,	Edward	F/Sgt	Pilot	1030473	126 Sqn	8 Jun 43
SWAIN,	Lawrence	F/Sgt	Pilot	1268639	185 Sqn	13 Sep 42
TAPPER,	Ralph	Sgt		528245		29 Apr 41
TAPPING,	Alfred	Cpl		1261303		9 Feb 42
TARBUCK,	James	Plt Off		136224	185 Sqn	1 Apr 43

ROLL OF HONOUR

TAYLOR,	James	LAC		1342823		30 Jun 43
TERRY,	Peter	F/Sgt	Pilot	1257673	185 Sqn	7 Jul 42
THOMAS,	Alban	Cpl		984976		2 Jul 42
THOMAS,	Desmond	Sgt	Pilot	929865		12 Jul 41
THOMAS,	Kenneth	Sgt	WOAG	985597		5 Apr 42
THOMPSON,	William	LAC		975619	126 Sqn	2 Sep 41
THORPE,	Robert	AC1		1082098		15 Sep 43
TIMMS,	William	Sgt	Pilot	740209	261 Sqn	11 Jan 41
TINDALL,	Leslie	AC1		1290496		27 Mar 42
TITHERINGTON,	William	AC1		1236550		24 Mar 42
TOMKINS,	Maurice	F/Sgt	Pilot	1169709		25 Jun 42
TOWNSEND,	Eugene	Sgt	Pilot	1001442		12 Jul 41
TURNER,	Valentine	LAC		1154551		9 Feb 42
TURNER,	William, MBE	Flt Lt		124581		9 Nov 44
TURPIN,	Clifford	LAC		622455	185 Sqn	24 Mar 42
TWEEDALE,	Gordon, DFM	Plt Off		404269	185 Sqn	9 May 42
TYM,	William	Flt Lt	Pilot	86364	23 Sqn	5 Jun 43
VAUGHAN,	Leonard, DSO, DFC	Flt Lt	Air Gnr	78666	138 Sqn	17 Dec 42
VELLA,	Anthony	AC1		776680		23 Jun 42
VERNEY,	Edgar	Cpl		349802		3 Jan 42
VINALL,	John	Sgt	Pilot	655947	185 Sqn	12 Oct 42
WADDINGHAM,	John, DFC	Flt Lt		40867	89 Sqn	27 Sep 42
WAGHORN,	Peter	Sgt	Pilot	745800	261 Sqn	11 Ap 41
WAGSTAFFE,	John	WO	Pilot	1219231	458 Sqn	19 Apr 44
WALKER,	Henry	Sgt		400312		8 Mar 42
WALLWORTH,	Jack	Sgt	Obs	1288982	217 Sqn	22 Jul 42
WALSH,	John	Flg Off		42547	261 Sqn	2 Mar 41
WARREN,	Wilfred	Sgt		349651	148 Sqn	28 Jan 41
WATERFIELD,	Arthur	Flt Lt		80704		21 Mar 42
WATSON,	William	AC1		1213575		7 Jan 42
WATT,	Alexander	Sgt	Flt Eng	571759	138 Sqn	17 Dec 42
WEBB,	Alexander	LAC		749925	185 Sqn	24 Mar 42
WEBB,	John	Sgt		333979		15 Feb 42
WEBLING,	Paul	Cpl		1134366		24 Jan 43
WEBSTER,	William	Sgt	Obs	1100851	235 Sqn	13 Jun 42
WEDGWOOD,	Jefferson, DFC	Sqn Ldr	Pilot	37645	92 Sqn	17 Dec 42
WEEDON,	Albert	Cpl		856015	185 Sqn	8 Apr 43
WELLS,	Peter	F/Sgt	Pilot	748775	69 Sqn	23 Dec 41
WHATMORE,	W	AC1		1204590		24 Mar 42
WHITE,	Gordon	LAC		632876	249 Sqn	13 Mar 42
WHITMORE,	Thomas	Sgt	WOAG	751136	98 Sqn	7 Nov 41
WILLIAMS,	Edward, DFC	Flt Lt		74346	69 Sqn	15 Jan 42
WILLIAMS,	John	WO	Nav/Radar	620740	108 Sqn	16 Jan 44
WILLIAMS,	Thomas	Sgt	WO	1123961	69 Sqn	2 Sep 43
WILLIAMSON,	Robert	F/Sgt	WOAG	1252008	458 Sqn	19 Apr 44
WILLS,	Dennis	Cpl		938306		1 Apr 42
WOODMAN,	Alan	Cpl		572591		24 Mar 42
WOODMAN,	William	WO	Nav	523248	23 Sqn	23 Mar 43
WOOR,	Thomas	Sgt	Obs	744940		4 Nov 40
WORSFIELD,	Arthur	Sgt	WOAG	924678		12 Jul 41
WOULDES,	Noel	Sgt	Obs	402234	59 Sqn	18 Jan 42
WRIGHT,	George	AC1		777018	249 Sqn	1 Mar 42
WRIGHT,	Jack	Sgt	WOAG	1314592	21 Sqn	9 Aug 43
WRIGHT,	Russell	Plt Off	Pilot	80402		1 Nov 42
WYLDE,	Paul	Flt Lt	Pilot	41342	69 Sqn	10 Aug 41
WYNNE,	Ernest	Sgt	Pilot	903314	185 Sqn	15 May 41

ROLL OF HONOUR

YAHOLNITSKY,	Walter	WO	Pilot	R/101915	249 Sqn	9 Apr 43
YATES,	Horace	Cpl		813260	69 Sqn	2 Aug 42

ROLL OF HONOUR

NAVY, ARMY AND AIR FORCE INSTITUTES

(This list contains the names of Maltese staff only)

AGIUS,	Joseph	*Glorious*	9 Jun 40
AGIUS,	Joseph	*Mohawk*	16 Apr 41
BARTOLO,	Emanuel	*Glorious*	9 Jun 40
CARBONE,	Augustine	*Glorious*	9 Jun 40
CHIRCOP,	Lawrence	*Manistee*	24 Feb 41
CIAPPARA,	Carmel	*Grafton*	29 May 40
CUESTA,	Ramon	*Glorious*	9 Jun 40
FALZON,	Anthony	*Fiona*	18 Apr 41
HOULTON,	James	*Grenville*	19 Jan 40
MICALLEF,	Carmel	*Glorious*	9 Jun 40
MICALLEF,	John	*Glorious*	9 Jun 40
MIFSUD,	Carmel	*Hotspur*	10 Apr 40
MIFSUD,	Joseph	*Juno*	21 May 41
MULLIGAN,	Joseph	*Hunter*	10 Apr 40
PSAILA,	Samuel	*Sydney*	19 Nov 41
SCHEMBRI,	George	*Rosaura*	18 Mar 41
SCIBERRAS,	Carmel	*Kipling*	11 May 42
SCICLUNA,	Charles	*Gallant*	11 Jan 41
VASSALLO,	William	*Airedale*	15 Jun 42
ZAMMIT,	Charles	*Diamond*	27 Apr 41
ZAMMIT,	Saviour	*Sydney*	19 Nov 41

ROLL OF HONOUR

MERCHANT NAVY

(This list contains the names of Malta-born seamen only)

ABELA,	Emanuel	Chief Std	*Empire Wave*	2 Oct 41
ABELA,	Paul	Std	*Retriever*	12 Apr 41
AGIUS,	Carmel	Boatswain	*Ascot*	29 Feb 44
AGIUS,	S P J	A.B.	*Nova Scotia*	28 Nov 42
ATTARD,	Anthony	A.B.	*Petrella*	4 Feb 41
ATTARD,	Carmelo	F & T	*Newbury*	15 Sep 41
ATTARD,	Coronato	F & T	*Newbury*	15 Sep 41
ATTARD,	Francis	F & T	*Glenlea*	7 Nov 42
ATTARD,	Giuseppe	Boatswain	*Thomas Walton*	7 Dec 39
ATTARD,	Giuseppe	F & T	*Newbury*	15 Sep 41
ATTARD,	John	F & T	*Holmbury*	5 May 43
ATTARD,	Joseph	A.B.	*Nova Scotia*	28 Nov 42
AZZOPARDI,	Alfred	Boatswain	*Zouave*	17 Mar 43
AZZOPARDI,	Emanuel	Donkeyman	*Shuntien*	23 Dec 41
AZZOPARDI,	Gerald	A.B.	*British Monarch*	19 Jun 40
AZZOPARDI,	Salvatore	Greaser	*San Fabian*	28 Aug 42
BARBARA,	Lorenzo	F & T	*Roch Ranza*	4 Feb 42
BLYE,	George	Donkeyman	*Brambleleaf*	10 Jun 42
BONANNO,	Annunziato	Donkeyman	*Caleb Sprague*	31 Jan 44
BONNICI,	Gio Maria	F & T	*Ashworth*	13 Oct 42
BORG,	Emanuel	F & T	*Langleford*	14 Feb 40
BORG,	George	Fireman	*Laconikos*	7 May 43
BORG,	Joseph	F & T	*Holmbury*	5 May 43
BORG,	Michael	F & T	*Newbury*	15 Sep 41
BORG,	Nicholas	Std	*Lady Glanely*	2 Dec 40
BOWDEN,	John	1st Rad O	*Rio Bianco*	12 Apr 42
BRINCAT,	Carmel	Greaser	*Ainderby*	10 Jun 41
BRINCAT,	John	F & T	*Linaria*	24 Feb 41
BUGEJA,	Giuseppe	Fireman	*Empire Collins*	17 Oct 44
BUGEJA,	Romeo	Carpenter	*Edwy R Brown*	18 Feb 41
BUHAGIAR,	John	Donkeyman	*Gothic*	12 Sep 40
BUHAGIAR,	J	Creaser	*Brambleleaf*	10 Jun 42
BUSUTTIL,		Rad Off	*Sarinikos*	7 Dec 42
BUSUTTIL,	Nazzareno	A.B.	*Manchester Citizen*	9 Jul 43
BUTTIGIEG,	Gerald	A.B.	*Cornish City*	29 Jul 43
BUTTIGIEG,	Publio	A.B.	*Glenlea*	7 Nov 42
CAFFARI,	Henri	Pantryman	*Shuntien*	23 Dec 41
CALIGARI,	Anthony	O S	*Empire Light*	7 Mar 43
CALLEJA,	Louis	Carpenter	*White Crest*	24 Feb 42
CALLUS,	Leonard	F & T	*Lock Ranza*	3 Feb 42
CAMILLERI,	Carmelo	F & T	*Corabella*	30 Apr 43
CAMILLERI,	Joseph	Sailor	*Empire Barracuda*	15 Dec 41
CAMILLERI,	Joseph	F & T	*Ashworth*	13 Oct 42
CAMILLERI,	Joseph	F & T	*Glenlea*	7 Nov 42
CAMILLERI,	Joseph		*Melbourne Star*	2 Apr 43
CAMILLERI,	William	Asst Std	*British Dominion*	10 Jan 43
CARABOTT,	Michael	Greaser	*Lady Glanely*	2 Dec 40
CARUANA,	Amadeo	Cook	*Gogovale*	4 Aug 40
CARUANA,	Felix	Sailor	*Lady Glanely*	2 Dec 40
CARUANA,	Giovanni	Donkeyman	*Ashbury*	8 Jan 45
CASSAR,	Carmel	F & T	*Ashbury*	8 Jan 45
CAUCHI,	Carlo	F & T	*Llanwern*	26 Feb 41
CAUCHI,	Coronato	Sailor	*Brambleleaf*	18 Jan 42
CAUCHI,	Rosario	Carpenter		

ROLL OF HONOUR

CINI,	Antonio	Sailor	*Koranton*	28 Mar 41
COSTA,	John	Fireman	*Glynn*	12 Oct 41
CUTAJAR,	Anthony	F & T	*Hazelside*	8 Nov 41
CUTAJAR,	Benjamin	Donkeyman	*Empire Amethyst*	14 Apr 42
CUTAJAR,	Carmel	Sailor	*Fiscus*	18 Oct 40
CUTAJAR,	John	Greaser	*Swiftpool*	5 Aug 41
CUTAJAR,	Salvatore	F & T	*Newbury*	15 Sep 41
DEBATTISTA,	John	Fireman	*Shuntien*	23 Dec 41
DEBONO,	Carmelo	A.B.	*Lancastrian Prince*	11 Apr 43
DEBONO,	Joseph	F & T	*Stonepool*	11 Sep 41
DEGIORGIO,	Giuseppe	Greaser	*Anglo Peruvian*	23 Feb 41
DEGUARA,	Carmel	F & T	*Ainderby*	10 Jan 41
DUCA,	George	F & T	*Frances Massey*	6 Jun 40
ELLUL,	Vincent	Fireman	*Pass of Balmaha*	17 Oct 41
EVANS,	James	Donkeyman	*Ashworth*	13 Oct 42
FALZON,	Carmelo	F & T	*Frances Massey*	6 Jun 40
FALZON,	Charles	F & T	*Ashbury*	8 Jan 45
FALZON,	Giuseppe	Carpenter	*Empire Engineer*	2 Feb 41
FALZON,	Joseph	Sailor	*Chelsea*	30 Aug 40
FALZON,	Michael	A.B.	*Chelsea*	30 Aug 40
FALZON,	Salvatore	O.S.	*Chelsea*	30 Aug 40
FALZON,	Salvatore	A.B.	*British Viscount*	3 Apr 41
FARRUGIA,	Coronato	Sailor	*Hawkinge*	27 Jul 41
FARRUGIA,	George	Mess Room Boy	*N.C. Monberg*	15 Dec 40
FARRUGIA,	Joseph	F & T	*Empire Lough*	24 Jun 44
FARRUGIA,	Nicholas	F & T	*Swiftpool*	5 Aug 41
FARRUGIA,	Salvatore	F & T	*Harcalo*	6 Jun 40
FARRUGIA,	Vincent	Fireman	*Ocean Crusader*	26 Nov 42
FAVA,	Carmelo	Fireman	*Durdham*	27 Jul 40
FENECH,	Carmelo	Greaser	*Empire Wildbeeste*	24 Jan 42
FENECH,	Edward	F & T	*Inventor*	13 Jan 45
FENECH,	James	Boy	*Sheaf Mead*	27 May 40
FENECH,	Vincenzo	Fireman	*Box Hill*	31 Dec 39
FERNANDEZ,	Manuel	Fireman	*Waziristan*	2 Jan 42
FORMOSA,	Charles	F & T	*Courland*	10 Feb 41
FORMOSA,	Giuseppe	Greaser	*Harpagon*	19 Apr 42
FORMOSA,	Michael	Fireman	*Kingston Hill*	7 Jun 41
FORTI,	Joseph	Donkeyman	*Empire Surf*	14 Jan 42
GALEA,	Anthony	Sailor	*Chelsea*	30 Aug 40
GALEA,	Consiglio	F & T	*Glendalough*	19 Mar 43
GALEA,	Edward	Fireman	*Knitsley*	12 Dec 42
GALEA,	Gerald	Asst Cook	*Culebra*	17 Jan 42
GALEA,	L	Fireman	*Shuntien*	23 Dec 41
GALEA,	Lucrezio	3rd Eng Off	*White Crest*	24 Feb 42
GASCIULLI,	Joseph	Fireman	*Ceramic*	7 Dec 42
GATT,	Nicholas	F & T	*Langleeford*	14 Feb 40
GAUCI,	Carmelo	Cook	*Newbury*	15 Sep 41
GLOVER,	Frank	Std	*King Lud*	8 Jun 42
GRAVINA,	Thomas	Donkeyman	*Tringa*	11 May 40
GRECH,	Anthony	F & T	*Loch Ranza*	3 Feb 42
GRECH,	Emanuel	Carpenter	*Tregenna*	17 Sep 40
GRECH,	George	Cook	*Western Chief*	14 Mar 44
GRECH,	Joseph	A.B.	*Fiscus*	18 Oct 40
GRECH,	Saverio	Cook	*Empire Wave*	2 Oct 41
GRIMA,	Coronato	F & T	*Ashbury*	8 Jan 45
GRIMA,	John	A.B.	*Lancastrian Prince*	11 Apr 43

ROLL OF HONOUR

GUSMAN,	Felix	O.S.	*Pass of Balmaha*	17 Oct 41
HABER,	Benigno	F & T	*Harcalo*	6 Jun 40
HERAGHTY,	Reginald	F & T	*Empire Crossbill*	11 Sep 41
INGUANEZ,	Joseph	Fireman	*Alderamin*	17 Mar 43
JONES,	Albert	Carpenter	*Baron Ogilvy*	29 Sep 42
LANE,	Leonard	3rd Eng Off	*Empire Light*	8 May 41
LONGO,	Albert	Chief Eng Off	*Lerwick*	13 Jan 42
MAGRI,	Charles	Chief Std	*Fowberry Tower*	12 May 41
MAGRI,	Ernest	Chief Std	*Norman Monarch*	20 May 41
MALENOIR-VICKERS,	Ruper	Rad Off	*Pearl Moor*	19 Jul 40
MALLIA,	Carmel	Sailor	*Friesland*	16 Apr 41
MALLIA,	Emanuel	A.B.	*Oropos*	21 Dec 42
MALLIA,	John	Fireman	*Coast Wings*	27 Sep 40
MAMO,	Emanuel	A.B.	*Maine*	6 Sep 41
MANGION,	Joseph	Motorman	*Buesten*	9 Apr 41
MARLOW,	Charles	Fireman	*Harley*	14 Nov 44
MERCIECA,	Dominic	Greaser	*Shuntien*	23 Dec 41
MERCIECA,	Emanuel	Greaser	*Ashbury*	8 Jan 45
MICALLEF,	Charles	Master	*Granville*	17 Mar 43
MICALLEF,	John	O.S.	*Rose Schiaffino*	3 Nov 41
MIFSUD,	Antoine	Donkeyman	*Empire Caribou*	10 May 41
MIFSUD,	Benedetto	Cook	*Harpagon*	19 Apr 42
MIFSUD,	Michael	F & T	*Llanwern*	26 Feb 41
MIZZI,	Alfred	Trimmer	*Alderamin*	17 Mar 43
MIZZI,	Anthony	Donkeyman	*Start Point*	22 Nov 42
MIZZI,	Gerald	Fireman	*Ceramic*	7 Dec 42
MONTEBELLO,	George	Asst Std	*Maine*	6 Sep 41
MOORE,	Emanuel	Fireman	*Derrynane*	12 Feb 41
MUSCAT,	Anthony	F & T	*Shakespear*	5 Jan 41
MUSCAT,	Carmelo	Fireman	*Thorold*	22 Aug 40
MUSCAT,	Emanuel	A.B.	*Pass of Balmaha*	17 Oct 41
MUSCAT,	Francis	F & T	*Ashbury*	8 Jan 45
MUSCAT,	Saverio	Greaser	*Loch Ranza*	3 Feb 42
MUSIN,	Joe	Donkeyman	*Empire Surf*	14 Jan 42
MUSU,	William	F & T	*Ashworth*	13 Oct 42
PACE,	George	Jr Refrig Engr	*Navasota*	5 Dec 39
PACE,	George	Chief Eng Off	*Dalveen*	28 Sep 40
PACE,	Joseph	Fireman	*Thorold*	22 Aug 40
PACE,	Sidney	Greaser	*Empire Attendant*	15 Jul 42
PACE,	William	Master	*Cressington Court*	19 Aug 42
PALMIER,	E	Chief Std	*Shuntien*	23 Dec 41
PAVIA,	Carmelo	F & T	*Newbury*	15 Sep 41
PHILLIPS,	John	Cadet	*King Lud*	8 Jun 42
PISANI,	Carmel	F & T	*Newbury*	15 Sep 41
PISANI,	Charles	Donkeyman	*Knitsley*	12 Dec 42
PISANI,	Giuseppe	Boiler Atttd	*Aviemore*	16 Sep 39
PISANI,	Salvatore	Cook	*Empire Wave*	2 Oct 41
PITHERS,	Francis	Std's Boy	*Rangitane*	27 Nov 40
PORTELLI,	Calcedonio	Donkeyman	*Ashbury*	8 Jan 45
PORTELLI,	Francis	F & T	*Newbury*	15 Sep 41
PORTELLI,	John	Boatswain	*Hawkinge*	27 Jul 41
PORTELLI,	J		*Sourabaya*	27 Oct 42
PORTELLI,	Joseph	Fireman	*Atland*	25 Mar 43
POUSTIE,	Gillian	Donkeyman	*Newbury*	15 Sep 41

ROLL OF HONOUR

PULIS,	Salvatore	F & T	*Langleeford*	16 Feb 40
RICKETTS,	Lewis John	Cadet	*Deptford*	13 Dec 39
SAFFARESE,	Romeo	F & T	*Ashbury*	8 Jan 45
SAID,	Emanuel	F & T	*Knitsley*	12 Dec 42
SAID,	John	Greaser,	*Shuntien*	23 Dec 41
SALIBA,	Francis	Sailor	*Roxby*	7 Nov 42
SAMMUT,	Joseph	F & T	*Loch Ranza*	3 Feb 42
SAVASTA,	Giovanni	A.B.	*Thomas Walton*	7 Dec 39
SCHEMBRI,	Nicholas	F & T	*Loch Ranza*	3 Feb 42
SCICLUNA,	Joseph	F & T	*Ainderby*	10 Jan 41
SCIFO,	Dominic	Donkeyman	*Lady Glanely*	2 Dec 40
SCORFNA,	Angelo	F & T	*Ashbury*	8 Jan 45
SKY,	Harry	F & T	*Katvaldis*	24 Aug 42
SINAGRA,	Nazzareno	Fireman	*Waziristan*	2 Jan 42
SMITH,	Alfred	1st Rad Off	*Athelsultan*	22 Sep 42
SMITH,	John	Fireman	*Shuntien*	23 Dec 41
SOLDATO,	Antonio	2nd Std	*Maine*	6 Sep 41
SPITERI,	Julian	Donkeyman	*Fabian*	16 Nov 40
SPITERI,	Michael	Std	*Atland*	25 Mar 43
SQUIBBS,	Robert	3rd Eng Off	*Slavol*	25 Mar 42
STELLINI,	Paul	F & T	*Newbury*	15 Sep 41
STELLINI,	Salvatore	F & T	*Loch Ranza*	21 Jan 45
STIVALA,	Anthony	Sailor	*British Viscount*	3 Apr 41
STIVALA,	Samuel	F & T	*Tennessee*	22 Sep 42
SULTANA,	Joseph	A.B.	*Lancastrian Prince*	11 Apr 43
TABONE,	George	Asst Std	*Ashworth*	13 Oct 42
TEUMA,	Emanuel	Carpenter	*Rose Schiaffino*	3 Nov 41
VASSALLO,	Amabile	F & T	*Baron Newlands*	16 Mar 42
VASSALLO,	Emanuel	Greaser	*Orangemoor*	31 May 40
VASSALLO,	Joseph	Greaser	*Ashbury*	8 Jan 45
VELLA,	Emanuel	Mess Room Boy	*Atland*	25 Mar 43
VELLA,	Giuseppe	Fireman	*Almeda Star*	17 Jah 41
VELLA,	Giuseppe	F & T	*Ashbury*	7 Jan 45
VELLA,	Joseph	Steward	*Retriever*	12 Apr 41
VELLA,	Joseph	Fireman	*Brambleleaf*	10 Jun 42
VELLA,	Paul	A.B.	*Blairangus*	21 Sep 40
VELLA,	Spiro	Greaser	*Box Hill*	31 Dec 39
XERRI,	Paul	A.B.	*Zouave*	17 Mar 43
XICLUNA,	Emanuel	A.B.	*Zouave*	17 Mar 43
ZAHRA,	Anthony	Carpenter	*Zouave*	17 Mar 43
ZAHRA,	Paul	F & T	*Ashbury*	8 Jan 45
ZAMMIT,	Francesco	Fireman	*Almeda Star*	17 Jun 41
ZAMMIT,	John	F & T	*Empire Lakeland*	11 Mar 43
ZAMMIT,	Maurizio	Fireman	*Polyana*	22 Apr 41
ZAMMIT,	Paul	F & T	*Anglo Peruvian*	23 Feb 41
ZAMMIT,	Raymond	Ch Std	*Empire Dryden*	23 Apr 22
ZARB,	Angelo	Fireman	*Primrose Hill*	29 Oct 42
ZARB,	Rosario	Greaser	*Western Chief*	14 Mar 41

(The Roll of Honour has been compiled by John A. Agius)

BIBLIOGRAPHY

A Short History of 7th Heavy A.A. Regiment in the Defence of Malta, Gale and Polden 1947.
Bader, Grp Capt Douglas, *Fight for the Sky*, Fontana/Collins 1975.
Bekker, Cajus, *The Luftwaffe War Diaries*, Corgi Books 1974.
Borghese, J. Valerio, *Decima Flottiglia Mas*, Garzanti 1967.
Cameron, Ian, *Red Duster White Ensign*, White Lion Publishers 1974.
Churchill, Sir Winston, *The Second World War*, Vol. IV, The Reprint Society 1956.
Combined Operations 1940-1942, HMSO 1943.
Crockett, George R., *The Airman is a Sailor*, unpublished manuscript.
Cunningham, Admiral of the Fleet, Lord, *A Sailor's Odyssey*, Hutchinson 1951.
Dobbie, Sybil, *Faith and Fortitude*, Maj P.E. Johnstone 1979.
Eisenhower, Gen Dwight D., *Crusade in Europe*, Doubleday 1948.
Emiliani, Chergo and Vigna, *Regia Aeronautica: Il Settore Mediterraneo*, Intergest 1976.
Fernyhough, Brig A.H., *History of the R.A.O.C. 1920-1945*, The Royal Army Ordnance Corps.
Gilchrist, Maj R.T., *Malta Strikes Back*, Gale and Polden.
Grossett, Harry, *Down to the Ships in the Sea*, Hutchinson 1953.
Gunther, John, *Procession*, Harper & Row 1965.
His Majesty's Submarines, HMSO 1945.
Johnstone, AVM Sandy, *Where No Angels Dwell*, Jarrolds 1969.
Jones, R.V., *Most Secret War*, Coronet Books 1979.
Kennett, Brig B.B., and Tatman, Col J.A., *REME — Craftsmen of the Army*, Leo Cooper 1970.
Kesselring, Field-Marshal Albert, *Memoirs*, William Kimber 1953.
Lazzati, Giulio, *Stormi d'Italia*, Mursia 1975.
Lipscomb, Cmdr F.W., *The British Submarine*, Conway Maritime Press 1975.
Lloyd, Air Marshal Sir Hugh, *Briefed to Attack*, Hodder and Stoughton 1949.
Malizia, Nicola, *Inferno su Malta*, Mursia 1976.
Marcon, Tullio, *Operazione Malta Due*, Rivista Marittima 1976.
Micallef, Rev Joseph, *Rahal Fi Gwerra*, 1978.
　　　　　　When Malta Stood Alone, 1981.
Mizzi, Laurence, *Ghall-Holma ta' Hajtu*, Edizzjoni Riveduta, Pubblikazzjoni Bugelli 1983.
Moorehead, Alan, *The March to Tunis*, Harper & Row 1967.
Official History of the Second World War, Army Medical Services, Campaigns in General History.
Playfair, Maj-Gen I.S.O., *The Mediterranean and Middle East*, Vol. II 1956.
Pyke, Magnus, *Teach Yourself Nutrition*, The English Universities Press Ltd 1965.
Ricci, Generale Corrado, *Vita di Pilota*, Mursia 1976.
Ships Company, Our Penelope, Guild Books 1943.
Sherwood, Robert E., *Roosevelt and Harry Hopkins*, Harper 1948.
Shores, Ring and Hess, *Fighters Over Tunisia*, Neville Spearman 1975.
Simpson, Rear-Adm G.W.G., *Periscope View*, Macmillan 1972.
Smith, Peter, *Pedestal: The Malta Convoy of August 1942*, William Kimber 1970.
Smith, Peter and Walker, Edwin. *The Battles of the Malta Striking Forces*, Ian Allan 1974.
The Institution of the Royal Army Service Corps, *The Story of the Royal Army Service Corps 1939-1945*, G. Bell & Sons Ltd 1955.
Times of Malta
The Malta Land Force Journal, Issue No 7.
Wagg, Alfred and Brown, David, *No Spaghetti for Breakfast*, Nicholson & Watson 1943.
Wheeler-Bennett, John W., *King George VI: His Life and Reign*, Macmillan 1958.
Wood, W.J.A., *Royal Air Force Year Book 1979*, RAF Benevolent Fund 1979.

INDEX

Abyssinian crisis, 5
Adelaide Cini Orphanage, Hamrun, 129
Adelphi Theatre, Rabat, 152
Afrika Korps, 37, 53, 56, 145, 160, 172, 173, 181
Agius, Lt. Joseph E., 34
Agius, Capt. Joseph, 144
Agius, Louis A., 14
Air Ministry Experimental Stations, 83, 84
Air Raid Precautions Organisation (ARP), 25, 63
Air raid shelters, 5
Air raid signals, 5
Air Raid Wardens, 73
Air-Sea Rescue, 46, 155, 156, 157, 158
Air supplies to Malta, 145
Aircraft pens, 79, 81, 82
Ala Littoria, 4
Albacore, 82, 177
Albermarle, 189
Alerts, number of, 179, 200
Alexander, Field-Marshal Sir Harold, 73, 187, 194, 202, 204
Alexander, Plt. Off. Peter B., 3
Alexandria, 20, 28, 48, 65, 67, 85, 86, 89, 118, 146, 176, 180, 181, 192
Algiers, 51, 135, 176, 180
Almeria Lykes, MV, 165
Amato Gauci, Lt. Bernard, 33
Amato-Gauci, Maj. Edgar, 87
Amato-Gauci, Maj. Gerald, 104, 109
Ambrosio, *Generale* Vittorio, 194
American scroll to Malta, 197
American Spitfires, 183
American Engineer, Company 'E', 182, 183
American 31st Fighter Group, 183
Ancient, Tug, 20, 67
Ancillary and Service Corps, 84
Anglo-Maltese League, 17, 18, 171
Anna Dacoutros, schooner, 147
Annunciation Church, Vittoriosa, 27
Anti-Aircraft Batteries, Heavy, 109
Apap, Robert, 143
Aphis, HMS, 6
Ara Fejn Hi, 36
Ardeola, MV, 176
Arethusa, HMS, 49
Argus, HMS, 22, 36, 64
Ark Royal, HMS, 36, 54
Armament Depot, 102
Aston, Isabella, 154
Aston, Simon, 154
Attard, N., Fitter, 175
Attard, Vincent, 190
Attendolo, Italian cruiser, 165
Attlee, Rt. Hon. Clement R., 2
Auchinleck, Gen. Sir Claude, 172
Auberge de Castille, 69
Augusta, Sicily, 41
Aurora, HMS, 53, 67, 82, 184, 185
Austrian internees, 87
Auxiliary power station, 91
Axisa, Police Commissioner Joseph, 121, 143, 144
Axum, Italian submarine, 164
Azzopardi, Mons. Michael, 35
Azzopardi, Sgt. S., 109

Badii, *Maresciallo* Mario, 164
Badoglio, *Maresciallo*, Pietro, 191, 194

Baltimore, 191
Band Clubs, Valletta, 194
Bantam, MV, 176
Barbara, Sgt., 44, 45
Barbaro of St. George, Marquis, 39, 176
Barber, Plt. Off. 'Jock', 31
Barioglio, *Tenente* Camillo, 51
Barla, *Sergente Palombaro* Luigi, 45
Bartolo, Salvatore, 89
Bates, L/Sgt., 45
Battle Honour 'Malta', 181
Battle of Britain, 33, 64, 112, 160
Bayliss, P.C. John, 124
Beasley, Tom, 201
Beaufighter, 51, 82, 172, 177
Beaufort, 161, 177
Beaverbrook, Rt. Hon. Lord, 18
Beckett, Maj.-Gen. C.T., 28, 171
Bedell-Smith, Maj.-Gen. W., 194, 197, 202
Beitz, *Unteroffizier* Gerhard, 158
Bekker, Cajus, 98, 100, 112
Bellenzier, *Tenente* Aldo, 32
Benedetti, *Tenente* Mario, 12
Benghajsa Point, 157, 158
Bergamini, *Ammiraglio d'Armata* Carlo, 192
Bernard, Lady Vera, 87
Bernard, Prof. Albert V., 129
Beurling, Sgt. Plt. George F., 152, 153, 154
Bighi, R.N. Hospital, 39
Bilocca, ARP Supt. Anthony, 132
Bisdee, Sqd. Ldr. John D., 135
Black market, 71
Blackman, W.O. Carmel, 46
Black-out, 14, 15
Blackwell, Lieut. Thomas W.T., 124
Blast walls, 15
Blenheim, 51, 54, 82, 158, 177
Blohm und Voss Bv222 flyingboat, 177
Blue Sisters Hospital, 128
Boettiger, Maj. John, 199
Boffa, Dr. Paul (later Sir), 25, 26, 59, 61
Bolton, Maj. L.G., 102
Bolzano, Italian cruiser, 165
Bomb Alley, 146
Bomb disposal, 29, 123, 124, 125, 126
Bomb tonnage dropped on Malta, 112
Bombo, Uganda, 90
Bombs, Hermann and Satan, 128
Bonello, G.M., 170
Bonello, Capt. Walter, 87, 88
Bonham-Carter, Gen. Sir Charles, 2, 73
Bonham-Carter, Lady, 73
Borg, Carmela, 175
Borg, H.H. Sir George, 90, 122, 132, 143, 195
Borg, William, 89
Borg Grech, Dr. Paul, 143
Borghese, *Principe* Valerio, 41, 42
Borghi, Caio, 142
Borg Olivier, Dr. George, 90
Borg Pisani, Carmelo, 142, 143, 144
Born, Fr. Harry, 109
Boston, 191
Botto, *Maggiore* Ernesto, 12
Box barrage, 25
Boy Scouts, 4, 71, 72
Boyd, Capt. Denis, 22

325

BR 20, 38
Bragadin, Marc'Antonio, 46
Brambilla, Nello, 38
Bramham, HMS, 167, 169, 170
Brand, David, 180
Bread rationing, 74
Bread supply, 61, 74, 146
Breakwater viaduct, 42
Breathing oxygen, 175
Breconshire, MV, 51, 65, 89, 90
Brincat, Can. Emanuel, 61, 185
Brisbane Star, MV, 165, 167, 170
British Army, 85, 163
British Army, enters Tripoli, 179
British Broadcasting Corporation, 172
British Cabinet, 2
British Commonwealth, 19, 119
British Empire, 18, 89
British Expeditionary Force, 132
British General Hospitals, 129
British Government, 18, 171
British Institute, 151
British Overseas Airways Corporation (BOAC), 145
British Press, 132, 170
British Sailors Society, 171
Bronze Cross, 72, 73
Brooke, Gen. Sir Alan, 200, 202
Brown, Sgt. A.R., 161
Buffs, The, 102, 180
Bugeja Hospital, 12, 129
Buhagiar, Ldg. Std. Anthony, 48
Burges, Flt. Lt. George, 3, 8, 12, 13
Buri, *Maggiore* Arduino, 51
Burrough, Rear-Adm. Harold, 163
Bus tragedy at Marsa, 12
Bush, Robert George, 27
Busuttil, Boy Philip, 6
Butterfly bombs (anti-personnel), 117, 124
Buttigieg, Sgt. M., 86

Cachalot, HM Sub., 48
Cairo, HMS, 164
Calorific value of food, 76
Calleja, Supt. Emanuel, 144
Camilleri, P.C. 347 Carmel, 22, 86
Camilleri, Sgt. Joseph, 108, 109
Camilleri, Maestro Joseph, 151
Camilleri, Judge Luigi, 90
Campbell, David, Lieutenant-Governor, 185, 186
Cant Z 501, 32
Cant Z 506, 161, 162
Cant Z 1007, 153, 164
Cape Bon, 20, 35, 140, 164
Captain Caruana's Smoking Divan, 151
Carabelli, *Sottotenente* Aristide, 43
Carabott, A., Fitter, 175
Carnes, Lieut.-Cmdr. Charles, 10, 46
Caruana, A., Skilled Labourer, 175
Caruana, Sgt. Maj. Carmel, 109
Caruana, Capt. Godfrey, 170
Caruana, H.G. Mgr. Dom Maurus, 74, 88
Casino Maltese, 61, 170
Cassar, P.C. 648 Carmel, 67, 86
Cassar, Joseph, 18, 171
Castillo, The Hon. Roger, 144
Catacombs, Rabat, 14
Catania, Sicily, 6, 22, 31, 94, 100, 159, 174
Cavallero, *Maresciallo* Ugo, 173
Central Civil Hospital, Floriana, 128
Chamberlain, Rt. Hon. Neville, 2
Chatfield, Adm. Lord, 171
Cheshire Regt., 43, 94, 180
Chiodi, *Capitano* Antonio, 13
Churchill, Maj. Randolph, 196
Churchill, Rt. Hon. Winston S., 2, 69, 116, 135, 136, 170, 172, 196, 197, 202, 203

Ciano, *Conte* Galeazzo, 53
Citation, George Cross, 119, 121
Civil Court, 88
Civil Prison, 88
Clan Campbell, MV, 65
Clan Ferguson, MV, 164
Clark, Capt. Franklin F., 102, 103
Clio, Italian torpedo-boat, 37
Clive, RASC launch, 156
Clyde, Scotland, 85, 170
Clyde, HM Sub., 48, 176
Coate, Flg. Off. E.E., 177
Cohen, Andrew, 59
Cohen, Sgt. Plt. Sidney, 181
Coins, shortage of, 59
Colonelcy-in-Chief, RMA, H.M. King George VI, 110
Combined Operations Pilotage Parties (COPP), 180
Comino, 32, 143
Comiso, 8, 22, 100
Command Fair, 150
Committee of Imperial Defence, 2
Communal Feeding Department, 67, 74, 77
Complimentary tickets to convoy crews, 170
Compulsory Service Regulations, 33
Concert Parties, 150, 170
Condachi, Dr. Irene, 35
Coningham, Air Marshal Arthur, 187
Connaught Home, 151, 170
Conscription, 33
Cooke, Vice-Adm. Charles N., 202
Cooper, Flt. Lt. Frank, 20
Copperwheat, Lieut. Dennis A., 67
Coppola, Inspector Charles, 86
Cordina, Gnr. Carmel, 6
Cork and Orrery, Earl of, 171
Cornwall, MV, 20
Corpo Aero Italiano (CAI), 38
Corradino Military Prison, 46
Costa, *Tenente di Vascello* Francesco, 45
Coster family, 96
'COSUP', Co-ordination of Supplies, 19
Cosulich, *Tenente di Vascello* Giuseppe, 142
Council of Government, 11, 14, 27, 55, 63, 89, 90, 91, 98, 185
Court of Appeal, 90
Cranborne, Viscount, 199, 200
Criminal Court, 143
Crockett, Flt. Lt. George R., 143, 155, 156, 157, 158
Crockford, Algernon, 18
Cunningham, Adm. Sir Andrew B., 19, 22, 28, 118, 187, 190, 192, 194, 202
Curfew, 14
Cutajar, Francis, 63

D'Agostino, Amadeo, 87
Dainty, HMS, 20
Dakota, 145, 180, 189
Davies, Flg. Off. George V., 20
da Zara, *Ammiraglio* Alberto, 192
De Angelis, *Secondo Capo Motorista Navale* Arnaldo, 142
Debattista, Act. P.O. Anthony, 82
Debono, George, 82
Debono, Gnr. Paul, 6
Decesare, Peter Paul, 132
Decima Flottiglia MAS, 41
Decontaminators, 73
De Courten, *Ammiraglio* Raffaele, 194
Defence Committee, 172
Defence Regulations, 15
Degiorgio, Louis J., 146
de Gray, Supt. Vivian, 144
Deichmann, *Oberst* Paul, 55
Delia, Can. Joseph, 17
Demolition and Clearance Section, PWD, 14, 26, 57
Denbighshire, MV, 176
Deportation Order, 89
Deucalion, MV, 164
Devonshire Regiment, 4, 181
Diamond, HMS, 20

326

Diana, Italian dispatch boat, 41
Di Blasi, *Capitano* Rosario, 8
Dick, Commodore Royar, 192
Dickinson, Sqd. Ldr., 126
Dill, Field-Marshal Sir John, 21
Dimech, Lt. Albert J., 179
Di Muro, *Capitano di Fregata* Mario, 41
Divisional Sea Transport Officer, Malta, 26
Dixon, Lieut. J., 67
Dixon, Plt. Off. Philip, 138
Dobbie, Sybil, 132
Dobbie, Lt.-Gen. Sir William, 6, 34, 39, 68, 87, 98, 110, 119, 121, 132
Dockyard, HM, 6, 21, 22, 25, 27, 84, 87, 91, 113, 124, 185, 196, 199
Dockyard Creek, 185, 192
Dockyard Defence Battery, 33, 102
Dorset, MV, 165
Dorsetshire Regiment, 4, 181
Douglas-Hamilton, Sqd. Ldr. Lord David, 102
Douhet, *Generale* Giulio, 100
D'Oyly-Hughes, Capt. Guy, 2
Dressing Stations, 129, 130
Drury, A/Maj. R.E.H., 85
Duce, (see Mussolini, Benito)
Duce, Lt., 89, 90
Dunkerley, Col. Arthur J., 4
Dunsmore, Plt. Off. W.M., 161
Durham Light Infantry, 180

E-boat attack, 41-47
Eagle, HMS, 64, 134, 135, 152, 163, 164, 169
Early Warning System, 104
Eastman, Lt. William M., 123
Eden, Rt. Hon. Anthony, 21, 199, 203
Eighth Army, 100, 173, 177, 190
Eisenhower, Gen. Dwight D., 182, 187, 189, 197, 202, 203
Electricity and water cuts, 148
Ellul, Bdr., 109
Emergency hospitals, 128
Empire flyingboats, 145
Empire Defender, MV, 51
Empire Guillemot, MV, 49
Empire Hope, MV, 164
Empire Patrol, MV, 176
Empire Pelican, MV, 51
Essex, SS, 26, 27
Eugenio di Savoia, Italian cruiser, 192
Evacuation of elderly to Gozo, 128

Faith Gloster Sea Gladiator, Presentation of, 195
Falcomatà, *Capitano Medico* Bruno, 41
Farrugia, Prof. Philip, 201
Fava, Salvatore, 59
Fenech, P.C. 509 Emanuel, 67, 86
Ferguson, Beatrice, 20, 21
Ferguson, Plt. Off. R.W., 20
Ferro, Col. Henry, 44, 46
Fiat CR 42, 12, 13, 21, 22, 25, 34
Field Marshal's baton, Presentation to Lord Gort, 185
Filfla, 143, 155
Fighter Operations Room, 83
Fighter pilots, 135, 151, 152
Fighter Plane Fund, The Malta, 18
Filippi, *Capitano* Luigi, 13
Filter Room, 83, 189
Final 'All Clear', Sounding of, 200
Fines for black-market offences, 147
Fleet Air Arm, 19, 22, 28, 36, 155
Fleming, Sgt., 140
Fliegerkorps II, 55
Fliegerkorps X, 22
Floating Dock, 12
Flour-mills, 117
Focacci, *Tenente* Guido, 51
Foggia, 32
Food Distribution Enforcement Officer, 176
Food Distribution Office, 39

Force 'B', 51
Force 'H', 54
Force 'K', 49, 51, 53
Ford, Vice-Adm. Wilbraham, 11, 45
Foresight, HMS, 164
Formosa, Fr. Raymond, 110
Fort Benghajsa, 4
Fort Bingemma, 4
Fort Campbell, 4
Fort Delimara, 4
Fort Madliena, 4
Fort Mosta, 84
Fort Ricasoli, 4, 10, 34, 43, 44
Fort St Angelo, 102, 170
Fort St Elmo, 4, 6. 10, 43, 44, 45, 117, 165
Fort St Leonardo, 4
Fort St Rocco, 4
Fort Salvatore, 87, 88
Fort Tignè, 4, 44, 109
Forward Interception Plan, 160
Fowlow, Plt. Off. Norman, 157
Franco, SS, 147
Frassetto, *Sottotenento di Vascello* Roberto, 42, 43, 46
Friedburger, Capt. W.H.D., 136, 138
Fuel shortage, 175
Führer (see Hitler, Adolf)
Fulmar, 20, 24, 25, 27
Funds, 18, 19, 171
Furious, HMS, 36, 138. 140, 163

Gabriele, Anthony, 147
Galea, Rev. Anton, 61
Galea, P.O. Francis, 10
Galea, Bdr. Joseph, 6
Galea, Salvino, 196
Gallant, HMS, 24
Ganado, Prof. Edgar, 143
Ganado, Dr. Herbert, 87, 88, 89, 90
Gas masks, 13
Gauci, Jane Amy, 73
Gauci, Joseph, 28
Geisler, *Generalleutnant* Hans-Ferdinand, 22
Gela, Sicily, 22, 33, 180
George VI, H.M. King, 11, 69, 110, 119, 184, 185
George Cross, Award of, 119, 121, 122
Gerbini, Sicily, 22, 100, 159
German, Augusto, 144
German internees, 87
German submarines, 54, 164, 180
Gharghur, 84
Ghajn Tuffieha, 180
Ghawdex Spitfire, W3212, 18
Gili, P.C. V., 86
Ginestra, Italy, 32
Giobbe, *Capitano di Corvetta* Giorgio, 42
Giraud, Gen. Henri, 199
Girl Guides, 72, 73
Gladiator, Gloster Sea, 3, 6, 8, 12, 13, 22
Glaucos, Greek submarine, 37
Glen Martin, 22, 32
Glenorchy, MV, 165
Glorious, HMS, 3
Gonzi, H.G. Mgr. Michael, 147, 182, 183, 206
Gorizia, Italian cruiser, 65
Gort, Lord, 72, 121, 122, 132, 144, 147, 148, 170, 185, 186, 190, 194, 196, 199, 201, 202
Gourgion Tower, Gozo, 182
Government Headquarters, 64
Government Information Centre, 150
Government School, Qormi, 35
Gozo, 5, 11, 28, 72, 84, 128, 143, 175, 187
Gozo airfield, 182, 183
Gracie, Sqd. Ldr. Edward J., 64
Grand Harbour, 20, 25, 26, 28, 31, 34, 39, 41, 43, 47, 49, 53, 65, 68, 102, 104, 124, 125, 146, 147, 158, 162, 165, 176, 184, 185, 190, 192, 194
Greenwood, Rt. Hon. Arthur, 2
Grossett, Harry, 68
Ground Control Interception (GCI), 83

Guggenberger, *Leutnant* Friedrich, 54
Guglielmo, *Palombaro* Giuseppe, 142
Gunners, 28, 31, 41, 46, 68, 101, 104, 116, 175
Gunther, John, 190

Hal Far, 3, 21, 27, 33, 36, 101, 109, 124, 135, 136, 157
Halifax, 189
Halifax, Lord, 2
Hampshire Regiment, 181
Hanlon, C.P.O. Leslie, 125
Hardeman, Sqd. Ldr., 126
Hardie, Grp. Capt. Edward, 46
Hardie, Flt. Lt. William, 155, 156
Harding, Judge William, 90, 143
Harrison, Austen St. B., 203
Hartley, Flt. Lt. Peter W., 3, 13
Harvest Day, 170
Harwood, Sir Henry H., 118
Heath, Capt., 25
Hebe, HMS, 167
Heinkel 111, 22
Heinkel 115, 40
Hemmings, Stoker, 25
Hermione, HMS, 49
Hetherington, Flt. Lt. Eric L., 153, 154
Hewlett, Frank S., 170
High Speed Launches, RAF, 132, 143, 155, 156, 157, 158, 161
Highland Division, 51st, 196
Hijack of Cant floatplane, 161, 162
Hili, Victor, 94
Hill, Lieut.-Cmdr. Roger, 165, 167
Hiscock, Lieut. William Ewart, 126
Hitler, Adolf, 1, 56, 159, 204
Holland, Flg. Off. Tony, 135
Home Guard, 14, 134, 202
Hopkins, Harry, 203
Horse-drawn carts, 81, 84, 148
Hospital for Mental Diseases, 89, 128
Houghton, Flg. Off. J.S., 161
Howard, George, 144
Hubbard, P. Pearce S., 203
Hudson, 20, 145
Hurricane, 12, 20, 22, 25, 26, 33, 35, 36, 37, 45, 49, 54, 64, 100, 101, 157, 177
Hutchinson, Capt. G.A.G., 51
Hypogeum, 15
Hythe, HMS, 167

Identification Friend or Foe (IFF), 83
Il-Bambina, 192, 194
Il-Berqa, 148
Illustrious, HMS, 20, 22, 24, 27, 28, 29, 30, 31, 79, 104, 192
Indomitable, HMS, 163, 164
Infantry Brigade, No. 231, 181, 190
Infantry Brigade, No. 234, 181
Information Service Bulletin, 150
Internment Camp, 87
I.O.Us, 59
Ismay, Gen. Sir Hastings, 202
Italy, 21, 31, 36, 42, 51, 73, 88, 90, 143, 177, 192
Italian Battle Fleet surrenders at Malta, 192

Jaccarini, Dr. Carmel, 61
Jackson, Sir Edward St. John, 11, 88, 98
Jamming of radar, 84
Japanese strategists, Advice of, 158
Jaunty, Tug, 20
Jephson-Jones, Capt. Robert L., 123
Jersey, HMS, 34
Jervis, HMS, 20
Jesus of Nazareth Orphanage, Zejtun, 129
Jodl, *General* Alfred, 206
Johnstone, Air Vice-Marshal Sandy, 177
Jones, Prof. Reginald V., 84
Junkers 52, 22, 181

Junkers 87, 21, 22, 24, 25, 27, 77, 96, 104, 108, 112, 138, 164, 165, 167, 169
Junkers 88, 22, 24, 25, 94, 98, 104, 112, 132, 138, 153, 165, 169, 173, 174
Juno, HMS, 20
Justice, Thomas L., 175

Kalafrana, 3, 4, 6, 21, 40, 109, 132, 143, 145, 155, 157, 158, 161, 162, 175
Kalkara, 94, 96
Keeble, Flt. Lt. Peter G., 3, 12
Kenya, HMS, 165
Kerkenna Islands, 181
Kesselring, *General-Feldmarschall* Albert, 55, 56, 82, 92, 159, 160, 173
Khenchela, Algeria, 164
Kimmins, Cmdr. Anthony, 172
King George V Hospital, 129
King George VI assumes Colonelcy-in-Chief of RMA, 110
King, Fleet Admiral Joseph, 202
King, Maj. R.J.W., 102
King's Own band, 194
King's Own Malta Regiment, 4, 49, 71, 96, 152, 181, 194
King's Own Malta Regiment, 1st Bn., 122
King's Own Malta Regiment, 2nd Bn., 'C' Company, 4
King's Own Malta Regiment, 3rd Bn., 33
Kingsway, 61, 179, 202
Kitney, Cpl. Arthur, 34
Knighthood for Archbishop Gonzi, 183
Knights of St. Columba, 151, 170
Knott, Lieut.-Cmdr. R.J., 67
Kordin Civil Prison, 88, 143
Kujawiak, Polish destroyer, 146
Kuter, Maj.-Gen. Lawrence S., 202

Laferla, Albert, 89, 90
Lamm, Lieut., 144
Lampedusa Island surrenders, 181
Lampione Island surrenders, 181
Lancashire Fusiliers, 132
Lance, HMS, 53
Lanner, HMS, 82
Lascaris, 11, 83
La Valetta band, 194
Laycock, Maj.-Gen. Robert, 202
Lazaretto, 8, 53, 128
Leatham, Vice-Adm. Sir Ralph, 118
Leathers, Lord, 202
Le Bargy, C.P.O., 126
Ledbury, HMS, 165, 167, 170
Legion, HMS, 116
Lehen is-Sewwa, 150
Levy Wine, International Variety Revue, 152
Lewis, R.H., 22
Life magazine, 172
Lija, Opening of first Victory Kitchen, 74
Linosa Island surrenders, 181
Lintorn Barracks, 123
Little Sisters of the Poor, 128
Littorio, Italian battleship, 65
Lively, HMS, 53
Lloyd, Air Vice-Marshal Hugh Pughe, 36, 38, 81, 126, 160
Lompa, *Unteroffizier* Johann, 157
Longmore, Air Chief Marshal Sir Arthur, 12
Longworth, A/Maj. S.D.G., 86
Louis Pasteur, MV, 85
Lucas, Wg. Cdr. P.B. 'Laddie', 134
Lucking, Stoker Ronald, 24, 25, 28
Luftwaffe, 27, 28, 30, 33, 34, 36, 49, 56, 65, 84, 94, 103, 146, 158, 164, 175
  Geschwader 1, 94
  Jagdgeschwader 3 (Udet), 100
  Jagdgeschwader 26 (7 Staffel), 33
  Jagdgeschwader 53 (Pik As), 64, 100, 135
  Kampfgruppen 52, 174
  Kampfgruppen 54, 100

Kampfgruppen 77, 100
Kampfgruppen 606, 98
Kampfgruppen 806, 98
Lufttransportstaffel See 222, 177
2 LG 1, 174
II Air Group, 135
III/ZG 26, 100
Luqa, 3
Luqa village, 31, 96
Lynch, Sqd. Ldr. John Joseph, 181

Macchi 200, 6, 12, 21, 22, 25, 27, 45
Macchi 202 *Folgore*, 49, 82, 153
Macfarlane, Capt. David, 170
Mackenzie, Rear-Adm. Kenneth, 185
Macmillan, Harold, 194
Magic Carpet Service to Malta, 48
Magri, Dr. Alberto, 143
Magri, *Sottotenente Pilota Puntatore* Elvio, 8
Magro, Rev. Salvatore, 111
Maitland Wilson, Field-Marshal Sir Henry, 202
Mallia, Frank, 22
Malta Auxiliary Corps, 85
Malta celebrates capture of Tripoli, 179
Malta Chronicle and Imperial Services Gazette, 150
Malta Convoy Fund, 171
Malta Defence Regulations 1939, 89, 143
Malta Lyric Company, 152
Malta makes history, 119
Malta Mobile Canteen (London) Fund, 18
Malta National War Museum, 46, 94, 195, 196
Malta Night Fighter Unit (MNFU), 37, 38
Malta Relief Fund, 18
Malta Review, 150
Malta Shipping Committee, 19
Malta Special Service Troops, 180
Malta Spitfire, W3210, 18
Malta Territorial Force (MTF), 84
Malta Volunteer Defence Force, 14
Malta War Headquarters, Lascaris, 83, 182, 189
Maltese colony in Tunisia, 20
Maltese internees, 87, 88, 89, 90
Maltzahn, *Major* Gunther Freiherr von, 64
Mamo's Garage, 84, 86
Manchester, HMS, 165
Manchester Regiment, 4
Manoel Island, 41, 109, 180
Manoel Theatre, 170
Manxman, HMS, 46, 49, 176, 179, 180
Maori, HMS, 86
Marcon, Tullio, 46
Marich's Smoking Divan, 151
Marie Georgette, Maltese schooner, 147
Marina Pinto, 84
Maritime Regiment of the Royal Regiment of Artillery, 171
Mars, Lieut. Alastair, 165
Marsamxett, 41, 118, 181
Marsascala, 10, 142
Marsaxlokk, 4, 10, 21, 65, 143, 192, 195
Marshall, Gen. George, 202
Martin, Sqd. Ldr. Alan C., 3
Martini, *General* Wolfgang, 84
Martins, L.A.C. C., 143
Maryland, 22, 51, 53, 82
Mason, Capt. Dudley, 169, 170
Mastrodicasa, *Tenente Pilota*, 161
Mater Boni Consilii School, Pawla, 129
Mavity, Charles Cyril, 91
Maynard, Air Commodore Forster H.M., 3, 12, 36
Mazzini, *Colonello* Umberto, 6
McCormick, Rear-Adm. Lynde Daniel, 202
McFarland, Brig.-Gen. A.G., 202
McMeekin, Capt. Terence, 25
Medical and Health Authorities, 129
Mediterranean, 41, 46, 47, 51, 53, 54, 56, 86, 122, 163, 170, 176, 185, 197
Melbourne Star, MV, 165, 170
Meli, P.C. J., 86

Merchant Navy, 19, 170, 175
Mercieca, Anthony, 39
Mercieca, Lady, 87, 89, 90
Mercieca, Lilian, 89, 90
Mercieca, Sir Arturo, 87, 89, 90
Message to People of Malta from Gen. Eisenhower, 190
Messerschmitt 109, 33, 64, 82, 132, 147, 153, 157, 175
Messerschmit 110, 22, 25, 27, 98, 100
Metcalfe, Sir Ralph, 202
Micallef, Maj. H.R., 186
Micallef, Gnr. Richard, 6
Micallef, Lt.-Col. Victor, 87
Middle East, 98, 163, 177, 180
Mifsud, Sgt.-Maj., 144
Mifsud, ARP Sgt.-Maj. John, 63
Mifsud, Sir Ugo, 89
Milestones, 56
Milford Haven, David, Third Marquess of, 169
Military Police, 45
Minesweepers, 118
Mining of approaches to Malta, 118, 146
Mitchell, 189
Mitchell, A.B. E., 54
Mizzi, Dr. Enrico, 87
Mizzi, Paul, 12
Mizzi, Willie, 25
Moccagatta, *Capitano di Fregata* Vittorio, 41, 45
Mohawk, HMS, 24
Monico Bar, 151
Montanaro Gauci, H.H. Mr. Justice Anthony, 89
Montgomery, Gen. Bernard Law, 177, 187
Montgomery House, 202
Moor, Mooring Vessel, 39
Moorehead, Alan, 111
More, Lieut., 40
Morgenthau, Henry, Jr., 199, 200
Mormacmoon, MV, 176
Mosquito, 177
Mosta, 92, 94
Mosta Church, 111
Mould, Sqd. Ldr. Peter W.O., 49
Mountbatten, Admiral of the Fleet, Earl, 169, 187
Müncheberg, *Oberleutnant* Joachim, 33
Murphy, Robert, 194
Muscat Azzopardi, Pio, 67
Musham, Commissioned Gunner C., 170
Mussolini, Benito, 1, 2, 53, 56, 142, 144, 159, 185, 191, 204

NAAFI, 5, 170
Nalder, Charles, 176
Narval, Free French submarine, 37
National Library, 17
National Museum, 17
National Service, 33
Nelson, HMS, 163, 169, 190, 194
Nelson, Col. John, 38
Nicholl, Capt. A.D., 113
Nicholls, Flt. Lt. Victor A., 156
Nigeria, HMS, 164
Nomis, Flg. Off. Leo, 154
North Africa, 21, 22, 36, 40, 51, 56, 113, 145, 159, 163, 173, 175, 177, 179, 181, 182, 189, 197
Nubian, HMS, 181
Nunn, Geoffrey N., 55

Observer Corps, 83
Offerdal, Lieut. Haakon, 40
Ohio, MT, 163, 164, 165, 167, 169, 170, 206
Oliva, *Ammiraglio* Romeo, 192
Oliver, Section Officer Sarah, 196
Olympus, HM Sub., 146
Omnibus, 148
Onslow, Adm. Sir Richard, 165
Operation 'Barbarossa', 36
Operation 'Calendar', 135
Operation 'Ceres', 170
Operation 'Colossus', 32
Operation 'Excess', 24

Operation 'Halberd' 48, 49
Operation 'Harpoon', 146
Operation 'Hats', 20
Operation *'Herkules'*, 56, 158, 160
Operation 'Hurry', 22
Operation 'Husky' 182
Operation 'MW 10', 65
Operation 'Pedestal' (WS 21S), 163, 169, 170, 171, 172
Operation 'Stoneage', 176
Operation 'Style', 49
Operation 'Substance', 48, 49
Operation 'Vigorous', 146
Operation 'White', 22
Operations Room, 83
Operazione C 3 : Malta, 158
Orari, MV, 146
Orion, HMS, 203
Oronsay, 5
Osborne, Plt. Off. A.F., 181
Osiris, HM Sub., 48
Ospizio, Floriana, 84
Otus, HM Sub., 48
Our Lady of Victories Basilica, Senglea, 27
Our Lady of Victories, Return of statue, 194
Oxley, Maj.-Gen. W.H., 196
Oxygen Plants, 175

Pace, L.A.C. Joseph, 143, 144
Pachino chemical factory, Spitfires attack on, 177
Palace, The, 17, 61, 64, 69, 90, 121, 185, 196
Palace, The Square, 121, 194, 195, 203
Palestine, 88
Pampas, MV, 65, 67, 68
Pantalleresco, Mons. Albert, 90
Pantelleria, 140, 141, 181, 189, 203
Pantelleria Island surrenders, 181
Panzavecchia, Scout Joseph, 72
Paper currency, 59
Parabolic Acoustic Mirror, 4
Paradise, Maj., 90
Park, Air Vice-Marshal Keith Rodney, 160, 182, 185, 187, 195, 197
Parker, Maj. Reginald, 29, 30, 123, 124
Parlatorio Wharf, 25, 89, 167
Parracombe, MV, 35
Parthian, HM Sub., 48, 176
Passenger ferry service, 147, 148
Passive Defence Corps, 13, 14, 25, 71, 72, 121
Patton, Gen. George, 182, 190
Pavesi, *Ammiraglio* Gino, 181
Pedretti, *Secondo Capo Palombaro* Alcide, 42
Penelope, HMS, 53, 67, 113, 116
Penn, HMS, 167, 169, 170
Pepperpot, 116
Pether, Lily, 73
Petrol, Restricted use of, 147
Petroni, Joseph, 82
Pezzi, *Tenente*, 38
Picchi, Fortunato, 32
Pilferage and other offences, 146, 147
Pilz, Franz, 132
Pinkney, Capt. Henry, 164, 170
Pinna, *Tenente* Mario, 12
Plotters, 83
Pluda, *Capitano* Mario, 49
Plumleaf, RFA, 20, 167
Police, Commissioner of, 5, 121
Police, C.I.D., 143, 144
Police, Malta, 14, 35, 63, 68, 121, 195
Polio outbreak, 129
Porpoise, HM Sub., 48
Port Chalmers, MV, 163, 165, 170
Port Sudan, 176
Portal, Air Chief Marshal Sir Charles, 202
Portelli, Lt. Bernard J., 45
Potsdam Meeting, 206
Pound, Adm. Sir Dudley, 2
Powell-Sheddon, Sqd. Ldr. George, 37
Power Station, 24, 102, 117

Prayers, 79
Price, Capt. E.J.F., 26, 65
Primary School, Birkirkara, 129
Prison Bakery, 61
Pritchard, Maj. T.A.G., 32
Public Works Department, 14, 91

Qormi, 21, 35
Quarantine Hospital, 128
Queen Alexandra's Imperial Military Nursing Service (QAIMNS), 130
Queen's Own Royal West Kent Regiment, 4, 180
Quincy, USS, 203

Radar, 37, 43, 83, 84, 104
Raffaelli, *Generale* Ferdinando, 164
Ransley, George, 147
Rationing, 39, 74, 146, 171, 172, 176, 200
Reconstruction grants, 204
Recruit Training Centre, 34
Red Flag signal, 67, 69
Rediffusion Relay System, 55, 71, 119, 148, 184
Reeves, Capt. J.W., 135
Regal Theatre, Pawla, 152
Regent Cinema, Valletta, 61
Regent, HM Sub., 48
Reggiane 2001, 82
Regia Aeronautica, 21, 30, 36, 164
Regia Aeronautica, 9 º Gruppo, 12
Regia Aeronautica, 9 º Gruppo, 4 Stormo, 49
Regia Aeronautica, 38 º Gruppo, 32 Stormo, 164
Regia Aeronautica, 130 º Gruppo Aerosilurante, 51
Regia Aeronautica, 11 º Stormo BT, 8
Regia Aeronautica, 36 º Stormo Aerosilurante, 51
Regia Aeronautica, 75 ª Squadriglia, 13
Regia Aeronautica, 139 ª Squadriglia Marittima, 161
Regia Aeronautica, 283 ª Squadriglia Aerosiluranti, 51
Regimental Aid Posts, 130
Requisition of transport, 84
Rexford Cabaret, Valletta, 87
Reynaud, Paul, French Prime Minister, 2
Ricci, *Generale* Corrado, 38
Riley, Capt. Frederick, 170
Roberts, H., Skilled Labourer, 175
Robin Locksley, MV, 175
Rochester Castle, MV, 165, 170
Rodney, HMS, 163, 169, 190
Roma, Italian battleship, 192, 194
Rommel, *Feldmarschall* Erwin, 51, 53, 56, 145, 159, 160, 172, 173, 179, 181
Roosevelt, President Franklin D., 135, 136, 196, 197, 199, 202, 203
Rorqual, HM Sub., 48, 176
Rosenbaum, *Leutnant* Helmut, 164
Ross Macintire, Rear-Adm., 197
Rowlands, Lieut. Cyril, 124
Roxy Theatre, Birkirkara, 152, 170
Royal Air Force, 18, 28, 36, 49, 64, 98, 101, 104, 110, 118, 121, 123, 126, 128, 145, 154, 162, 172, 175, 177, 181, 189, 191, 195
Royal Air Force, 418 Flight, 22
Royal Air Force, 431 Flight, 22
Royal Air Force, 1430 Flight, 36
Royal Air Force, 23 Squadron, 177
Royal Air Force, 24 Squadron, 145
Royal Air Froce, 71 *Eagle* Squadron, 154
Royal Air Force, 78 Squadron, 32
Royal Air Force, 126 Squadron, 36, 64
Royal Air Force, 185 Squadron, 36, 45, 49, 64, 177
Royal Air Force, 217 Squadron, 161
Royal Air Force, 229 Squadron, 154
Royal Air Force, 249 Squadron, 36, 64, 134, 153
Royal Air Force, 261 Squadron, 22, 36
Royal Air Force, 272 Squadron, 177
Royal Air Force Rest Camp, 151
Royal Army Medical Corps, 130
Royal Army Ordnance Corps, 84, 102, 123

Royal Army Service Corps, 46, 85, 156
Royal Army Service Corps, 32 (GT) Company, 85
Royal Army Service Corps, 651 (GT) Company, 85
Royal Army Service Corps, 178 (Palestinian GT) Company, 85
Royal Army Service Corps, 468 (Palestinian GT) Company, 85
Royal Artillery, 33, 104, 152, 171, 173
Royal Artillery, 4th Heavy Regiment, 4, 103
Royal Artillery, 7th Heavy AA Regiment, 85, 103
Royal Artillery, 10th Heavy AA Regiment, 103
Royal Artillery, 59th Light AA Battery, 102
Royal Auxiliary Air Force, No. 601 (County of London), 135
Royal Auxiliary Air Force, No. 603 (City of Edinburgh), 102
Royal Corps of Signals, 180
Royal Electrical and Mechanical Engineers, 84
Royal Engineers, 4, 29, 83, 84, 123
Royal Irish Fusiliers, 4, 180
Royal Lady, Gozo ferry-boat, 147
Royal Malta Artillery, 4, 6, 47, 103, 104, 110, 143, 152, 165, 170, 173, 186, 197
Royal Malta Artillery, 1st Coast Regiment, 1st Coast Battery, 4
Royal Malta Artillery, Anti Parachute Squadron, 6
Royal Malta Artillery, 2nd HAA Regiment, 7th Battery, 103, 109
Royal Malta Artillery, 3rd LAA Regiment, 33, 103, 110
Royal Malta Artillery, 3rd LAA Regiment, 30th LAA Battery, 33
Royal Malta Artillery, 11th HAA Regiment, 103, 108
Royal Malta Artillery, 11th HAA Regiment, 23rd Battery, 104
Royal Malta Artillery, 3rd Battery, 45
Royal Malta Artillery, 10th LAA Battery, 102, 109, 195
Royal Marines, 47, 87, 102, 194
Royal Naval Torpedo Depot, 175
Royal Navy, 19, 41, 49, 87, 123, 129, 163, 167, 169, 170, 175
Royal Navy, Force 'B', 51
Royal Navy, Force 'H', 54, 190
Royal Navy, Force 'K', 49, 51, 53
Royal Navy, 8th Destroyer Flotilla, 192
Royal Navy, 14th Destroyer Flotilla, 51
Royal Opera House, 111
Royal Signals, 4
Royal Tank Regiment, 85, 86
Rye, HMS, 167

Sacco, Dr. Henry, 98
Sacred Heart Convent, St. Julian's, 129
Sadler, Brig. Norman, 25
Safari, HM Sub., 180
St Agatha's Convent, 88, 90
St Aloysius College, Birkirkara, 129
St Andrew's Hostel, 151
St Angelo, HMS, 10, 102, 126
St Edward's College, 84
St George's Barracks, 126
St George's Bay, 147, 156
St James Cavalier, 5
St John's Ambulance Brigade, 72, 73
St John's Co-Cathedral, 17, 56, 206
St Lawrence Church, Vittoriosa, 26
St Luke's Hospital, 128
St Julian's, 74, 128, 170
St Julian's Tower, 132
St Paul's Bay, 74, 151, 161, 192, 195
St Paul's Home for the Elderly, Hamrun, 128
St Peter's HAA gun position, 104, 109
St Philip's Church, Senglea, 192
St Philip's Square, Zebbug, 201
St Publius Church, Floriana, 116
St Vincent de Paule Hospital, 128
Saliba, Gnr. Michael A., 6
Salomone, Lt.-Col. E.J., 103, 110
Salvation Army, 151, 171
Sammut, Special Constable J., 86
Sammut, Lt.-Col. Joseph A., 103
Samut-Tagliaferro, Brig. Alfred, 195
San Anton Palace, 170
Sansom, C.H., 13
Santa Elisa, MV, 165
Santa Marija, Il-Convoy ta', 170, 184

Santarosa, Italian submarine, 177
Santoro, *Generale* Giuseppe, 173
Santo Spirito Hospital, 128, 143
Satchell, Wg. Cdr. Jack, 100, 101
Savoia Marchetti 79, 6, 8, 12, 20, 21, 22, 24, 51, 164
Savoia S.84, 51, 164
Sawra Hospital, 129
Schembri, Joseph, 148
Scicluna, Marquis and Marchioness, 152
Schreiber, Lt.-Gen. Sir Edmond, 90, 202
Secretary of State, 87, 98, 121
Senglea, 27, 59, 61, 116, 142, 143, 170, 185, 192
Sicily, 20, 22, 30, 32, 33, 36, 39, 41, 45, 49, 55, 84, 135, 143, 158, 159, 163, 173, 174, 177, 180, 181, 189, 190, 196
Sicily, Invasion of, 181, 187
Sicily occupied, 190
Siebe-Gorman anti-gas hood, 13
Siege Kitchens, 77
Sikorski, Gen. Wladyslaw, 199, 200
Simpson, Capt. G.W.G., 53, 118
Skye, Scotland, 46
Sliema, 44, 69, 87, 125, 132, 143, 150, 156, 161
Smith, Sgt. A.T. 22
Smith, Lieut. Bob, 180
Smith, Brig. Kenneth P., 160
Smoke screen, 138
Smuts, Gen. Jan Christiaan, 199
Sokol, Polish submarine, 37
Solimena, *Tenente* Francesco, 12
Somers, Lord, Chief Scout, 72
Somerville, Adm. Sir James, 202
Somerwell, Lt.-Gen. Breban B., 202
Soroti, Uganda, 90
Soup Kitchens, 74
Spaatz, Gen. Carl, 197
Special Coast Watchers, 72
Special Constabulary, 14, 25, 86, 121, 202
Speedy, HMS, 167
Spitfire, 64, 82, 100, 101, 135, 138, 141, 152, 157, 158, 161, 162, 165, 172, 173, 174, 177, 181, 195, 197
Springs, Margory, 20, 21
Stettinius, Edward, 203
Stilon, Albert, 89, 90
Stirling, 189
Stokes-Roberts, Capt., 67
Storace, ARP Supt. Joseph, 25
Strever, Lt. Edward T., 161
Student, *General* Kurt, 159
Stuka (see Junkers 87)
Styles, Maj., 83
Submarine Base, 41, 128
Submarine Flotillas, 48, 53, 117
Sunday Times of Malta, 148
Sunderland, 21, 132
Superfortress, 206
Surman, Flg Off J. Max, 83
Sweeny, Maj. Charles W., 206
Sword of Honour, 201
Swordfish, 19, 22, 40, 46, 82, 124, 155, 158, 177, 181
Syfret, Vice-Adm. Neville, 163

Ta' Qali, 3, 21, 36, 37, 82, 98, 100, 101, 111, 129, 135, 136, 138, 148, 154
Tadorna, MV, 176
Talabot, MV, 65, 67, 68, 86
Talbot, HMS, 53
Talbot, Lt., 123
Tamir Sholmo, 85
Tanks, 85, 86
Tapestry Chamber, 63, 64
Taranto, 22, 73, 161, 192
Target Date, 121, 170
Teacher, Lieut.-Cmdr. Norman, 180
Tedder, Air Chief Marshal Sir Arthur, 187, 194, 200
Telephone Manager's 'Most Secret' Circular, 160
Tench, R. Wingrave, 74
Tenth Light Flotilla, Italian, 41

Terror, HMS, 6
Tesei, *Maggiore* Teseo, 41, 42
Theuma, Marcel, 147
Thunderbolt, HM Sub., 177
Tibbets, Col. Paul W., Jr., 206
TIME Newsmagazine, 173
Times, The, (of London), 119
Times of Malta, The, 14, 18, 76, 77, 130, 148, 171
Titov Lik, 73
Toc H, 151, 170
Travel Permits, 148
Trento, Italian cruiser, 65
Treves, Frederick, 169, 171
Tribuna Illustrata, La, 144
Tripoli, 51, 177, 179, 181
Triumph, HM Sub., 33
Troilus, MV, 146
Tucker, Mr Justice, 171
Tunisia, 20, 51, 138, 181, 182
Tunnelling Companies, RE, 91
Typhoid, Outbreak of, 129

Uganda, 89, 90
Ultra, 47, 51
Umberto Primo School, 142
Unbending, HM Sub., 180
Unbroken, HM Sub., 165
Under Twenty Club, 151, 170
Unexploded radio-controlled bomb, Recovery of, 29, 30
Ungarelli, *Sottotenente di Vascello* Ongarillo, 142
Union Clubs, 151, 170
United, HM Sub., 180
United Kingdom, 64, 76, 83, 112, 123, 124, 154, 177
United Nations, 73, 122, 190
Unrivalled, HM Sub., 180
Upholder, HM Sub., 53
Upper Barracca Gardens, 5, 39

Valenzia, Hon. Ercole, 18
Valiant, HMS, 192
Valletta, 15, 17, 25, 28, 39, 44, 56, 61, 63, 77, 83, 108, 111, 117, 148, 150, 151, 173, 184, 191, 196, 200, 206
Vella, Giovanna, 92
Venables, Cmdr. A.G., 163
Ventura Lockheed, 189
Verdala Palace, 86, 185
Vernon Club, 151, 170
Vian, Rear-Adm. Philip, 65
Vichy French, 20
Vickers Terni field-gun, Presentation of, 196
Victoria, Gozo, 175
Victorious, HMS, 36, 163
Victory Kitchens, 74, 76, 77, 146
Victory Thanksgiving Service, 206
Villa Apap, Hamrun, 86
Villa Portelli, Sliema, 87
Vittorio Emanuele III, King, 191
Vittoriosa, 26

Volo, MV, 20
Voluntary Aid Detachment, 73, 130
von Arnim, *General* Alexander, 181

Waco gliders, 189
Wagg, Alfred, 186
Waimarama, MV, 165, 169, 171
Wairangi, MV, 165
Walcott, Sgt., 135
Walrus, 158
Wanklyn, Lieut.-Cmdr. Malcolm D., 53
War Cabinet, 172
War Headquarters, Lascaris, 83, 182, 189
Warburton, Flg. Off. Adrian, 32
Warren, Maria, 189
Warrington, Capt. Tommy, 143, 144
Warspite, HMS, 190, 192
Wasp, USS, 135, 136
Waters, Flg. Off. John L., 3, 12
Wellington, 21, 31, 51, 81, 172, 177
Welshman, HMS, 136, 176, 180
Westgate, Boom Defence Vessel, 39
Whitley V, 32, 145
Wied il-Kbir Cold Stores, 3
Wied Qirda, 134
Wigglesworth, Air Vice-Marshal H.E.P., 187
Wilkinson, Sgt. J.A., 161
Williams, Plt. Off. John W., 153
Willis, Vice-Adm. Algernon, 194
Willy's jeep 'Husky', Presentation of, 197
Wilson, Gen., 197
Wilson, Brown, Rear-Adm., 197
Winton, Plt. Off. Denis, 45. 46
Woods, Flg. Off. William J., 3. 12
Woolley, Lieut. Edward D., 125, 126
Women's Auxiliary Reserve, 73
Wren, Capt. Richard, 170

Xaghra, Gozo, 182
Xewkija, Gozo, 182
Xghajra, 10

Yalta, 202
Yalta Conference, 203
Yugoslav Partisans, 200, 201
Yugoslav sick and wounded, 73
Yellow Garage, Valletta, 15
York, HMS, 41

Zabbar, 190
Zammit, Spr. Spiro, 27
Zammit, Sgt. V., 43
Zaniboni, *Comandante* Pietro, 46
Zarb, L/Sgt. Fedele, 109
Zebbug, 134, 201